LET'S GO

www.letsgo.com

AMSTERDAM & BRUSSELS

researcher-writers
Beatrice Franklin
Joshua McTaggart

staff writers
Sophia Angelis
William N. White
Qichen Zhang
Dwight Livingstone Curtis
Elias Berger

research managers
Joseph B. Gaspard
Chris Kingston

editors
Teresa Maria Cotsirilos
Bronwen Beseda O'Herin

managing editor
Marykate Jasper

D1153792

RESEARCHER-WRITERS

BEATRICE FRANKLIN. A walk through the Red Light District was like a stroll through a tulip field after Beatrice's last gig as an RW for *Let's Go Thailand*. She dug out her one orange sundress to celebrate *Oranje* success at the World Cup and turned a well-trained eye toward everything from the diviest hostel to the smartest smartshop.

JOSHUA MCTAGGART. Josh has a surprisingly good British accent—we promise it has nothing to do with the fact that he grew up just outside Bristol, UK. Researching Brussels, Bruges, and Maastricht (as well as France), Josh certainly got his fill of continental Europe. Josh researched with the aplomb of fellow Brit James Bond, though he sampled more wine than martinis on his travels.

CONTENTS

The Netherlands and Belgium

N
LG

0   20 kilometers
0   20 miles

North Sea

Waddenzee

Emden

GRONINGEN
Leeuwarden   Groningen

FRIESLAND

Den Helder

DRENTHE

NORTH HOLLAND

FLEVO LAND

Lelystad

OVERIJSSEL

Amsterdam ✪

NETHERLANDS   Hengelo

The Hague   Utrecht

SOUTH HOLLAND   **GELDERLAND**

Hoek van Holland   **UTRECHT**

Rotterdam   Arnhem   Emmerich

Waal R.

Maas R.   Nijmegen   **Essen**

Rhine R.

ZEALAND

NORTH BRABANT   **LIMBURG**

Eindhoven   Venlo

Zeebrugge   Ostende   **ANTWERP**   Düsseldorf

Bruges   **EAST FLANDERS**   **LIMBURG**   Köln

WEST FLANDERS   **FLEMISH BRABANT**   Hasselt   Maastricht

BELGIUM   ✪ Brussels   Aachen

HAINAUT   **WALLOON BRABANT**   Liège

Lille   Namur   **LIÈGE**   **GERMANY**

Arras   Mons   Meuse R.

Cambrai   **NAMUR**

La Roche

St. Quentin   **LUXEMBOURG**

FRANCE   Charleville Mézières   **LUXEMBOURG**

Laon   Luxembourg City ✪   Trier

Longwy

Soissons   Thionville

AMSTERDAM & BRUSSELS

There are few places in the world that can pull off the Low Countries' unique combination of reefer-clouded progressiveness and folksy, earnest charm. Like your ex-hippie high school math teacher, this part of Europe somehow manages to appeal both to tulip-loving, wooden-shoe-lusting grandmas and ganga-crazy, Red-Light-ready students. However, such an over-simplified analogy overlooks the Parisian elegance of Europe's capital, Brussels, another facet of the Low Countries' inimitable character. So, like every other college student, come to Amsterdam to gawk at the coffeeshops and prostitutes, but don't leave thinking that's all there is to this quirky region. Take some time to cultivate an appreciation for the Flemish masters; people will think you're so cool when you declare that the Northern Renaissance was really the site of Western culture's rebirth. If you need to satisfy a case of the munchies, take the opportunity to indulge in this region's specialty: comfort food. Various interpretations of waffles, French fries, chocolate, and white beer are all waiting for your discerning palate. Most of all, take time to pick the brains of the friendly, largely English-speaking natives of the region. Obviously, most Dutch people aren't pot-heads—they'll tell you that if marijuana was legalized in the States, 700,000 fewer people would need to be incarcerated annually. Put that in your pipe and smoke it. Consider what it would be like to live in a place where hookers are unionized and public works like windmills, dikes, canals, and bike lanes define the national character, and get ready to go Dutch!

when to go

The Low Countries reach their tourist peak in the summer (July and August), and for good reason: this is when the weather is sunniest, the days are longest, and most people are on vacation. Spring is another popular time to hit the region, especially if you're a flora fanatic dying to see Holland's tulips in bloom or a jazz junkie hoping to soak up some jams at Brussels's Jazz Marathon.

Temperatures very rarely rise to intolerable levels here, but rainy, gray skies are a fairly common occurrence in the Low Countries' fluctuating climate. Called "Low" due to the large amount of land that lies below sea level, the Netherlands are graced by a classic ocean fog that usually dissolves by midday.

top five places to go dutch

5. MANNEKEN PIS: Eat a chocolate-covered waffle, toss back some Belgian beer, then do your own imitation of Brussels's iconic little dude.

4. AMNESIA: Smoke a Cannabis Cup winner while discussing the pros and cons of legalized *wiet* with this Amsterdam coffeeshop's friendly budtender.

3. RED LIGHT DISTRICT: March with the Amsterdam prostitutes' union.

2. ANNE FRANK HOUSE: You read her diary in eighth grade, now see the building in which her inspiring story was written.

1. LEIDSEPLEIN: Bike your way home after a late night spent partying in this neighborhood that never sleeps. You'll earn more local street cred than the bros on the Leidseplein Pub Crawl will ever possess.

what to do

LET'S (VAN) GOGH

Forget Italy and its Renaissance—the Dutch Golden Age inspired serious strides in architecture, literature, and painting. Leonardo, Donatello, Raphael, and Michelangelo? The Ninja Turtles *should* have been named Rembrandt, Vermeer, Hals, and Brueghel. Amsterdam even has more canals than Venice, and Brussels's Manneken Pis (the little peeing boy fountain) certainly has something over the Trevi Fountain when it comes to ironic understatement.

In all seriousness, were you to put Italian and Dutch art up against one another in a cage match, there'd be no decisive winner (probably because the Dutch side would either find a way to subsidize itself out of the problem or wouldn't pass the drug test, but that's beside the point). While not nearly as chick-flick-ready as the art and architecture of Italy, the paintings and buildings you'll find in Amsterdam and Brussels are sure to reward the sightseer with an eye for quirky details. Check out the ingenuity of the Dutch designers who built tall, supermodel skinny buildings along Amsterdam's

canals to capitalize on real estate opportunities. The canals themselves are a marvel of city planning. In Brussels's medieval Grand Place, enjoy architectural grandeur that's a little less quaint. And we weren't kidding when we suggested renaming the Ninja Turtles. Dutch art may be "quieter" than its Italian counterparts, but after studying it in places like the Rijksmuseum and The Hague's Mauritshuis, you'll agree that it's got a certain something. Don't forget the more recent artistic luminaries of the region. Van Gogh, who despite his decampment to sunny France, was born and passed his early life in Holland, and Surrealist star Magritte was also Belgian.

- **JORDAAN:** Tour this neighborhood to get your best view of canalside architecture. Make sure to check out a *hofje* for an example of Dutch concern for social security that dates back to the Middle Ages. (Amsterdam; p. 49.)

- **THE RIJKSMUSEUM:** *The* museum of Dutch art. Come here to marvel at *Night Watch*, Rembrandt's gargantuan tableau that rivals Leonardo's *Last Supper,* and at the blank-verse poetry of Vermeer's intimate domestic scenes. (Amsterdam; p. 52.)

- **VAN GOGH MUSUEM:** Compared to the Rijksmuseum, this collection of Van Gogh masterpieces is far more intimate and manageable. Due to the chronological arrangement of the master's works, a tour through the exhibit can help enrich your understanding of Van Gogh's biography. (Amsterdam; p. 51.)

- **GRAND PLACE:** Admire the architecture of Brussels's beautiful square during the day, but don't miss it at night when the buildings' illumination makes the sight even more magical. (Brussels; p. 132.)

- **MAGRITTE MUSEUM:** This new museum presents the story of the artist's life using his own sketches, notes, and even snippets from drawing games with friends. (Brussels; p. 135.)

A CASE OF THE MUNCHIES

Raw herring is a specialty in Amsterdam, which says a lot about what you can expect from the city's cuisine scene. That said, the "Venice of the North" is populated by numerous ethnic eateries, making its particular brand of seafood a bit more bearable. Once you've gotten tired of traditional Dutch fare, give Indonesian, Algerian, and Middle Eastern cuisines a try (or two, or three...).

Belgium has a reputation for producing top-rate waffles, chocolate, and French fries. Satisfy any munchies lingering from your stay in the Netherlands by slurping down mussels, gobbling up the twice-fried *frites* (go local, dipping them in mayonnaise rather than ketchup), popping warm waffles into your eager mouth, and eating as many pralines as you can. Those with a particularly strong sweet tooth should take extra care when visiting Brussels's Grand Place, where multiple chichi chocolate shops stand ready to accommodate a self-induced case of early-onset diabetes.

For those too timid to sample some of the hash capital's wares, perhaps Belgium's world-renowned beers will provide a satisfying substance alternative. Coming in a dazzling array of varieties, Belgian brews can be explored endlessly. They're taken seriously, too, often served in a glass specifically designed to bring out the flavor of their particular type. This kind of refined appreciation for a staple of the bro diet should come as no surprise in Belgium, which is sandwiched between France and Germany. In this best-of-both-worlds, you can eat as heartily as the Germans and be as snobby about it as the French.

- **DELIRIUM BAR:** Sample the best of Belgian beers (there are over 2000 to choose from) at this overcrowded and extremely busy watering hole. (Brussels; p. 152.)

- **MUSÉE DU CACAO ET DU CHOCOLAT:** Bone up on your chocolate IQ at this museum that aims to do justice to everyone's favorite dark gold: the Aztecs actually used the stuff as currency back in the day. (Brussels; p. 131.)

- **RAINARAI:** Discover Algerian cuisine at this combination eatery and specialty grocer. Spicy lamb meatballs get the mouth watering in a way that pickled herring can't. (Amsterdam; p. 77.)

FUNKY FOLKLORE

Humble *Nederlanders* certainly have the right to exhibit a little national pride. Their hard work has turned below-sea-level earth into arable land for fields of tulips to cheerfully bloom in the spring. Dikes, canals, and windmills dot the landscape of the Low Countries, testifying further to the earnest ingenuity of its clog-shod inhabitants. While you'll get a feel for this kind of charming folk heritage as you live it up in Amsterdam, you'll want to leave the big-city cosmopolitanism of Europe's liberal capital and head to some of the Netherlands's other cities for a more down-home, old-school Holland experience. Utrecht, Maastricht, and The Hague are hardly rural farm towns—heck, The Hague is home to the International Court of Justice—but they do offer a fair share of classic Dutch cuteness.

The best thing about the Low Countries' folk traditions is that they exist easily alongside the über-modernity of Rotterdam architecture, legalized drug use, and Prostitution Info Centres. Like the strange peeing boy of Brussels's famous Manneken Pis, folksiness here is unapologetic, earthy, completely at home in an urban setting, and just a little tongue-in-cheek. So don't bat an eye if you see a practical *Nederlander* toking up after a long day of traditional cheese making; slip on your wooden clogs and join the party.

- **MADURODAM:** Be Godzilla to the Netherlands in this miniature recreation of Holland's big sites. Windmills, the Domtoren, working trains: they're all here! (The Hague; p. 191.)

- **SMARTLAPPEN:** Come to Utrecht during the second week of November to indulge in the city's folk-singing and beer-drinking festival. Luckily, all the drinking means you can probably fudge your way through the unfamiliar lyrics. (Utrecht; p. 206.)

student superlatives

- **MOST EMBARRASSING MUSEUM TO VISIT WITH YOUR FAMILY (ESPECIALLY CREEPY UNCLE NICK):** The Amsterdam Sex Museum.

- **BEST PLACE TO PONDER WHY SOMEONE WOULD EVER CUT OFF HIS EAR:** The Van Gogh Museum.

- **BEST WAY TO CHECK YOUR MATE:** Playing oversized chess at Max Euweplein.

- **MOST LIKELY TO EXPAND YOUR WAISTLINE:** Antoine's *friterie*, Brussels's oldest.

- **BEST PLACE TO START YOUR OWN BUSINESS:** Amsterdam's Red Light District.

- **BEST FAILED RELATIONSHIP REMEDY:** A night partying it up in Rotterdam, where over half of the population aged 20-40 is unmarried.

- **BEST PLACE TO MAKE THE CONNECTIONS NECESSARY FOR YOUR NEXT ATTEMPT AT WORLD DOMINATION:** The suave Place du Luxembourg next to the European Parliament.

Let's Go

www.letsgo.com

- **TOONE:** See Shakespeare as never before: the Toone puppet theater stages adaptations of the bard's works performed by marionettes. These puppets are a traditional Belgian art form. (Brussels; p. 162.)

BEYOND TOURISM

Given this region's visible social conscience and the frequency of spoken English throughout the Netherlands, the Low Countries provide ample opportunity for visitors to travel as volunteers or students. Future revolutionaries, imagine the social justice issues to be tackled in a place where pot and prostitution are legal. Cheapskates, imagine how much you'll save on your semester tuition in a place where a year at university will set you back only $1000. Food snobs, imagine how jealous your friends will be when you come back home a Gouda cheese-making expert. Then, imagine doing all of these and smoking a joint afterward. Now book your plane ticket.

While getting down and dirty with the Dutch is made easier due to their comfortable facility with English (a language that's compulsory from elementary school on for them), you can still turn your native tongue into a money-making asset by setting up shop as an English tutor or au pair. Adults are still eager to perfect their command of the language, and many parents are in need of a good babysitter, no matter what language he or she speaks. While you won't be able to take your kids to the Heineken Brewery, they will give you an excuse to swing shamelessly on the monkey bars at Vondelpark.

- **INTERNATIONAL TRAINING CENTER FOR WOMEN:** Intern with this NGO to promote gender equality within the Dutch workforce and potentially fight for the male prostitutes. (Amsterdam; p. 252.)

- **LEIDEN UNIVERSITY:** Study at the Netherlands's oldest university. Also has an outpost in Amsterdam, so you can get high on knowledge...and other things. (Leiden; p. 249.)

- **HOTELSCHOOL:** Enter the hospitality industry and apprentice at Le Début restaurant in Amsterdam or Hotel Skotel's outpost in The Hague. (The Hague; p. 250.)

what to do . beyond tourism

suggested itineraries

BEST OF AMSTERDAM & BRUSSELS IN 9 DAYS

By connecting stays in Amsterdam and Brussels with stopovers in The Hague, Rotterdam, and Bruges, you'll be getting a sense of all the delights the Low Countries have to offer, from Dutch internationalism and progressiveness to Belgian cuisine and fine living.

1. AMSTERDAM (3 DAYS): Hit the Rijksmuseum and the Van Gogh Museum first thing. Follow them up with some time in Vondelpark before a night in Leidseplein. Start **day two** early to beat the crowds at the Anne Frank House; check out Westerkerk as you head for Nieuwmarkt and onward to the Red Light District for some early evening entertainment. Pack **day three** with a morning at the Zuiderkerk and Museum Het Rembrandt, an afternoon at the Jewish Historical Museum, and a full night in Rembrandtplein.

2. THE HAGUE (1 DAY): Brush up on international law in this city, home to the Dutch royal family, the impressive Mauritshuis, and the Netherlands's seat of government.

3. ROTTERDAM (1 DAY): The biggest port city in Europe is ready to dazzle you with modern architecture, diversity, and a lively nighttime scene.

4. BRUSSELS (2 DAYS): In the morning, explore the Grand Place and Magritte Museum. Tour the European Parliament on **day two,** and return to Brussels's center for a beer night.

Best Of Amsterdam & Brussels In 9 Days

5. BRUGES (2 DAYS): Climb the Belfort and spend the rest of your morning at the Groeninge Museum. After lunch, hit the Church of Our Lady to view Michelangelo's *Madonna and Child.* On **day two,** learn about fried delicacies at the Friet Museum.

NORTHERN NICETIES

The best of the northern Low Countries, this "tour" can be done as a series of side trips from Amsterdam thanks to easy train connections.

1. AMSTERDAM (2-3 DAYS): Make this fabulous city your home base—after a few days here, you'll be saying Amster-*damn.* Take day one as an opportunity to tour the plentiful selection of coffeeshops in the Nieuwe Zijd and Jordaan neighborhoods. Then head to Electric Ladyland for a psychedelic trip before filling up on grub at one of the many restaurants in Scheepvaartbuurt. Spend your second day in the De Pijp neighborhood, getting kitschy at the Heineken Experience, shopping the eclectic collection at Albert Cuypstraat's outdoor market, and enjoying the neighborhood's cheap eats and hipster nightlife. Culture yourself on day three with visits to the Canal Ring's FOAM and Van Loom Museums, an exploration of the Golden Bend, and an evening excursion to either the Concertgebouw or Muziektheater for first-rate opera, ballet, or classical music.

2. UTRECHT (1 DAY): Only 30min. away by train, this home to the Universiteit Utrecht is blessed with a college town feel... and a museum devoted to clocks and street organs.

Northern Niceties

3. THE HAGUE (1 DAY): The Netherlands's center of government also boasts Andrew Carnegie's Vredespaleis (Peace Palace).

4. ROTTERDAM (1 DAY): Rebuilt after the devastation of World War II, Europe's largest port city houses the Netherlands's tallest structure.

OLD WORLD ESCAPE

Connect the following three cities for a taste of classic European fine living.

1. BRUGES (1 DAY): Continue your Fatty McFat-Fat ways with a stop in Bruges and splurge on mussels. Admire the city's canals and Northern Renaissance buildings.

2. BRUSSELS (2 DAYS): Delight in the delicious delicacies of this culinary capital (there's even a charming chocolate museum) and appreciate its elegant architecture in a day spent wandering about the Grand Place and environs, making sure not to miss the Manneken Pis. On your second day, spend the morning at the Musical Instrument Museum and the afternoon at the Belgian Center for Comic Strip Art.

3. MAASTRICHT (1 DAY): At the crossroads of the Netherlands, Belgium, and Germany, this cobblestoned city housed the signing of the EU treaty.

how to use this book

CHAPTERS

In the next few pages, the travel coverage chapters—the meat of any *Let's Go* book—begin with Amsterdam. From there, we head south to (no surprise) Brussels. In our third chapter, "Excursions," you'll find coverage on a collection of cities throughout the Low Countries, such as Rotterdam and Bruges, that we think you should check out if you're in the area and can spare the time.

But that's not all, folks. We also have a few extra chapters for you to peruse:

CHAPTER	DESCRIPTION
Discover Amsterdam & Brussels	Discover tells you what to do, when to do it, and where to go for it. The absolute coolest things about any destination get highlighted in this chapter at the front of all *Let's Go* books.
Essentials	Essentials contains the practical info you need before, during, and after your trip—visas, regional transportation, health and safety, phrasebooks, and more.
Beyond Tourism	As students ourselves, we at *Let's Go* encourage studying abroad, or going beyond tourism more generally, every chance we get. This chapter lists ideas for how to study, volunteer, or work abroad with other young travelers in Amsterdam and Brussels to get more out of your trip.

LISTINGS

Listings—a.k.a. reviews of individual establishments—constitute a majority of *Let's Go* coverage. Our Researcher-Writers list establishments in order from **best to worst value**—not necessarily quality. (Obviously a five-star hotel is nicer than a hostel, but it would probably be ranked lower because it's not as good a value.) Listings pack in a lot of information, but it's easy to digest if you know how they're constructed:

ESTABLISHMENT NAME ✈☺♿⊘((ŋ))♈✿☂▼ type of establishment ❶
Address ☎phone number ▣website
Editorial review goes here.
✂ *Directions to the establishment.* *i* *Other practical information about the establishment, like age restrictions at a club or whether breakfast is included at a hostel.* ⑨ *Prices for goods or services.* ⌚ *Hours or schedules.*

ICONS

First things first: places and things that we absolutely love, sappily cherish, generally obsess over, and wholeheartedly endorse are denoted by the all-empowering 🅰**Let's Go thumbs-up**. In addition, the icons scattered throughout a listing (as you saw in the sample above) can tell you a lot about an establishment. The following icons answer a series of yes-no questions about a place:

✈	Credit cards accepted	☺	Cash only	♿	Wheelchair-accessible
⊘	Not wheelchair-accessible	((ŋ))	Internet access available	♈	Alcohol served
✿	Air-conditioned	☂	Outdoor seating available	▼	GLBT or GLBT-friendly

The rest are visual cues to help you navigate each listing:

☎	Phone numbers	▣	Websites	✂	Directions
i	Other hard info	⑨	Prices	⌚	Hours

OTHER USEFUL STUFF

Area codes for each destination in the "Excursions" chapter appear opposite the name of the city and are denoted by the ☎ icon. Area codes for Amsterdam and Brussels can be found in boxes titled "Call Me!" at the beginning of those cities' respective chapters. Finally, in order to pack the book with as much information as possible, we have used a few **standard abbreviations.** "Avenue" has been abbreviated "Av.," and Boulevard becomes "Bld." in this book.

PRICE DIVERSITY

A final set of icons corresponds to what we call our "price diversity" scale, which approximates how much money you can expect to spend at a given establishment. For **accommodations,** we base our range on the cheapest price for which a single traveler can stay for one night. For **food,** we estimate the average amount one traveler will spend in one sitting. The table below tells you what you'll *typically* find in Amsterdam and Brussels at the corresponding price range (Amsterdam and other Dutch cities on the left, Brussels and Bruges to the right), but keep in mind that no system can allow for the quirks of individual establishments.

ACCOMMODATIONS	RANGE		WHAT YOU'RE LIKELY TO FIND
❶	under €36	under €25	Campgrounds and dorm rooms, both in hostels and actual universities. Expect bunk beds and a communal bath. You may have to provide or rent towels and sheets.
❷	€36-55	€25-40	Upper-end hostels or lower-end hotels. You may have a private bathroom, or there may be a sink in your room and a communal shower in the hall.
❸	€56-77	€41-60	A small room with a private bath. Should have decent amenities, such as phone and TV. Breakfast may be included.
❹	€78-100	€61-80	Should have bigger rooms than a ❸, with more amenities or in a more convenient location. Breakfast probably included.
❺	over €100	over €80	Large hotels or upscale chains. If it's a ❺ and it doesn't have the perks you want (and more), you've paid too much.

FOOD	RANGE		WHAT YOU'RE LIKELY TO FIND
❶	under €8	under €15	Probably street food or a fast-food joint, but also university cafeterias and bakeries (yum). Usually takeout, but you may have the option of sitting down.
❷	€8-12	€15-25	Sandwiches, pizza, appetizers at a bar, or low-priced entrees. Most ethnic eateries are a ❷. Either takeout or a sit-down meal, but only slightly more fashionable decor.
❸	€13-17	€26-35	Mid-priced entrees, seafood, and exotic pasta dishes. More upscale ethnic eateries. Since you'll have the luxury of a waiter, tip will set you back a little extra.
❹	€18-22	€36-45	A somewhat fancy restaurant. Entrees tend to be heartier or more elaborate, but you're really paying for decor and ambience. Few restaurants in this range have a dress code, but some may look down on T-shirts and sandals.
❺	over €22	over €45	Your meal might cost more than your room, but there's a reason—it's something fabulous, famous, or both. Slacks and dress shirts may be expected. Offers foreign-sounding food and a decent wine list. Don't order a PB and J!

AMSTERDAM

Tell someone you're going to Amsterdam, and you'll be met with a chuckle and a knowing smile. Yes, everyone will think you're after hookers and weed, but the tolerant laws here are shared by many Dutch cities that can't claim Amsterdam's title as the liberal capital of the West. Its characteristic tolerance has defined the city for centuries, long before the advent of drug tourism and prostitutes' unions. A refuge for Protestants and Jews fleeing Belgium in the 16th century, this center of sea trade and capital of a formerly imperialist nation has grown to be a tremendously diverse and progressive place that is more remarkable for letting its residents (and visitors) be whoever they please than for being a pothead's paradise.

As you stroll the streets, appreciate the culture and vitality of this pretty city. You can walk it in under an hour, moving from the peaceful canals of the **Jordaan** to the leering men and gaudy porn stores of the **Red Light District.** Old trading money lives on in graceful canal houses, while a few blocks away, repurposed squats are now clubs and cinemas. The city makes a strong effort to aid its burgeoning arts and culture scene, so Amsterdam is truly getting cooler by the day. And as long as you really like beer, food and drink here are far cheaper than the fare in other European cities.

Whether you're obsessed with Dutch painting, want to dance all night at a GLBT club, or just want to sit in a coffeeshop and get high, you're guaranteed to have a good time in Amsterdam. If you're the stoner, make sure to mix it up and go to Vondelpark every once in a while. And if you're the art student, we hear that *Sunflowers* looks really cool when you're high.

greatest hits

- **LEID THE WAY.** Leidseplein (p. 92) has possibly the highest concentration of great bars and clubs you'll find anywhere. Well, except perhaps for its clubbing cousin, Rembrandtplein (p. 96).

- **MUSEUMPLENTY.** The area around Museumplein features not one, but two of the world's greatest art museums. Savor the Dutch Golden Age at the Rijksmuseum (p. 52) or *Sunflowers* at the Van Gogh Museum (p. 51).

- **CENTRAAL PERK.** It's no cliché to say that Amsterdam's coffeeshops are like no others in the world. No matter what your tastes, a visit to even just one is sure to be an enlightening experience (p. 57).

It's hard to think of many cities anywhere in the world that are as friendly to students as Amsterdam. You could never call it a "college town," though; it's got too much going on to be reduced to that. This means that the city is perfect for young travelers looking for a student scene, while also allowing them to transcend such concerns. The city's remarkable culture is extremely accessible. Purchase a **Museumjaarkaart** for unlimited access to Amsterdam's numerous museums—it comes at half price for anyone under 26. Hostels are dotted throughout town and often offer the chance to meet a great community of people. For food, try **'Skek** in Oude Zijd, where you'll receive a 33% discount by showing a student ID. This might be the first place in the world where people try to borrow IDs from people *under* 21.

Of course, the two most (in)famous attractions in Amsterdam are its coffee-shops and its nightlife. Fortunately, neither disappoint, and both are key reasons why this is such a great student city. Coffeeshops are everywhere, but pick care-fully, as quality varies enormously. Check out our extensive listings to help you decide where to visit. After the coffeeshops have closed, the parties rage nightly in **Leidseplein** and **Rembrandtplein,** while the central areas like the **Red Light District** offer a seedier, but uniquely "Amsterdam," experience.

Amsterdam is a young person's city, but it doesn't force the under 30 crowd to conform to any stereotype. No matter what your interests, you can find somewhere here to indulge them, and probably a boat-load of friends to tag along with you.

orientation

The first step to getting a handle on Amsterdam's geography is to learn about its canals. The **Singel** encloses the heart of the Centrum, made up of the **Oude Zijd, Red Light District,** and **Nieuwe Zijd** from east to west. Barely 1km in diameter, the Centrum overflows with bars, brothels, clubs, and tourists wading through wafts of marijuana smoke. **Centraal Station** sits at the northern end. After that, running in concentric circles you have the **Herengracht, Keizergracht,** and **Prinsengracht,** a somewhat classier area filled with good restaurants and intriguing museums. **Rembrandtplein** and **Leidse-plein** are nestled into the central part of the ring. To the east of the canal ring is **Jodenbuurt and Plantage,** the city's historically Jewish district. Continuing around the south of the canal ring to the west, you've got **De Pijp,** an artsy neighborhood filled with immigrants and hipsters, then **Museumplein and Vondelpark,** home to some of the city's most important museums and its biggest central park. Moving farther clock-wise, you'll find the **Oud-West** and **Westerpark,** two largely residential neighborhoods that are experiencing a boom in popularity and culture. In between Westerpark and the canal ring is the lovely **Jordaan,** north of which (and just west of Centraal Station) lies **Scheepvaartbuurt.**

The phone code for Amsterdam is ☎020.

OUDE ZIJD

Many will delight in telling you that the Oude Zijd ("Old Side") is in fact newer than the Nieuwe Zijd ("New Side"). That doesn't really say much about the character of the neighborhood, which manages to encapsulate many of Amsterdam's multifaceted qualities in a narrow stretch of real estate. The northern strip, centered around **Zeedijk,** is as close as Amsterdam gets to having a Chinatown, though just as many Thai restaurants and faux-British pubs fill this part of the neighborhood as do Chinese establishments. Zeedijk spills into **Nieuwmarkt,** a lovely square dominated by a medieval ex-fortress. The bars and cafes lining Nieuwmarkt's perimeter are popular places for tourists and locals to rub elbows over a beer. Farther south is **Kloveniersburgwal,** a canal lined with genteel 17th-century buildings (many now occupied by the University of Amsterdam). You can find a number of fancy hotels and cafes where the canal hits the Amstel. The Oude Zijd is bordered on one side by the Red Light District and on the other by Jodenbuurt and represents something of a balance between those starkly different neighborhoods.

RED LIGHT DISTRICT

Like it or not, the Red Light District is what draws many travelers to Amsterdam. This is a bit of a reversal from the days of the sex industry's origin back in the 13th century. In those days, the sailors who frequented Amsterdam's port came to the city as a result of their work in the shipping industry, not the draw of loose women. However, the business opportunity created by this surplus of sex-starved young men did not go unnoticed, and prostitutes soon emerged to capitalize on the needs of the city's lonely seafarers. Today, the neighborhood goings-on are remarkably well regulated and policed, but the area is definitely no Disneyland (though the number of families with children sightseeing here during the day might surprise you). The **Oudezijds Achterburgwal,** with its live sex shows and porn palaces, is the Red Light's main artery. Most of the working-girl-filled windows line the streets perpendicular to this main thoroughfare and stretch to **Oudezijds Voorburgwal** and **Warmoesstraat.** Lots of sex stores and some theaters have set up camp on these western streets, but for the most part, they provide male tourists with bars where they can get liquored up before venturing through one of the neon-lit doors. Don't get us wrong, though—yes, this is very much a neighborhood about sex, but the high concentration of hotels on Warmoesstraat means that there is an industry here for the less red-blooded traveler as well. In fact, you'll find many bars and coffeeshops that have nothing to do with prostitution. If you want to see the neighborhood at its most hedonistic, come on a Friday or Saturday night; to be less overwhelmed, try strolling through on an afternoon, especially midweek.

NIEUWE ZIJD

Older than the Oude Zijd (but home to a church that's younger than the Oude Kerk, thus explaining the neighborhoods' confusing name swap), the Nieuwe Zijd offers a mix of history, culture, and a whole lot of tourists. **Damrak,** its eastern edge, stretches from **Centraal Station** to **Dam Square** and then turns into **Rokin.** These are some of the busiest streets in the city, full of souvenir shops and shawarma stands. As you head west, the streets become less crowded and more hip. **Spuistraat,** in particular, is loaded with artsy cafes and boutique stores. **Kalverstraat,** for centuries one of the city's prime shopping streets, now offers a high concentration of department stores and international chains. Massive hostels and a veritable universe of coffeeshops are sprinkled throughout this hopping part of town, making youthful backpackers a good segment of the area's crowds. All in all, the Nieuwe Zijd is a not-to-be-missed microcosm of the city as a whole. Either **Dam Square,** lined by the **Nieuwe Kerk** and **Koninklijk Palace,** or cafe- and bookstore-filled **Spuistraat,** make good starting points for an exploration of the area.

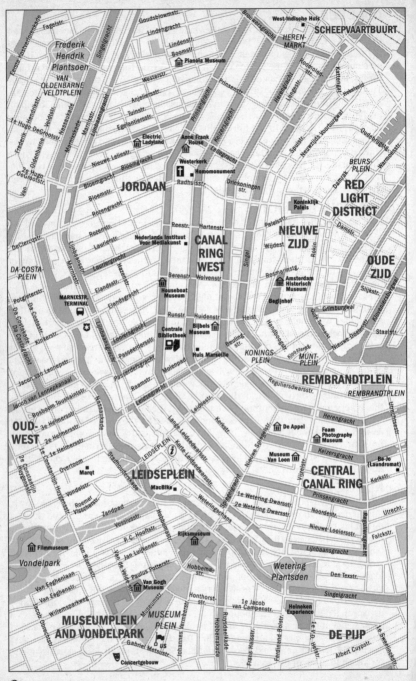

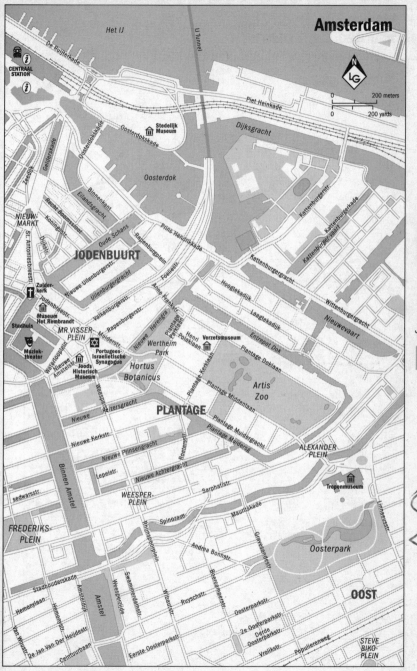

Amsterdam

Het IJ

U Tunnel

CENTRAAL STATION

De Ruijterkade

Piet Heinkade

Dijksgracht

Stedelijk Museum

Oosterdokskade

Oosterdoksdkade

Gelderskade

Oosterdok

Binnenkant

Eilandsgracht

Recht Boomssloot

Koningstr.

NIEUW-MARKT

Oude Schans

Zeedijk

Dijkstr.

St. Antoniesbreestr.

JODENBUURT

Nieuwe Uilenburgerstr.

Uilenburgerstr.

Valkenburgerstr.

Rapenburgerstr.

Jodenbreestr.

Zuider-kerk

Museum Het Rembrandt

Stadhuis

MR VISSER-PLEIN

Muiderstr.

Muzlek-theater

Waterlooplein

Nieuwe Amstelstr.

Portuges-Israelietische Synagogue

Joods Historisch Museum

Weesperstr.

Keizersgracht

Nieuwe

Nieuwe Herengracht

Wertheim Park

Hortus Botanicus

PLANTAGE

Nieuwe Kerkstr.

Nieuwe Prinsengracht

Lepelstr.

Nieuwe Achtergracht

Binnen Amstel

sedwarsstr.

WEESPER-PLEIN

Sarphatistr.

Spinozastr.

FREDERIKS-PLEIN

Rhingsporenplein

Andrea Bonnstr.

Stadhouderskade

Hemonylaan

Hemonystr.

Amsteldijk

Amstel

Weesperzijde

Swammerdamstr.

Ruyschstr.

Van Woustr.

De Jan Van Der Heijdestr.

Ceintuurbaan

Eerste Oosterparkstr.

Prins Hendrikkade

Rapenburgplein

Foeliestr.

Anne Frankstr.

Plantage Parklaan

Henri Polaklaan

Verzetsmuseum

Plantage Kerklaan

Plantage Middenlaan

Plantage Muidergracht

Plantage Muiderstr.

Roetersstr.

Hoogtekadijk

Laagtekadijk

Entrepot Dok

Plantage Doklaan

Kattenburgergracht

Kattenburgerstr.

Kattenburgervaart

Kattenburgerkade

Wittenburgergracht

Nieuwevaart

Nieuwwevaart

Artis Zoo

ALEXANDER PLEIN

Tropenmuseum

Mauritskade

Oosterpark

OOST

Oosterparkstr.

2e Oosterparkstr.

Dérde Oosterparkstr.

Populierenweg

STEVE BIKO-PLEIN

Vrolikstr.

Beukenweg

Wibautstr.

Beeverstr.

Gravesandestr.

Linnaeusstr.

Linnaeusstr.

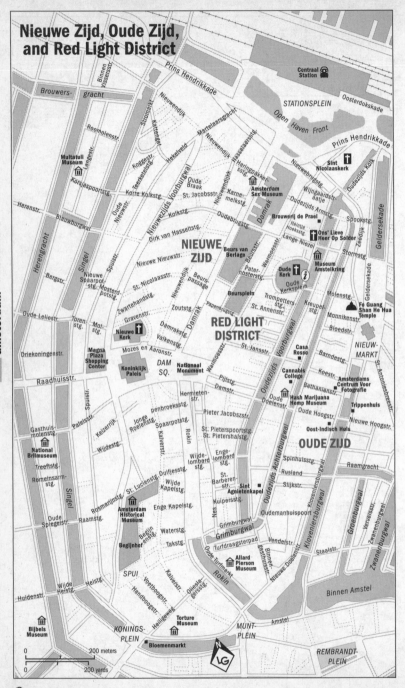

Nieuwe Zijd, Oude Zijd, and Red Light District

Centraal Station

STATIONSPLEIN

Oosterdokskade

Open Haven Front

Prins Hendrikkade

Brouwers- gracht

Binnen Wisserstr.

Prins Hendrikkade

Roomolenstr.

Nieuwendijk

Martelaarsgracht

Stromarkt

Katengat

Haarlemmerstr.

Nieuwebrugsteeg

Sint Nicolaaskerk

Oudezijds Kolk

Multatuli Museum

Langestr.

Korsjaspoortstg.

Teerkelstg.

Koggestr.

Nieuwendijk

Hekelveld

Haringpakkers- steeg

Amsterdam Sex Museum

Wijngaardt- aatje

Oudezijds Armstr.

Spookstg.

Zeedijk

Gelderskade

Herenstr.

Blauwburgwal

Oude Nieuwstr.

Nieuwezijds Voorburgwal

Oude Braak

St. Jacobsstr.

Karne- melksstg.

Brouwerij de Prael

Heintje Hoeksstg.

Lange Niezel

Ons' Lieve Heer Op Solder

Korte Kolkstg.

Kolksteeg

Oudebrugsteeg

Stormstr.

Gelderskade

Singel

Nieuwe Spaarpot- stg.

Mosterd- potstg.

Dirk van Hasseltstg.

NIEUWE ZIJD

Beurs van Berlage

Damrak

Warmoesstr.

Pater- nosterstg.

Oude Kerk

Museum Amstelkring

Bergstr.

Nieuwe Nieuwstr.

St. Nicolaasstr.

Beurs- passage

Oude Kerksplein

Molensteeg

Fo Guang Shan He Hua Temple

Oude Leliestr.

Toren- stg.

Mol- stg.

Zwartehandstg.

Beurs- plein

Trompetters- stg.

Kreupel- stg.

Monnikenstr.

Bloedstr.

Herengracht

Driekoningenstr.

Gravenstr.

Zoutstg.

Papenbrugstg.

St. Annenstr.

NIEUW- MARKT

Nieuwe Kerk

Damraksteeg

Valkenstg.

RED LIGHT DISTRICT

St. Jansstr.

Barndesteeg

Raadhuisstr.

Magna Plaza Shopping Center

Mozes en Aaronstr.

Koninklijk Paleis

DAM SQ.

Nationaal Monument

Warmoesstr.

Oudezijds Voorburgwal

Casa Rosso

St. Antoniesbreestr.

Pijlstg.

Damstr.

Cannabis College

Amsterdams Centrum Voor Fotografie

Gasthuis- molenstg.

National Brilmuseum

Palelsstr.

Keizerrijk

Jonge Roelenstg.

Spaarpotstg.

Pieter Jacobszstr.

Bethanienstr.

Hash Marijuana Hemp Museum

Oude Doelenstr.

Trippenhuis

Treeftstg.

Romeinsarm- stg.

Wijdestg.

Kalverstr.

Oude Hoogstr.

Nieuwe Hoogstr.

St. Pieterspoortstg.

St. Pietershalstg.

Oost-Indisch Huis

OUDE ZIJD

Singel

Oude Spiegelstr.

Rosmarijnstg.

Amsterdam Historical Museum

Begijn ensstg.

Waterstg.

Spinhuissteeg

Wijde- lombard stg.

Enge- lombard stg.

Rusland

Raamgracht

St. Barberen str.

Sint Agnietenkapel

Slijkstr.

Raamstg.

Begijnhof

Takstg.

Enge Kapelstg.

Kuipersstg.

Nes

Oudemanhuispoort

Oudezijds Achterburgwal

Kloveniersburgwal

Groenburgwal

Verversstr.

Zwanenburgwal

SPUI

Voetboogstr.

Handboogstr.

Heiligeweg

Olieslagerstg.

Grimburgwal

Grimburgwal

Vendelstr.

Binnen gasthuisstr.

Nieuwe Doelenstr.

Staalstr.

Zwanenburgwal

Wijde Heistg.

Heistg.

Oude Turfmarkt

Turfdraagsterpad

Allard Pierson Museum

Rokin

Binnen Amstel

Huidenstr.

Bijbels Museum

KONINGS- PLEIN

Kalverstr.

Torture Museum

Bloemenmarkt

MUNT- PLEIN

Amstel

REMBRANDT- PLEIN

0   200 meters

0   200 yards

LG

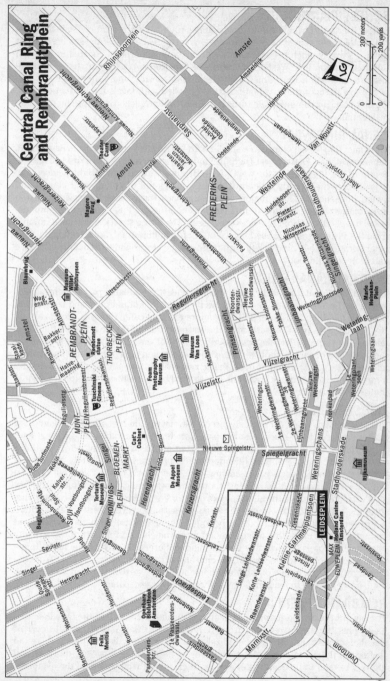

Central Canal Ring and Rembrandtplein

200 meters
200 yards

SCHEEPVAARTBUURT

Scheepvaartbuurt, which would create quite a round of *Wheel of Fortune*, is the city's old shipping quarter. At its northern edge, you can feel a hint of the sea breeze, but today it's pretty much become another ordinary neighborhood, located in between Centraal Station and Westerpark, north of the Jordaan. Its main street, **Haarlemmerplein,** is worth a visit—lined with restaurants, stores, and coffeeshops, it's one of the few parts of the city center that is crowded with locals rather than tourists. Farther east, Haarlemmerplein turns into Haarlemmerdijk and becomes increasingly residential.

CANAL RING WEST

The Canal Ring West comprises—spoiler alert—a ring of three canals: the **Herengracht, Keizersgracht,** and **Prinsengracht** (helpful hint: they go in alphabetical order from the center of the city towards the west), from Brouwersgracht down to the Leidseplein. It is an extremely pretty stretch of the city, chock-full of grand canal houses and quaint houseboats. Three major sights—the **Anne Frank House, Westerkerk,** and the **Homomonument**—are located in this neighborhood as well as smaller museums devoted to everything from Bibles to eyeglasses. The ⬛**Nine Streets,** small lanes running from the Prinsengracht to the Singel, south of Raadhuisstraat, are a highlight of the neighborhood. They are packed with more unique stores and vibrant cafes than we can fit in our guidebook.

CENTRAL CANAL RING

The Central Canal Ring is, in some ways, the least remarkable part of central Amsterdam. The Museumplein overshadows its sights, Rembrandtplein and Leidseplein outdo its nightlife, and De Pijp offers a more exciting culinary scene. However, the "CCR"—the area from **Leidsestraat** to the **Amstel,** bordered on the north by the **Singel** and on the south by **Weteringschans**—touches all of these neighborhoods, enjoying the best parts of each without suffering the crowds and high prices. **Utrechtsestraat** is an especially great stretch of lively cafes, restaurants, and stores, all frequented by a mix of locals and tourists, and the **Golden Bend** boasts some of Amsterdam's most impressive architecture.

LEIDSEPLEIN

The Leidseplein, an almost exclusively commercial rectangle south of the main canal ring, is bordered by the Nassaukade, Spiegelgracht, Prinsengracht, and Leidsegracht. A busy and touristy region, this part of Amsterdam has a polarizing effect on those who pass through it, inspiring devotion or disapproval but very rarely anything in between. If you tell locals you're staying here, they're likely to pity you, but don't be put off, as this can be a fascinating, though overwhelming, neighborhood. The few streets running through the Leidseplein's interior are packed with ethnic restaurants, theaters, bars, and clubs. Among the sushi and salsa, however, there are also a number of very Dutch establishments to be found. Numerous transport connections and vibrant nightlife make this neighborhood a convenient and fun part of town; many comfortable hotels (though few hostels) line its border. By day and by night, it is a great place to observe the flow of the city, and sitting just across the river from the wonderful cultural points of the Museumplein and the verdant paths of Vondelpark, the Leidseplein's at times garish atmosphere is easily escapable.

REMBRANDTPLEIN

For our purposes, the Rembrandtplein neighborhood comprises the actual square itself, plus the area stretching from Herengracht to the Amstel and the part of Reguliersdwarsstraat coming from Vijzelstraat towards the Bloemenmarkt. Like the **Leidseplein,** this is an area most renowned for its nightlife; however, the bars and clubs here tend to be even larger and more exclusive, while some of the establishments outside of the main square can be a little seedy. In addition to a generally more diverse crowd, Rembrandtplein has a far higher concentration of GLBT nightlife than its southwestern cousin. Food and accommodations in Rembrandtplein often cost more than they're worth, although there are a few good value options. There are no sights to speak of—except for the nightly display that goes on in the neighborhood of bars and clubs. Rembrandtplein has to be seen to be believed, and believe us: you really should see it.

JORDAAN

Once upon a time, this was a staunchly working class neighborhood. Today, it's one of Amsterdam's prettiest and most fashionable. The Jordaan provides a good transition from the pretty-as-a-postcard Canal Ring to its east and the really residential Westerpark to the west. Streets are narrow, canals are leafy, and gabled houses are squashed together in colorful rows. You won't find any of the sights that make Amsterdam famous here (well, except for maybe **Electric Ladyland**), but the restaurants and cafes are not to be missed. Establishments in the northern part of the neighborhood are more often filled with locals, while tourists tend to wander over from Westermarkt into the area near **Rozengracht**.

WESTERPARK AND OUD-WEST

Westerpark is a residential neighborhood northeast of the main city center; its eponymous park is a serene stretch of green that makes for a pleasant break from the urban jungle. It has a loyal and vocal—but don't expect to hear any English—community and is becoming increasingly popular among young people and artists, bringing ever-exciting cultural projects and nightlife to its streets. South of Westerpark lies the Oud-West, still dominated by locals but with a few large streets (**Kinkerstraat** and **Overtoom** in particular) full of small ethnic cafes and cheap chain stores that keep the area busier. Perpendicular to the main thoroughfares lie smaller roads lined with beautifully traditional Dutch houses. The northern part of Oud-West is a little grungy, but further south close to the Leidseplein and north of Vondelpark is probably the most tourist-friendly part of the neighborhood, with a number of excellent restaurants and affordable hotels.

MUSEUMPLEIN AND VONDELPARK

Museumplein and Vondelpark lie south of the main canal ring, but that doesn't make them any less worthy of a visit. Vondelpark is a gorgeous, green space with some fine hostels and convenient proximity to Leidseplein and the ethnic food of the Oud-West. Museumplein feels distinctly different from the rest of the city center. With its excellent cultural sites, it draws larger groups of older and more affluent tourists than do the backpacker-filled areas to the north. **P. C. Hooftstraat** is lined with designer stores like Prada, Gucci, and Tiffany and Co.—the number of fancy French brasseries reflects the cash thrown around here. Just because you're young and poor doesn't mean you should avoid the area though. Museumplein itself is a large, grassy field lined with some of the best museums in the world—it may be the obvious touristy thing to do, but no visit to Amsterdam is complete without a trip to the Van Gogh Museum or Rijksmuseum. Come here to get some space, culture, and class, three things that feel very far away when you're downing Heineken in a hostel bar on Warmoesstraat.

DE PIJP

De Pijp may lack in traditional history or cultural sights, but it more than makes up for that in terms of modern culture. A mix of different immigrant communities, students, and artists enjoy the relatively inexpensive (for the pre-gentrified moment) housing, the excellent ethnic restaurants, and the fun cafes of the area. **Albert Cuypmarkt,** one of the largest markets in the city, is a focal point, as is **Sarphatipark** whenever the weather is nice. Still a little bit rough around the edges, De Pijp has all the charm of the Jordaan spiked with an urban edge.

JODENBUURT AND PLANTAGE

Jodenbuurt and Plantage are two of the less-touristy neighborhoods that travelers are still likely to visit. A high concentration of sights and museums is the real draw here, but don't overlook the few excellent restaurants and small bars that dot the area. Jodenbuurt, centered around **Waterlooplein,** takes its name from its history as a 17th-century Jewish immigrant neighborhood. The Holocaust tragically devastated Amsterdam's Jewish population, lowering the population from 55,000 to just over 5000. Today, many moving and informative museums recount the Dutch Jewish community's experience. Stretching around Jodenbuurt to the east is **Plantage,** with its large streets and many lovely parks. Most commercial establishments can be found in the streets near the **Artis Zoo.**

accommodations

Unless you're going to be shelling out for one of the glitzy, multi-star hotels in Amsterdam, chances are you'll either be staying in a big backpacker hostel or a small hotel in a converted canal house. For the most part, pretty much anything you find in the city center will be a decent option, but there's a huge variety in value—some rooms are simply small white boxes with a bed, while others are lovingly decorated with modern elegance or a cool theme. To stretch your euro the most, consider staying in one of the neighborhoods outside of the main canal ring. Otherwise, the hostels in the center are well-maintained and home to vibrant social scenes.

Room rates fluctuate wildly according to season and time of the week. The closer you get to the cold of winter, the cheaper your room will be (except for the days surrounding Christmas and New Year's, when prices skyrocket). To visit Amsterdam in the more pleasant summer months and still save money, try scheduling your trip from a Monday to a Thursday. Always call or check the website of a prospective hotel for any new discounts or last-minute deals. While in the high season it's unadvised to show up in the city without having booked a room, owners with too many beds unoccupied have been known to radically slash prices at less busy times.

Virtually all accommodations these days provide Wi-Fi, and most have computers with internet available. Few are wheelchair-accessible, however, thanks to the city's proliferation of tall, teetering staircases. Most establishments take credit cards, but some will charge a 3-5% fee to compensate for what the credit card companies bill them. A city accommodations tax is usually included in the advertised price, but confirm with the management before paying to avoid any nasty surprises.

OUDE ZIJD

Most accommodations are concentrated in the Red Light District and Nieuwe Zijd, leaving the Oude Zijd with slim pickings. However, it's here that you can find two of the city's best and most affordable hostels.

■ SHELTER CITY
⟳⊗⁽ᵗ⁾ HOSTEL ❶

Barndesteeg 21 ☎062 532 30 ▣www.shelter.nl

Shelter City is a large and friendly Christian hostel (with no religious requirements for guests) in the heart of the Oude Zijd. Dorms range in size from 4 to 16 beds per room. All are single-sex, and most come with shared baths. However, some 4-bed rooms have ensuite baths. The rooms have high ceilings and colorful bunks which imbue the place with a playful feel. There are many comfortable common spaces, including a cafe and courtyard garden in this hostel that's extremely popular with young backpackers from all over.

⚑ Ⓜ*Nieuwmarkt. Just off the southwestern edge of the square.* **i** *Breakfast included. No drugs or alcohol allowed. Free Wi-Fi.* Ⓢ *Beds €14.50-32.50. Discounts available for longer stays.* ⚉ *Security 24hr.*

STAYOKAY AMSTERDAM STADSDOELEN (HI) ☞⊗⑺ HOSTEL ❶
Kloveniersburgwal 97 ☎062 468 31 ▧www.stayokay.com/stadsdoelen

Located in a tranquil part of the Oude Zijd, this hostel is nearer to Jodenbuurt but still a short walk from Dam Square, the Red Light District, and Rembrandtplein. Rooms are plain and clean, with a slightly older feel than many of the other Stayokays because this one is housed in an old canal building. Comfortable common spaces, like the TV room and bar, are good places to socialize with your fellow travelers.

⚑ *Tram #4, 9, 16, 24, or 25 to Muntplein. Walk down Nieuwe Doelenstraat; Kloveniersburgwal will be on the right over the bridge.* **i** *Breakfast included. Internet €1.50 per 15min., €3 per hr.* Ⓢ *Co-ed or single-sex 8- to 20-bed dorms €15-27.50; private rooms €39-70. HI discount.*

RED LIGHT DISTRICT

Lined with popular hotels and hostels, **Warmoesstraat** is great if you're looking for a place with a bustling backpacker atmosphere. While the prices here vary seasonally as they do in most of the city's neighborhoods, rates in the Red Light District also tend to fall drastically during the middle of the week.

THE GREENHOUSE EFFECT HOTEL ☞⊗⑺ HOTEL ❸
Warmoesstraat 55 ☎062 449 74 ▧www.greenhouse-effect.nl

The Greenhouse Effect has some of the nicest rooms in all of Amsterdam, so they're definitely miles above the Red Light District average. Each room is decorated according to its own whimsical theme: there's *1001 Nights*, which has gauzy wall hangings and an exotic chandelier; the *Sailors' Cabin*, done up ship-shape with deep blue walls and brass accents; the *Outer Space* room, with a translucent neon green sink that lights up, and many more. The hotel's location above a welcoming bar and next door to a great coffeeshop is also special, particularly since guests receive discounts at both establishments. Between the furnishings, the fun, and the breakfast served until noon, the staff here try to help their customers enjoy their stays to the fullest.

⚑ *From Centraal Station, go south on Damrak, turn right onto Brugsteeg, and veer left onto Warmoesstraat.* **i** *Breakfast included. Most rooms ensuite; some with shared bath. Free Wi-Fi in the bar.* Ⓢ *Singles €65-75; doubles €95-110; triples €130.*

DURTY NELLY'S HOSTEL ☞⊗⑺ HOSTEL ❶
Warmoesstraat 115-117 ☎063 801 25 ▧www.durtynellys.nl

A deservedly popular hostel over an equally convivial pub, Durty Nelly's boasts co-ed dorms that are, ironically, very clean. They aren't terribly spacious, but the rooms feel more cozy than cramped. Then again, why worry about your bunk bed when Nelly's is bound to get you out and about? Guests receive a discount on food and drink at the pub below, and the staff is happy to help arrange sightseeing around the city.

⚑ *From Centraal Station, go south on Damrak, turn right onto Brugsteeg, and veer right onto Warmoesstraat.* **i** *Breakfast included. Large lockers included. Free Wi-Fi.* Ⓢ *4- to 10-bed dorms €25-50.*

HOTEL WINSTON ☞♿⑺ HOTEL, HOSTEL ❶
Warmoesstraat 129 ☎062 313 80 ▧www.winston.nl

Hotel Winston feels more modern and continental European than the other boozing-and-snoozing complexes on the street, thanks in part to its sleek bar and surprisingly good club. Cutting-edge artwork lines the halls and private rooms, and dorms are less excitingly decorated but still bright and quite clean.

accommodations • red light district

➡ *From Centraal Station, go south on Damrak, turn right onto Brugsteeg, and veer right onto Warmoesstraat.* i *Breakfast included. 1 wheelchair-accessible room. Free Wi-Fi.* $ *Dorms €32-40; singles €73-95; doubles €88-114.*

MEETING POINT YOUTH HOSTEL 💳🚭📶 HOSTEL [1]

Warmoesstraat 14 ☎062 774 99 🖥www.hostel-meetingpoint.nl

The cheapest prices and most spacious dorms in the Red Light District—you know this place is gonna be popular with young backpackers. The eight- or 18-bed co-ed dorms are plain but very large and airy. The bar downstairs is open 24hr.

➡ *From Centraal Station, turn left onto the far side of Prins Hendrikkade, then bear right onto Nieuwebrugsteeg, then a right onto Warmoesstraat.* i *Breakfast €2.50. Locker rental €2 per stay. Free Wi-Fi.* $ *18-bed dorms €18-25; 8-bed €25-30.*

HOTEL INTERNATIONAAL 💳🚭📶 HOTEL [3]

Warmoesstraat 1-3 ☎062 455 20 🖥www.hotelinternationaal.com

Similar to many of the other small bar-hotel setups along the street, Hotel Internationaal nevertheless stands out thanks to its extra-amicable staff and extra-pastel-green walls. The rooms are otherwise a bit nondescript—though those on the top floor have cool Tudor-style exposed beams—but perfectly functional and comfortable. A computer is available for use, and all rooms come with a sink. Some have ensuite baths.

➡ *From Centraal Station, turn left onto the far side of Prins Hendrikkade, then bear right onto Nieuwebrugsteeg, then a right onto Warmoesstraat.* i *Free Wi-Fi.* $ *Doubles €65-85, with bath €85-110; quads €120-140.*

HOTEL VIJAYA 💳♿📶 HOTEL [2]

Oudezijds Voorburgwaal 44 ☎062 694 06 🖥www.hotelvijaya.com

This hotel at the edge of the Red Light District and not far from the Oude Kerk has nicely decorated rooms with artful lamps and pretty bedspreads. Singles can be somewhat small but are still a good bargain, especially midweek when prices fall drastically. Guests can enjoy a discount at the Indian and Indonesian restaurants owned by Vijaya's proprietors.

➡ *From Centraal Station, turn left onto Prins Hendrikkade and then bear right onto Nieuwebrugsteeg; continue straight, and Nieuwebrugsteeg will become Oudezijds Vorburgwaal.* i *Breakfast included. Bath and ensuite. Free Wi-Fi.* $ *Singles €35-80; doubles €50-105.*

OLD NICKEL HOTEL 💳🚭📶 HOTEL [3]

Niuewebrugsteeg 11 ☎062 419 12 🖥www.oldquarter.com/oldnickel

At the northern tip of the Red Light District, Old Nickel remains quite close to the, er, action. The plaid coverlets on the beds and nature prints on the walls can almost fool you into thinking you're in a British country inn—the pub downstairs certainly adds to that impression. Slanted ceilings make the rooms on the top floor extra cozy.

➡ *From Centraal Station, turn left onto the far side of Prins Hendrikkade, then bear right onto Nieuwebrugsteeg.* i *Breakfast included. All rooms with shared bath. Wi-Fi in the pub.* $ *Singles €50-75; doubles €60-85.*

NIEUWE ZIJD

The Nieuwe Zijd is packed with accommodations, making it easy to stumble straight from **Centraal Station** into your room. Hotels here tend to be pricey for what you're getting. Luckily, top-notch hostels abound.

👍 **FLYING PIG DOWNTOWN** 💳🚭📶 HOSTEL [1]

Nieuwendijk 100 ☎042 068 22 🖥www.flyingpig.nl

A lively bar (it doesn't call itself a "party hostel" for nothing), a comfy smoking lounge with couches and pillows, and spacious dorms make this a perennial favorite among backpackers. The young and cheerful staff makes the place feel like home, and frequent events, like live DJs three times a week, drink specials, and televised sports games enhance the sociable atmosphere. Guests are referred to as "piggies," which we find tremendously endearing.

*➔ From Centraal Station, walk toward Damrak. Pass the Victoria Hotel and take the 1st alley on your right, which leads to Nieuwendijk. **i** Breakfast included. Free towels. Kitchen available. Free Wi-Fi and computers. Ⓢ 4- to 18-bed dorms €20-30. Significant discounts can be found online and in the low season.*

👍 AIVENGO YOUTH HOSTEL
💳🚭📶 HOSTEL [1]

Spuistraat 6 ☎042 136 70

If you find the white walls and minimal decoration in most hostels a little boring, this is the place for you. Deep colors and gauzy purple curtains give the dorms a decadent, *Arabian Nights* sort of vibe. A mix of bunks and normal beds fills the large and sociable dorms. Somewhat humorously (misogynously, some might say), the all-female dorms are the only ones equipped with a kitchen. Fridge and microwave are available for the guests in co-ed dorms. Two private doubles can be booked, one with roof terrace and hot tub.

*➔ From Centraal Station, walk down Martelarsgraacht; keep straight onto Hekelveld, which will turn into Spuistraat. **i** Free Wi-Fi and computers. Ⓢ Dorms €20-35; in winter prices as low as €12. Private rooms €70-110.*

👍 BOB'S YOUTH HOSTEL
🍸🚭📶 HOSTEL [1]

Nieuwezijds Voorburgwal 92 ☎062 463 58 💻www.bobsyouthhostel.nl

A slightly hippie-er counterpart to the Flying Pig, Bob's Youth Hostel attracts flocks of young travelers who enjoy lounging in the graffiti-filled bar area or outside on the steps (often with acoustic guitars) when the weather is nice. Dorm rooms have recently been tattooed with cheeky and colorful murals by visiting artists. An apartment with a kitchen and bath for two or three people is also available. To leave room for more spontaneous travelers, only a small number of reservations are taken.

*➔ From Centraal Station, go down Martelaarsgracht and bear left as it becomes Nieuwezijds Voorburgwal. **i** Breakfast included. Wi-Fi €3 per hr., €4 per day. Ⓢ 4- to 16-bed dorms €22; apartment €90 for 2 people, €120 for 3. ⏰ Bar open until 3am.*

👍 HOTEL BROUWER
🍸🚭 HOTEL [4]

Singel 83 ☎062 463 58 💻www.hotelbrouwer.nl

If you want to get a sense of what it would be like to live in an old Dutch canal house, this is your best bet (and value). Of all the rooms (each named after a Dutch artist), the small double Bosch room is the real delight, with a living room space featuring antique furniture and a traditional box bed set into the wall. The other rooms, all with canal view, are less distinctive but still spacious and well-decorated. Delft tiles line the staircase, and the breakfast room is adorned with lush oil paintings.

*➔ From Centraal Station, cross the water, go right on Prins Hendrikkade, and left onto Singel. **i** Breakfast included. Free Wi-Fi. Ⓢ Doubles €100; triples €120.*

HOTEL GROENENDAEL
💳🚭📶 HOTEL [1]

Nieuwendijk 15 ☎062 448 22 💻www.hotelgroenendael.com

Simple, slightly worn rooms are more than just bed-filled boxes thanks to lovely touches like molding around the wall edges, large windows, and a few small terraces. Breakfast is served in a cozy common area.

*➔ From Centraal Station, turn right, go left at Martelaarsgracht, and then head right onto Nieuwendijk. **i** Breakfast included. Most rooms with shared bath, 1 ensuite double available. Free Wi-Fi. Ⓢ Singles €35; doubles €60; triples €90.*

HOSTEL AROZA
🍸🚭 HOSTEL [1]

Nieuwendijk 23 ☎062 091 23

The "dorms" here are really just quads with twin beds that can be booked individually. It's a nice break if you dislike the institutional feeling of larger hostels with rows and rows of bunk beds. Rooms are extremely plain, but the trippy murals in the halls give the place definite charm. The bar downstairs is a popular hangout.

🧭 From Centraal Station, turn right, go left at Martelaarsgracht, and then head right onto Nieuwendijk. ℹ Breakfast included. No Wi-Fi, but computer with internet in the bar. $ Beds €25-30.

HOTEL BRIAN
💳♿📶 HOTEL [2]

Singel 69 ☎062 446 61 💻www.hotelbrian.com

If you can manage to get over the vertiginous (even by Amsterdam standards) stairs, you'll be surprised by the pleasant purple-walled rooms and their lacy curtains. The hotel has recently undergone renovation, so bathrooms, TVs, and paint are minty fresh. Rooms with canal view come at no extra cost.

🧭 From Centraal Station, cross the water, go right on Prins Hendrikkade, and left onto Singel. ℹ Breakfast included. Sinks ensuite, but shared bath. Free Wi-Fi. $ Doubles €60-90; triples €80-120.

HOTEL HOKSBERGEN
💳🚭📶 HOTEL [3]

Singel 301 ☎062 660 43 💻www.hotelhoksbergen.nl

Hotel Hoksbergen's pretty rooms in neutral shades aren't super-sized, but some have leafy canal views framed by lace curtains. They're also nicely situated on the southern end of the Nieuwe Zijd, close to both Spui and the Nine Streets. Family-size apartments with kitchens are also available.

🧭 Tram #1, 2, or 5 to Spui/Nieuwezijds Voorburgwal. Walk down Heisteeg and make a right onto Singel. ℹ Breakfast included. All rooms with bath. Free Wi-Fi. $ Singles €60-98; doubles €72-120; 5-person apartments €110-249.

SCHEEPVAARTBUURT

👍 FREDERIC RENT-A-BIKE
🍸🚭 HOTEL, APARTMENTS [2]

Brouwersgracht 78 ☎062 455 09 💻www.frederic.nl

Three amazing, homey rooms, each named after a different artist, sit at the back of Frederic's bike rental shop. The Picasso and Chagall rooms are smaller and more romantically decorated, with the artists' prints on the walls and wrought-iron chairs. The magnificent Mondrian room, however, steals the show with a double waterbed and a 👍**hot tub** in the brightly tiled bathroom. The rooms are surrounded by the cozy shop that's filled with pianos, statues, and other knick-knacks (including a small suit of armor). Frederic also rents out a number of houseboats and apartments in the area, and though they vary in size, each is spectacularly furnished in a combination of modern and antique styles. Pictures and descriptions of all of the housing possibilities are on Frederic's website. You can end up saving quite a bit by staying in these impeccable apartments which come at a price that's more than competitive given their quality and location. The convenience of a kitchen space (which all but one apartment have) only increases these rooms' value for a budget traveler. Adding to the experience are the supremely helpful owners, who know the city inside and out and will give you some of the best Amsterdam advice you can find. They also have some great stories to tell; make sure to ask them about their experiences with other luminaries of the travel-writing world.

🧭 Leaving Centraal Station, make a right, cross the Singel, then walk 2 blocks down Brouwersgracht. ℹ Croissant breakfast included with hotel rooms. Small rooms have shared bath. $ Smaller rooms €40-50 as singles, €60-70 as doubles; Mondrian room €90-100. Apartments and houseboats range from €100 for 2 people to €225 for 6, with 15% reservation fee.

HOTEL MY HOME

⊗⊗⁽ᵖ⁾ HOTEL ❶

Haarlemmerstraat 82   ☎062 423 20 ▣www.amsterdambudgethotel.com

This place has been around for a while, as you can tell by their prime piece of internet real estate. The rooms are small and simple, but yellow walls and patterned bedspreads brighten things up a bit. The common space with pool table is a relaxed hangout.

⚡ *From Centraal Station, make a right; after a few blocks, cross the Singel and continue onto Haarlemmerstraat.* ***i*** *Breakfast included. All rooms with shared bath. Free Wi-Fi.* Ⓢ *Bed in a triple or quint room €28-33; doubles €55-70.*

RAMENAS HOTEL

🛏⊗⁽ᵖ⁾ HOTEL ❷

Haarlemmerdijk 61   ☎062 460 30 ▣www.hotelramenas.nl

Near Haarlemmerplein, Ramenas sits above a cafe of the same name. Rooms are nothing special, but slightly lower ceilings and wooden window frames help them to feel cozy. Some rooms have shared baths, while ensuite bathrooms are small and include sinks in the room proper.

⚡ *Tram #3 to Haarlemmerplein. Reception is in the cafe downstairs.* ***i*** *Breakfast included. Free Wi-Fi.* Ⓢ *Singles €50-75; doubles €60-95.*

CANAL RING WEST

Raadhuisstraat is a row of hotel after hotel, making it a great place to try and find a room if everywhere else is full. For a quieter and more picturesque location, try one of the places in the **Nine Streets** or along a canal.

🔲 HOTEL CLEMENS

⊗⊗⁽ᵖ⁾ HOTEL ❷

Raadhuisstraat 39   ☎062 460 89 ▣www.clemenshotel.com

Every room in this small hotel is lovingly decorated with French patterned wallpaper and tiered curtains. Some rooms have cushioned window seats, and all of them have a fridge and a safe. Enjoy breakfast on the balcony with a view of the Westerkerk. Best of all: it's cheap.

⚡ *Tram #13, 14, or 17 to Westermarkt.* ***i*** *Breakfast included. Rooms with shared bath have sinks. Free Wi-Fi.* Ⓢ *Singles €40-60; doubles €60-120; triples €120-150.*

🔲 NADIA HOTEL

🛏⊗⁽ᵖ⁾ HOTEL ❸

Raadhuisstraat 51   ☎062 015 50 ▣www.nadia.nl

Nadia Hotel boasts luxurious rooms with elegant bedspreads, large windows, and built-in wooden shelves. The breakfast room is full of hanging plants and looks over Westermarkt. The double overlooking the canal will make you feel like you're on a 🔲**boat**. Some deluxe rooms have balconies and views of the canal or Westerkerk. All rooms have desks, coffee and tea makers, a safe, and ensuite bath.

⚡ *Tram #13, 14, or 17 to Westermarkt.* ***i*** *Breakfast included. Free Wi-Fi.* Ⓢ *Singles €50-90; doubles €65-100.*

HOTEL PAX

🛏⊗ HOTEL ❷

Raadhuisstraat 37B   ☎062 497 35 ▣www.hotelpax.nl

The common spaces in Hotel Pax are brightly painted and hung with mirrors and prints, giving it a much nicer feel than many other budget hotels in the neighborhood. The no-frills rooms are outfitted with plain metal-frame beds but remain spacious and airy. Both ensuite and shared-bath rooms available.

⚡ *Tram #13, 14, or 17 to Westermarkt.* ***i*** *Computer available for a fee.* Ⓢ *Singles from €35; doubles €60-90; quads €120-150.*

HOTEL HEGRA

🛏⊗⁽ᵖ⁾ HOTEL ❷

Herengracht 269   ☎062 378 77 ▣www.hotelhegra.nl

Although just as central as the other hotels in the neighborhood, Hegra's pretty canalside location sets it apart from the Westermarkt activity. Rooms are clean and simple, with plush red carpeting underfoot and pretty floral tiles surrounding the ensuite sinks (most have sink and shower but share a toilet). Some rooms have canal views.

🚊 Tram #1, 2, 5, 13, 14, or 17 to Dam; continue along Raadhuisstraat and make a left onto Herengracht. i Breakfast included. Free Wi-Fi. $ Doubles €49-119, averaging around €89.

HOTEL BELGA
💳🚭📶 HOTEL ❷

Hartenstraat 8 ☎062 490 80 💻www.hotelbelga.nl

Tucked among hip cafes and quirky shops on one of the Nine Streets, this hotel basks in the same fun and youthful feeling. The rooms are large, if a bit plain, but abstract floral paintings brighten up the white walls. Some have slightly slanted floors, which can seem either charming or disorienting depending on your degree of spatial dyslexia.

🚊 Tram #13, 14, or 17 to Westermarkt; cross Keizersgracht, make a right, and then a left onto Hartenstraat. i Breakfast included. Free Wi-Fi. $ Singles (shared bath) €45-55; doubles (some ensuite) €60-100.

HOTEL WESTERTOREN
💳🚭📶 HOTEL ❶

Raadhuisstraat 35b ☎062 446 39 💻www.hotelwestertoren.nl

The most exciting room here is the seven-person ensemble, which has two lofted double beds, a single bed underneath, and another double against the opposite wall. Have fun building a fort with your friends—it definitely beats the average hostel. Each room is decorated with traces of the old luxe charm that once characterized this canal house (think red curtains, floral bedspreads, and romantic paintings).

🚊 Tram #13, 14, or 17 to Westermarkt. i Breakfast included. All rooms with fridge and coffee and tea makers; some with balcony. Free Wi-Fi. $ 7-person dorms €35 per person (must be booked as a group); singles €45-55.

CENTRAL CANAL RING

Despite the neighborhood's slim hotel pickings, the Central Canal Ring is an excellent place to call home. You'll be close to Museumplein, Leidseplein, Rembrandtplein, and the Nieuwe Zijd—pretty much wherever you might want to go in Amsterdam. To top it all off, these relatively quiet hotels come at a much better value than those in the city center.

👍 HEMP HOTEL
💳🚭📶 HOTEL ❸

Fredericksplein 15 ☎062 544 25 💻www.hemp-hotel.com

Each of Hemp Hotel's rooms has a different geographic theme—the Caribbean, Tibet, and India are regions represented—brought to life by hemp fabrics, handmade wood carvings, and vibrant pictures. The Hemple Temple bar downstairs serves about a dozen kinds of hemp beer, along with drinks derived from less infamous crops. It's a great place to hang out and meet fellow travelers. Book far in advance—the hotel is deservedly popular and fills up quickly. Make sure to try the hemp rolls at breakfast.

🚊 Tram #4, 7, 10, or 25 to Fredericksplein. Walk diagonally across the square. i Breakfast included. Free Wi-Fi. $ Singles €60; doubles €70, with bath €75.

👍 THE GOLDEN BEAR
💳🚭📶▼ HOTEL ❸

Kerkstraat 37 ☎062 447 85 💻www.goldenbear.nl

Since 1948, this has been Amsterdam's premier openly gay hotel (about 75% of the guests are male, though women and straight couples are certainly welcome). Besides its forward-thinking attitude, the hotel is notable for its welcoming staff and elegantly modern rooms at excellent prices. Management changed in late 2010, so call ahead to find out if policies remain the same.

🚊 Tram #1, 2, or 5 to Keizersgracht. Continue down Leidsestraat and make a right. i Breakfast included. Free Wi-Fi. $ Singles without bath €63-70; doubles €73-90, with bath €90-130.

HOTEL KAP
💳🚭📶 HOTEL [2]

Den Texstraat 5b ☎062 459 08 🖥www.kaphotel.nl

In the summer, when you can eat breakfast or simply relax in the leafy garden out back, Hotel Kap is a really lovely option. The rooms have high ceilings and great windows, though the furnishings are rather plain.

🚋 Tram #4, 7, 10, 16, 24, or 25 to Weteringcircuit. Walk down Weteringschans, make a right at 2e Weteringplantsoen, and then a left at Den Texstraat. ℹ Breakfast included. Singles with shared bath; doubles available shared bath or ensuite. Wi-Fi €5 per stay. $ Singles €40-65; doubles €60-95.

HOTEL ASTERISK
💳🚭 HOTEL [3]

Den Texstraat 16 ☎062 417 68 🖥www.asteriskhotel.nl

Hotel Asterisk offers great rooms for the price, thanks to its location on a side street in a pocket of calm between touristy neighborhoods. The space is kept very clean, with good furniture, pretty paintings on the walls, and nice curtains. The deluxe rooms with bath are quite spacious, but the simpler twins and singles might feel a little small. The hotel seems to pad its profit margin by charging for Wi-Fi.

🚋 Tram # 4, 7, 10, 16, 24, or 25 to Weteringcircuit. Walk down Weteringschans; turn right at 2e Weteringplantsoen and then left at Den Texstraat. ℹ Breakfast included. Wi-Fi €5 per hr., €30 per 10hr. $ Singles €59-68; doubles €60-79, deluxe €89-129.

LEIDSEPLEIN

The best hotels in the Leidseplein are found down **Marnixstraat** and around the bend of the **Leidsekade.**

👍 BACKSTAGE HOTEL
💳🚭📶 HOTEL [2]

Leisegracht 114 ☎062 440 44 🖥www.backstagehotel.com

We at Let's Go may not be rock stars, but even without Keith Richards' life experience under our belts, we can safely say that there is no way in hell any backstage area is as glorious as the rooms of this hotel. The decor adheres strictly to a concert-venue theme: backboards are made to look like trunks, lamps like spotlights, ceiling lights have drum lampshades, and certain rooms have dressing tables that even Lady Gaga would envy. Some suites are quads and quints big enough to house your whole band. Concert posters, many of them autographed by artists who have played local venues, line the walls and stairways; the reception desk is accompanied by a bar (open until 1am), pool table, and piano. Open-mike nights are held here every Tuesday. And we saved the best for last: one room has been sponsored by Activision and is Guitar Hero themed, with your very own Xbox and game setup. Perhaps even better, the staff is happy to talk up Amsterdam as well as the hotel's concert schedule (informal and regularly scheduled).

🚋 Tram #1, 2, or 5 to Leidseplein; #7 or 10 to Raamplein. ℹ Free Wi-Fi. $ Singles €35-85; doubles €47.50-145; quints €150-250.

👍 FREELAND
💳🚭📶❄ HOTEL [3]

Marnixstraat 386 ☎062 275 11 🖥www.hotelfreeland.com

Freeland is an unbelievably fresh and cheerful hotel, miles away in character from the crowds and grit of the Leidseplein, though the neighborhood's bustling center is just a block away. Rooms are airy and floral, but in a pastel take on modern design that's breezier than the cloying sweetness of your great-aunt Mildred's living room. Each room is stocked with amenities like DVD players and coffee makers. The staff is welcoming and ready to guide the inquisitive traveler to all kinds of Amsterdam hotspots. Ask if the special double with sunroom is available. Book early, as this place's charm isn't exactly a well-kept secret.

🚋 Tram #1, 2, 5, 7, or 10 to Leidseplein; #7 or 10 to Raamplein. ℹ Breakfast included. Free Wi-Fi. $ Singles €58-70; doubles €78-120.

INTERNATIONAL BUDGET HOSTEL 💳🚭📶 HOSTEL [1]

Leidsegracht 76 ☎062 427 84 💻www.internationalbudgethostel.com

On the opposite side of the Leidsegracht from the Leidseplein in a classic, narrow canal house sits this student-friendly hostel. Rooms are plain, but the exposed beams on the ceiling give them charm. Each dorm has four single beds—no bunk beds, a boon for those prone to either hitting their heads on or rolling off the top bunk—and lockers. Two private doubles (with shared facilities) are also available. Sparkling clean toilets and showers grace each floor. Breakfast served until noon in the canteen *(dishes €3-8);* there is also a lounge with couches, TV, and vending machines. Very welcoming and friendly staff.

🚋 Tram #7 or 10 to Raamplein. Continue walking down Marnixstraat and make a left at the canal. Tram #1, 2, or 5 to Prinsengracht. Make a right and walk along Prinsengracht and then turn left after you cross the bridge. i Free Wi-Fi. $ Dorms €20-32.

KING HOTEL 💳🚭📶 HOTEL [2]

Leidsekade 85-86 ☎062 496 03 💻www.hotel-king.nl

Warmly decorated, impeccably clean rooms with glossy wood and orange curtains fill this hotel, located in an old canal house along the bend of the Leidsekade. Some rooms have spectacular views over the water (though you'll pay extra to enjoy them).

🚋 Tram #1, 2, 5, 7, or 10 to Leidseplein. Walk down Marnixstraat and make a left at the canal; the hotel is around the bend. i Breakfast included. Free Wi-Fi. $ Singles €49-75; doubles €75-125.

HOTEL QUENTIN 💳🚭📶 HOTEL [2]

Leidsekade 89 ☎062 275 11 💻www.quentinhotels.com

Located in a beautiful renovated mansion overlooking the Leidsekade, this hotel sets itself apart with comfortable and stylish rooms filled with funky, abstract furniture and posters of musicians. Some have excellent views. The hotel bar serves coffee, alcohol, and soft drinks, and lounge seating can be found in the lobby.

🚋 Tram #1, 2, 5, 7, or 10 to Leidseplein. Walk down Marnixstraat and make a left at the canal; the hotel is around the bend. i Free Wi-Fi. $ Singles €35-55, with bath €40-60; doubles €50-70/€65-85.

MARNIX HOTEL 💳♿📶 HOSTEL [1]

Marnixstraat 382 ☎061 606 61 💻www.marnixhotel.nl

Certainly not the most charming of accommodations, but if you're just looking for a cheap place to lay your weary head after exploring the city, this is one of your best options. Rooms are extremely simple, essentially just metal-frame bunk beds packed into a box with a window or two. Eight- and 10-person rooms have ensuite bathrooms, while six-person rooms have bathrooms outside. Prices can hit as low as €9 per bed in the low season.

🚋 Tram #1, 2, or 5 to Leidseplein; #7 or 10 to Raamplein. i Breakfast included. Free Wi-Fi. $ Dorms €9-30. ⏰ Reception 24hr.

BOUTIQUE HOTEL VIEW 💳🚭📶 HOTEL [4]

Leidsekade 77 ☎052 896 68 💻www.boutiquehotelview.com

This is one of the more expensive hotels in the neighborhood (save for the massive four- and five-star ones lining the canals), but you'll still be getting your money's worth if you stay here. The rooms are palatial in size and style; with the large, gilt-framed mirrors and black leather couches, you can count on feeling classy to the max. There are no singles, but some smaller doubles can function as single-occupancy rooms.

🚋 Tram #1, 2, 5, 7, or 10 to Leidseplein. Walk down Marnixstraat and make a left at the canal; the hotel is around the bend i Breakfast €10 per person per day. Free Wi-Fi. $ Small doubles €89-129, large doubles €129-189.

REMBRANDTPLEIN

Rembrandtplein's reputation as a popular nightspot can be both a blessing and a curse. On the one hand, living here means it's easy to stumble home after a long night; on the other, prices and noise levels can be high (especially so on weekends). The **City Hotel** is a good option, but unless you are dead set on partying nearby, you may be better off staying elsewhere.

◼ CITY HOTEL
Utrechtstraat 2

✆062 723 23 ◼www.city-hotel.nl

●❖⊗(ŋ)) HOTEL ❸

Large, brightly decorated, and perfectly clean rooms with colorful bedspreads and oversized pictures of flowers characterize this beautiful hotel. Some rooms have balconies, and those on the top floor have great views of Rembrandtplein and the rest of the city. Many of the rooms are made for five to eight people (some with bunk beds), but none feel cramped. Since there are no singles and City Hotel's multi-person rooms are a great value for groups of travelers, the place is popular with a young backpacking crowd. Breakfast is available in a chic dining area with red leather seats.

✴ *Tram #9 or 14 to Rembrandtplein; off the southeast corner of the main square. i Breakfast €7.50 per day. All rooms have ensuite safe. Free Wi-Fi; free public computer in dining room. ⑤ Doubles €135; triples €150; 6-person rooms €270.*

HOTEL MONOPOLE
Amstel 60

✆062 462 71 ◼www.hotel-monopole.nl

●❖⊗(ŋ)) HOTEL ❸

A few blocks removed from the madness of Rembrandtplein, this hotel has simple but pretty pastel rooms, many with canal views (ask ahead). Rooms have the added luxury of breakfast delivered to your door. There's also a cushy common space on the first floor.

✴ *Tram #9 or 14 to Rembrandtplein; cut through one of the alleyways on the northern side of the square to get to the canal side. i Breakfast included. Free Wi-Fi. ⑤ Singles €65-105; doubles €75-125.*

HOTEL THE VETERAN
Herengracht 561

✆062 026 73 ◼www.veteran.nl

●❖⊗(ŋ)) HOTEL ❷

Hotel the Veteran is a bare-bones establishment, but all the essentials are here. The rooms are clean and cozy with floral bedspreads and wood paneling. It also sits right at the corner of a beautiful stretch of the Herengracht and the bar strip of Thorbeckeplein. Be advised that to enter some rooms you must climb an external staircase next to a bunch of bars, which may be uncomfortable for some travelers returning to their room at night. That said, this is one of the cheapest places to stay around Rembrandtplein.

✴ *Tram #9 or 14 to Rembrandtplein. At the corner of Thorbeckeplein and Herengracht. i Breakfast included. Singles all have shared bath; both shared and ensuite doubles available; triples all ensuite. Wi-Fi available in 1st fl. rooms and reception area. ⑤ Singles €35-65; doubles from €50.*

JORDAAN

If you want to live like a local but not commute like one, camp out here.

◼ SHELTER JORDAAN
Bloemstraat 179

✆062 447 17 ◼www.shelter.nl

●❖⊗(ŋ)) HOSTEL ❶

Smaller and in a quieter location than its sister hostel in the Oude Zijd, the Shelter Jordaan has the same excellent prices, clean facilities, and comfortable atmosphere. Single-sex rooms are large and bright, with colorful beds and lockers that avoid the somewhat institutional feel to which many hostels succumb. A large cafe and garden provide popular hangout spots, and the included breakfast features such luxuries as pancakes and french toast.

🚋 *Tram #10 to Bloemstraat or tram #13, 14, or 17 to Westermarkt. Follow Lijnbaansgracht for 50m, then turn right onto Bloemstraat.* ℹ *Breakfast included. All rooms with shared bath. Free Wi-Fi.* Ⓢ *4- to 8-bed dorms €16.50-30.50.*

HOTEL VAN ONNA
⊛⊘(ᵗ) HOTEL ❷

Bloemgracht 104 ☎062 658 01 🖳www.vanonna.nl

The rooms on the top floor of this hotel are truly remarkable, with slanted ceilings and exposed wood beams, plus a view over the rooftops of the whole Jordaan. You'll need to hike up the stairs a bit in order to reach them, but at least the staircase is lined with lovely black-and-white pictures of the city. Rooms are impeccably clean, though the ones downstairs feel a bit blah compared to the lovely rooms upstairs.

🚋 *Tram #10 to Bloemgracht or tram #13, 14, or 17 to Westermarkt. Cross Prinsengracht and make a right; Bloemgracht is 2 blocks away.* ℹ *Breakfast included. Free Wi-Fi.* Ⓢ *Singles €45; doubles €90; triples €135.*

HOTEL ACACIA
⬅⊘(ᵗ) HOTEL ❸

Lindengracht 251 ☎062 214 60 🖳www.hotelacacia.nl

Tucked in a lovely and tranquil corner of the northern Jordaan, Acacia has simple rooms decorated in shades of pink and red; ask for one with a canal view. Small studio apartments, complete with a kitchenette and living area, are also available. Alas, they no longer rent houseboats because of new regulations, but in the future, that may be subject to change.

🚋 *Tram #3 or 10 to Marnixplein. Cross the small canal and make a left onto Lijnbansgracht; Acacia will be on the right.* ℹ *Breakfast included. All rooms with ensuite bath. Free Wi-Fi.* Ⓢ *Doubles €60-90; studios €70-110.*

WESTERPARK AND OUD-WEST

Westerpark is almost exclusively residential and has relatively few accommodations. The section of the Oud-West closest to the Leidseplein has a smattering of small hotels that put you in close proximity to the neighborhood center via foot and tram; prices are not much lower than those of hotels across the canal, but accommodations here are far less crowded and noisy.

🏨 HOTEL JUPITER
⊛⊘(ᵗ) HOTEL ❷

2nd Helmersstraat 14 ☎061 871 32 🖳www.jupiterhotel.nl

Charming both inside and out, this hotel sits on one of the small streets parallel to Overtoom, leaving it close enough for easy access to transportation and grocery shopping but removed from the bustle and noise of the main thoroughfare. The rooms are a welcome break from the usual monochromatic hotel palette, with colorful walls and sleek modern furniture, and they're only a 5min. walk from the Leidseplein. Breakfast included, served in a pretty little room.

🚋 *Tram #3 or 12 to Overtoom. From Overtoom, walk 2 blocks away from Vondelpark on 1e C. Huygensstraat and make a right. Tram #1 to 1e C. Huygensstraat. On 1e C. Huygensstraat, walk 2 blocks away from Vondelpark and turn right.* Ⓢ *High-season singles €54, with bath €64; doubles €74/99. Low-season singles €39/49; doubles €59/79. Triples and quads also available.*

HOTEL DE FILOSOOF
⬅⊘(ᵗ) HOTEL ❹

Anna van den Vondelstraat 6 ☎068 537 50 🖳www.hotelfilosoof.nl

No two philosophers think the same, and fittingly, each room in this hotel is themed in homage to its own great thinker(s). The "Cloud" room maintains a blue sky with fluffy white puffs on even the grayest of days (it's dedicated to Socrates and Magritte), while the "Eros" room (we didn't know he counts as a philosopher, but what the heck) boasts a pretty antique dressing table and ostrich-feather lamp. Other rooms channel Nietzsche, Wittgenstein, and more. A round of Monty Python's Philosophers' Drinking Song would certainly not be out of place at the small bar in the lobby, where busts of the ancients benevolently stare you in the face. A small garden area is attached, but with Vondelpark directly behind the hotel, you won't be at a loss for greenery. Breakfast is €15 extra per day—even those deep in thought have to eat.

🚋 *Tram #1 to J. P. Heijestraat. Walking towards the center along Overtoom with Vondelpark on your right, the small street will be on your right 2 blocks after J. P. Heijestraat.* $ *Rooms from €79-189, depending on date and room.*

HOTEL ABBA 💳🚭📶 HOTEL [2]

Overtoom 116-122 ☎061 830 58 💻www.hotel-abba.nl

The rooms here are simple, with white walls and bedding, but many are spacious and have a TV as well as a table and chairs to boot. This "smoker-friendly" hotel has an especially appropriate location—when your hotel's above an Albert Heijn supermarket, grabbing munchies couldn't be easier. Free safety deposit boxes are available at reception, where the friendly staff is happy to help you arrange trips and tours.

🚋 *Tram #1 to 1e C. Huygensstraat. Above the Albert Heijn.* $ *High-season singles €50, with bath €60; doubles €70/85. Low-season singles €35/40; doubles €60/70.*

MUSEUMPLEIN AND VONDELPARK

You can get your hostel fix without having to face the noise and crowds of the Centrum at one of Vondelpark's two excellent backpacker options. Hotels in the neighborhood are removed from the city's best food and drink but ooze residential luxury. And, of course, they put you a stone's throw from Museumplein, so you can go back and see *Night Watch* again and again and again.

👍 **STAYOKAY AMSTERDAM VONDELPARK** 💳♿📶 HOSTEL [1]

Zandpad 5 ☎058 989 96 💻www.stayokay.nl/vondelpark

This is a large, slightly institutional-feeling hostel in between Vondelpark and Leidseplein. The dorms are spacious and incredibly clean, and each room has its own bathroom (the larger rooms have two). Staff are more than willing to help with any questions you may have about the city. Downstairs, a bar with frequent deals is a popular hangout. Guests tend to be on the younger side of the backpacker set.

🚋 *Tram #1, 2, 5, 7, or 10 to Leidseplein. Walk across the canal toward the Marriott, take a left, then make a right onto Zandpad after 1 block.* *i* *Breakfast included. Single-sex dorms available. Internet €1.50 per 15min., €3 per hr.* $ *2- to 20-bed dorms €20-34; singles €50-80.*

👍 **FLYING PIG UPTOWN** 💳🚭📶 HOSTEL [1]

Vossiusstraat 46-47 ☎040 041 87 💻www.flyingpig.nl

We find it a little confusing that the Flying Pig Uptown is actually south of Flying Pig Downtown in Nieuwe Zijd, but then again, we can't quite wrap our heads around the fact that the Nile runs south to north—no matter. This is the original Flying Pig, and with a tranquil location across from Vondelpark, this winged swine is a little less rowdy than its younger sibling. Nevertheless, it's still a phenomenally popular and friendly hostel. Dorms vary from those with plain walls and metal-frame bunks to ones that are more colorful (literally—not in the Amsterdam sense this time), but all are comfortable and clean and with their own bathroom. The downstairs boasts a bar with a TV lounge on one side and a smoking room on the other. With proximity to the Leidseplein, guests frequently start off here before going pubbing and clubbing—and then nurse their hangovers the next day.

🚋 *Tram #2, 3, 5, or 12 to Van Baerlestraat. Walk down Van Baerlestraat toward Vondelpark and make a right onto Vossiusstraat.* *i* *Breakfast included. Linens and towel included. Free Wi-Fi.* $ *2- to 10-bed dorms €14-40.* ⏰ *Bar open until 3am.*

👍 **HOTEL BEMA** 💳🚭📶 HOTEL [2]

Concertgebouwplein 19b ☎067 913 96 💻www.bemahotel.com

Just across from the stunning **Concertgebouw** and the grassy expanse of Museumplein, Hotel Bema boasts rooms with incredible romantic elegance boosted by high ceilings, crystal chandeliers, and old-fashioned floral wallpaper. Chambers on the ground floor have antique-style furniture to boot. Topping off the luxury, breakfast is brought to your room between 8:30am and 9am. We could get used to living like this, especially at such low prices.

➔ Tram #3, 5, 12, 16, or 24 to Museumplein. Walk down the left side of the Concertgebouw and cross the street. ***i*** *Breakfast included. Free Wi-Fi.* $ *Singles without bath €35-45; doubles €65-75, with bath €75-85.*

APPLE INN 💳🚭📶 HOTEL ❷

Koninginneweg 93 ☎066 278 94 💻www.apple-inn.nl

On a map, this hotel may seem a bit out of the way, but it's just a few minutes from Museumplein. Plus, the neighborhood surrounding it is a lovely spot with elegant houses. The rooms match the surroundings: all have geometric moldings on the lower half of the walls, and some even have stained-glass skylights. Each is spacious, with solid, modern furniture. A couple have access to a small garden.

➔ Tram #2 to Emmastraat. Koninginneweg is the left-hand fork in the road; continue on about 200m. ***i*** *Breakfast €9.50 per day. Most rooms with ensuite bath. Free Wi-Fi.* $ *Singles €40-99; doubles €50-129.*

HOTEL MUSEUMZICHT 💳🚭📶 HOTEL ❷

Jan Luykenstraat 22 ☎067 129 54

A bit like staying in your cool grandmother's house—if your grandmother had a perfect view of the temporary wing of the Rijksmuseum. The breakfast room, with its two sides full of windows, is a great vantage point to creep on Museumplein and the people milling below. Old wooden furniture, Oriental-patterned rugs, and decorative curtains adorn each room. Most have shared bath, but they're some of the nicest shared baths we've ever seen, with detailed mosaic tiling on the walls. No double beds, but twins can be pushed together to form a pseudo-double.

➔ Tram #2 or 5 to Hobbemastraat. Walk away from the Rijksmuseum and make a left onto Jan Luykenstraat. ***i*** *Breakfast included. Free Wi-Fi.* $ *Singles €55; doubles €75-85, with bath €85-125.*

HOTEL OMEGA 💳♿📶 HOTEL ❷

Jacob Obrechtstraat 33 ☎066 451 82

Tucked just behind the main commercial area of Museumplein, Hotel Omega advertises its rooms as colorful, and they certainly are (though not garish)—bright orange curtains, deep red carpets and bedspreads, and gilt mirrors round out the luxurious look. The hallways are a bit dim but decorated in a fun Art Deco style.

➔ Tram #2 or 16 to Jacob Obrechstraat. ***i*** *Breakfast included. All rooms with ensuite bath. Free Wi-Fi.* $ *Singles from €50; doubles from €60; triples from €90.*

DE PIJP

Though far from the city's true center, De Pijp has character and easy transport options, making it the perfect place to see what it's like to be the hip, young thing living in an up-and-coming 'hood.

BICYCLE HOTEL 💳🚭📶 HOTEL ❷

Van Ostadestraat 123 ☎067 934 52 💻www.bicyclehotel.com

A certain current of yuppie environmentalism runs through De Pijp, so it's appropriate that this eco-conscious hotel sits within its borders. And we couldn't be happier: not only does the hotel have solar panels and a "green roof" (something about plants growing on it and saving energy—the owners explain it better than we can), but the whole theme of clean freshness permeates the building. The rooms have lavender sheets and pastel prints on the walls to match, while large windows overlooking leafy gardens let in light and air. There are even some real balconies to sit on. Plus, the per-day bicycle rental costs almost exactly equal the price of a 24hr. transport ticket, so there's no excuse for you not to go green as well.

Tram #3, 12, or 25 to Ceinturbaan/Ferdinand Bolstraat. Continue 1 block farther and make a left onto Van Ostadestraat. i Breakfast included. Free Wi-Fi. $ Singles €35-70; doubles €40-85, with bath €60-120. Bike rental €7.50 per day.

SARPHATI HOTEL — HOTEL 3

Sarphatipark 58 ☎067 340 83

This bright and modern hotel is just across the street from Sarphatipark and a few blocks away from Albert Cuypmarkt. Rooms have bright yellow walls and high ceilings; all are impeccably clean.

Tram #3 or 25 to 2e van der Helstraat. Walk along the park. i Breakfast included. Free Wi-Fi. $ Singles €60-90; doubles €80-140.

HOTEL VIVALDI — HOTEL 3

Stadhouderskade 76 ☎057 763 00

Location is everything at this hotel, which sits at the beginning of the main part of De Pijp and just across the canal from the Central Canal Ring. The rooms aren't lavish and are minimally furnished (don't worry, there's still a bed), but some surprise with touches of stained glass in the windows or great canal views.

Tram #16 or 24 to Stadhouderskade. i Breakfast included. Free Wi-Fi. $ Singles €45-90; doubles €60-110.

JODENBUURT AND PLANTAGE

Slightly removed from the city center (though in pocket-sized Amsterdam you're never really far from anything), these establishments will make for a more tranquil and local-feeling stay.

BRIDGE HOTEL — HOTEL 4

Amstel 107-111 ☎062 370 68 www.thebridgehotel.nl

The massive, comfortable rooms in this family-run hotel are well worth the splurge. Done up in a mod palette of black, red, and white, rooms are large enough for a table and chairs and some have a view of the Amstel outside. The location may feel remote, but you're just across the bridge from Rembrandtplein.

Tram #9 or 14 to Waterlooplein or Mr. Visserplein. Walk down Weesperstraat; make a right onto Nieuwe Prinsengracht, then a left onto Amstel. i Breakfast included. Free Wi-Fi. $ Singles €85-115; doubles €98-140.

HERMITAGE HOTEL — HOTEL 3

Nieuwe Keizersgracht 16 ☎062 382 59 www.hotelhermitageamsterdam.nl

A newer addition to the street, Hermitage also has a younger feel than most of the neighboring hotels. Somehow managing to combine two of Amsterdam's predominant hotel aesthetics, modern minimalist and old-fashioned floral, Hermitage covers its walls in stylized silver-and-black flowered wallpaper, and the rooms continue the cozy yet urban look.

Tram #9 or 14 to Waterlooplein or Mr. Visserplein. Walk down Weesperstraat and make a right onto Nieuwe Keizersgracht. i Breakfast €9 per day. Free Wi-Fi. $ Singles €44-90; doubles €55-120.

HOTEL PLANTAGE — HOTEL 3

Plantage Kerklaan 25 ☎062 055 44 www.hotelplantage.nl

Hotel Plantage consists of two buildings filled with plain but comfortable rooms. Across from the Artis Zoo, it is popular with a younger crowd of travelers. No singles are available, but smaller doubles can be used for single occupancy at a 5% discount. The staff goes out of their way to make your trip as smooth as possible.

☼ Tram #9 or 14 to Plantage Kerklaan. *i* Free Wi-Fi. Sandwiches and snacks can be bought from reception. ⑤ High season doubles €75-110, low-season €55-90.

HOTEL REMBRANDT
✦⊗⁽ᵗ⁾ HOTEL ❸

Plantage Middenlaan 17
☎062 727 14 ▣www.hotelrembrandt.nl

This elegant hotel near pretty Wertheim Park with the transport convenience of Waterlooplein boasts rooms that wouldn't be out of place in a country inn, decorated as they are with rustic wooden or wrought-iron furniture and floral wallpaper. One large double has a particularly natural feel due to patio access. The supremely luxurious breakfast room is full of oil paintings that will remind you of the hotel's namesake.

☼ Tram #9 or 14 to Plantage Kerklaan. *i* Breakfast €10 per day. Safe and minibar ensuite. Free Wi-Fi. ⑤ Singles €75; doubles €95-150. Extra bed in large doubles €20.

sights

Walking around Amsterdam, you'll come across more than enough sights to fill your visit. Between old churches, quaint houses, and peaceful canals, this is one of the prettiest modern cities around. Behind those picturesque walls, however, there's a whole lot more waiting to be explored. The large, famous galleries on Museumplein are rightly celebrated for their collections of new and old Dutch art; modern photography exhibitions are held in 17th-century canal houses or 14th-century churches; and a whole host of excellent museums and monuments are reflections upon the Netherlands's tribulations during WWII. Most historical museums focus on Dutch or colonial topics, while the newer art exhibitions have an international bent. Of course, there are also a few less highbrow options like the Sex Museum and the Hash, Marijuana, and Hemp Museum. Plus the First Museum of ▣Fluorescent Art, which is just too awesome to be sufficiently honored by mere prose.

If you're planning on visiting a number of museums, it's strongly recommended to invest in the **Museumjaarkaart** (▣www.museumjaarkaart.nl). For €40, or €20 if you're under 26, you get free entrance to most museums in Amsterdam and the Netherlands for a whole year. Though only a few museums have admission fees of more than €10, the little €5 and €7 tickets do add up. With the Museumjaarkaart, there's nothing to stop you from popping into one of the smaller or weirder museums and then skipping right out if it's not up to snuff. You *cannot* get the card at the tourist office, but instead should go to one of the participating museums, such as the Bijbels Museum, the Rijksmuseum, or the Van Gogh museum. If, on the other hand, you're only in town for a few days, consider getting the **I Amsterdam card** (▣www.iamsterdam.com) at the tourist office, which is more expensive and only valid for 24-72hr. but also gives you access to public transport.

OUDE ZIJD

The Oude Zijd doesn't have many traditional sights or museums, but it is home to a number of interesting architectural landmarks.

▨ NIEUWMARKT
♿ ☕ ⛪ SQUARE

Nieuwmarkt

Dominated by the largest still-standing medieval building in Amsterdam, Nieuwmarkt is a calm square lined with diverse cafes and bars, making it one of the best places in the city for some relaxed people-watching. **De Waag,** the 15th-century castle-like structure in Nieuwmarkt's center, was originally a fortress gate. When the walls surrounding the city were demolished to enable Amsterdan sion, the fortress became a weighing house. In later centuries it house for surgical dissections (Rembrandt's *The Anatomy Lesson of Dr. Tu* one such event), the **Jewish Historical Museum,** and, now, a restauran Nieuwmarkt is beloved by tourists and locals alike: in the 1970s, a plan ... Metro and highway going through the neighborhood triggered the demolition of many surrounding buildings, which in turn prompted heavy rioting here in 1975. The highway idea was scrapped, but the Metro plan persisted, the product of which you can see in the corner of the square. Daily markets selling everything from souvenirs to organic food take place daily here and are at their largest on the weekends.

➜ *[M]Nieuwmarkt or from Centraal Station walk 10min. down Zeedijk.*

SINT NICOLAASKERK 🚫 CHURCH

Prins Hendrikkade 73 ☎062 487 49 💻www.nicolaas-parochie.nl/nicolaaskerkamsterdam.html

If the austere Protestant churches around town are getting you down, head to this relatively new (opened in 1887) Catholic building. Adrianus Bleijs designed the church in a combination of neo-Renaissance and neo-Baroque styles. The dark stone exterior and interior are complemented by beautiful stained glass, mosaics, and murals depicting the life of St. Nicholas (the patron saint of sailors). Take a look at the cupola, made entirely from Belgian glass. It's the only glass cupola in the Netherlands. The organ, designed by William Sauer, is also impressive in size and sound. Stop by one of the church's frequent concerts to hear it played.

➜ *2min. walk from Centraal Station; make a left when leaving Stationsplein.* ⏰ *Open to tourists M noon-3pm, Tu-F 11am-4pm, Sa noon-3pm. Mass held throughout the week in Dutch, Latin, and Spanish; check website for schedule.*

AMSTERDAMS CENTRUM VOOR FOTOGRAFIE ♿ GALLERY

Bethanienstraat 39 ☎062 248 99 💻www.acf-web.nl

Tucked in a small street between Nieuwmarkt and the Red Light District, this gallery showcases the work of young Dutch photographers, many of whom are just out of art school. Exhibits vary greatly in topic, but it's certainly worth poking your head in to see what's on the walls. The center also holds lectures, workshops, and master classes—all in Dutch.

➜ *[M]Nieuwmarkt. Walk south on Kloveniersburgwal and make a right.* $ *Exhibits are free.* ⏰ *Open Th-Sa 1-5pm.*

FO GUANG SHAN HE HUA TEMPLE 🚫 TEMPLE

Zeedijk 106-118 ☎042 023 57 💻www.ibps.nl

You can't miss this brightly painted, gabled building along Zeedijk. It's Europe's largest palace-style Buddhist temple. Queen Beatrix herself officially opened the temple, associated with the Taiwan-based Fo Guang Shan Buddhist order, in 2000. The goals of the temple include both spiritual development and cultural exchange. Most travelers come to peek inside the temple at the ornate Buddha statues, but the building also hosts lectures on Buddhism and Chinese as well as holiday and festival celebrations.

➜ *[M]Nieuwmarkt.* $ *Free.* ⏰ *Open Tu-Sa noon-5pm, Su 10am-5pm. Services Su 10:30am open to the public.*

OOST-INDISCH HUIS ♿ DUTCH HISTORY

Kloveniersburgwal 48

For almost two centuries, the *Vereenigde Oostindische Compagnie*, or Dutch East India Company, wielded quasi-governmental powers and a whole lot of cash. Beginning in 1606, this building along Kloveniersburgwal was where they set up shop. Its Dutch Renaissance design is a trademark of Hendrik de Keyser,

the architect to whom the building has been convincingly attributed. Today, the University of Amsterdam cares for this national monument, though the students loitering and smoking outside the building take away a bit of its gravitas.
🚶 Ⓜ Nieuwmarkt.

RED LIGHT DISTRICT

No one comes to the Red Light District to go museum-hopping. However, if you decide to take a break from pretending not to look at the window prostitutes, there are a few sights here that you can examine without feeling nearly as embarrassed.

👍 OUDE KERK — 🚫💳 ♿ CHURCH

Oudekerksplein 23 — ☎062 582 84 💻www.oudekerk.nl

Since its foundation in 1306, Oude Kerk, the oldest church in Amsterdam, has endured everything from the Protestant Reformation to the growth of the Red Light District which today encroaches naughtily on its very square. Oude Kerk didn't escape all this history unscathed: during the Alteration of the 16th century, the church lost much of its artwork and religious figures. However, it remains a strikingly beautiful structure, with massive vaulted ceilings and gorgeous stained glass that betray the building's Catholic, pre-Calvinist roots. The grandiose **Vater-Muller organ** wasn't around when Rembrandt married his first wife, Saskia van Uylenburgh, within these walls, but if you come for one of the concerts played on this instrument that dates back to 1724, make sure to look for where she is buried. Oude Kerk is now largely used for art and photography exhibitions, including the display of the prestigious **World Press Photo** prizewinners.

🚶 From Centraal Station, walk down Damrak, take a left onto Oudebrugsteeg, and turn right onto Warmoesstraat; the next left leads to the church. i Check the website for a calendar of organ concerts and other performances. $ €7.50; students, seniors, and under 13 €5.50; with Museumjaarkaart free. 🕐 Open M-Sa 10am-5:30pm, Su 1-5:30pm. Last entry 30min. before close.

ONS' LIEVE HEER OP SOLDER — 💳 🚫♿ MUSEUM

Oudezijds Voorburgwal 40 — ☎062 466 04 💻www.opsolder.nl

In contrast to the typical Catholic lavishness of **Oude Kerk** around the corner, Ons' Lieve Heer op Solder—the name translates to "Our Lord in the Attic"—highlights the more muted Catholicism of the 17th century, when openly practicing the religion was prohibited and churches such as this one were hidden in canal house attics. Despite its clandestine location, the church still managed to maintain the traditional Catholic concern for spaces of worship whose beauty honors the glory of God. Surprisingly large, it contains an impressive organ and a beautiful altarpiece by the famous painter **Jacob de Wit.** Unfortunately, the church is undergoing restorations until 2012, so much of the artwork is currently being stored elsewhere. However, the church is still open, allowing you to get a feel for the place. Additionally, the excellent planned route up and down the three houses that are joined by the attic church gives a detailed glimpse into 17th-century Dutch life and is enhanced by a great collection of art and furniture from the period.

🚶 From Centraal Station, turn left onto Prins Hendrikkade and then bear right onto Nieuwebrugsteeg; continue straight as Nieuwebrugsteeg becomes Oudezijds Vorburgwaal. $ €7, students €5, under 18 €1, under 5 and Museumjaarkaart holders free. 🕐 Open M-Sa 10am-5pm, Su 1-5pm.

BROUWERIJ DE PRAEL — 🚫💳 🚫♿ BREWERY

Oudezijds Voorburgwal 30 — ☎040 844 70 💻www.deprael.nl

A brewery that does more than just make beer, de Prael was founded by two former psychiatrists who now employ over 60 people with a history of mental illness to staff the brewery. The owners' backgrounds have made it into other elements of the company, particularly the names they give their brews. Each beer on tap shares its moniker with a popular singer of *levensliederen*, which are essentially sappy Dutch ballads that, apparently, exert a special pull on these brewers' heartstrings. The beers are all organic, unfiltered, and non-pasteurized. On a tour, you can learn about the brewery and opt to try one beer or a tasting menu of four. A store that sells de Prael's beers and other merchandise is attached.

From Centraal Station, turn left onto Prins Hendrikkade and then bear right onto Nieuwebrugsteeg; continue straight as it becomes Oudezijds Vorburgwaal. i Reservations recommended for large group tours. $ Tour €4, with 1 beer €6.50, with tasting menu €14.50. ⏰ Open M 12:30-5pm, Tu-W 10am-6pm, Th 10am-9pm, F 10am-6pm, Sa-Su noon-6pm.

HASH MARIJUANA HEMP MUSEUM MUSEUM

Oudezijds Achterburgwal 148 ☎062 359 61 💻www.hashmuseum.com

No matter how much weed you've encountered in Amsterdam, this place probably has something you haven't seen before. More valuable for the kitsch factor than for actual information (if you want that, go a few doors down to **Cannabis College**), this museum explores the history and myriad uses of the cannabis plant. Displays detail ancient mentions of smoking marijuana, the importance of the hemp industry in the 17th and 18th centuries, the science of THC, and the costs of America's war on drugs—among much other ganga-related information. You can see a collection of pipes from around the world and a copy of the Declaration of Independence printed on hemp paper. Scattered somewhat incongruously throughout are Bible verses that could be liberally interpreted as support for the freedom to toke up. Hey, take backing from anywhere you can get it, especially when it's of the divine variety. A grow room sits adjacent to the main display area. Check out a few large, leafy specimens of the plants that you may or may not be smoking throughout the city's coffeeshops.

From Dam Square, walk east on Dam and make a left onto Oudezijds Achterburgwal. $ €9, groups of 10 or more €7 per person. ⏰ Open daily 10am-11pm.

CANNABIS COLLEGE INFORMATION CENTER

Oudezijds Achterburgwal 124 ☎042 344 20 💻www.cannabiscollege.com

Get your druggie "diploma" (a bachelor's in blunts? a master's in marijuana? a doctorate in doobies?) by taking a short quiz on all things cannabis-related. Don't just come to pad your credentials, though: this is a repository of any and all information you could ever want about the funny stuff. Friendly volunteers on staff are happy to answer any questions visitors may have about the history, science, and usage of the drug. They're so knowledgeable that they run training programs for coffeeshop staffers, and they're hoping to expand with even more educational opportunities in the future. Downstairs, a wide variety of plants grow in a lovingly tended organic garden.

From Dam Square, walk east on Dam and make a left onto Oudezijds Achterburgwal. $ Free. Garden €2.50. ⏰ Open daily 11am-7pm.

NIEUWE ZIJD

The Nieuwe Zijd (despite the name) is one of the oldest parts of the city. Both important historical architecture and museums dedicated to the past can be found within its borders. Some of the more recent and gimmicky museums, such as **Madame Tussaud's** and the **Amsterdam Dungeon,** are located here as well.

NIEUWE KERK ♿ CHURCH, MUSEUM

Dam Sq. ☎063 869 09 💻www.nieuwekerk.nl

Built in 1408 when the Oude Kerk became too small for the city's growing population, the Nieuwe Kerk is a commanding Gothic building that manages to hold its own amid the architectural extravaganza that is Dam Sq. Inside, the church is all vaulted ceilings and massive windows. Don't miss the intricate organ case designed by **Jacob van Campen,** Koninklijk Palace's architect. Today, the church is no longer used for religious purposes but is the site of royal inaugurations (the last one being that of **Queen Beatrix** in 1980) and some royal weddings (**Prince Willem-Alexander,** the heir to the Dutch throne, was married here in 2002). Most of the year, however, the space serves as a museum. Each winter, the church holds exhibits on foreign cultures, with a specific focus on world religions, and recent topics have included Islam and Ancient Egypt. Other times during the year, the space is used for temporary exhibits by prominent Dutch museums like the **Stedelijk** and **Rijksmuseum.** Organ concerts are held here every Sunday, while shorter and more informal organ recitals are performed on Thursday afternoons.

Any tram to Dam. Nieuwe Kerk is on the northeastern edge of the square. $ €5, students €4, with Museumjaarkaart free. Organ concerts €8.50, recitals €5. Open daily 10am-5pm. Recitals Th 12:30pm. Concerts Su 8pm.

BEGIJNHOF — COURTYARD, CHURCH

Begijnhof — www.begijnhofamsterdam.nl

The **Beguines** were medieval groups of Roman Catholic laywomen who took vows of chastity and chose to serve the Church without retreating from the world and formally joining a convent. After seeing this beautiful 14th-century courtyard (the Beguines lived in the houses surrounding it), you'll agree that they made a good call: this is a pretty sweet crib. Tour groups, bicycles, and photographs aren't allowed, so you can get some sense for the place's original tranquility. During the Alteration, the original chapel was turned into a Protestant place of worship. The women responded by using a secret Catholic church, the **Begijnhofkapel,** built within two of the houses. Today, the cute but unremarkable chapel is an English Presbyterian church that is open to respectful visitors.

Tram #1, 2, or 5 to Spui/Niuewezijds Voorburgwal. Walk down Gedempte Begijnsloot; the gardens are on the left. $ Free. Open daily 9am-5pm.

AMSTERDAM HISTORICAL MUSEUM — MUSEUM

Nieuwezijds Voorburgwal 357, Kalverstraat 92 — ☎052 318 22 www.amh.nl

People, schmeople. This place is about Amsterdam, the *city.* Watch the introductory video that shows how this northern powerhouse has grown from a tiny settlement by the Amstel to a familiar horseshoe ring of canals to the recognizable urban destination of the past century. Then, proceed on the museum's **"Grand Tour,"** which begins in 1350 with **"The Young City,"** continues through the growth of trade, art, and turbulent politics of **"The Golden Age,"** and finishes off with the period from the Industrial Revolution to **"The Modern City."** The path is a little unnecessarily winding, but the collection of paintings, artifacts, and multimedia presentations that lines the way are well-presented and informative. Don't miss the room dedicated to Golden Age art, with some stomach-churningly gruesome paintings of the anatomy lessons that were fashionable during the 17th century. Also fascinating is the corner that shows various city planning designs from the past century, driving home the fact that Amsterdam is an entirely manmade city and that building more housing today entails building more land. At the exit, you'll quickly be thrown back into the present by the glossy vending machine selling historically relevant souvenirs.

Tram #1, 2, or 5 to Spui/Niuewezijds Voorburgwal. Head up Niuwezijds Voorburgwal; the museum is on the right. $ €10, seniors €7.50, students and ages 6-18 €5, under 6 and with Museumjaarkaart free. Audio tour €4.50 Open M-F 10am-5pm, Sa-Su 11am-5pm.

DAM SQUARE — SQUARE

Dam Sq.

Once upon a time, lively Amsterdam was just two small settlements on either side of the Amstel River. Then one day, the settlers decided to connect their encampments with a dam. Three guesses where that dam was built. Since then, Dam Square has been the heart of the city, home to markets, a church, the town hall, and a weigh house (until Napoleon's brother had it torn down because it blocked his view). The obelisk on one end is the **Nationaal Monument,** inside of which soil from all twelve Dutch provinces and the Dutch East Indies is stored. The monument was erected in 1956 to honor the Dutch victims of WWII. Across from the monument, next to the Nieuwe Kerk, you'll find the **Koninklijk Palace,** which is currently closed for restoration. Louis Napoleon took it over in 1808, deciding that the building, constructed in the 17th century as Amsterdam's town hall, would make an excellent fixer-upper. Since then, it has been an official royal palace of the Netherlands, though Queen Beatrix only uses it for official functions and actually lives elsewhere. Too bad—she's wasting a unique view of the crowds, street performers, and occasional concert-type events that take place in the square.

🚋 *Tram #1, 2, 4, 5, 9, 13, 14, 16, 17, 24, or 25 to Dam. Yeah, it's pretty easy to get here.*

BEURS VAN BERLAGE
♿ DUTCH HISTORY, ARCHITECTURE

Damrak 277 ☎053 041 41 🖥www.beursvanberlage.nl

The first stock and commodities exchange was established in Amsterdam during the 17th century, and at the end of the 1800s, the exchange got a spiffy new home. **Hendrik Petrus Berlage** won the task of designing the exchange's new digs, and after initially entering the competition with a Neoclassical design that matched the trend of the period, he scrapped it all and came up with what was to become this hulking brick building on the Damrak. To put it mildly, not everyone was thrilled at the time, but Berlage's Modernist innovation paved the way for important Dutch architectural movements like that of the Amsterdam School. (Learn more about them at the **Museum het Schip.**) Nowadays, there's no stock market to be found here. Instead, look for music and dance performances (see **Arts and Culture**), conferences, and other private events. This fulfills the socialist Berlage's prediction that capitalism would eventually fail, the stock market would no longer exist, and the building in which it was housed would become a cultural 🖼"**palace of the people.**" (Well, at least that last one is kind of true.) And if we're being honest, the Beurs van Berlage isn't too public—your best bet for getting a peek inside the building is to contribute to the capitalist economy and visit the cafe on the south side.

🚋 *From Centraal Station, walk straight down Damrak.* 🕐 *Cafe open M-Sa 10am-6pm, Su 11am-6pm.*

ALLARD PIERSON MUSEUM
♠♿ MUSEUM

Oude Turfmarkt 127 ☎052 525 56 🖥www.allardpiersonmuseum.nl

Had too much of the modern city's hustle and bustle? Step back a few millennia at the archaeological museum of the University of Amsterdam, named after the school's first professor of Classical Archaeology. The artifacts here are drawn from Egypt, the Middle East, the Roman Empire, Etruria, and the Greek world. It's not an overly large collection, but there are graceful statues, a large collection of pottery, and even a mummy. Small, specialized displays like the ones on the Coptic church or the role of animals in antiquity are quirkily informative. Unfortunately, some display cards are only written in Dutch, but larger informative displays are bilingual.

🚋 *Tram #4, 9, 14, 16, 24, or 25 to Spui/Rokin. The museum is just across the canal.* 💲 *€6.50; ages 4-16, seniors, and students €3.25; under 4 and with Museumjaarkaart free.* 🕐 *Open Tu-F 10am-5pm, Sa-Su 1-5pm.*

AMSTERDAM SEX MUSEUM
👁🚫 MUSEUM

Damrak 18 ☎062 283 76 🖥www.sexmuseumamsterdam.nl

Unless you were previously unaware that people have been having sex since the species's origin, there is not much information about sex or sexuality to be had at this museum. (The brief "Sex Through the Ages" presentation is hilariously simplistic, though the elegant British accent narrating it is priceless.) Instead, there's a lot of pornographic paintings, photographs, books, and statues, mainly from the late 19th and early 20th centuries, though most historical periods are represented in some form or another. Scattered throughout are models of various sexual icons: there's Marilyn Monroe with her skirt fluttering over the subway vent, a 1980s pimp, and even a 🦟flasher who thrills the audience like clockwork every few seconds. If you really want to see a parade of pictures of people having sex, you could just walk through the Red Light District and get it for free. At least this place charges a low rate for the high kitsch factor.

⚑ *From Centraal Station, walk straight down Damrak.* ⓘ *Must be 16+ to enter.* ⓢ *€4.* ⓩ *Open daily 9:30am-11:30pm.*

SCHEEPVAARTBUURT

Scheepvaartbuurt, or the Shipping Quarter, was once one of Amsterdam's most important neighborhoods. In the 18th and 19th centuries, its location along the banks of the IJ made the area an ideal base for the city's flourishing trade companies. Alas, toward the end of the 1800s, the center of the shipping industry shifted and spread, leaving the neighborhood a shell of its former glory. For a long time, this was one of the rougher parts of Amsterdam, full of little more than criminals and junkies. Urban renewal efforts have had their effects here as well, though, and now Scheepvaartbuurt is a perfectly pleasant area. As for remnants of the neighborhood's salty seadog days, bronze ship-related monuments like propellers, anchors, and nautical steering wheels dot the sidewalks. We like to think that you can also detect a faint whiff of the sea breeze that blew ships to and from this shore oh so long ago. Otherwise, the only real sight in the neighborhood is the West-Indische Huis building.

WEST-INDISCHE HUIS
        ♿ DUTCH HISTORY
Haarlemmerstraat 75

Back when the Dutch ruled the seas, the *Geoctroyeerde Westindische Compagnie*, or **Chartered West India Company,** was a pretty big deal. This building in Herenmarkt was their headquarters from 1623-1647, and it was here that New York City was born when the company's board of governors decided to construct a fort on the island of Manhattan in 1625. Before and after its tenure as the West India Company's headquarters, the building served as a meat market, a hotel, and a home for orphans and the elderly. Today, different companies and organizations as well as private parties rent the space. It's not open to the public, but the elegant white building's exterior gives you a sense of the company's power back in the days when Scheepvaartbuurt was still the city's shipping quarter.

⚑ *Make a right when leaving Centraal Station; the building's on your left a few blocks after crossing the Singel.*

CANAL RING WEST

The Canal Ring West has none of the city's large art museums, but it is where you'll find some of Amsterdam's quirkiest spots as well as the notable **Anne Frank House** and nearby **Westerkerk.**

▨ ANNE FRANK HOUSE
        ✎⊗ MUSEUM
Prinsengracht 267   ☎055 671 00 🖥www.annefrank.nl

From July 6, 1942, until they were betrayed by a still unknown informant and arrested on August 4, 1944, Anne Frank and her family, along with four others, lived in a "secret annex" above the warehouse of her father's company in this building. Since its publication in 1950, the diary Frank kept during her stay in the annex has become one of the world's most-read books; it stands as one of the most moving accounts of war and persecution to date as well as a testament to the strength and depth of the human spirit. This wonderfully presented museum illustrates the story of Frank and her fellow annex inhabitants and accompanies their tale with more information about the fate of Jews in the Netherlands and throughout Europe under Nazi oppression. Many traces of the annex's clandestine residents have been preserved, including the pictures Anne glued to the walls in hopes of cheering up the place and the pencil marks that tracked the growth of the children throughout their years in hiding. The rooms are no longer furnished, but models of their earlier setup (as well as blacked-out windows and the size of the rooms themselves) give some idea of the close quarters Anne struggled with in her diary. Pages from her original journal are on display in one of the rooms, and throughout the museum, quotes from it (in Dutch and English) accompany the exhibits. Video interviews with Anne's father, a childhood friend, and one of the factory workers who helped the family are also available for viewing. The museum route takes you through the entirety of the family's hiding place, starting behind the moveable bookcase that masked the annex; after going through the annex, there are displays describing the fates of the Franks and the millions of other Jews who were sent to the concentration camps across Europe. Further on is an exhibit that brings forth one of Otto Frank's main motives for establishing the museum: not just to remember the victims of the Holocaust, but to use that memory to work for a future in which such atrocities remain a thing of the past.

*🚋 Tram #13, 14, or 17 to Westermarkt. **i** Lines are shortest before 10am and after 6pm. $ €8.50, ages 10-17 €4, under 10 free. 🕐 Open daily July-Aug 9am-10pm; Sept 1-14 9am-9pm; Sept 15-March 14 9am-7pm; March 15-June 9am-9pm.*

☑ WESTERKERK — CHURCH

Prinsengracht 281 — ☎062 477 66 💻www.westerkerk.nl

The 85m tower of the Westerkerk stands out starkly amid the relative height uniformity of central Amsterdam's buildings. This church was completed in 1631 according to a design by **Hendrik de Keyser.** On the top of the tower is the symbol of the crown of Maximilian of Austria, a gift he gave to the city in thanks for Amsterdam's support of the Austro-Burgundian princes. Despite the apparent narcissism of the gesture, Maximilian's crown and the tower it caps have become an enduring symbol of the city. On the outside, the church's brick-and-stone exterior is a fine example of Dutch late Renaissance style. Inside, its plain white walls and clear glass windows are an example of the clean Calvinist aesthetic. The only real decorations are the shutters on the organ, beautifully painted by **Gerard de Lairesse.** Nevertheless, the church is by no means restricted to perpetual austerity: Queen Beatrix and Prince Claus were married here in 1966, which must have been quite the event. Rembrandt is buried somewhere within the church, although no one seems to know exactly where. (Yeah, we don't know how they forgot where they put one of the most famous painters of all time either.)

A trip up the **Westerkerkstoren** (part of a 30min. guided tour) is a must, affording phenomenal views of the surrounding city. Also up in the tower's heights is an astounding set of 47 bells, one of which weighs in at an astonishing 7509kg, making it Amsterdam's heaviest. On Tuesdays, the carillon plays from noon to 1pm. Free organ concerts are held every Friday at 1pm, and the church hosts many other concerts throughout the year.

🚋 Tram #13, 14, or 17 to Westermarkt. $ Free. Tower tour €5. 🕐 Open Apr-Oct 11am-3pm. Tower tours every 30min.

☑ HOMOMONUMENT — ♿▼ MONUMENT

Westermarkt — 💻www.homomonument.nl

Designed by Karin Daan and officially opened in 1987, the Homomonument was the culmination of a movement to erect a memorial dedicated to those who were persecuted by the Nazis for their sexuality, but it is also meant to stand for all homosexual men and women who have been and are being oppressed because of their sexual orientation. The monument is constructed of three pink granite triangles (in remembrance of the symbol the Nazis forced homosexuals to wear) that are connected by thin lines of pink granite to form a larger triangle. Built so that it would merge seamlessly with the daily life of the city, the Homomonument can, in fact, be hard to discern under picnicking tourists and whizzing bikes. One triangle is set down into the water of the Keizergracht and points towards the **National War Monument** in Dam square, representing the present. The raised triangle stands for the future and points toward the headquarters of the COC, a Dutch gay rights group that was founded in 1946, and, as such, is the oldest continuously operating gay and lesbian organization in the world. The third triangle points toward the **Anne Frank House,** symbolizing the past; it is engraved with the words *"Naar Vriendschap Zulk een Mateloos Verlangen"* ("such an endless desire for friendship") from the poem *To a Young Fisherman* by Jacob Israel de Haan (1881-1924), a gay Dutch Jewish poet.

✈ *Tram #13, 14, or 17 to Westermarkt. The Homomonument is between Westerkerk and the Keizersgracht.* Ⓢ *Free.*

BIJBELS MUSEUM
⊛Ġ MUSEUM

Herengracht 366-368   ☎062 424 36 ▧www.bijbelsmuseum.nl

This informative museum provides glimpses into two radically different worlds: ancient Biblical culture and 17th-century Dutch life. The top floor has Egyptian artifacts—sculptures, sarcophagi, even a mummy—that are meant to illustrate the Israelite presence in Egypt. There is also a model of the Tabernacle, constructed by the minister Leendert Schouten (1828-1905) over the span of 20 years; it was Schouten who founded the museum, with public viewings of the Tabernacle as its core. Also on display are some memorabilia from Schouten's life. The next floor down houses the Temple Mount Room, which displays the history of the city of Jerusalem and illustrates how Islam, Judaism, and Christianity have interacted there. On the ground floor are rooms adorned by phenomenal ceilings painted courtesy of Jacob de Wit; they contain a collection of ornately bound prayer books. The ground-floor introduction to the domestic life that once filled these 17th-century buildings is continued below, where a refurbished traditional Dutch kitchen stands ready for your perusal. Adjacent are two large and comfortable reading rooms (with a variety of books and pamphlets free for browsing) and the somewhat perplexing **Aroma Room,** which has samples of Biblical scents like cedar and myrrh free for the sniffing. At the back is a lovely and peaceful garden. Many of the rooms in the museum are devoted to temporary special exhibitions.

✈ *Tram #1, 2, or 5 to Koningsplein. Make a right onto Herengracht.* Ⓢ *€8, students €4.75, ages 13-17 €4.* ⏱ *Open M-Sa 10am-5pm, Su 11am-5pm.*

MULTATULI MUSEUM
⊛⊗ MUSEUM

Korsjespoortsteeg 20   ☎063 819 38 ▧www.multatuli-museum.nl

In 1820, this unassuming house saw the birth of **Eduard Douwes Dekker,** considered the Netherlands's most significant writer. Dekker was a rather unsuccessful lad, and after failing at school and a trade clerkship, he was carted off to Indonesia by his sea captain father. Here, he finally exhibited some talent in the civil service (maybe all dropouts should be rewarded with a one-way ticket to Java), rising through the ranks and marrying a baroness along the way, until he was stationed in a town overseen by an indigenous leader known to be cruel and corrupt. Finally able to recognize the abuses engendered by imperialism, Dekker tried to prosecute the leader and push for reform, much to the disapproval of his superiors. Despite their resistance, Dekker stuck to his morals and quit his job rather than acquiesce to the system, returning to a penniless life in

Europe. He wasn't willing to go down without a fight either: under the pen name Multatuli (Latin for "I have endured much"), Dekker wrote the autobiographical novel *Max Havelaar* to expose the evils of colonialism and the Dutch East India Company. Some also say that Dekker published the book in order to show what an upstanding, ethical person he had been. Ironically, *Max Havelaar* became a massive hit, not due to its message of reform (which was largely ignored by the contemporary public) but as a result of Dekker's entertaining, well-written prose. In time, however, the work came to be cited as an influence promoting fairer government policies and colonial nationalist movements. Dekker continued to write and was an early proponent of women's equality, workers' rights, parliamentary reform, and atheism. Today, *Max Havelaar* is the most popular Dutch novel, existing in over 40 translations. Dekker is considered a crucial intellectual forefather to the atmosphere of tolerance for which the Netherlands is renowned today.

Dekker's second wife probably guessed that he was going to be a big deal, so after his death she kept a collection of his papers and belongings, which in 1910 were given to the newly founded Multatuli Society, which runs the museum. On the ground floor of the building, you will find a collection of Dekker's works in numerous translations, plus shelves of secondary sources—criticisms, biographies, and the like. The first floor (up a classically narrow and vertiginous staircase) holds furniture and a few belongings from Dekker's later years, including the couch where he died. Also on display is his personal library, with 19th-century editions of everything from Dickens to *The History of the Decline and Fall of the Roman Empire*. Terrifically friendly and knowledgeable staffers are happy to show you around the small exhibit and tell you all about Dekker's fascinating life and legacy.

�znⁿ *Tram #1, 2, 5, 13, or 17 to Nieuwezijds Kolk. Walk to the Herengracht and make a right.* Ⓢ *Free.* ◨ *Open Tu 10am-5pm, Sa-Su 10am-5pm.*

HUIS MARSEILLE
♿⊘ MUSEUM

Keizersgracht 401   ☎053 189 80 ▣www.huismarseille.nl

Located in a lovely 17th-century canal house, this museum holds three-month-long photographic exhibitions arranged by theme or artist. The multiple floors have rooms that are sparsely decorated, allowing the photos themselves to shine. Works are mostly by contemporary photographers from a variety of international backgrounds. Downstairs, visitors may explore the museum's library with books on photography and a nice little garden that is open to the public.

✞ⁿ *Tram #1, 2, or 5 to Keizersgracht (Leidsestraat). Walk about 1½ blocks north along Keizersgracht.* Ⓢ *€5, seniors €3, with Museumjaarkaart free.* ◨ *Open Tu-Su 11am-6pm.*

NEDERLANDS INSTITUUT VOOR MEDIAKUNST
⊘⊘ MUSEUM

Keizersgracht 264   ☎062 371 01 ▣www.nimk.nl

The Netherlands Media Art Institute puts on four approximately 10-week exhibitions per year showcasing the works of Dutch and international artists who use film, video, the internet, and other media technology. Brilliant and cutting-edge projects fill the half-dozen rooms upstairs, with box-like seats provided so that you can linger over each piece. The Institute also runs a number of smaller exhibitions that involve more experimental performances or symposia. Housed in the same building is the **Mediatheque,** which holds a collection of books and media pieces numbering in the thousands; it also manages the video collections of De Appel and many other Dutch museums.

✞ⁿ *Tram #13, 14, or 17 to Westermarkt.* Ⓢ *€4.50, students and seniors €2.50. Mediatheque free.* ◨ *Open Tu-F 11am-6pm, Sa and every 1st Su 1-6pm. Mediatheque open M-F 1-5pm.*

NATIONAAL BRILMUSEUM (NATIONAL SPECTACLES MUSEUM) MUSEUM

Gasthuismolensteeg 7 ☎042 124 14 💻www.brilmuseumamsterdam.nl

Wandering the halls of this quirky museum is a bit like wandering through a cluttered antiques store. Housed in a 17th-century building, the Brilmuseum displays 700 years of eyewear history, art, and culture. You can learn about the developments in optics and glasses-making technology and track the trends of ocular fashion through the ages—some of our favorites were the jewel-toned, rectangular 👍**"railway glasses"** and a pretty crazy set of **monocles.** Hundreds of glasses are packed in alongside opticians' tools, old-fashioned advertisements, and models of the eye. Try to spot the pairs that once belonged to stars like **Schubert** and **Dame Edna.** If, after viewing this remarkable collection of eyewear, your own spectacles are beginning to develop a bit of an inferiority complex, you can make a visit to the eye-poppingly well-stocked store on the ground floor.

⇟ Tram #13, 14, or 17 to Westermarkt. Walk east on Raadhuisstraat, make a right after crossing Herengracht, and then a left onto Gasthuismolensteeg. $ €4.50, under 12 €2.50. ⏰ Open W-F 11:30am-5:30pm, Sa 11:30am-5pm.

CENTRAL CANAL RING

The grand buildings in the center of the canal ring, architectural landmarks themselves, house some excellent historical museums as well as galleries highlighting more cutting-edge culture.

👍 **FOAM PHOTOGRAPHY MUSEUM** ♿ MUSEUM

Keizersgracht 609 ☎055 165 00 💻www.foam.nl

Foam—the **Fo**tografiemuseum **Am**sterdam—showcases photography exhibits on pretty much every topic imaginable, from ultramodern, gritty documentary shots to glossy fashion photos. Both renowned and up-and-coming photographers are shown here in a sparse wood-and-metal space. A place for study as well as exhibition, the cafe reading room has books and magazines for your perusal. No need to feel ashamed for simply grabbing a coffee and feeling like one of the artsy Dutch students who hang out here though.

⇟ Tram #4, 16, 24, or 25 to Keizersgracht. FOAM is about 50m east of the stop. $ €8, students and seniors €5.50, under 12 and with Museumjaarkaart free. ⏰ Open M-W 10am-6pm, Th-F 10am-9pm, Sa-Su 10am-6pm. Cafe open daily 11am-5pm.

MUSEUM VAN LOON MUSEUM

Keizersgracht 672 ☎062 452 55 💻www.museumvanloon.nl

The Van Loons have been so integral to the city's history, their family tree might as well be drawn on a map of Amsterdam. One of the family's earlier members was a founder of the Dutch East India Company, and since then many have been mayors, political advisors, and the like. However, this house was not originally owned by this powerful lineage. Its first resident, **Ferdinand Bol,** was Rembrandt's most famous student. The house as you see it now, though, is clearly of the Van Loon tenure, with family portraits lining the walls. Indeed, while here, it's easy to feel as if you're creeping around someone's house (which, really, you are). Set up to look like the elegant, upper-class home it was when the Van Loons still lived here, the museum preserves a record of what traditional wealthy Dutch life was like, as per the intentions of the family when they donated their residence to the city. Weird last name or no, you'll wish that you had grown up a Van Loon after seeing this place—everything is stunningly beautiful. Don't miss the Mediterranean wall paintings in the **Drakensteyn Room.** Downstairs by the kitchen a video about the house and its inhabitants is narrated by one of the Van Loon descendents.

⇟ Tram #4, 16, 24, or 25 to Keizersgracht. The museum is about 50m east of the stop. $ €7, students €5, with Museumjaarkaart free. ⏰ Open M 11am-5pm, W-Su 11am-5pm.

GOLDEN BEND ♿ ARCHITECTURE

Herengracht, between Leidsestraat and Vijzelstraat

If the tiny, teetering canal houses of Amsterdam are beginning to make you feel a bit claustrophobic, head to this scenic stretch of the Canal Ring. In the 17th century, the ring canals were extended all the way to the Amstel. This required a fair bit of cash, so in order to encourage investment, the city decided to loosen restrictions on house width and allow Amsterdam's rich to build homes that were twice as wide as had been previously allowed. Termed the "Golden Bend" for the wealth that subsequently flocked here, this is a grand and beautiful stretch of former residences, all featuring Neoclassical facades and glimpses of sparkling chandeliers through latticed windows. Today, most are inhabited by banks, life insurance agencies, and the occasional philanthropic organization, though you can sneak a peek inside one at the **Cat's Cabinet.** Otherwise, during just a few days in June, it's possible to tour many of the houses' gardens on the **Open Garden Days.** For more information, check out 🖥**www.opentuinendagen.nl.**

🚊 Tram #1, 2, or 5 to Koningsplein.

MUSEUM WILLET-HOLTHUYSEN MUSEUM

Herengracht 605 ☎052 318 70 🖥www.willetholthuysen.nl

Not technically on the "Golden Bend" but still an extremely elegant canal house, this building has been preserved by the **Amsterdams Historisch Museum** to demonstrate what wealthy Dutch life was like in the 19th century as seen through the eyes of **Abraham Willet** and **Louisa Willet-Holthuysen,** the house's last inhabitants. Three opulently decorated floors feature many of the pieces acquired by this couple of avid art collectors. Painted by **Jacob de Wit,** the ceiling in the Blue Room was poached from a house on Keizersgracht. Throughout the museum, small paragraphs detail the culture and customs of life in the Willets' time. The top floor contains the most specific information about the Willets themselves and their circle, including audio recordings (available in English) of excerpts from a friend's diary. It makes a striking contrast to some of the other historic house museums such as **het Rembrandt** due to its grandeur and scale. A lovely garden in the back is open to museum visitors.

🚊 Tram #9 or 14 to Rembrandtplein. Walk down Utrechtsestraat and make a left. $ €7, students and ages 6-18 €3.50, under 6 and with Museumjaarkaart free. ⏰ Open M-F 10am-5pm, Sa-Su 11am-5pm.

CAT'S CABINET MUSEUM

Herengracht 497 ☎062 653 78 🖥www.kattenkabinet.nl

J. P. Morgan shows up as an important figure in many museums. No exception here—oh, except that this J. P. Morgan is a tabby cat who lived an illustrious life from 1966-83. His devoted owner (and we mean *really* devoted) dedicated two floors of this canal house to his less historic fat cat and all things feline-related. By now, the museum has racked up a pretty interesting collection of artwork involving cats: there are statues from Ancient Egypt, those Toulouse-Lautrec posters that adorn every college student's wall, a drawing by Picasso, and a series of paintings by **Karel Appel.** Look for Morgan's portrait in the fake dollar bill on the staircase, which was given to the tabby on his 15th birthday. Six real-live cats roam throughout the exhibits. Even if you're more of a **dog person,** a visit to the museum provides your best chance to get inside a building on the Golden Bend. The rooms are decorated in a decadent style that evokes the general majesty of the area.

🚊 Trams #1, 2, or 5 to Koningsplein. Walk to Herengracht and make a left. $ €5. ⏰ Open M-F 10am-4pm, Sa-Su noon-5pm.

LEIDSEPLEIN

The whole of Leidseplein is really a sight unto itself, presenting a unique combination of gaudy bars and stately old theaters. During the day, the square is packed with street performers as well as promoters for pub crawls and other assorted nightlife; at night, the revelry continues in a bath of neon light and cheap beer. A walk down the **Weteringschans** will take you past some beautiful buildings, including the church that has been repurposed as the nightclub **Paradiso** and the **Barlaeus Gymnasium,** an extremely famous Dutch secondary school dating from the 19th century.

MAX EUWEPLEIN
&⚴ SQUARE

Max Euweplein

🖥️www.maxeuweplein.net

This small square tucked in the corner of a space dominated by megabar patios remains the heart of the Leidseplein. Somewhat inexplicably, the inscription above the pillars of the main entrance to the square reads *Homo sapiens non urinat in ventum* ("A wise man does not piss into the wind")—perhaps a useful reminder to the barflies of the Leidseplein. The sight to be seen is a large chessboard with oversized pieces (Max Euwe was a famous Dutch chess master), generally presided over by a cluster of grizzled old men as younger chess enthusiasts eagerly watch every move. The square occasionally plays host to live music and dance performances.

🚋 *Tram #1, 2, 5, 7, or 10 to Leidseplein. Facing the ABN-Amro bank, make a left along Weteringschans; the square will be on your right.* Ⓢ *Free.*

REMBRANDTPLEIN

Rembrandtplein lacks the museums and other cultural spots that fill the rest of Amsterdam, but underneath the beer and bumping bass there is some history to be found even here.

REMBRANDTPLEIN
&⚲⚴ SQUARE

Rembrandtplein

Once upon a time (a.k.a. the late 17th century), the area now known as Rembrandtplein was home to Amsterdam's butter market *(Botermarkt)*. Unless there are things we don't know about the dairy trade, we suspect that the neighborhood was quite a bit tamer than it is today. Around the end of the 19th century, hotels and cafes began to spring up around the square, which led to more tourists visiting the area, which led to people trying to figure out how to get more money from the tourists, which meant trying to get tourists drunk: thus, the explosion of bars and clubs nearby. Rembrandtplein is now home to Amsterdam's largest club, **Escape,** underneath Europe's largest LCD TV screen. From the middle of the square, **Rembrandt van Rijn** looks benevolently down at the madness.

🚋 *Tram #9 or 14 to (surprise!) Rembrandtplein.*

THORBECKEPLEIN
&⚲⚴ SQUARE

Thorbeckeplein

In between Rembrandtplein and Herengracht is another bar-lined square named after a historical figure, Mr. **Johan Rudolph Thorbecke** (1798-1872)—he's the one on the pedestal by the river. Thorbecke was a member of the Dutch parliament who led the constitutional reforms of 1848, restricting the power of the monarchy and giving it to the States-General of the Netherlands. He became minister of internal affairs in 1849, making him for all intents and purposes the first prime minister of the Netherlands. His parliamentary career went through many ups and downs owing to constant political conflicts, but today he is remembered as one of the greatest Dutch political figures. No surprise, then, that he got a square named after him. Thorbeckeplein, in turn, gave its name to a song written by the popular Dutch singer **Robert Long** about a bittersweet gay love affair.

🚋 *Tram #9 or 14 to Rembrandtplein. It's on the opposite side of Rembrandtplein from the giant TV screen.*

JORDAAN

ELECTRIC LADYLAND

MUSEUM

2e Leliedwarsstraat 5 ☎042 037 76 🖥www.electric-lady-land.com

The "First Museum of Fluorescent Art" and a sight unlike any other, Electric Ladyland deserves a good chunk of your sightseeing time. The endearingly eccentric and passionate owner, Nick Padalino, will happily spend hours explaining the history, science, and culture of fluorescence and fluorescent art to each and every visitor who walks through the door. He's collected a spectacular assortment of rocks and minerals, many exceedingly rare, that hail from New Jersey to the Himalayas and glow all kinds of colors under the different light Padalino expertly shines upon them. A case full of ordinary objects that fluoresce under blacklights includes a credit card with a hidden face of Einstein. Other artifacts tell the history of fluorescence and its popularity in the early part of the century: paintings made from fluorescent paint or ground mineral pigments, some dating to as early as the 1940s, hang on the walls. Most intriguing, though, is the fluorescent cave-like sculpture that Padalino terms "participatory art"—don a pair of foam slippers and poke around the glowing grottoes and stalactites, flick the buttons on and off to see different fluorescent and phosphorescent stones, and look for the tiny, hidden Hindu sculptures. Completing the psychedelic trip is a quiet soundtrack of classic rock from Hendrix to The Beatles. Upstairs, you can buy your own fluorescent art or blacklight kits to take home a part of the experience.

🚋 *Tram #13, 14, or 17 to Westermarkt. Cross Prinsengracht and walk 1 block down Rozengracht, then make a right and walk a few blocks—the museum is just before you reach Egelantiersgracht.* $ *€5.* 🕒 *Open Tu-Sa 1-6pm.*

STEDELIJK MUSEUM BUREAU AMSTERDAM

♿ MUSEUM

Rozenstraat 59 ☎042 204 71 🖥www.smba.nl

As the Stedelijk Museum's project space, the Stedelijk Museum Bureau Amsterdam (SMBA) seeks to promote cutting-edge contemporary art, primarily from the Netherlands. The bright white room hosts around six exhibitions a year, with everything from sculpture to painting to performance art represented. Lectures and discussions are also organized by the gallery. Check the website to see what's currently running. Given the free admission, there's no reason not to drop by.

🚋 *Tram #13, 14, or 17 to Westermarkt. Cross Prinsengracht, make a left, and walk 1 block.* $ *Free.* 🕒 *Open Tu-Su 11am-5pm.*

HOFJES

♿ GARDENS, DUTCH HISTORY

Located in the northern third of the Jordaan

One theory regarding the origin of the Jordaan's name speculates that the moniker is derived from the French word *jardin* (garden), as a number of French Huguenots immigrated here in the 17th century. Such a hypothesis may provoke skepticism, however, since Jordaan is one of Amsterdam's few areas that doesn't have a park—it all starts to make sense, though, once you've stepped behind some of the neighborhood's closed doors. Here, you will find a number of *hofjes*, courtyards surrounded by almshouses that were originally designed to provide housing for poor older women. Nowadays, the buildings have been turned into private houses, but many of the gardens are still open to the public. In the northern part of the Jordaan, at Palmgracht 28-38, you can find the **Raepenhofje,** named after the founder (Pieter Raepe) who had it built in 1648 for orphans and widows to enjoy. A few blocks down is the **Karthuizerhof,** at Karthuizersstraat 21-131. This larger *hofje* has two flowering gardens dotted with benches and a pair of old-fashioned water pumps. Finally, head to Egelantiersgracht 107-145 for the **Sint-Andrieshof** *(🕒 Open M-Sa 9am-6pm.)*, another oasis of tranquility. These gardens are surrounded by residences, so be quiet and respectful.

➡ To start off at the Raepenhofje, take tram #3 to Nieuwe Willemstraat, cross Lijnbaansgracht, make a left, and then a right onto Palmgracht. $ Free.

HOUSEBOAT MUSEUM

MUSEUM

Prinsengracht, facing #296 ☎042 707 50 💻www.houseboatmuseum.nl

You can't avoid seeing **houseboats** floating in the canals as you wander through Amsterdam, and this museum is designed to answer the inevitable questions that arise when landlubbers contemplate living on the water. The museum *is* a houseboat, and it appears deceptively large—it's actually the same size as the average Amsterdam apartment. It's cozily set up to look like a real home, too, but it's more than just a model: the informative guide available in dozens of languages, slideshows, and photos tell you all about the history, construction, and maintenance of the boats. If you're inspired to get on the water yourself, you can always rent a houseboat from **Frederic Rent-a-Bike.**

➡ Tram #13, 14, or 17 to Westermarkt; cross Prinsengracht, make a left, and walk to the intersection with Elandsgracht. $ €3.50, with Museumjaarkaart €2.75. 🕒 Open Mar-Oct Tu-Su 11am-5pm; Nov-Jan 3 F-Su 11am-5pm; Jan 30-Feb F-Su 11am-5pm.

PIANOLA MUSEUM

MUSEUM

Westerstraat 106 ☎062 796 24 💻www.pianola.nl

Vying with **Electric Ladyland** for the title of Weirdest Museum in the Jordaan, Pianola began as a private collection and now fills a space on busy Westerstraat with a glimpse into early 20th-century music and culture. What's a pianola, you ask? Commonly referred to as a player piano, it's an upright piano whose internal mechanism has been partially replaced with machinery that lets it play automatically. Different songs are recorded on paper rolls and inserted into the instrument. The museum holds over 25,000 such rolls, most of which can be played on the instruments that fill the place. A 1920s feel pervades the exhibition, as this was the time when these instruments were at their peak popularity (though we expect a resurgence any day now). Regular concerts are held here: check the website or posters outside for details.

➡ Tram #3 or 10 to Marnixplein. Cross Lijnbaansgracht and walk up Westerstraat. $ €5. 🕒 Open Su 2-5pm. Group visits by appointment.

WESTERPARK AND OUD-WEST

MUSEUM HET SCHIP

♿ MUSEUM

Spaarndammerplantsoen 140 ☎041 828 85 💻www.hetschip.nl

As Amsterdam expanded at the turn of the 20th century, its workers lived in increasingly cramped and squalid conditions. Socialist movements led to laws regulating housing (requiring, for example, that apartments have windows) and to the construction of affordable, higher-quality living spaces. **Het Schip** ("The Ship") was one such housing project, built in 1919 and designed by Michel de Klerk. Its unusual design makes it a leading example of the Amsterdam School, an expressionist movement in architecture and design. You can get a feel for the characteristics of the Amsterdam School just by walking around the large building: notice the unusual curves inspired by organic shapes, the creative use of different kinds of brick and roof tiles, and the intricate sculptural decorations lurking in various corners. A visit to the museum, however, is worth the extra time, as it provides you with the opportunity to explore inside the remarkable post office nestled in one corner as well as an example of one of the building's original apartments (the rest are still in use). On the apartment's first floor, you'll find an exhibit on the Amsterdam School. Try to arrive on the hour to take advantage of the excellent and informative free tour that will point out building details which are otherwise easy to miss. The staff are sometimes able to squeeze in visitors who arrive at other times. Across the street, a lunchroom serves food amid an exhibit of Amsterdam School photography and sculptures.

Tram #3 to Haarlemmerplein. Walk across the canal toward Westerpark, up Spaarndammerstraat, and left onto Zaanstraat; the building will be a few blocks down the street. $ €7.50, students €5, with Museumjaarkaart free. ⏰ Open Tu-Su 11am-5pm. Tours every hr. 11am-4pm.

WESTERPARK ♿ PARK

The park that gives the neighborhood its name is small but worth a visit on a sunny day. Along the Haarlemmerweg grassy slopes roll down to the water and invite lounging; dirt paths around the park are great for biking, walking, or jogging. In the middle, a duck-filled pond accompanied by some very curious statues, including a headless woman in fancy dress, presides. Towards the northeastern corner is a playground filled with happy kiddies.

Tram #10 to Van Limburg Stirumstraat. Walk up V. L. Stirumstraat, cross the Haarlemmerweg, and enter the park on the right. Main entrance on Spaarndammerstraat, across from the Naussauplein (buses #22 and 348). $ Free.

WESTERGASFABRIEK ♿🍸 CULTURAL PARK

Pazzanistraat 41 ☎058 607 10 💻www.westergasfabriek.nl

A "cultural park" right next to the traditional verdant kind. Westergasfabriek was originally a 19th-century gasworks, but its abandonment after the discovery of natural gas in the northern part of the Netherlands left its infrastructure available for other uses in the 1960s. Westergasfabriek's buildings, most designed by Isaac Goschalk, form an imposing brick cluster in the Dutch Renaissance style. Spaces are open to any and all cultural projects, and currently house art studios and galleries, restaurants, theaters, and nightclubs. Some buildings are also available to rent for events. Check the website for a list of current programs; recent ones have included an Asian film festival and the so-called "Funky Spring Market."

Just east of Westerpark. Tram #10 to Van Hallstraat. Cross the bridge and make a right to get to the main cluster of buildings.

MUSEUMPLEIN AND VONDELPARK

Surprise! The Museumplein is filled with museums. Good ones, at that, with two of the city's best and most famous just a few steps away from each other. Besides the listings that follow, the beautiful **Concertgebouw** at the southern end of Museumplein is a concert hall worth visiting even when the music isn't playing (see **Arts and Culture**).

VAN GOGH MUSEUM ♿ MUSEUM

Paulus Potterstraat 7 ☎057 052 00 💻www.vangoghmuseum.nl

We think this may be the best museum in Amsterdam—unfortunately, so do a lot of other people. The lines can get pretty painful, so to avoid them, reserve tickets on the museum's website or arrive around 10:30am or 4pm. By all means, don't let the fear of crowds deter you: this museum is absolutely worth the wait. Van Gogh was an artist for only about 10 years, yet he left a remarkable legacy of paintings and drawings—most of which are owned by this museum. The exhibit is arranged in chronological order, and wall plaques do an excellent job of describing and analyzing each phase of Van Gogh's life. On the ground floor, you'll find works from the **French Barbizon School** and the **Dutch Hague School,** both of which were influential to Van Gogh's early development. The next floor up contains the bulk of Van Gogh's works. His early phase is exemplified by dark, gloomy works like the *Potato Eaters* and *Skull of a Skeleton with Burning Cigarette.* After moving to Paris and becoming more involved in the modern art movement there, Van Gogh began to experiment with a different, brighter tone.

Some clearly show the influence of the late 19th-century Orientalism craze and the period's popular Japanese woodblock prints. Others reflect his friendships with Modernist painters like **Paul Gauguin** (more on him and others later). The eye-catching works in this later period include paintings like *Bedroom at Arles* (undergoing restoration at the time of press) with its bright impasto hues and the delicate *Branches of an Almond Tree in Blossom.* It's particularly poignant to track the theme of Van Gogh's descent into depression and suicide which threads throughout the commentary accompanying the paintings.

The second floor contains works from the **Mesdag Museum,** one of Holland's earliest museums of modern art whose collection is now in the hands of the Van Gogh Museum. More works by the Barbizon and Hague schools are also on display here. While you won't find any blockbuster names, the works are incredibly diverse and provide a helpful overview of Impressionism's precursors. One more flight up, works of Van Gogh's French contemporaries are displayed, with some of Van Gogh's works hanging among them to emphasize their connection. There are lovely works by Toulouse-Lautrec, Gauguin, Renoir, Manet, Seurat, and Pissarro. Following these, works by artists influenced by Van Gogh, such as **Derain** and **Picasso** are featured. Finally, a small exhibition on Symbolism explains what besides Impressionism was going on in the French art world of the 19th century. Temporary traveling exhibitions fill an adjacent space.

All in all, the museum presents a remarkable concentration of top-quality art in an accessible dose.

🚋 Tram #2, 3, 5, or 12 to Van Baerlestraat. Walk 1 block up Paulus Potterstraat. $ €14, 17 and under and with Museumjaarkaart free. Audio tour €5. 🕐 Open M-Th 10am-6pm, F 10am-10pm, Sa-Su 10am-6pm.

★ RIJKSMUSEUM — 🎟♿ MUSEUM

Jan Luijkenstraat 1 — ☎067 470 00 💻www.rijksmuseum.nl

If something feels familiar when you see the Rijksmuseum for the first time, don't be surprised: the palatial building was designed by **Pierre Cuypers,** the architect responsible for Centraal Station. The museum has been under construction for years and, at the time of writing, plans to fully reopen in 2013. For now, highlights of the collection are on display in the **Philips Wing.** As the national museum of both history and art, the Rijksmuseum holds vast stores of art and artifacts from the Middle Ages through the 19th century, a comprehensive exhibit on Dutch history, a collection of Asian art, and an enormous selection of furniture, Delftware, silver, and decorative objects (including two detailed 👍**dollhouses** that probably cost more than many student apartments). Some of this stuff is temporarily on loan to other European museums, but a good cross-section remains in the Philips Wing on the ground floor. Here, the museum tells the story of the Netherlands as it grew from Dutch Republic to world power, commanding a fair share of the seas and international trade. However, the real heart of the museum is the art on the floor above, where the outstanding Dutch paintings of the Golden Age are housed. Numerous still lifes (cheese figures prominently, typical Dutch), landscapes, and portraits set the tone for 17th-century Dutch art, reflecting the trends and culture of the history lesson on the first floor. Next up, they pull out the big guns in a room full of deep, beautiful works by **Rembrandt van Rijn** and his pupils, evocative landscapes by **Jacob van Ruisdael,** and four luminous paintings by **Vermeer,** including *The Milkmaid.* A whole room is devoted to the *Night Watch*, probably Rembrandt's most famous painting, which depicts a military company on a gargantuan scale. Finally, a spot for temporary exhibits often connects these early Dutch masters to more modern painters. A recent show displayed the influence 17th-century Dutch painters exerted on the Spanish Modernist **Joan Miró.**

Two audio tours are available to guide you through the museum. One is more traditional and led by the museum director, while the other is narrated by the Dutch artist, actor, and director **Jeroen Krabbé,** who gives a more personal view of the artists and paintings.

🚋 *Tram #2 or 5 to Hobbemastraat. Or tram #7 or 10 to Spiegelgracht. Museum is directly across the canal. You can't miss the giant building.* Ⓢ *€12.50, under 18 and with Museumjaarkaart free. Audio tour €5.* Ⓧ *Open daily 9am-6pm.*

🖼 VONDELPARK
Vondelpark

♿ ♼ PARK

One hundred and twenty acres of rolling streams, leafy trees, and inviting grass—in the summer, at least—make Vondelpark central Amsterdam's largest and most popular open space. Founded in the 1880s to provide a place for walking and riding, the park is now a hangout for skaters, senior citizens, stoners, soccer players, sidewalk acrobats, and more. Head here on the first sunny day of the spring and you'll see the whole city out in full force. The park is named after **Joost van den Vondel,** a 17th-century poet and playwright often called the Dutch Shakespeare. Not only is Vondelpark a great outdoor space, but it also has some excellent cafes, a weekly group roller skate that leaves every Friday at 8pm in front of the Filmmuseum, and an open-air theater *(🖥www.openluchttheater.nl)* with free music and theater performances in the summer. If you're looking for a different sort of outdoor entertainment, be happy to know that it was determined in 2008 that 🖥**having sex** would be legal in Vondelpark—provided that it wasn't taking place near the playground. Local police, however, decided that they wouldn't let this fly. We're not too sure what the law's status is today, so we recommend playing it safe and exhibiting restraint (or letting us know what happens if you try taking advantage of the 2008 measure). Even without a bit of afternoon delight, you can still spend a delightful afternoon here taking a break from the rest of the city.

🚋 *Tram #2, 3, 5, or 12 to Van Baerlestraat. Walk down Van Baerlestraat to the bridge over the park and take the stairs down.*

DE PIJP

De Pijp's sights are of a decidedly different variety than those in nearby Museumplein. Rather than staring at paintings you'll never have a chance to own, haggle for wares at **Albert Cuypmarkt,** and instead of contemplating what life would be like in the Dutch Golden Age, find out what it's like being a bottle of beer at the Heineken Experience.

SARPHATIPARK
Sarphatipark

♿ PARK

In the 1860s, Amsterdam's chief architect was convinced that the center of the city would move south, and that this spot in De Pijp (then just marshlands and a windmill or two) would be the ideal place for Centraal Station. We all know how that one turned out (though one wonders what would have happened to the Red Light District if visitors couldn't stumble straight into it from the station). Not one to be deterred, the architect decided to build a park instead. And not a bad one, either. Sarphatipark is fairly small, but its crisscrossing paths and central monument give it a genteel, 19th-century feel. It's rarely as crowded as Vondelpark, so you can have more grassy sunbathing space to yourself. The monument commemorates the same guy who gave his name to the park, the Jewish philanthropist and doctor **Samuel Sarphati.** Under the Nazi occupation, his statue was removed and the park was renamed for a Hegelian philosopher; one of the first acts after the liberation was to restore the park to its rightful name.

🚋 *Tram #3 or 25 to 2e Van der Helstraat.*

HEINEKEN EXPERIENCE

MUSEUM

Stadhouderskade 78 ☎052 392 22 www.heinekenexperience.com

Beer hasn't been made here since 1988 (if you want an actual brewery tour, check out **Brouwerij 't IJ** or **Brouwerij de Prael**), which is why this is an "experience." And what an experience, indeed. Four floors of holograms, multimedia exhibits, and virtual reality machines tell you everything you'll ever want to know about the green-bottled beer. We particularly enjoyed the ride that replicates the experience of actually becoming a Heineken beer. (There's something very Zen-alcoholic about the whole "in order to enjoy the beer you must BE the beer" idea.) And don't worry—it would be inhumane to be surrounded with all of that beer-related information without actually letting you drink, so the ticket includes two oat sodas of your very own. Lines can be long in the afternoon, so the best time to arrive is before 1pm. Yeah, you'll be drinking early, but we won't judge. It *is* Amsterdam, after all.

Tram #16 or 24 to Stadhouderskade, or tram #4, 7, 10, or 25 to Weterincircuit. Cross the canal and you'll see the building. $ €15. Open daily 11am-7pm, last entry 5:30pm.

JODENBUURT AND PLANTAGE

Jodenbuurt and Plantage are filled with some of the city's lesser-known but no less interesting museums. Due to its history as the Jewish Quarter, Jodenbuurt has its share of museums focusing on Jewish culture and history. Spacious Plantage offers the open spaces of the **Botanical Gardens** and **Artis Zoo.** The phenomenal **Brouwerij 't IJ** can be found north, by the water.

VERZETSMUSEUM (DUTCH RESISTANCE MUSEUM)

MUSEUM

Plantage Kerklaan 61 ☎062 025 35 www.verzetsmuseum.org

Nazi Germany occupied the Netherlands for five years during WWII, and this museum is designed to present the various responses of Dutch people during that time to the question "What do we do?" The permanent exhibition begins in the 1930s, painting a picture of what life was like during that time and building a backdrop to the traditions and conflicts within Dutch society. In the early days of the occupation, many struggled with the decision of whether to adapt to their relatively unchanged life under Nazi rule or to openly resist the occupiers. As time went on, the persecution of Jews, gypsies, and gays intensified, and numerous political and social regulations were put into place; as a result, the forces of the resistance grew. This museum does a masterful job of combining the ordinary and the extraordinary by placing visitors in the shoes of average Dutch citizens and also sharing the stories of individuals who risked (and often lost) their lives to publish illegal newspapers, hide Jews, or pass information to Allied troops. An extensive collection of artifacts and video footage brings the period to life in vivid detail. A smaller portion of the exhibit details the effects of the war on Dutch colonies in East Asia.

Tram #9 or 14 to Plantage Kerklaan. Across from Artis Zoo. $ €7.50, ages 7-15 €4, under 7 and with Museumjaarkaart free. Open M 11am-5pm, Tu-F 10am-5pm, Sa-Su 11am-5pm.

JOODS HISTORISCH MUSEUM (JEWISH HISTORICAL MUSEUM)

MUSEUM

Nieuwe Amstelstraat 1 ☎053 103 10 www.jhm.nl

Four 17th- and 18th-century Ashkenazi synagogues were incorporated to form this museum dedicated to the history and culture of the Jews of the Netherlands. One part of the museum highlights the religious life of the community using artifacts (including a number of beautifully decorated Torahs), explanations of Jewish traditions, and videos that recount personal anecdotes. Above this section, an exhibit details the history of the community from 1600-1900, from the first settlements in Amsterdam under the city's unusually early religious tolerance to the struggles Jews faced in gaining full civil and political liberties.

Paintings and documents detail different aspects of Dutch Jewish life. Particularly noteworthy is the small display on Spinoza, including an early copy of the *Tractatus Theologico-Politicus.* The next part of the museum chronicles 1900 to the present, showing the growth of the Jewish community up until WWII, the persecution and devastation of the war period, and then the rebuilding efforts after the war's end. The museum also holds two temporary exhibition spaces which host art shows related to the Jewish experience in the Netherlands or elsewhere in Europe. The JHM Children's Museum introduces kids to Jewish life and culture through the reconstruction of a typical Jewish family, with friendly Max the Matzo as their guide.

🚋 Trams #9 or 14 or [M]Waterlooplein. $ €9, students and seniors €6, ages 13-17 €4.50, under 13 and with Museumjaarkaart free. ⏰ Open daily 11am-5pm.

TROPENMUSEUM ✎♿ MUSEUM

Linnaeusstraat 2 ☎056 882 00 💻www.tropenmuseum.nl

In a palatial building that is part of the Koninklijk Instituut voor de Tropen (Dutch Royal Institute of the Tropics), this museum provides an anthropological look at disparate "tropical" regions from the distant past to today. A running theme throughout the exhibits is the complicated relationship between Europe and these areas during the rise and fall of Western imperialism. Starting on the second floor, you can explore Central and South America, Africa, and the Middle East; the first floor exhibits India, Southeast Asia, and Oceania. From Thai bridal jewelry to African presidential folk cloths, an astounding collection of cultural artifacts is on display, while videos give a sense of what current life is like in the different regions. An extensive portion of the first floor is devoted to the Dutch colonial experience in Indonesia (from the perspective of both colonizers and colonized), from which a large part of the museum's collection was initially drawn. For the other side of the coin, see **Oost-Indisch Huis.** A space for temporary exhibitions can be found on the ground floor, like the recent exhibits on Africa and the 2010 World Cup.

🚋 Tram #9, 10, or 14 to Alexanderplein. Cross the canal and walk left along Mauritskade. $ €9, students €5, under 18 and with Museumjaarkaart free. ⏰ Open daily 10am-5pm.

BROUWERIJ 'T IJ ⊗♿🍷🍺 BREWERY

Funenkade 7 ☎062 283 25 💻www.brouwerijhetij.nl

What could be more Dutch than drinking beer at the base of a windmill? What's even better is that the beer brewed and served here is much, much tastier than more internationally famous Dutch brands (we won't name any names). Once a bathhouse, this building was taken over as a squat in the 1980s. Today, its brewers craft 10 different beers, some seasonal but all organic, unfiltered, and non-pasteurized. You can try a glass or three of their wares at the massive outdoor terrace of the on-site pub or at a few cafes and bars in the city. Brews range from the *Zatte*, a golden triple beer, to the *Plzen*, their pilsner, to a variety of bocks and a delicious wheat beer. If you're at the bar, make sure to notice the long collection of bottles on the shelves—it's one of Europe's largest.

🚋 Tram #10 to Hoogte Kadijk or #14 to Pontanusstraat. Head toward the windmill. $ Beer €1.90-2.30. ⏰ Pub open daily 3-8pm. Free tours of the brewery F 4pm, Su 4pm.

MUSEUM HET REMBRANDT ✎⊗ MUSEUM

Jodenbreestraat 4 ☎052 004 00 💻www.rembrandthuis.nl

Flush with success at the height of his popularity, Rembrandt van Rijn bought this massively expensive house in 1639. Twenty years later, after a decline in sales and failure to pay his mortgage, he sold the house along with his possessions. It probably sucked to be him, but his misfortune turned out to be a great boon for historians—the inventory of Rembrandt's worldly goods taken at the time of sale meant that hundreds of years later curators were able to reconstruct his house almost exactly as it was when he lived there. Now visitors can see where Rembrandt slept, entertained guests, sold paintings, made paintings, and got attacked by his mistress after a fight over alimony (that would be in the kitchen). The most interesting rooms are those on the top floor: Rembrandt's massive studio (with many of his original tools still there) and the room where he stored his *objets d'art*—armor, armadillos, and everything in between. Throughout the house paintings by many of Rembrandt's very talented contemporaries and students adorn the walls. The museum also holds a hundred-fold collection of Rembrandt's etchings, a rotating selection of which are on display. Every 45min. on the third floor, guides reenact Rembrandt's etching and printing techniques. An exhibition space for rotating collections of more contemporary art is attached to the main building.

Tram #9 or 14 or Ⓜ Waterlooplein. $ €9, ages 6-17 €2.50, under 6 and with Museumjaarkaart free, with ISIC card €6. ⏰ Open daily 10am-5pm.

ARTIS ZOO ZOO

Plantage Kerklaan 38-40 ☎0900 278 4796 www.artis.nl

If all of Amsterdam's culture is blowing your brain, join the animals at this zoo, one of Europe's oldest. The sprawling complex includes an aquarium, a planetarium, and a geological museum in addition to the critters themselves. Areas are devoted to regions like the South American Pampas and the African Savannah, and all the classics like elephants, lions, leopards, giraffes, and a variety of monkeys can be found among the hundreds of species living here. Some of our favorites include the teeny black-footed penguins, playful sea lions, and **Lemurland,** a special island where visitors can get up close and personal with the fuzzy beasts. Watch for zookeepers giving presentations about the animals throughout the day, as they often end with an opportunity to see the animals being fed.

Tram #9 or 14 to Plantage Kerklaan. $ €18.50, ages 3-9 €15, seniors €17. Detailed guidebook €3. ⏰ Open daily Apr-Oct 9am-6pm; Nov-Mar 9am-5pm. Zookeeper presentations daily from 11am-3:30pm.

PORTUGEES-ISRAELIETISCHE SYNAGOGUE SYNAGOGUE

Mr. Visserplein 1-3 ☎062 453 51 www.esnoga.com

This beautiful synagogue has remained largely unchanged since the local community of Sephardic Jews constructed it in 1671. Most of them had fled persecution in the Iberian peninsula—hence the common practice of calling the synagogue an *Esnoga*, the Portuguese word for synagogue. The building's large vaulted interior is dominated by massive stone pillars and hung with brass candelabra. Sand is scattered on the floor in the Dutch tradition to absorb dirt and muffle the noise of footsteps. Information and artifacts from the Dutch Jewish community's past 300 years are on display, but this is still very much a space of worship—services are held on Sabbaths and holidays. The highly informative and free audio tour describes the construction and architecture of the synagogue in addition to recounting stories of important figures and events in the community's history.

Trams #9 or 14 or Ⓜ Waterlooplein. $ €6.50; students, seniors, and with Museumjaarkaart €5; ages 13-17 €4. ⏰ Open M-F 10am-4pm, Su 10am-4pm. Closed on Jewish holidays.

HORTUS BOTANICUS GARDENS

Plantage Middenlaan 2A ☎063 816 70 www.dehortus.nl

These botanical gardens started out as a place for medicinal herbs (no, not *that* kind) in 1638 and have now grown to include over 4000 species of leafy plant life. Thanks to the Dutch East India Company, exotic species began arriving here over 300 years ago, and some of those original plants (such as the Eastern Cape giant cycad) are still around today. The gardens and greenhouses are arranged by climate and class, allowing you to find everything from algae to palm trees to carnivorous plants with relative ease. The "crown jewels" section is the place to go to catch a glimpse of extremely rare species such as the *Victoria amazonica*, a water lily that only opens at dusk. Well-landscaped ponds and paths make this a pleasant place for a wander. The cafe, located in the Orangery, is a stunning spot to munch on organic snacks.

🚊 *Tram #9 or 14 to Waterlooplein.* 💲 *€7.50, seniors and ages 5-14 €3.50. Su tours €1.* 🕙 *Open July-Aug M-F 9am-7pm, Sa-Su 10am-7pm; Sept-Nov 9am-5pm, Sa-Su 10am-5pm; Dec-Jan 9am-4pm, Sa-Su 10am-4pm; Feb-June 9am-5pm, Sa-Su 10am-5pm. Tours Su 2pm.*

coffeeshops and smartshops

The first experience of walking into a store, reading a menu, and ordering a few grams of weed as casually as you would a sandwich may feel surprising to those used to buying their magic **dragon** from a shady guy with an unregistered cell phone number and a 1970s car. Sure, there are plenty of ways to enjoy yourself in Amsterdam without lighting up, and lots of people won't set foot in a coffeeshop over the course of their entire visit. Nevertheless, it's undeniable that liberal drug laws *do* draw people to the city from far and wide.

However, just because you can do things here that you'd get arrested for elsewhere doesn't mean that anything goes. Certified coffeeshops will have a green-and-white **BCD sticker** that denotes their credibility. Shops aren't allowed to advertise the fact that they sell marijuana or hash, and in theory, you're supposed to have to ask for the menu, though in most places they'll have it on the bar as long as it's towards the back of the store. You are only allowed to buy 5g of drugs from an establishment per day. It's recently become illegal to smoke tobacco indoors in most places, though some coffeeshops have special smoking areas where you can indulge in a mixed joint. Don't walk down the street smoking a blunt—just because the Dutch are OK with THC doesn't mean that they smoke all that much of it, and doing so will mark you as an obvious tourist. (And a stoned one, at that—hi, pickpockets!) If you do want a smoke in the open air, find a store with an outdoor patio or hit up one of the city's parks.

The variety at many shops can be overwhelming for those who aren't used to choosing what strain they're smoking. Ask coffeeshop staff for advice if you have any questions, as they are usually used to explaining their wares. In general, the more expensive a brand is, the stronger or better you can expect it to be. If you want to smoke some really good stuff, look for prestigious **Cannabis Cup winners.** When it comes to hash, most places stock blonde (Moroccan), which is lighter than black (Indian). Neither of them is anywhere near as potent as the special varieties of Dutch **ice-o-lator.** It can cost €20-50 per gram, but that's because it's basically purified THC and will, to put it "blunt"-ly, fuck you up. Europeans generally stick to smoking joints, but quite a few stores provide bongs or even vaporizers for tourists. If you want to roll a doobie yourself, most stores will let you take a few papers for free. You can also buy pre-rolled joints with a limited selection of strains. If there's something you really want to try that doesn't come pre-rolled, many shops offer paper cones that allow the truly lazy (or uncoordinated) to simply pop the weed in and be set to light up. Coffeeshops also sell space cakes, muffins, and brownies. As cute as they sound, these should be eaten with caution, as it's impossible to verify how strong they are and the effects often don't kick in for 1hr. or more—and then can last for up to a day.

Smartshops do not sell weed and hash, though they usually stock marijuana seeds and smoking accessories. What they do offer in terms of instant psychedelic gratification are truffles (the only type since the banning of hallucinogenic psilocybin

top 10 coffeeshops

These are our picks for the best of Amsterdam's famous coffeeshops. As totally groovy as they are, *Let's Go* definitely does not recommend trying to hit all of these in one day...

- **AMNESIA.** Feel classy as you smoke in this shop nestled on a row of stately canal houses. The location is good, but the selection of their own specialty brands is better.

- **THE BUSH DOCTOR.** Rembrandtplein tends to be more about drinking than smoking, but the crazy selection of potent strains here makes it a worthwhile stop. You might want to leave plenty of time between smoking and hitting the clubs, though, or the strobe lights could be a bit overwhelming.

- **DE TWEEDE KAMER.** Probably stocks the widest selection of weed in Amsterdam. This coffeeshop is run by the same people as the more famous Dampkring, but here you'll find fewer tourists and a cozier atmosphere. Plus, there's a certain pleasurable irony in smoking in a store named after one of the Dutch chambers of Parliament.

- **GREY AREA.** One of the only coffeeshops in Amsterdam run by Americans. These guys really know their stuff, as do many of the loyal patrons. Try one of their vaporizers. With many celebrities frequenting the store, there's a chance you'll be able to say that you've used the same one as Willie Nelson.

- **HILL STREET BLUES.** With so many smokers in Amsterdam, you may feel a little insignificant. Leave your mark on the graffiti-filled wall here (markers are provided for the purpose) as you listen to the excellent hip-hop soundtrack and dig into an ice cream sundae.

- **KANDINSKY.** Enjoy their specialty house blend in a sleek, elegant space that feels more like a club than a coffeeshop.

- **PARADOX.** Feels more like an artsy cafe than a coffeeshop, with a welcoming owner to boot. It's a good place to pick up a pre-rolled joint and hit one of the beautiful nearby canals in the Jordaan. Or, head to Electric Ladyland and poke around the fluorescent cave sculpture.

- **RUSLAND.** One of the city's oldest shops offers a unique Russian-themed setting with a remarkable selection of teas to combat that pesky dry mouth.

- **STIX.** If you want to feel like a local, come to this uncrowded shop in the Central Canal Ring where the drugs are cheap and strong. Don't forget to get a slice of pie with whipped cream from Zuivere Koffie next door.

- **YO YO.** Come for the high-quality organic weed, stay for the fresh apple pie and the remarkably peaceful, art-filled interior. Nearby places to enjoy your high include grassy Sarphatipark and the ethnic eateries of De Pijp.

mushrooms that are still legal), salvia, and all sorts of herbs and extracts that can promise everything from ecstasy-like effects to heightened sexual arousal.

If you have any questions regarding the effects or legality of drugs options in Amsterdam, hit up **Cannabis College** or the **Jellinek Clinic,** both of which keep extensive, up-to-date information.

It is *imperative* to keep in mind that hard drugs (ecstasy, cocaine, heroin, etc.) are not legal in the Netherlands, despite what dealers approaching you on the street at 3am might try to tell you. Seriously, there are stores with DRUG MENUS here. Isn't that enough?

Finally, though we may list a wide array of coffeeshops and smartshops in this guidebook, *Let's Go* does not recommend drug use in any form.

OUDE ZIJD

A number of bustling coffeeshops can be found around **Nieuwmarkt,** but if you want better atmosphere and value, head away from the square.

RUSLAND — COFFEESHOP

Rusland 17 ☎062 794 68

According to some, this is the oldest coffeeshop in Amsterdam. We won't take a stance on that issue, but we will say that this is definitely one of the city's better shops. Two floors inside are decorated with stenciled images of the Kremlin and other Moscow buildings, and the low ceilings combined with comfy cushion-lined seating will make you feel as cozy as you might while sitting inside on a snowy Russian day. The drug menu isn't terribly extensive, but it is complemented by an astonishing selection of teas, fresh juices, and milkshakes.

Tram #4, 9, 14, 16, 24, or 25 to Muntplein. Walk up Nieuwe Doelenstraat and make a left. $ Weed €4-12 per g; joints €2.50-4.50; hash €3-30 per g; space muffins €5. ⏰ Open daily 10am-midnight.

SOLO — COFFEESHOP

Korte Koningsstraat 2

A truly simple, out-of-the-way shop that has a surprisingly good selection of smoke-ables. The store is large and hardly decorated, nothing more than a long bar, a number of tables, and some booths. About a dozen kinds of marijuana are for sale, however, including popular names like Bubblegum, Cheese, and Diesel. Varieties of both local and imported hash are available as well.

[M]Nieuwmarkt. Walk down Koningsstraat, which becomes Korte Koningsstraat. $ Weed €7-14 per g; joints €10, with tobacco €3.20-3.80; hash €9-25 per g; space cakes €5. 10% discount on purchases of at least 5g. ⏰ Open daily 10am-midnight.

RED LIGHT DISTRICT

HILL STREET BLUES — COFFEESHOP

Warmoesstraat 52 ☎063 879 22 www.hill-street-blues.nl

So named because of its location next to a police station, Hill Street Blues benefits from a great view over the water at the back of its smoking room, reached through a narrow entrance that hides the large two-level shop. Every inch of the walls, floor, and ceiling is covered with graffiti—you can add to it yourself (buy a marker at the counter if you happened to forget your own). The place, like everywhere on Warmoesstraat, is busy but manages to remain relaxed. There's a well-priced selection of many popular weed and hash varieties, and at the separate bar you can get coffee, juice, fresh shakes, and ice cream sundaes.

From Centraal Station, walk down Damrak; make a left onto Oudebrugsteeg and then a left onto Warmoesstraat. $ Weed €3-14 per g; joints €10, with tobacco €3-5; hash €4-20 per g. ⏰ Open daily 9am-1am.

CONSCIOUS DREAMS KOKOPELLI — SMARTSHOP

Warmoesstraat 12 ☎042 170 00 www.consciousdirect.com/shops/kokopelli/

A bright emporium for all kinds of consciousness-altering substances and souvenirs, this smartshop sells sex toys, lava lamps, and trinkets. On the drug-related side, they offer a huge array of herbal substances like Philosopher's Stones, salvia, and herbal XTC. They also sell drug-testing kits that can evaluate the composition of the drugs you're going to take or the state of your body after you've already taken them. Ask the well-informed staff any questions you may have regarding psychedelic substances.

➜ From Centraal Station, turn left onto Prins Hendrikkade, bear right onto Nieuwebrugsteeg, and then keep right onto Warmoesstraat. $ Philosopher's Stones €12.50-20; salvia, herbal XTC, and most other substances around €9-17. ⏰ Open daily 11am-10pm.

THE GREENHOUSE EFFECT COFFEESHOP

Warmoesstraat 53 ☎062 374 62 🖥www.greenhouse-effect.nl

Next door to the bar and hotel of the same name. The very friendly staff stays smiling, despite all the crowds that cycle through this popular spot. Particularly comfortable couches at the back enhance the already relaxed atmosphere. Half a dozen well-priced, popular strains each of weed and hash are available.

➜ From Centraal Station, walk down Damrak, make a left onto Oudebrugsteeg, and then a left onto Warmoesstraat. $ Weed €3-14 per g; joints €8, with tobacco €3-4; hash €4-20 per g. ⏰ Open daily 9am-1am.

NIEUWE ZIJD

Lots of tourists (especially backpackers) means a lot of coffeeshops. Don't just settle for the first one you see: it's worth seeking the Nieuwe Zijd's star establishments. Prices are slightly higher here, but the selections tend to be more impressive.

👍 **DE TWEEDE KAMER** ♿ COFFEESHOP

Heisteeg 6 ☎042 222 36

Looks just like a classic Dutch *bruin cafe*, but don't be fooled—De Tweede Kamer has one of the most extensive menus of any coffeeshop in Amsterdam, categorized by type, smell, flavor, and quality of the high. It is the parent shop of **Dampkring** but generally less packed with tourists.

➜ Tram #1, 2, or 5 to Spui/Nieuwezijds Voorburgwal. Walk down to Spui, up Spuistraat, and left onto Heisteeg. $ Weed €4-13 per g; joints €3-9; hash €8-40 per g; space cakes and muffins €6. ⏰ Open daily 10am-1am.

👍 **KANDINSKY** COFFEESHOP

Rosmarijnsteeg 9 ☎062 470 23

Eschewing the Rasta-psychedelic-jungle themes of many neighboring coffeeshops, Kandinsky has a multilevel interior with sleek leather booths, mod tables, and tastefully colored lighting that make it feel like some sort of hip lounge club. No pretension in the attitude, though: the staff is chatty and cheerful. Menu includes all the most popular strains, plus their own house blend.

➜ Tram #1, 2, or 5 to Spui/Nieuwezijds Voorburgwal. Walk up Nieuwezijds Voorburgwal and make a left onto Rosmarijnsteeg. $ Weed €8.25-13 per g; joints €4.50, with tobacco €3.70; hash €7.50-35 per g. ⏰ Open daily 9:30am-1am.

👍 **DAMPKRING** ♿ COFFEESHOP

Handboogstraat 29 ☎063 807 05 🖥www.dampkring.nl

The same extensive menu as Tweede Kamer but a very different atmosphere. Scenes from *Ocean's Twelve* were filmed in the warmly painted, psychedelic lounge. This newfound celebrity and the quality of options on the menu have catapulted Dampkring to a stardom that brings in the crowds. Has smoking-accessories shop on Prins Hendrikkade and an extensive online store.

➜ Tram #1, 2, or 5 to Koningsplein. Cross the canal and continue onto Heiligeweg, then make a left onto Handboogstraat. $ Weed €4-13 per g; joints €3-9; hash €8-40 per g; space cakes and muffins €6. ⏰ Open M-Sa 10am-1am, Su 11am-1am.

👍 **ABRAXAS TOO** ♿📶 COFFEESHOP

Spuistraat 51 🖥www.abraxas.tv

A newer offshoot of the popular Abraxas coffeeshop nearby, this smaller shop has the same comfort and quality of selection as the main store, just shrunk down a few sizes. Beautiful mosaics decorate the walls, and there's also a lounge upstairs and a patio outside. The house specialties like Kushadelic, Applejack, and John Sinclair come recommended by the staff.

⇞ Tram #1, 2, 5, 13, or 17 to Nieuwezijds Kolk. Walk down Korre Kolksteeg to Spuistraat and make a left. ℹ Free internet and Wi-Fi. $ Weed €10-14 per g; joints €3.50-6; hash €10-35 per g; space cakes and muffins €4.50. ⏰ Open daily 10am-1am.

ROUTE 99 🚫⊗ COFFEESHOP

Haringpakkerssteeg 8 ☎032 075 62

Often one of the first shops tourists stumble into from Centraal Station, Route 99 keeps them coming back to its two large floors and tobacco-friendly room upstairs. A Western theme permeates the place, replete with paintings of cowboys and Elvis. Quality selection of weed and hash, including favorites like Bubblegum, Blueberry, and various hazes.

⇞ From Centraal Station, walk down Damrak and make a right onto Haringpakkerssteeg. $ Sold in €15 bag increments; will get you 1-2.2g of weed or 1.4-2g of hash. Joints €7.50, with tobacco €5; space cakes and muffins €5. ⏰ Open M-Th 9am-midnight, F-Sa 9am-1am, Su 9am-midnight.

MAGIC MUSHROOM GALLERY 💳♿ SMARTSHOP

Spuistraat 249 ☎042 757 65 💻www.magicmushroom.com

Large smartshop with all kinds of herbal extracts, dried herbs, mushroom seeds, and grow kits, plus more knick-knacks than you can shake a stick at. Patient staff will walk you through the book of all their options, or you can peruse it yourself in the small seating area. Another, smaller location is on the Singel, by the Bloemenmarkt.

⇞ Tram #1, 2, or 5 to Spui/Nieuwezijds Voorburgwal. Walk down to Spui and then right up Spuistraat. $ Salvia €12-30; mushroom seeds €22-30. ⏰ Open daily 10am-10pm.

SCHEEPVAARTBUURT

BARNEY'S 🚫⊗ COFFEESHOP

Haarlemmerstraat 102 ☎062 597 61 💻www.barneys.biz

An Amsterdam institution with a coffeeshop, souvenir and seed stores, and a bar across the street. The recently renovated interior is quite modern and free of the exotic psychedelica or faux-*bruin cafe* designs of so many Amsterdam stores. Instead, there's a row of tables of varying sizes, each with its own TV screen and vaporizer. Strong selection of weed and hash, with seven Cannabis Cup winners of each.

⇞ Make a right when leaving Centraal Station; Barney's is on your right, a few blocks after crossing the Singel. $ Weed €10-17 per g; joints €6.50-8, with tobacco €4-5.50; hash €10-26 per g, ice-o-lators €32-55 per g; space cakes €6.50. ⏰ Open daily 7am-1am.

CANAL RING WEST

👍 **AMNESIA** 🚫⊗⛅ COFFEESHOP

Herengracht 133 ☎063 83 03

One of Amsterdam's best decorated coffeeshops, in all senses of the word. The spacious interior has long couches and tables done up in black and purple; picturesque canalside seating is available outside. The menu, highlighted by nine Cannabis Cup winners, includes both standard fare and specialty brands. Vaporizers are available. It also has a big coffee bar for those who prefer the stimulating effects of caffeine to those of the other drugs on offer. Those whose greatest vice is dessert should try Amnesia's frothy shakes.

⇞ Tram #1, 2, 5, 13, 14, or 17 to Dam/Radhuisstraat. Continue along Radhuisstraat and make a right onto Herengracht. $ Weed €8.50-13 per g, specialty brands €13-17 per g; joints €4-6. ⏰ Open daily 10am-1am.

GREY AREA COFFEESHOP

Oude Leliestraat 2 ☎042 043 01 💻www.greyarea.nl

Grey Area is a small, sticker-covered shop popular with locals, tourists, and celebrities ranging from Willie Nelson to Flavor Flav. No questions as to why: the ever-rotating selection of marijuana and hash sold here is peppered with plenty of award-winners, and the atmosphere is friendly and unfussy. A helpful assortment of smoking supplies is available as well. The store is conveniently located in the Nine Streets area, where mouth-watering eateries abound.

🚋 Tram #1, 2, 5, 13, 14, or 17 to Dam/Radhuisstraat. Continue on Radhuisstraat, make a right onto the far side of the Singel; it will be on your left. [S] Marijuana €8.50-13 per g; joints €5. ⏰ Open daily noon-8pm.

XTREME COFFEESHOP

Huidenstraat 13 ☎977 356 98

This small basement coffeeshop with mosaic-covered walls, chill reggae, and comfortable couches offers a limited selection (five types of weed, four of hash) but includes popular classics like White Widow, Super Pollen, and AK47.

🚋 Tram #1, 2, or 5 to Koningsplein. Cross Herengracht; continue up and left onto Huidenstraat. [S] Weed €7-11 per g; joints €6.50-8.50, with tobacco €3.50-5; hash €6-10 per g; brownies €6.50. ⏰ Open daily 11am-midnight.

CENTRAL CANAL RING

👍 **STIX** COFFEESHOP

Utrechtsestraat 21 💻www.stix.nl

Stix is a simple shop—no big smoking rooms with couches and Ganesh statues here, just picnic-table seating and a bright, airy atmosphere. Staff cheerfully welcomes both newcomers and loyal regulars. No separate smoking room for tobacco. The weed selection includes perennial favorites like Amnesia Haze and Bubblegum, while hash options feature some Moroccan varieties and their own house blend.

🚋 Tram #9 or 14 to Rembrandtplein. Walk down Utrechtsestraat; the store is near Herengracht. [S] Weed €6-13 per g; joints €10, with tobacco €3.20-3.80; hash €9-25. ⏰ Open daily 11am-1am.

👍 **AZARIUS** SMARTSHOP

Kerkstraat 119 ☎048 979 14 💻www.azarius.net

The physical manifestation of the largest online smartshop, Azarius sits in the building once inhabited by the city's oldest smartshop (Conscious Dreams). Azarius is a small and friendly store, with a knowledgeable staff ready to answer any questions about their many products. They sell magic truffles, salvia, herbal XTC, and many other herbs and extracts in addition to cannabis seeds and smoking-related accessories. If you can't find what you're looking for in the store, you can always check online.

🚋 Tram #1, 2, or 5 to Prinsengracht. Walk 1 block up Leidsestraat and make a right onto Kerkstraat. [S] Truffles €10-14 per dose. ⏰ Open in summer daily noon-9pm; fall, winter, and spring M-Tu noon-9pm, Th-Sa noon-9pm.

THE DOLPHINS COFFEESHOP

Kerkstraat 39 ☎062 591 62

This is a fun place to relax amid the vibrant sea creature murals and other underwater-themed decorations. The house special, **"White Dolphin,"** is quite popular, as are the vaporizers available for free use. One of the rare places where they advertise the dosage of drugs in their space cakes, which strikes us as a rather wise idea.

🚋 Tram #1, 2, or 5 to Prinsengracht. Walk 1 block up Leidsestraat; it's on the corner. [S] €10 will get you 1-1.5g of weed or 1-1.3g of hash; small joints €6.50, large €8; space muffins €7.50, space tea €7. ⏰ Open M-Th 10am-1am, F-Sa 10am-3am, Su 10am-1am.

THE NOON

Zieseniskade 22

Renowned for their house specialty marijuana, **Blueberry,** which is a two-time Cannabis Cup award-winner. Popular with those escaping the packed tourist spots in Leidseplein, The Noon becomes, ironically, rather crowded as well. Enjoy the Buddha mural, pillows, and **⬛dragons** that give the store an Asian lounge-y atmosphere.

🚋 *Tram #7 or 10 to Spiegelgracht. Walk up Spiegelgracht and left onto Zieseniskade. Ⓢ Weed €6-13 per g; joints €7-10, with tobacco €3-5; hash €6-14 per g, ice-o-lators €20-50 per g; space cakes €3.50. ⓩ Open daily 9am-1am.*

DUTCH PASSION

Utrechtsestraat 26

The people at Dutch Passion were the first to figure out how to engineer seeds that only produced female plants, and their tradition of excellence continues today. You can find a huge variety of indoor and outdoor cannabis seeds from all over the world here in addition to the special seeds that are the fruits of their continued explorations into the science of weed. This is one of the few companies that actually advertises the amount of THC in each strain, which, again, strikes us as a good idea. The staff can also help you learn about the finer points of growing your own plants and sells kits to help you along.

🚋 *Tram #9 or 14 to Rembrandtplein. Walk down Utrechtsestraat; the store is just after Herengracht. Ⓢ 10 seeds €20-120. ⓩ Open M-Sa 11am-6pm.*

LEIDSEPLEIN

The coffeeshops around the Leidseplein are surprisingly unpopulated given how packed the area is. Prices do tend to be slightly higher, reflecting the neighborhood's more central location.

EASY TIMES

Prinsengracht 476

This coffeeshop feels a bit like a hip club, with sleek furnishings, purple lights, and trance-y house music playing on the stereo—like a hip club, but minus the exclusive attitude. Extensive selection of indica, sativa, and hash as well as space cookies, brownies, and cakes. Carries the infamous Dutch ice-o-lator. Also serves coffee and juices.

🚋 *Tram #1, 2, or 5 to Prinsengracht. Make a left and continue along the canal. Ⓢ Weed €8-15 per g; joints €7-10, with tobacco €3.50-5.50; hash €6-13, ice-o-lator €22 per g; baked goods €6-10. Buy 4g or more, get a 10% discount. ⓩ Open daily 8:30am-1am.*

ROOKIES

Korte Leidsedwarsstraat 145-147

This super-chill coffeeshop in the heart of the Leidseplein will welcome you into its unusually large smoking room, which is filled with the dulcet tones of laid-back hip hop (and, obviously, clouds of smoke). Small but quality selection of marijuana and hash; pre-rolled joints are available with Northern Lights (weed) and Super Pollen (hash). Also sells space cakes, coffee, and juices.

🚋 *Tram #1, 2, 5, 7, or 10 to Leidseplein. Ⓢ Weed €5.50-13 per g; joints €3.50; hash €7.40-15, ice-o-lator €24 per g; space cakes €5. ⓩ Open daily 10am-1am.*

TATANKA

Korte Leidsedwarsstraat 151

This smartshop sells a variety of mushrooms, marijuana seeds, salvia, and all kinds of smoking accoutrements—pipes, grinders, and anything else you might need. Also sells T-shirts and other souvenirs. Very helpful staff will walk you through the mechanics of any prospective purchase.

🚋 *Tram #1, 2, 5, 7, or 10 to Leidseplein. Ⓢ Mushrooms €12-20; seeds from around €30 to over*

€100. ⏰ Open daily 11am-10pm.

REMBRANDTPLEIN

👍 THE BUSH DOCTOR

COFFEESHOP

Thorbeckeplein 28

☎033 074 75

A small, colorfully psychedelic store with two floors and outdoor seating spilling into Thorbeckeplein. This is one of the best places to try specialty strains of weed and hash: not only do they have a variety of their own potent mixes, various fruity options, and organic wares, but they also carry over half a dozen kinds of the infamous ice-o-lator hash.

🚋 Tram #9 or 14 to Rembrandtplein. Thorbeckeplein is across the square from the giant TV screen. $ Weed €7.50-12.50 per g; joints €4-6.50; hash €10-12 per g, ice-o-lator €22-55 per g; space cakes €7. ⏰ Open daily 9am-1am.

THE OTHER SIDE

COFFEESHOP

Reguliersdwarsstraat 6

☎042 110 14

A cafe atmosphere, with bright decor and muted jazzy music, makes this a hip and pleasant place to stop for a smoke. The Other Side also serves some of the best coffee and tea in Amsterdam. Carries nine types of weed and 10 types of hash, sold in €10, €20, and €35 increments. Pre-rolled joints (with Super Skunk or Pollen) are available.

🚋 Tram #9 or 14 to Rembrandtplein or tram #1, 2, or 5 to Koningsplein. $ €10 will get you 1.4-1.8g weed, depending on strain; 1-3g hash, depending on strain. €20 will get you 2-4.4g weed/2-5g hash, €35 will get you 5.5g/3-4.8g. Joints €3.75. ⏰ Open daily 11am-1am.

COFFEESHOP SEVILLA

COFFEESHOP

Utrechtstraat 14

☎062 448 20

A pint-sized, relaxed, and not particularly busy coffeeshop around the corner from the main square of Rembrandtplein, Sevilla offers some tables and chairs outside, while indoors you'll find a foosball table and arcade game machines. The selection of weed and hash includes standards like White Widow, Amnesia Haze, Strawberry, and Super Pollen.

🚋 Tram #9 or 14 to Rembrandtplein. Utrechtstraat is off the southeast corner of the square. $ Marijuana €7-12 per g; 3 joints of White Widow or Super Pollen €10; hash €6-12 per g. ⏰ Open daily 10am-1am.

JORDAAN

Coffeeshops in the Jordaan provide the perfect settings for a relaxed and peaceful smoke. However, few have the kind of award-winning selections available at establishments in central Amsterdam.

👍 PARADOX

COFFEESHOP

1e Bloemdwarsstraat 2

☎062 356 39 💻www.paradoxcoffeeshop.com

Paradox boasts a wonderfully laid-back atmosphere with the staff to match. A smattering of wooden tables and chairs fill the cafe-like space, and the chill feel is continued in a soundtrack that tends toward reggae and other types of world music. Over a dozen types of weed and hash are available, with a wider variety of strains in the pre-rolled joints than can be found elsewhere.

🚋 Tram #13, 14, or 17 to Westermarkt. Cross Prinsengracht and continue on Rozengracht, then make a left onto 1e Bloemdwarsstraat. $ Weed €5.50-11 per g; joints €3-4; hash €7-15 per g; space cakes €6. ⏰ Open daily 10am-8pm.

👍 LA TERTULIA

COFFEESHOP

Prinsengracht 312

💻www.coffeeshopamsterdam.com

For over 20 years, people have been enjoying this mother-and-daughter-run shop. Fresh and relaxed, the store is filled with plants and crystals. In good weather, white garden tables sit on the sidewalk for patron use. Impressive selection of weed and hash; their Bubblegum is especially popular.

Tram #7, 10, or 17 to Elandsgracht. Walk down Elandsgracht and make a right onto Prinsengracht. Most weed and hash €10-12 for 1-1.3 g; 5g medallion of ice-o-lator hash €100. Open Tu-Sa 11am-7pm.

SANEMENTERENG

COFFEESHOP

2e Laurierdwarsstraat 44 ☎062 520 41

Don't be deceived by the vintage clutter outside—this is a coffeeshop, not an antiques store. The rickety building (it's supported by some leaning tree trunks) does provide one of the most unique places to smoke in the city: everything from Indonesian puppets to old kitchen utensils is scattered about. Decent selection of weed and hash at very low prices.

Tram #10, 13, 14, or 17 to Marnixstraat/Rozengracht. Walk east on Rozengracht and left onto 2e Laurierdwarsstraat. Weed €3.50-8 per g; joints €3; hash €3.50-20 per g; space cakes €5. Open daily 11am-1am.

WESTERPARK AND OUD-WEST

Coffeeshops in these primarily residential neighborhoods tend to be few and far between; the following, however, is one of Amsterdam's standouts.

DE SUPERMARKT

COFFEESHOP

Frederik Hendrikstraat 69 ☎068 322 68 www.coffeeshopdesupermarkt.nl

A breath of (figuratively) fresh air from the dark atmosphere that characterizes most Amsterdam coffeeshops, De Supermarkt is clean and bright, with the colorful work of local artists decorating the walls. The extremely helpful staff is happy to answer questions as you select items from their small but varied menu of weed and hash. Pure marijuana can be smoked in the main area, while a small smoking room is available for smokes mixed with tobacco. The clientele tends toward the local and laid-back.

Tram #13. Just north of the roundabout at the intersection with 2e Hugo de Grootstraat. Marijuana and hash from €4; pre-rolled joints €3.50. Open daily 11am-11pm.

MUSEUMPLEIN AND VONDELPARK

Simply put, this is the rare part of Amsterdam where you *won't* find a coffeeshop on every corner, so plan ahead if you hope to smoke in Vondelpark or before seeing the sunflowers at the Van Gogh museum.

TWEEDY

COFFEESHOP

2e Constantijn Huygensstraat 76 ☎061 803 44

The most important thing this shop has going for it is its proximity to Vondelpark—it's a great place to refuel if you're on a stoner's picnic and have run out of stuff to smoke. Other than that, this is a pretty nondescript store with a small (though cheap) selection of wares.

Tram #1 to 1e C. Huygensstraat or tram #3 or 12 to Overtoom. Walk down Overtoom and make a left onto 2e C. Huygensstraat. Weed €5-11 per g; joints €3.50; hash €6-10 per g. Open daily 11am-11pm.

DE PIJP

YO YO

COFFEESHOP

2e Jan van der Heijdenstraat 79 ☎066 471 73

The kind of store where they take their weed seriously, but you'd never tell from the supremely laid-back attitude. Only sells outdoor, organic marijuana and hash. Pastel green walls and large windows letting in lots of light continue the whole earth-happy theme. It's a nice place to come for a slice of pie and a coffee, even if you don't plan on smoking.

🚊 Tram #3, 4, or 25 to Ceinturbaan/Van Woutstraat. Walk north on Van Woutstraat, then make a right onto 2e Jan van der Heijdenstraat. $ €5 gets you 0.6-1g of weed or 0.8-1.1g of hash; joints €2.50. ⏰ Open M-Sa noon-7pm.

KATSU

COFFEESHOP

1e Van der Helstraat

💻www.katsu.nl

In the middle of a clutch of hipster bars, this shop matches the lively and fun atmosphere to a "T." The inside is painted in warm, tropical colors, and there's a communal table in the front where you can meet your fellow smokers. A wide selection of weed graces its selection, including a few Cannabis Cup winners.

🚊 Tram #16 or 24 to Albert Cuypstraat. Walk 1 block through the market and then right on 1e Van der Helstraat. $ Only sold in €5 and €10 denominations. €5 will get you 0.6-1g of weed, 0.5-1g of hash; €10 gives 0.8-3g of weed, 0.7-2.25g of hash. €20 for 0.4g of ice hashes. Joints €4, 3 for €10. ⏰ Open M-Th 11am-11pm, F-Sa 11am-midnight, Su noon-11pm.

COFFEESHOP CARMONA

COFFEESHOP

2e Jan van der Heijdenstraat 43

☎040 040 26

A few blocks away from Albert Cuypmarkt in a fairly residential neighborhood, this isn't the place to come if you want a huge choice of weed or lavishly themed smoking rooms, but for inexpensive stuff and a fairly private smoke in a vaguely Moroccan-looking room, it's ideal. It boasts a half-dozen types of weed (a few hazes, one bio option, and a house special) and three of hash.

*🚊 Tram #3, 4, or 25 to Ceinturbaan/Van Woutstraat. Walk north on Van Woutstraat, then make a right onto 2e Jan van der Heijdenstraat. **i** Internet €2 per hr. $ Weed €4-12 per g; joints with tobacco €2.50, Amnesia joints €4; hash €6-11 per g. ⏰ Open daily 10am-1am.*

amsterdam

JODENBUURT AND PLANTAGE

BLUEBIRD

COFFEESHOP

Sint Antoniesbreestraat 71

☎062 252 32

What's the point of visiting a city where weed is decriminalized if you're just going to smoke it in a place that looks like a basement from 1977? That's the look far too many Amsterdam coffeeshops go for, but fortunately, Bluebird is here to buck the trend. Dispensing with the blacklight paintings and lava lamps that define many of its competitors, this spot instead provides peaceful blue walls, wooden tables, and in-demand leather couches on the second floor. It has an extensive menu of weed and hash, with special cakes and muffins also available. The bar serves coffee, fresh juices, and smoothies to keep the non-smoking friend you dragged along with you happy.

🚊 Tram #9 or 14 to Mr Visserplein. Cross Valkenburgerstraat and walk straight. $ Most weed and hash €5-12.50 per g; joints €5, with tobacco €3; cakes €4, muffins €5. ⏰ Open daily 9:30am-1am.

REEFER

COFFEESHOP

Sint Antoniesbreestraat 77

☎062 336 15

This otherwise ordinary coffeeshop's massive glass chandelier alone makes it worth a look-see. Its upper-floor smoking area overlooks the canal, providing an exceptional view for lighting up. Reefer offers a smallish selection of wares, but many classics like AK47, White Widow, and Polm will leave blaze aficionados happy. Rarely as crowded as neighboring Bluebird.

🚊 Tram #9 or 14 to Mr Visserplein. Cross Valkenburgerstraat and walk straight. $ Weed €7-12.50 per g; joints €6.50, with tobacco €3; hash €4.50-15 per g. ⏰ Open M-Th 11am-10pm, F-Sa 11am-midnight, Su 11am-10pm.

food

For some reason, when we think "Northern Europe," we don't think "awesome food." Now, that's a little bit prejudiced, but it's telling that in the vast world of Amsterdam restaurants, very few of them actually serve Dutch cuisine. (Here's a quick run-down of what that looks like: pancakes, cheese, herring, and various meat-and-potato combinations.) Instead, most of the terrific food you'll find comes from the cuisines of all the others who, just like you, have been drawn to Amsterdam by its reputation of awesome. Large immigrant populations have brought **Indonesian, Surinamese, Ethiopian, Algerian, Thai,** and **Chinese** food to the banks of the city's canals. There are also many Italian, Spanish, French, pan-Mediterranean, and other nouveau-European fusion combinations that range from the homey to the ultra-chic. Finally, Amsterdam has this thing with sandwiches—they are everywhere, and they tend to be really, really good. Vegetarians and vegans should have no problem finding a meal, as there are quite a few exclusively vegetarian restaurants and most other places have plenty of veggie options.

De Pijp, Jordaan, and the Nine Streets in Canal Ring West boast the highest concentration of quality eats. De Pijp is the cheapest of the three. If you really want to conserve your cash though, **Albert Heijn** is the largest and most visible chain of supermarkets in the city *(find your nearest location at ▧www.ah.nl)*. For even cheaper eats, the basic budget store **Dirk van den Broek** *(Marie Heinekenplein 25 ☎067 393 93 ▧www.dirk.nl ⊡ Open M-Sa 8am-9pm, Su 10am-7pm.)* can keep your wallet and stomach full at the same time. On the other end of the spectrum, the **Natuurwinkel** *(Haarlemmerdijk 160-165 ☎062 663 10 ▧www.natuurwinkel.nl ⊡ Open M-F 8am-7pm, Sa 8am-6pm, Su 11am-6pm.)* chain of stores sells organic produce and other yuppie-ish natural products at fairly high prices. Keep in mind that most supermarkets close around 8pm. If you need groceries late at night (we can only guess why), try **De Avondmarkt** near Westerpark.

dutch desserts

Whether it's from roaming through museums or lazing in coffeeshops, sightseeing in Amsterdam is bound to make you a bit peckish. You can continue the cultural immersion *and* satiate your hunger with these traditional sweets.

- **STROOPWAFELS.** Literally "syrupwaffles," these crunchy-on-the-outside, gooey-on-the-inside Dutch treats are made from two thin waffle-like cookies glued together by a brown sugar and butter syrup. You won't be able to go a block in the Netherlands without finding a store that sells them in some form.

- **HAGELSLAG.** Breakfast in the Netherlands tends to be quite an affair, and one of the things that may stand out most is a box of these chocolate (or fruit-flavored) sprinkles. The common way to eat them is on buttered toast, so the sprinkles don't roll off. The name *hagelslag* is derived from the Dutch word for "hail," surely fueling dreams of chocolate falling from the sky in the minds of many a Dutch child.

- **OLIEBOLLEN.** A somewhat unappealing name—"oil balls"—comes with a fun story. Legend has it that the Germanic goddess Perchta would fly around during midwinter, slicing the belly off anyone she met. Germanic tribes ate *oliebollen* so that the oil in their stomachs would cause her sword to slide off. The science may be dubious, but these balls of dough studded with raisins, deep-fried, and then dusted with powdered sugar are certainly delicious.

food

OUDE ZIJD

Zeedijk is overwhelmingly packed with restaurants of all shapes and sizes, so be careful to compare menus when selecting a place to eat, since some can be touristy rip-offs. Don't cross the neighborhood off your list for fear of that possibility though—there are some really great places.

👍 'SKEK
👍♿📶🍸☀ CAFE, GLOBAL [2]

Zeedijk 4-8 ☎042 705 51 💻www.skek.nl

A "cultural eetcafe" where all students with ID get a 33% discount, 'Skek prepares food that is a sort of European fusion, with options like a Greek hamburger with *tzatziki* mayonnaise, grilled vegetable lasagna, or salmon with lentils. This is a place that begs you to stay a while—tables are painted with whimsical fantasy board games, student art lines the walls, and live music is featured many nights. The free Wi-Fi is a draw as well.

➔ At the beginning of Zeedijk, near Centraal Station. Ⓢ Appetizers €4.25-5; entrees €12.50-13.50. Did we mention the 33% student discount? ⏰ Open M-Th noon-1am, F-Sa noon-3am, Su noon-1am.

👍 LATEI
👍🚭 CAFE [1]

Zeedijk 143 ☎062 574 85 💻www.latei.net

Colorful and eccentric, Latei is filled with mismatched furniture and interesting knick-knacks—every single one of which is for sale. Save your money for the simple and impeccable food, though: sandwiches are made with artisan bread and the cafe's own olive oil and filled with everything from chorizo to hummus and grilled eggplant. Indian cuisine makes a guest appearance at dinner Thursday to Saturday nights.

➔ ⓂNieuwmarkt. Ⓢ Sandwiches €3-5. ⏰ Open M-W 8am-6pm, Th-F 8am-10pm, Sa 9am-10pm, Su 11am-6pm.

BIRD
👍🚭🍸 THAI [3]

Zeedijk 72-74 ☎062 014 42 💻www.thai-bird.nl

Zeedijk might be considered Amsterdam's Chinatown, but the best Asian restaurant is arguably Thai eatery Bird. Seriously, this is the most authentic Thai food you can get outside the Land of Smiles. The main restaurant is large and exotically decorated, while across the street (at Zeedijk 77) a simpler snack bar sells the same dishes to be eaten off the premises or at the counter for a few euros less. The menu's got all the Thai classics, including some special dishes from the northeast. *Let's Go* really likes their green curry.

➔ ⓂNieuwmarkt. i Snack bar cash only. Ⓢ Entrees €11-14, at snack bar €9-11. ⏰ Open daily 5-11pm. Snack bar open daily 2-10pm.

IN DE WAAG
👍🚭🍸☀ FRENCH, DUTCH [4]

Nieuwmarkt 4 ☎045 277 72 💻www.indewaag.nl

Located in Nieuwmarkt's distinctive 15th-century building, this restaurant presents quite the dining experience. In the summer, sit on the large terrace and admire the buildings and the bustle of the square. When it's cold out, the modernized medieval interior, lit by hundreds of candles, is just as enticing. The food is Mediterranean with a Dutch twist—lots of lamb, beef, and fish, with some vegetarian pastas and polentas.

➔ ⓂNieuwmarkt. Ⓢ Lunch entrees €7.50-14; dinner entrees €18-22. ⏰ Open daily 10am-1am.

RED LIGHT DISTRICT

Gluttony is one of the few sins you can't indulge in the Red Light District. There are some good, reasonably-priced cafes, but if you're looking for a quality meal, head next door to the Oude Zijd.

☑ **DE BAKKERSWINKEL** 🍴♿ CAFE ❶

Warmoesstraat 69 ☎048 980 00 🖥www.debakkerswinkel.nl

As cute and homey as the surrounding streets are neon and sordid. In the large pastel dining room you can enjoy terrific quiches, breakfast menus, or homemade sourdough bread and cheese. High tea is also available, replete with different combinations of scones, sweets, and sandwiches. Don't miss the fresh cakes and organic juices, either.

🚇 From Centraal Station, walk down Damrak, make a left onto Oudebrugsteeg, and then a right onto Warmoesstraat. $ Sandwiches €4. Slice of quiche €5.20. Breakfast menus €5.95-12.25. High teas €13.95-40. ⏰ Open Tu-F 8am-6pm, Sa 8am-5pm, Su 10am-5pm.

THEEHUIS HIMALAYA 🍴♿ CAFE, VEGETARIAN ❶

Warmoesstraat 56 ☎062 608 99 🖥www.himalaya.nl

At the back of a New Age-y bookstore, this surprisingly large cafe with welcoming staff and a tranquil canal view offers an all-vegetarian menu with many vegan options. Choose from a selection of sandwiches, bagels, and desserts or try the special vegan Himalaya burger. This may be the one place where you can find inner peace in the Red Light District.

🚇 From Centraal Station, walk down Damrak, make a left onto Oudebrugsteeg, and then a left onto Warmoesstraat. $ Sandwiches and bagels €3-5. Burgers €7.95. ⏰ Open M noon-6pm, Tu-W 10am-6pm, Th 10am-8pm, F-Sa 10am-6pm, Su noon-5:30pm.

NEW SEASON 💳♿🍸 CHINESE ❷

Warmoesstraat 39 ☎062 561 25

Come here for a sit-down meal in the Red Light District if you want something a bit more substantial than a sandwich. There's a wide selection of meat, fish, vegetable, rice, and noodle dishes. Most are Chinese, but some Thai curries and Malaysian dishes also make their way onto the menu. Plate options (combining an entree and rice) are a particularly good deal.

🚇 From Centraal Station, walk down Damrak, make a left onto Oudebrugsteeg, and then a left onto Warmoesstraat. $ Small entrees €6.50-11, full-size €9-14. ⏰ Open daily 11am-11pm.

NIEUWE ZIJD

Eating in the Nieuwe Zijd is less than ideal: it tends to be packed with overpriced, low-quality tourist traps. Try the southern half of **Spuistraat** or head to La Place for a quick lunch. Otherwise, save your money and walk a little farther to the Canal Ring West.

☑ **LA PLACE** 💳♿🍸🌳 CAFETERIA ❶

Kalverstraat 203 ☎062 201 71 🖥www.laplace.nl

In most parts of Amsterdam, it's often the cute cafes that have the best informal food. In the Nieuwe Zijd, many of those cafes will try to charge you €10 for a sandwich, so embrace the rampant commercialism in the area and head to this cafeteria inside the giant **Vroom and Dreesmann** department store. You'll be rewarded by a vast buffet of pizzas, pastas, salads, sandwiches, meats, and pastries for incredibly reasonable prices. Grab a tray and help yourself, then head to one of the multiple floors of seating, one of which includes an outdoor terrace.

🚇 Tram #4, 9, 14, 16, 24, or 25 to Muntplein. You'll see the giant V and D store; enter through the Kalverstraat door; the entrance to the cafeteria is on the left. $ Sandwiches €3-5. Pizzas €7. Other dishes depend on weight, but an entree will probably be €3-8. ⏰ Open M 11am-8pm, Tu-W 10am-8pm, Th 10am-9pm, F-Sa 10am-8pm, Su noon-8pm.

CAFE SCHUIM 💳♿🍸🌳 CAFE ❷

Spuistraat 189 ☎063 893 57

With bright, abstract shapes on the wall and massive padded-leather chairs surrounding small tables, this artsy spot is the antithesis of the McDonald's a few blocks away. Try sandwiches like the club with smoked chicken and avocado at lunch, or their creative pastas, steak, and entrees at dinner. The place is popular at night as well, when young professionals and hipsters crowd the bar and picnic tables outside. Enjoy the live music and DJs a few times a month.

➔ *Tram #1, 2, 5, or 14 to Dam/Paleisstraat. Walk down Paleisstraat toward Singel and make a left onto Spuistraat.* Ⓢ *Sandwiches €4-7. Pastas €9.50-12.50. Beer from €2.20.* ⏰ *Open M-Th noon-1am, F-Sa noon-3am, Su 1pm-1am.*

RISTORANTE CAPRESE

💳🚭🍸🌳 ITALIAN [3]

Spuistraat 259-261 ☎062 000 59

The service here is leisurely at best, but that just makes it feel more authentically Italian. With the massive wall mural of a Neapolitan bay view, you might even be convinced that you're a few countries to the south (at least in the summer). Traditional Italian food done well, from the excellent tomato sauce to the organically raised meat.

➔ *Tram #1, 2, or 5 to Spui/Nieuwezijds Voorburgwall. Cross over to Spuistraat and make a right.* Ⓢ *Pastas €9-14. Meat entrees €18-22. House wine from €4 per glass.* ⏰ *Open daily noon-11pm.*

SIE JOE

💳♿🌳 INDONESIAN [2]

Gravenstraat 24 ☎062 418 30 🖥www.siejoe.com

This unassuming Indonesian spot in the shadow of the Nieuwe Kerk is one of the better value options in the Nieuwe Zijd. The limited menu contains a half-dozen rice dishes, some soups, and meat satays. For vegetarians, the *gado gado* (mixed vegetables and tofu in peanut sauce) is a good option.

➔ *From Dam Square, walk up Nieuwezijds Vorburgwaal and make a left onto Gravenstraat. Sie Joe is directly behind the church.* Ⓢ *Entrees €6.75-8.75.* ⏰ *Open M-W 11am-7pm, Th 11am-8pm, F-Sa 11am-8pm.*

HUMPHREY'S RESTAURANT

💳♿🍸 FRENCH [3]

Spuistraat 267 ☎062 435 55 🖥www.humphreys.nl

A Dutch chain restaurant that doesn't really look it. The interior is spacious and elegant at Humphrey's, certainly one of the area's most affordable options for a sit-down meal in a nice setting. For €22.50, you get a three-course meal with around six choices for each course. Appetizers are along the lines of beef *carpaccio*, prawn tempura, or asparagus soup. For an entree, you might have steak with truffle sauce, salmon, or asparagus with roasted potatoes and a watercress salad. Dessert options include fresh strawberries and *crème brulée*.

➔ *Tram #1, 2, or 5 to Spui/Nieuwezijds Voorburgwal. Cross the square and walk up Spuistraat.* Ⓢ *3-course meal €22.50.* ⏰ *Open M-Th 5-10pm, F-Sa 5-10:30pm.*

SCHEEPVAARTBUURT

Haarlemmerstraat and **Haarlemmerdijk** are lined with restaurants, from cheap sandwich joints to upscale bistros. You'll have no problem finding somewhere to eat, but don't disregard a few of the quality options off the main streets.

★ OPEN CAFE-RESTAURANT

💳♿🍸🌳 FRENCH, ITALIAN [3]

Westerdoksplein 20 ☎062 010 10 🖥www.open.nl

This restaurant inhabits one of the coolest locations in Amsterdam—a renovated segment of a train bridge perched high above the waters between Westerdok and the IJ. Seating is available in the glossy mod interior lined with windows and green leather booths, on a walkway terrace, or on the sidewalk right by the water. The Mediterranean-style food is elegant, with dishes like lamb ravioli, stewed oxtail, and sea-bass salad. Conveniently, most dishes come in both half and full portions, so you can enjoy the view without breaking the bank.

➔ *From Haarlemmerstraat, walk from Korte Prinsengracht through the tunnel under the train tracks and then cross the bridge; you can't miss the restaurant on your right.* Ⓢ *Sandwiches and salads €7-14. Half-entrees €7-14, full €14-22.* ⏰ *Open daily 10am-10:30pm.*

HARLEM: DRINKS AND SOUL FOOD

💳♿🍸☀ AMERICAN [2]

Haarlemmerstraat 77 ☎033 014 98

No, they didn't leave out a vowel: this place is the Dutch outpost of good ol' American soul food. Here, you can indulge your culinary homesickness without the shame of being seen in a Burger King. Fill up on a variety of club sandwiches, soups, and salads at lunch or sup on dishes like macaroni and cheese and fried chicken at dinner. As the night wears on, patrons stick around to imbibe and listen to the grooving soul and funk on the stereo, making Harlem one of Scheepvaartbuurt's livelier places come nightfall.

🚶 Make a right when leaving Centraal Station, cross the Singel, and walk down Haarlemmerstraat a few blocks; Harlem's on the corner with Herenmarkt. $ Sandwiches €5-8. Entrees €12-18. ⏰ Open M-Th 10am-1am, F-Sa 10am-3am, Su 10am-1am. Kitchen closes 10pm.

SMALL WORLD

🍴♿☀ SANDWICHES [1]

Binnen Oranjestraat 14 ☎042 027 74 💻www.smallworldcatering.nl

The world may be small, but the sandwiches here are anything but. In this deli-style shop, you can choose from a long list of inspiring combinations like prosciutto with artichoke and lemon oil, roasted pumpkin and goat cheese, and a classic BLT, all available on a variety of hearty breads. Small World also sells coffee, fresh juices, salads, and sweets. Many locals get their sandwiches to go, but you can also enjoy them at the window counter or in the few seats under the awning outside.

🚶 In between Haarlemmerdijk and Brouwersgracht. $ Sandwiches €5.75-6.75. ⏰ Open Tu-Sa 10:30am-8pm, Su noon-8pm.

JAY'S JUICES

🍴♿ SMOOTHIE BAR [1]

Haarlemmerstraat 14 ☎062 312 67 💻www.jaysjuices.nl

Serving up juices "from the heart," Jay works magic with fresh fruit and a blender. Choose from dozens of combinations of strawberries, bananas, limes, papayas, and every fruit imaginable—plus some more unusual ingredients like chili pepper. Boosters like ginseng and guarana available, as is fresh wheatgrass juice made from Jay's own crop.

🚶 From Centraal Station, make a right; Jay's is on your right after you cross the Singel. $ Juices €2.50-3.50. ⏰ Open daily 8am-7pm.

LE SUD

🍴🚭 VEGETARIAN, MEDITERRANEAN [1]

Haarlemmerdijk 118 ☎062 258 88 💻www.lesud.nl

This store near Haarlemmerplein sells vegetarian sandwiches filled with things like hummus, grilled eggplant, and falafel. The "salad" selection includes your standard Greek, Italian, and pasta salads but also features a tremendous array of deli items like olives, cheeses, more hummus, dolmades (stuffed grape leaves), tapenades, and more. It is primarily a takeout location with Westerpark conveniently nearby.

🚶 Tram #3 to Haarlemmerplein. $ Sandwiches €2.95. Salads €1.25-2.50 per 100g. ⏰ Open M-Sa 10am-6pm.

CANAL RING WEST

This is one of the best places for high-quality eats in Amsterdam; restaurants in this neighborhood take food and style very seriously. The Nine Streets area is especially packed with hip and delicious cafes. Below is a starting point for exploring some of the neighborhood's choicest spots.

👍 FOODISM

💳🚭 SANDWICHES, ITALIAN [1]

Oude Leliestraat 8 ☎042 751 03 💻www.foodism.nl

This lovely little joint is bursting with color, from the lime green walls to the glossy cherry tables. The food is even brighter: choose from a menu of creative sandwiches like chicken and mango chutney or hummus with alfalfa or go for one of the daily homemade pastas—past offerings have included ravioli varieties such as chorizo, potato, and paprika and spring asparagus and mushroom. The baked goods are sinfully delicious. They also serve breakfast and soups.

✚ Tram #1, 2, 5, 13, 14, or 17 to Dam/Radhuisstraat. Continue on Radhuisstraat and make a right on the far side of the Singel; it will be on your left. ⑤ Sandwiches €5.50. Pastas €10-12. ☼ Open M-Sa noon-10pm, Su 1-6pm.

'T KUYLTJE
Gasthuismolensteeg 9

⊗⊘ SANDWICHES ❶
☎062 010 45 ▣www.kuyltje.nl

A no-frills takeout spot that makes tremendous, filling Belgian *broodjes*. The proprietor used to be a butcher, a fact which is immediately evident from the fresh and flavorful meat products (roast beef, pastrami, speck, and more)—no prepackaged cold cuts here.

✚ Tram #1, 2, 5, 13, 14, or 17 to Dam/Radhuisstraat. Continue down Radhuisstraat and make a left at the Singel. ⑤ Sandwiches €3.50. ☼ Open M-F 7am-4pm.

I QUATTRO GATTI
Hartenstraat 3

⊗⊗¥ ITALIAN ❸
☎042 145 85

One of the most popular restaurants in the neighborhood. The tiny restaurant serves up Italian dishes exquisitely made by a native-born chef. Menus change to reflect seasonal ingredients, and everything is homemade. It boasts a great wine selection; ask the staff to suggest something that will complement your meal.

✚ Tram #13, 14, or 17 to Westermarkt. Make a right after crossing Keizersgracht and then a left onto Hartenstraat. *i* Reservations strongly recommended. ⑤ Entrees €12-20. ☼ Open Tu-Sa 6-10pm.

ENVY
Prinsengracht 381

✦⊗¥⊜ ITALIAN ❹
☎034 464 07 ▣www.envy.nl

Envy (no relation to **Lust** on Runstraat, but owned by the same group as **Vyne**, a few doors down) immerses you in its culinary experience from the moment you walk through the door. Immediately after the entrance, the kitchen awaits, totally open to gawking customers, while a series of glass-fronted refrigerators displaying fruits, vegetables, cheeses, and oils—every ingredient involved in the menu—runs along an entire side of the restaurant. While dining, you may see a cook dash over to one of the transparent fridges to pick up a lime or a cauliflower. The rest of the restaurant's decor is stylishly minimalist, the better to put the focus on the food. And what food! The menu consists of small plates highlighting traditional Italian delicacies: artisan prosciuttos and cheeses, risottos, zucchini cannelloni with truffles, and so on. Most guests find two to three plates sufficient for a meal. The accommodating staff is eager to talk about the menu or suggest a wine pairing.

✚ Tram #13, 14, or 17 to Westermarkt. Walk down Prinsengracht. ⑤ 5-course tasting menu €52.50, 4-course €45; meats and cheeses €4-6 per portion. Entrees €8-14. ☼ Open M-Th 6pm-1am, F-Sa noon-3pm and 6pm-3am, Su noon-3pm and 6pm-1am. Kitchen closes daily at 11pm.

THE PANCAKE BAKERY
Prinsengracht 191

✦⊗¥⊜ DUTCH ❷
☎062 513 33 ▣www.pancake.nl

Many swear that this canalside restaurant serves the best pancakes in Amsterdam. The menu has a dizzying list of sweet and savory options, from the standard ham and cheese to international concoctions like the Indonesian (with chicken, peanut sauce, and sprouts). Enjoy these flaky, gooey wonders in the traditional wooden interior or at a table by the water.

✚ Tram #13, 14, or 17 to Westermarkt. Make a right up Prinsengracht. ⑤ Pancakes €7-14. ☼ Open daily noon-9:30pm.

DE KAASKAMER
Runstraat 7

⊗⊗ CHEESE ❶
☎062 334 83 ▣www.kaaskamer.nl

Wallace and Gromit's greatest dream, this store is packed floor-to-ceiling with hundreds of different types of cheese. Hard cheese, soft cheese, French cheese, Dutch cheese, red cheese, blue cheese—if you can make it out of milk, they have it. Because man cannot live on cheese alone (though we may have had an ill-fated *Let's Go* Researcher try that one year), the shop also sells wine, bread, olives, and other cheese-complementing snacks.

✚ Tram #13, 14, or 17 Westermarkt. Walk down Prinsengracht; Runstraat will be on the left. ⑤ Most cheese around €2-3 per 100g, or €7-9/500g. ⌚ Open M noon-6pm, Tu-F 9am-6pm, Sa 9am-5pm, Su noon-5pm.

TASCA BELLOTA
Herenstraat 22

●⊗☕ SPANISH ❸
☎042 039 46 🖥www.tascabellota.nl

At this tapas and wine bar, patrons perch on colorfully cushioned benches and treat themselves to dishes like spicy lamb meatballs, peppers filled with lentils and Manchego cheese, and dates with bacon. Strongly recommended by locals, Tasca Bellota hosts live music some nights.

✚ Tram #1, 2, 5, 13, or 17 to Nieuwezijds Kolk. Cross Spuistraat and the Singel and continue on Herenstraat. ⑤ Small dishes €5-10. ⌚ Open Tu-Th 6-10pm, F-Sa 6-11pm, Su 6-10pm.

SUSHI ME
Oude Leliestraat 7

●&☕ JAPANESE ❷
☎062 770 43 🖥www.sushime.nl

Super-cool sushi spot where the dishes are made fresh to order. Boasts a large variety of combination menus *(€7-17)* with every possible union of maki, nigiri, and sashimi. Sushi pieces can also be ordered a la carte.

✚ Tram #1, 2, 5, 13, 14, or 17 to Dam/Radhuisstraat. Continue on Radhuisstraat and make a right onto the far side of the Singel; it will be on your left. *i* Free delivery available with €14 min. order. ⑤ Maki €3.10-3.90 per 3 pieces; nigiri €1.40 per piece. ⌚ Open daily 4-10:30pm.

VENNINGTON
Prinsenstraat 2

●⊗♨ CAFE ❶
☎062 593 98

Vennington is an inexpensive, diner-esque place to enjoy breakfast and lunch. Their yolk-yellow tables are perfect for grabbing a quick snack if you're in the northern part of the Canal Ring. They have an extensive selection of sandwiches (simple ones, like ham and cheese or avocado and tomato, are the cheapest), breakfast options, coffee, and shakes.

✚ From the Westerkerk, walk up Prinsengracht and make a right. ⑤ Sandwiches €2.50-7. Coffee from €1.50. Shakes €3-4. ⌚ Open daily 8am-5:30pm.

CENTRAL CANAL RING

You'll eat well in the Central Canal Ring, where restaurants are affordable, tourist crowds are low, and you're never too far from Amsterdam's major sights. **Utrechtsestraat** in particular boasts a high concentration of diverse restaurants.

◪ GOLDEN TEMPLE

●&((•))♨ VEGETARIAN ❷

Utrechtsestraat 126
☎062 685 60 🖥www.restaurantgoldentemple.com

An exotically decorated spot with a wide range of vegetarian cuisine, Golden Temple gets increasingly exciting as you climb the stairs up its three floors. The ground level has standard tables and chairs, the first floor has low tables with sheepskin rugs for lounging, and the top floor has a tiny roof terrace with benches, sofas, and even more sheepskin, plants, and Indian artwork—you'll feel as though you've found a magical oasis in the midst of the city. Lunch consists of sandwiches, salads, and some hot Indian dishes, while dinner offers everything from Italian pizzas to Mediterranean *mezze*. The fresh juices are remarkably delicious.

✚ Tram #4, 7, 10, or 25 to Fredericksplein. Walk diagonally through the square and up Utrechtsestraat. *i* Free Wi-Fi. ⑤ Sandwiches and soups €3.75-4.75. Lunch entrees €7.25-11.25. Dinner entrees €8-17. ⌚ Open M 5-9:30pm, Tu-Sa noon-3pm and 5-9:30pm, Su noon-3pm.

food . central canal ring

B AND B LUNCHROOM

Leidsestraat 44 — CAFE, SANDWICHES [1]
☎063 815 42

It's hard to walk by this storefront and not be drawn in by the window heaped high with pastries and muffins. The shop sells filling sandwiches that go beyond the ordinary offerings with combinations like roast beef and "citron mayonnaise" or gorgonzola and asparagus. Soups and salads complete the menu that covers multiple blackboards in the store. At lunchtime, you may have to take your food to go: despite the touristy surroundings, many Dutch people pour in from the offices in the neighborhood to grab lunch.

Tram #1, 2, or 5 to Keizersgracht. The cafe is on the southwestern corner. $ Sandwiches €3.50-6. Salads €6.50-7.50. ⏰ Open daily 10am-6pm.

LOS PILONES

Kerkstraat 63 — MEXICAN [3]
☎032 046 51 🖥www.lospilones.com

While popular with tourists, locals, and expats from all over, this restaurant remains steadfastly Mexican—their website is only in Spanish, and you should have seen the crowds here watching Mexico play in the World Cup. The menu is full of tacos, enchiladas, and other entrees like *pollo con mole.* With an impressive selection of tequilas and Mexican beers, it's also a choice place to enjoy a drink and some chips. Plus, there's always the chance that a mariachi band will turn up for a serenade.

From Leidseplein, walk up Leidsestraat and make a right on Kerkstraat. $ Appetizers €3-8; entrees €15-17. Margaritas €7.25. ⏰ Open Tu-Th 4pm-1am, F-Sa 4pm-2am, Su 4pm-1am.

ZUIVERE COFFEE

Utrechtsestraat 39 — CAFE [1]
☎062 499 99

There's an expression in Dutch, "*dat is geen zuivere koffie,*" which literally translates to "that's no pure coffee" but really means something along the lines of "that's totally suspicious." This store, then, is the opposite, offering not only good coffee, but also unquestionably good homemade cakes and pastries. The apple pie is a thing of beauty: you can actually tell that it is made from apples, not some dubious apple-flavored gelatinous filling with chunks of an apple-like product. It also serves sandwiches, croissants, and the like. Enjoy treats in the garden seating area out back.

Tram #4, 16, 24, or 25 to Keizersgracht. Walk east on Keizersgracht and make a left onto Utrechtsestraat. $ Sandwiches €5. Apple pie €3.50. Coffee €1.80-3. ⏰ Open M-F 8am-5pm, Sa 9am-5pm.

GO FRESHSHOP

Vijzelstraat 135 — SANDWICHES, ITALIAN [2]
☎052 869 85 🖥www.gofreshshop.nl

"For pure food and drinks" is their motto, and this store certainly delivers. Combine a sandwich or hearty salad with one of their freshly-squeezed juices and you'll feel purged of the city's grit. At dinner, the many pasta options at least *feel* a lot healthier and fresher than those of your typical Italian restaurant. They have tons of vegetarian options as well as meat and fish.

Tram #4, 16, 24, or 25 to Keizersgracht. Walk south on Vijzelstraat; the store is at the corner with Prinsengracht. $ Sandwiches €4-4.50. Salads and pastas €9.50. ⏰ Open M-Sa 11am-10pm, Su noon-10pm.

LEIDSEPLEIN

Korte and Lange Leidsedwarsstraat are stuffed to the gills with restaurants from every corner of the globe. With so many options, few are ever extremely crowded, and most are certainly passable. However, many do tend to be overpriced. For the best values, look for restaurants that have special set menus or daily deals, or grab a sandwich and snack from a grocery store. At night, places like **Maoz** and **Wok to Walk** (both on Leidsestraat, toward Prinsengracht) stay open late and are surprisingly tasty as well as affordable. Of course, there's always Burger King and McDonald's, but if it's not White Castle, why bother?

👍 EAT AT JO'S

⊛♿🍸 AMERICAN [2]

Marnixstraat 409 ☎063 833 36 💻www.eatatjos.com

This cafe inside the **Melkweg** complex gives you the opportunity to rub elbows with performers and locals over outstanding, impeccably fresh food. The menu changes daily, accommodating seasonal variation and the chef's multiethnic whims, but always with a vegetarian and vegan option. Sandwiches are available at lunch, full menu at dinner. Note the Green Bay Packers mug behind the bar: owner Mary Jo hails from Wisconsin, having come to Melkweg initially with her musician husband.

🚋 Tram #1, 2, 5, 7, or 10 to Leidseplein. Make a right down Marnixstraat. $ Sandwiches €5. Salads €7. Entrees €13. ⏰ Open W-Su noon-9pm. Dinner service begins at 5:30pm.

BOJO

💳⊗🍸☁ INDONESIAN [2]

Lange Leidsedwarsstraat 49 ☎064 344 43

Come here for great deals on delectable Indonesian cuisine. Special deals include a noodle or rice dish, meat, and a satay skewer for only €10. The portions are ample, and the staff knows it—they post a note on the menu encouraging visitors to ask for a doggy bag. The bamboo walls and low-hanging lanterns enhance the authenticity of the food; you'll think you're oceans away from chilly Amsterdam.

🚋 Tram #1, 2, 5, 7, or 10 to Leidseplein. $ Entrees €8-14. ⏰ Open M-F 4-9pm, Sa-Su noon-9pm.

J. J. OOIJEVAAR

⊛⊗🍸 DELI [1]

Lange Leidsedwarsstraat 47 ☎062 355 03

This is the place for the cheapest sandwiches on the Leidseplein—perhaps in all of Amsterdam. Rolls start at €1.30, and all manner of fillings are available to stuff them with: cheeses, meats, vegetables, etc. The store also sells many grocery and convenience items.

🚋 Tram #1, 2, 5, 7, or 10 to Leidseplein. $ Sandwiches €1.30-3.50. 6-pack of beer €6. ⏰ Open M-F 8:30am-6pm.

DE ZOTTE

⊛♿🍸☁ BELGIAN [2]

Raamstraat 29 ☎062 686 94 💻www.dezotte.nl

Among the infinite alcohol-focused establishments on or around the Leidseplein, De Zotte is one of the few that cares about quality, not just quantity. It offers an incredible selection of Belgian beers and a menu full of hearty Belgian food to go with them. Choose from steak, sausages, and pâté or cheese served with wonderful country bread. Less artery-clogging options such as quiche are also available. The place is all dark wood and old beer posters, completing the authentic feel.

🚋 Tram #7 or 10 to Raamplein. Raamstraat is 1 block away from the Leidsegracht. Or tram #1, 2, or 5 to Leidseplein. Walk down Marnixstraat and Raamstraat will be on your right after the canal. $ Appetizers (some are filling enough to be a meal) from €3; entrees €10-17. ⏰ Open M-Th 4pm-1am, Sa-Su 4pm-3am. Kitchen open daily 6-9:30pm.

THE PANTRY

💳⊗🍸☁ DUTCH [3]

Leidsekruisstraat 21 ☎062 009 22 💻www.thepantry.nl

Designed to hint at the feel of an old Dutch living room, with traditional paintings and cozy wooden tables, this is one of the most popular restaurants among locals. A great place to try some authentic Dutch dishes, like *boerenkoolstamppot* (mashed potatoes mixed with kale, served with a smoked sausage or a meatball) or salted herring.

*🚋 Tram #1, 2, 5, 7, or 10 to Leidseplein. Make a right onto Korte Leidsedwarsstraat and Leidsekruisstraat will be on your left. **i** Reservations strongly recommended. $ Entrees €12-17. ⏰ Open daily noon-9pm.*

MAI THAI

99 Korte Leidsedwarsstraat

🍴♿🍸☀ THAI [2]

☎062 342 59

A small and cozy spot compared to the vast ethnic eateries that line Korte and Lange Leidsestraat, Mai Thai serves up really flavorful and authentic Thai food in hefty portions—the pad thai alone could fill up the hungriest backpacker. Daily meat and fish specials are a treat, but there are also plenty of vegetarian choices.

🚋 Tram #1, 2, 5, 7, or 10 to Leidseplein. $ Entrees €9-17. ⏰ Open daily noon-10pm.

CAFE AMERICAIN

Leidsekade 97

🍴🚭🍸☀ FRENCH [4]

☎055 631 16 💻www.amsterdamamerican.com

Cafe Americain stands as an extremely grand monument to Art Deco elegance, with original Tiffany glass lamps hanging from its vaulted ceiling arches. This makes it a great place to grab a coffee or cocktail in style; dinner is a relatively formal affair, with dishes ranging from lamb to lobster. The restaurant's large patio provides a superb place to observe the plebes on the Leidseplein, so soak up the snooty while you can—we all know you'll be partying with the peasants later on.

🚋 Tram #1, 2, 5, 7, or 10 to Leidseplein. $ Appetizers €9.50-14.50; entrees €16.50-32.50. Mixed drinks €9. ⏰ Open daily 10:30am-midnight.

REMBRANDTPLEIN

Rembrandtplein, like the Leidseplein, is packed with enormous international restaurants and oversized cafes, but here there are fewer small, affordable eateries scattered into the mix. Many of the area's chic bars have expensive menus as well, though some of their snacks can make a budget-friendly but still luxurious treat. Bottom line: if you're looking for Amsterdam's best food, you're better off elsewhere.

✓ RISTORANTE PIZZERIA FIRENZE

Halvemaansteeg 9-11

🍴♿🍸 ITALIAN [1]

☎062 733 60 💻www.pizzeria-firenze.nl

The wine bottles sitting on every table and the murals of Italian scenery on the walls will make you feel like you're actually in *Italia*. Not the world's most gourmet pizza, but with large pies beginning at €5, no one's complaining. Dozens of choices for both pizza and pasta, as well as some meat and fish dishes. Definitely one of the best values for a restaurant meal around Rembrandtplein.

🚋 Tram #9 or 14 to Rembrandtplein. Halvemaansteeg is the street to the left of the line of buildings with the giant TV screen. $ Pizza and pasta €5-9. House wine €2.50 per glass, €10 per L. ⏰ Open daily 1-11pm.

✓ VAN DOBBEN

Korte Reguliersdwarsstraat 5-9

🍴♿📶 SANDWICHES [1]

☎062 442 00 💻www.eetsalonvandobben.nl

An old-school deli and cafeteria that is everything most restaurants in Rembrandtplein are not: cheap, fast, and simple. The black and white ceramic tiling and chrome accents are a good match for the food's simplicity. Choose from a long list of sandwiches or a more limited selection of soups, salads, and omelettes. Coffee and other drinks are available as well. We're not sure how this place stays in business, seeing as how everywhere else seems to charge five times as much, but we hope they keep the magic going.

🚋 Tram #9 or 14 to Rembrandtplein. The easiest way to find the small street is to get onto Reguliersdwarsstraat and then look for where the street veers off on the right. ℹ Free Wi-Fi. $ Sandwiches €2.50-4.25. ⏰ Open M-Sa 9am-6pm.

TOMO SUSHI

Reguliersdwarsstraat 131

🍴🚭🍸 JAPANESE [4]

☎052 852 08

One of Amsterdam's more highly regarded (and more expensive) sushi restaurants. The inside is sleek and pale, with futuristic pod-like white chairs. Patrons nibble to hip music ranging from ambient stuff to salsa. There are many combinations of freshly made sushi and sashimi as well as pieces available for ordering a la carte; don't forget the array of sake options, too.

🚊 *Tram #9 or 14 to Rembrandtplein.* $ *Combinations €17-27. A la carte pieces €2-4.* ⏰ *Open daily 5:30-11:30pm.*

💳♿🍸☀ MEXICAN [3]

ROSE'S CANTINA

☎062 597 97 💻www.rosescantina.com

Reguliersdwarsstraat 40

A big and bright interior with lively salsa music makes this a more fun version of the somewhat overpriced restaurants near Rembrandtplein. Check out the great selection of appetizers and the standard entrees (burritos, fajitas, enchiladas, etc.). The combination deal *(€17.50)* lets you choose two from a selection of quesadillas, enchiladas, and tacos served with rice, beans, and guacamole. The large bar serves up a long list of summery cocktails.

🚊 *Tram #9 or 14 to Rembrandtplein or tram #1, 2, or 5 to Koningsplein.* $ *Appetizers €5.50-7.50; entrees €14-21. Mixed drinks €7-9.50.* ⏰ *Open M-Th 5-10:30pm, F-Sa 5pm-2am, Su 5-10:30pm. Kitchen closes F-Sa 11pm.*

JORDAAN

The Jordaan has very few truly budget options for food, but very few overpriced ones either. Area establishments are frequented more by loyal regulars than by tourists.

🥗🚭 ALGERIAN [2]

RAINARAI

☎062 497 91 💻www.rainarai.nl

Prinsengracht 252

Walk into this small restaurant and take a look at the food counter: the dishes here change daily, and the staff will explain the day's offerings to you. Next, gauge your hunger level and select a plate size. Medium is standard and comes with generous servings of rice or couscous, a meat dish, and a vegetable dish. The Algerian fare means you can count things like spicy lamb meatballs, grilled asparagus, stuffed artichokes, and curry among your options. No matter what the daily dishes are when you arrive, you won't be disappointed—everything is delicious. You can also get your meal to take away. Additionally, the stores sells food products such as olive oils, beans, and canned vegetables, plus their own cookbook if you want to try and recreate your meal back at home.

🚊 *Tram #13, 14, or 17 to Westermarkt. Cross Prinsengracht and make a left.* $ *Entrees €10-14.50.* ⏰ *Open Tu-Su noon-10pm.*

💳♿🍸 ITALIAN [4]

TOSCANINI

☎062 328 13 💻www.diningcity.nl/toscanini

Lindengracht 75

Quite a few locals will swear backwards and forwards that this is the best Italian food in Amsterdam. The menu is strongly authentic: instead of pizza you'll find homemade pastas like ravioli with lemon and saffron or *secondi* along the lines of pan-fried pork with *vin santo*. The bright, sky-lit interior similarly lacks the gimmickry of faux-Italian trattorias found the world over. In the neighborhood for over 20 years, this restaurant is no longer a secret, so reservations are virtually required.

🚊 *Tram #3 to Nieuwe Willemstraat. Cross Lijnbaansgracht to Willemstraat, make a right onto Palmdwarsstraat, and then left onto Lindengracht.* $ *Appetizers €11-14.50; primi €8-14.50; secondi €18-22.50.* ⏰ *Open M-Sa 6-10:30pm.*

🥗♿🍸 VEGETARIAN [2]

DE VLIEGENDE SCHOTEL

☎062 520 41 💻www.vliegendeschotel.com

Nieuwe Leliestraat 162-168

It's a little unclear what aliens have to do with vegetarian cuisine (this restaurant's name translates to "The Flying Saucer"), but we'll let the mystery slide because this restaurant is down-to-earth even if its food is out-of-this-world good. The cuisine is organic and macrobiotic, with many vegan choices, too. Dishes change seasonally, but might include an Ayurvedic curry, seitan goulash, or lasagna.

🚊 *Tram #10 to Bloemgracht. Cross Lijnbaansgracht, make a left, and then a right onto Nieuwe Leliestraat.* $ *Entrees €11-13.* ⏰ *Open daily 4-11:30pm. Kitchen closes at 10:45pm.*

WINKEL 🚫💳🚫♿🍸⛅ CAFE [2]

Noordermarkt 43 ☎062 302 23 💻www.winkel43.nl

On the corner of Noordermarkt, with a lovely view of the church from its outdoor patio, Winkel serves up a cuisine that's hard to classify: you can get miso soup, a club sandwich, or lamb stew depending on your whim. No matter how you're feeling, you should do as everyone else does and order the apple pie. Renowned across the city, it's served with a heap of fluffy whipped cream. Winkel occasionally hosts live music and dancing.

➡ Tram #3 or 10 to Marnixplein. Cross Lijnbaangracht, walk up Westerstraat, and make a left onto the square. $ Entrees €6-15. ⏰ Open M 7am-1am, Tu-Th 8am-1am, F 8am-3am, Sa 7am-3am, Su 10am-1am.

DE BOLHOED 🚫💳♿🍸⛅ VEGETARIAN [2]

Prinsengracht 60-62 ☎062 618 03

Looking exactly as you would expect a healthy vegetarian establishment to look, with vines outside and a colorful floral theme within, de Bolhoed serves great vegetarian fare at reasonable prices. Lunch consists mostly of sandwiches and omelettes, while dinner features more substantial dishes like pasta or enchiladas. Fresh juices and vegan desserts round out the offerings.

➡ Tram #13, 14, or 17 to Westermarkt. Cross Prinsengracht, make a right, and walk a few blocks. $ Sandwiches €5-7. Entrees €13-17. ⏰ Open M-F 11am-10pm, Sa 10am-10pm, Su 11am-10pm.

PASO DOBLE 💳♿🍸 SPANISH [3]

Westerstraat 86 ☎042 126 70 💻www.dobson-uzcudun.com/tapas/pasodoble.htm

Owned by the Spanish food empire that runs **Rose's Cantina** near Rembrandtplein and a number of the gargantuan steakhouses in Leidseplein, Paso Doble is one of the group's more intimate and less touristy offshoots. Enjoy the wide selection of tapas while sitting on colorful chairs surrounded by lovely Spanish art. The tapas are split into meat, fish, and vegetarian sections of the menu, so you can try everything from dates with bacon to a potato omelette. If you're with a group of seven or more, consider opting for the €19.50 per person tasting menu.

➡ Tram #3 or 10 to Marnixplein. Cross Lijnbaansgracht and continue along Westerstraat. $ Most tapas €3.75-6. ⏰ Open M-F 5-11pm, Sa-Su noon-11pm.

WESTERPARK AND OUD-WEST

Some of the quirkiest eats, most unique spaces, and highest-quality food can be found in these neighborhoods. In this residential area, you're likely to be the only foreigner at the table.

👍 **TOMATILLO** 💳♿ MEXICAN [1]

261 Overtoom ☎068 330 86 💻www.tomatillo.nl

Tomatillo bills itself as "Tex-Mex to go," but its crisp, clean interior and fresh ingredients set it apart from the rest of the ethnic fast food eateries along Overtoom. There are a few small tables available for eating in the restaurant, where you can enjoy watching the chefs at work in the open kitchen. The food steers clear of the greasy, over-cheesiness of many gringo attempts at Mexican cuisine (though we suspect the friendly proprietors would give you extra cheese if you asked—this is the Netherlands, after all). The tacos are an especially good deal, consisting of two small tortillas and a heap of fillings that adds up to a satisfying lunch. Six types of salsa, salads, drinks, and desserts round out the menu.

➡ Tram #1 to J. P. Heijestraat. Tomatillo is between Jan Pieter Heijestraat and G. Brandstraat, a block north of Vondelpark. $ Burritos and tostadas €7.50-9.50. Tacos €2.75-3.50. Desserts €2-4. ⏰ Open Tu-Su noon-9pm.

👍 **BELLA STORIA** 🚫💳♿🍸⛅ ITALIAN [2]

Bentinckstraat 28 ☎048 805 99 💻www.bellastoria.info

For people who miss their Italian granny's home cooking (or missed out on having an Italian granny entirely), this is the place to be. It's truly a family affair, run by a mother and her sons who chatter in Italian as they roll out dough. Since the restaurant sits smack in the middle of an extremely residential area, expect to have the place to yourself during a weekday lunch and get ready to be surrounded by locals at dinner. Some standard sandwiches and entrees can be found on the menu, but the real standouts are the fresh pizzas and pastas, all handmade, that may not be listed on the hard menu. These offerings change daily, so check out the blackboard or ask the waitress what's cooking when you come in. We promise you won't be disappointed.

Tram #10 to Van Limburg Stirumplein. Facing Limburg Stirumstraat, Bentinckstraat is on your right. $ Pastas €10-17. Open daily 10am-10pm.

DE AVONDMARKT
GROCERY STORE ❶

De Wittenkade 94-96 ☎068 649 19 www.deavondmarkt.nl

One of the most frustrating things about the Netherlands can be the lack of 24hr. stores, but "The Evening Market" helps fill the bellies of night owls, until midnight at least. The store sells standard but high-quality grocery items (bread, juice, snacks, fruits, vegetables), wine, and beer as well as a wide variety of cheeses and prepared foods like lasagna and meats. Good selection of organic products.

Tram #10 to De Wittenkade. On the mainland side of De Wittenkade, at the corner with Van Limburg Stirumstraat. Open M-F 4pm-midnight, Sa 3pm-midnight, Su 2pm-midnight.

WESTERGASTERRAS
GLOBAL ❸

Klonne plein 4-6 ☎068 484 96 www.westergasterras.nl

This modern restaurant and bar is tucked away behind the Westergasfabriek by a surprisingly rural stretch of greenery. A massive terrace is available to enjoy in fresh air and sunshine, but with an interior space as open and airy as this one, you can still feel some semblance of the outdoors even when the weather is bad. Popular with young professional types for after-work relaxation, Westergasterras offers a menu that is ambiguously ethnic but unquestionably delicious, with offerings like an avocado and smoked paprika sandwich, daily risotto, and beef sashimi. Also has a small, carefully-selected wine list.

Tram #10 to Van Limburg Stirumstraat. Continue along V. L. Stirumstraat, cross the Haarlemmerweg, and turn away from the Westergasfabriek. On your right, there will be a path next to the giant round silo-looking thing. $ Lunch dishes €4.50-9.50; dinner appetizers €7.50-12; entrees €19.50. Wine from €4 per glass. Open M-Th 11am-1am, F 11am-3am, Sa 10am-3am, Su 10am-1am. Kitchen closes at 10pm.

PEPERWORTEL
DELI ❷

140 Overtoom ☎068 510 53 www.peperwortel.nl

The type of packed, bountiful store you would expect to find in Italy or France, with all manner of prepared food and delicacies from Europe and beyond, Peperwortel presents options that include, but are by no means limited to, quiches, pastas, hummus and other dips, soups, and more exotic dishes like Indonesian beef. Order an entree as a meal, and it comes with a starch and vegetable. It has an excellent variety of vegetarian offerings and a good wine selection. Limited seating is available outside, but the grass of Vondelpark a few blocks away makes for an even better table.

Tram #1 to C. Huygensstraat. Peperwortel is on the corner of Overtoom and 2nd C. Huygensstraat. $ Entrees €8.50-13.50. Desserts €3. Wines from €7. Open daily 4-9pm.

KADE 58
CAFE, GLOBAL ❶

58-60 Jacob van Lennepkade ☎061 807 57 www.kade58.nl

In our experience, establishments that name themselves after their addresses are either too hip for their own good or unselfconsciously laid-back. This place is the latter. Amsterdam is full of bar-and-restaurant combinations that line the canals, but Kade 58 holds the happy distinction of being in a more residential neighborhood—meaning your seat will actually have a view of the river, and you won't cry your own when the check comes. The spacious and relaxed interior is also available when the weather isn't going your way. Kade 58 gets extra brownie points for one of the most eclectic selections of bar snacks we've ever seen, from bread with aioli to dim sum to nachos. Lunch and dinner dishes that include both tuna melts and Thai beef salad continue the international theme. It also has a full bar and a limited but classic selection of mixed drinks.

⚲ *Tram #3 or 12 to Kinkerstraat. On the corner of Bilderdijkstraat and Jacob van Lennepkade.* ⑤ *Sandwiches €5.25-6.25. Dinner appetizers €4-6.50; dinner entrees €13.75-17.50. Snacks €4-8.50.* ⚇ *Open M-Th 3pm-1am, F 3pm-3am, Sa noon-3am, Su noon-1am. Kitchen closes at 10:30pm.*

CAFE NASSAU

⬦❧🚫♨🅿 CAFE, ITALIAN, DUTCH ❶

De Wittenkade 105A ☎068 435 62

This riverside cafe's kitchen pumps out a simple but creative menu of sandwiches, tostis, and soups, plus a daily selection of more substantive entrees (often pastas and seasonal vegetables). Ingredients are fresh and fillings are bountiful; try the *broodje* with spicy Italian sausage, grilled eggplant, parmesan, and arugula. Plenty of seating is available in the warm wood interior, but when the weather is nice, you can sit at the ample patio or even at picnic benches across the road, right next to the canal. Coffee and drinks from the cafe's full bar are available.

⚲ *Tram #10 to De Wittenkade. It is at the corner of De Wittenkade and 2e Nassaustraat.* ⑤ *Sandwiches from €5. Entrees from €10.*

CAFE-RESTAURANT AMSTERDAM

⬦⊗(ⁿ)♨🅿 DUTCH, CAFE ❸

Watertorenplein 6 ☎068 226 66 🖳www.cradam.nl

Housed in an old industrial building, this restaurant has a vast interior dining space with high ceilings and long windows as well as a stretch of outdoor seating along a small, mossy canal in a corner of the Westerpark neighborhood. The menu matches the establishment's minimalist charm, offering a seasonal selection of unfussy plates like steaks, ravioli, and a remarkable variety of seafood. Part of the restaurant is a cafe section, with bare tables and free Wi-Fi. The whole place is popular with families.

⚲ *Tram #10 to Van Hallstraat. Directly behind the tram stop.* ⑤ *Appetizers €4-9.50; entrees €13-18.50.* ⚇ *Open M-F 11am-midnight, Sa-Su 11am-1am. Kitchen open M-F 11:30am-10:30pm, Sa-Su 11:30am-11:30pm.*

MUSEUMPLEIN AND VONDELPARK

Museumplein seems to be the one area of the city that attracts real grown-ups, so it stands to reason that the food is a little bit pricier. A long day of museum-hopping can be strenuous though, and if you need to refuel on the cheap, the **Albert Heijn** supermarket at the edge of the park across from the Concertgebouw is at your service. When you're not picnicking at Vondelpark, we hope you're still enjoying its greenery while dining at Cafe Vertigo.

🛡 CAFE VERTIGO

⬦⊗♨🅿 CAFE, MEDITERRANEAN ❶

Vondelpark 3 ☎061 230 21 🖳www.vertigo.nl

Cafe Vertigo finds itself in a remarkable, ornate building with a seemingly endless patio that makes the place look like it should be a lot more expensive than it is. On a summer day, there's no better place to enjoy a sandwich and a drink (except, perhaps, for the grass of Vondelpark itself). Though the cafe sits on the edge of the park, it faces an expanse of green that will make you feel quite outside the city. Sandwiches (lamb with artichokes, ham and cheese, goat cheese with red onion compote) and soups (try the chickpea with lamb) make a great lunch. There's a full coffee and alcohol bar as well, so you can enjoy the atmosphere without filling up.

✉ Tram #1, 3, or 12 to 1e Constantijn Huygensstraat/Overtoom. Walk down 1e C. Huygensstraat, make a right onto Vondelstraat, and enter the park about 1 block down; the cafe is on your left. ⑤ Soups and sandwiches €3.50-6.75. Entrees €11.75-19.50. ② Open daily 10am-1am.

▧ BAGELS AND BEANS

●⊗& CAFE ❶

Van Baerlestraat 40

☎067 570 50 🖳www.bagelsbeans.nl

This charming chain now has over 40 stores across the Netherlands, but this is where it all began. You can get something as simple as a bagel with cream cheese (though with dozens of bagels and cream cheese options, it's not as simple as it sounds), or go for one of their creative sandwiches like chicken and avocado or goat cheese, honey, and walnuts. Given the dearth of affordable food around here, this place is magical.

✉ Tram #2, 3, 5, or 12 to Van Baerlestraat. ⑤ Bagel with cream cheese €3.35. Sandwiches €3.95-6.50. ② Open May-Sept M-F 7:59am-6:02pm, Sa-Su 9:31am-6:02pm; Oct-Apr M-F 8:28am-6:01pm, Sa-Su 9:31am-5:59pm. No, we're not joshing you; yes, these are their real opening times.

SAMA SEBO

●&¶& INDONESIAN ❸

P. C. Hooftstraat 27

☎066 281 46 🖳www.samasebo.nl

Just next to the temporary entrance to the **Rijksmuseum,** this restaurant exemplifies the Dutch fondness for Indonesian food—authentic *rijsttafels* are served in a place that looks like a quintessential Dutch pub. Not the cheapest meal available, but the lunch deals are a good value for the neighborhood. They come with rice or noodles, a couple of vegetables, some different kinds of meat, a satay, and some fried tasties—all in all, a filling place. You can also build your own *rijsttafel* piece by piece from their a la carte menu.

✉ Tram #2 or 5 to Hobbemastraat. Walk down the street with the Rijksmuseum on your right; the restaurant is at the intersection with P. C. Hooftstraat. ⑤ Entrees €2.50-8. Lunch menus €16. Rijsttafel €30 per person. ② Bar open M-Sa 9am-1am. Kitchen open noon-3pm and 5-10pm.

PASTA TRICOLORE

●& ITALIAN ❶

P. C. Hooftstraat 52

☎066 483 14 🖳www.pastatricolore.nl

A long list of Italian sandwiches with filling combinations of salami, cheeses, grilled vegetables, and the like can be found at the back of this shop, while a counter brimming with different kinds of salads and *antipasti* is at the front. No real seating to speak of, but it's a good place to grab supplies for a picnic in Vondelpark or Museumplein (if you want something a bit snazzier than the Albert Heijn).

✉ Tram #2 or 5 to Hobbemastraat. Walk down Hobbemastraat away from the Rijksmuseum and make a left onto P. C. Hooftstraat. ⑤ Sandwiches and salads from €4. ② Open M-Sa 9am-7pm, Su noon-7pm.

DE PIJP

If you could somehow work it so that you ate every meal in De Pijp during your time in Amsterdam, you would be a happy 🎒camper. In a radius of just a few blocks, you'll find a tremendous variety of cuisines dished up at significantly lower prices than in most other parts of the city. **Albert Cuypstraat** and **Ferdinand Bolstraat** are good places to start looking, but don't neglect the smaller side streets that radiate off of them as well. Many of the places listed in **Nightlife** also whip up surprisingly good food.

▧ CAFE DE PIJP

●⊗¶& MEDITERRANEAN ❶

Ferdinand Bolstraat 17-19

☎067 041 61 🖳www.goodfoodgroup.nl

20-somethings linger over drinks, dinner, or more drinks at Cafe De Pijp, something of a catch-all local hotspot. The menu is filled with tapas-esque offerings,

food • de pijp

like Merguez sausage with Turkish bread and aioli, or more Italian-inspired dishes along the lines of eggplant parmesan. On weekend nights, DJs spin dance tunes to help you work off your meal.

 # Tram #16 or 24 to Stadhouderskade. Walk 2 blocks down Ferdinand Bolstraat. $ Entrees €5.50-8. ⏰ Open M-Th 3:30pm-1am, F 3:30pm-3am, Sa noon-2am, Su noon-1am.

BAZAR

MIDDLE EASTERN ❷

Albert Cuypstraat 182

☎067 505 44 www.bazaramsterdam.com

The crush of Albert Cuypmarkt feeling a little overwhelming? Pop into this former church where the vaulted ceilings remain, now decorated with Arabic Coca-Cola signs and old Dutch advertisements. Seating is available both on the ground and in the old balconies above. Bazar serves inexpensive and super tasty Middle Eastern food.

 # Tram #16 or 24 to Albert Cuypstraat. Walk through the market a few blocks. $ Sandwiches and lunch entrees €4-10. Dinner entrees €12-16. ⏰ Open M-Th 11am-midnight, F 11am-1am, Sa 9am-1am, Su 9am-midnight.

WARUNG SPANG MAKANDRA

INDONESIAN ❶

Gerard Doustraat 39

☎067 050 81 www.spangmakandra.nl

Imperialism may have been a pretty terrible thing, but at least it has given us delicious culinary combinations like the Indonesian-Surinamese mix at this neighborhood favorite. Enjoy noodle and rice dishes, satays, and *rotis*—pancakes with different meat or vegetable fillings—for incredibly low prices. Plenty of vegetarian options.

 # Tram #16 or 24 to Albert Cuypstraat. Walk 1 block north on Ferdinand Bolstraat and make a left. $ Entrees €5.50-9. ⏰ Open M-Sa 11am-10pm, Su 1-10pm.

DE SOEPWINKEL

SOUP ❶

1e Sweelinckstraat 19F

☎067 322 83 www.soepwinkel.nl

Modern minimalism meets home cooking at this soup shop. Sit at picnic-esque tables in the airy store or at a patio table outside and enjoy one of their six marvelous rotating specialty soups (always at least one vegetarian option). They prepare quiches, tarts, and sandwiches as well.

 # Tram #3, 4, or 25 to Ceinturbaan/Van Woutstraat. Walk towards the park, make a right onto Sarphatipark, and continue for 1½ blocks. Or tram #16 or 24 to Albert Cuypstraat. Walk a few blocks through the market and make a right onto 1e Sweelinckstraat. $ Soups from €4. Menu with soup, a slice of quiche, and a drink €7.90-8.40. ⏰ Open M-Sa 11am-8pm, Su 11am-6pm.

BURGERMEESTER

BURGERS ❶

Albert Cuypstraat 48

☎067 093 39 www.burgermeester.eu

Thankfully, the burgers here are better than the store's punny name (*burgemeester* is "mayor" in Dutch). This is something of a designer-burger bar—you can get a patty made from fancy beef, lamb, salmon, falafel, or Manchego cheese and hazelnuts, then top it with things like Chinese kale, truffle oil, or buffalo mozzarella. Burgers can be ordered normal-sized or miniature, because food is always more fun when it's tiny. They sell salads, too, but who goes to a burger joint for a salad?

 # Tram #16 or 24 to Albert Cuypstraat. Walk down the street away from the market. $ Burgers €6.50-8.50. Toppings €0.50-1. ⏰ Open daily noon-11pm.

DE TAART VAN M'N TANTE

DESSERT ❶

Ferdinand Bolstraat 10

☎077 646 00 www.detaart.com

What started as a customized cake bakery now has its own restaurant where you can try slices of delicious cakes and pies—apple, pecan, and all kinds of more exciting combinations (including ones made "tipsy" with dashes of Amaretto and other liqueurs). The pink, sparkly, and floral interior is how we think a female

Mad Hatter would decorate a tea party and complements the kitschy sweetness of the cakes themselves.

🚊 *Tram #16 or 24 to Stadhouderskade/Ferdinand Bolstraat. The store is on the corner.* Ⓢ *Tart slices €4.30-5.20.* ☼ *Open daily 10am-6pm.*

WILD MOA PIES
⊕♿ PIES ❶

Van Ostadestraat 147
☎064 291 4050 🖳www.pies.nu

We didn't really know that New Zealand had much of a national cuisine, but apparently it does at least have pie. This Kiwi-owned store sells six types of meat pie (one made from real New Zealand beef) and three types of vegetarian (we like the 3 Ps—Pumpkin, sweet Potato, and Paprika). One largish table is available if you want to eat your pies in the store, but you can also take them to Sarphatipark just across the street.

🚊 *Tram #3 or 25 to 2e Van der Helstraat. Walk 1 block south, away from the park.* Ⓢ *All pies €3.* ☼ *Open Tu-Sa 9am-5:30pm.*

HET IJSPALEIS
⊕♿ ICE CREAM ❶

1e Sweelinckstraat 20
☎061 204 1617

A gleaming white "Ice Palace" that looks awfully tempting on a hot day, especially after trawling through the crowds of Albert Cuypmarkt. Serves about a dozen fresh, homemade flavors in cups or cones. Also has a fine selection of coffee and teas. Keeping to the neighborhood's hipster ambience, they even have exotic choices like **rooibos.**

🚊 *Tram #16 or 24 to Albert Cuypmarkt. Walk through the market and make a right.* Ⓢ *Servings from €1.10.* ☼ *Open daily 11am-8pm.*

SIRIPHON
🍴♿☕☂ THAI ❷

1e Jacob van Campenstraat 47
☎067 680 72

Offering tasty Thai cuisine in a small, exotically decorated restaurant with welcoming staff, Siriphon has the usual selection of curries, noodles, soups, salads, and rice dishes. Food is served with chili oil, so you can adjust the spiciness to your taste. Things come out of the kitchen reasonably fiery, so proceed with caution.

🚊 *Tram #16 or 24 to Stadhouderskade. Walk down Ferdinand Bolstraat and make a right.* Ⓢ *Entrees €10-14.* ☼ *Open daily 3-10:30pm.*

JODENBUURT AND PLANTAGE

🏛 EETKUNST ASMARA
⊕♿☂ ERITREAN ❷

Jonas Daniel Meijerplein 8
☎062 710 02

Jodenbuurt started out as a neighborhood of immigrants, and this East African restaurant is a testament to the area's continuing diversity. The menu consists of different types of meat or vegetables cooked in delicately blended spices, all served with *injera*, a traditional spongy, slightly tangy bread. Each dish is accompanied by an assortment of lentils and other veggies, so one entree could comfortably feed two people. This is thus one of the cheapest meals around and a nice break from Amsterdam's unending parade of sandwiches.

🚊 *Tram #9 or 14 or Ⓜ Waterlooplein. Restaurant is just after the Jewish Historical Museum.* Ⓢ *Entrees €9.50-11.50. Beer €1.50.* ☼ *Open daily 6-11pm.*

ROSARIO
🍴⊗☂ ITALIAN ❹

Peperstraat 10
☎062 702 80 🖳www.restaurantrosario.nl

If you're in the neighborhood and ready to drop a tidy sum, then this is the place to come. Everything from the bread to the pasta is fresh and homemade. Dishes are classic Italian with a twist, like curry *tagliatelle* with salmon or avocado *panna cotta*. Downstairs, a small lounge room faces directly into the canal. Believe it or not, people often come in from passing 🚤**boats.**

➥ Tram #9 or 14 or Ⓜ Waterlooplein. Walk along Nieuwe Uilenburgerstraat until it becomes Peperstraat. Ⓢ Antipasti €11-12.50; primi €13.50-15; secondi €22-24. ⏰ Open W-Su 6-10:30pm.

PLANCIUS

💳♿🍸☀ CAFE, SANDWICHES, FRENCH [2]

Plantage Kerklaan 61A ☎033 094 69 💻www.restaurantplancius.nl

Capturing that elusive stylish yet unpretentious feeling, Plancius is a one-stop-shop for everything from breakfast to after-dinner drinks. The menu rotates seasonally, but trust that lunch will have a selection of creative spins on the traditional sandwich (as well as some soups and salads), while dinner tends toward more formal French fare like lamb shank or shrimp croquettes.

➥ Tram #9 or 14 to Plantage Kerklaan. Directly across from Artis Zoo. Ⓢ Sandwiches €2.65-8.50. Dinner appetizers €8; entrees €15-19. ⏰ Open daily 11am-11pm. Cheaper items served until 6pm.

SOEP EN ZO

🥗♿☀ SOUP [1]

Jodenbreestraat 94A ☎042 222 43

This small takeout counter serves up fresh soups and a few salads. Free bread accompanies the brothy deliciousness, which you gussy up with various toppings ranging from coriander to cheese. Take advantage of their outside patio when the weather's nice.

➥ Tram #9 or 14 or Ⓜ Waterlooplein. Ⓢ Soups €3-7. ⏰ Open M-F 11am-8pm, Sa-Su noon-7pm.

NAM TIN

💳♿🍸 CHINESE [2]

Jodenbreestraat 13 ☎042 885 08 💻www.namtin.nl

A gargantuan dining room bedecked in 📷**dragons** and Confucian statues is the setting for this eatery's tasty, tiny Cantonese treats. Dim sum is served daily from noon-5pm. Peruse the special book that lists all the treats available and mark your choices of juicy soup dumplings, pillowy pork buns, and slippery rice noodles on the ordering cards. Other Cantonese cuisine is also available in a separate menu.

➥ Tram #9 or 14 or Ⓜ Waterlooplein. Ⓢ Dim sum €3-5. Most entrees €7-14. ⏰ Open daily 11:30am-11pm.

LÖFEL AND BURKE

🥗🚭📶🍸☀ CAFE [1]

Plantage Kerklaan 2 ☎075 291 81 💻www.lofelenburke.nl

This popular, cool cafe serves lunch (mostly sandwiches and salads) until 4pm and snacks and drinks until late. It's a good place to grab a quick bite before hitting up the area's museums or linger over your choice of coffee or cocktail after a day of sightseeing.

➥ Tram #9 or 14 to Plantage Kerklaan. ℹ Free Wi-Fi. Ⓢ Sandwiches €3.50-6.50. Salads €9. ⏰ Open M-Th 10am-1am, F 10am-3am, Sa noon-3am, Su noon-1am.

nightlife

It goes without saying that experiencing the nightlife in Amsterdam is an integral part of any trip to the city. Certainly, you can go to the Rijksmuseum and see a dozen Rembrandts, but there's nothing like stumbling out of a bar at 5am and seeing the great man staring down at you from a pedestal in the middle of **Rembrandtplein.** That's one of the main after-dusk hotspots, where you can find glitzy clubs lined up next to raucous tourist bars and dance spots where the music invites choruses of drunken revelers to sing along. **Leidseplein** offers a similar mix of quality dance venues with live DJs, cool cocktail spots, and rowdy pubs. The crowds here tend to be a bit younger and more local. A few additional clubs are scattered throughout the city, but mostly what you'll find in the way of nightlife are some hipper lounge bars and a whole lot of *bruin cafes*, cafe-pub combinations populated by old Dutch men and hipster students, depending on what neighborhood you're in (though sometimes both demographics share the same table space). The closer you get to the **Red Light District**, the more the local presence fades away and is taken over by groups of large British men on bachelor party trips wearing matching T-shirts. No matter where you are, the Amsterdam post-dinner scene is free of the pretension sometimes found in other European cities. Lines may occasionally be long at some of the more popular clubs, but as long as you seem sober and aren't with a huge group of men (unless you're going to a gay club) you should have little problem eventually entering.

☑**GLBT nightlife** is very visible and prominent. Around Rembrandtplein, especially on Reguliersdwarsstraat, you'll find both gay clubs and bars that cater primarily to men, though some women often turn up, too. The northern part of **Zeedijk** also has a couple of gay bars, and on the end of Warmoesstraat, near Dam, you'll find smaller, darker clubs that are strictly men-only and feature a fair bit of rubber and leather. Fewer spots cater to lesbian audiences, though such establishments do exist. And it's worth bearing in mind that in this city famous for tolerance, virtually every bar and club is ☒**GLBT-friendly.**

There are a number of ways to keep informed about upcoming evening events in the city. *NL20* is a free weekly publication that keeps extensive listings of what's on in Amsterdam. Though it's only in Dutch, it's pretty easy to decipher the names of clubs and DJs. You can find *NL20* outside most stores, supermarkets, and tobacco shops. *Time Out Amsterdam*, an English-language publication, can be purchased at newsstands and bookstores and lists monthly calendars of nightlife, live music, and other events. The city is also plastered with **posters** advertising concerts, festivals, and club events. Read these. They are helpful.

bruin cafe

Heading to a "brown cafe" may not sound like the most appetizing way to spend an evening. If we at *Let's Go* were going to name a kind of bar with a color, we'd have gone for something with a bit more punchy. Like "turquoise bar." Or "indigo bar." Or "bright shiny bar." But the Dutch are what they are, so *bruin cafes* dot the Amsterdam social scene. Fortunately, they're actually not dull, muddy, boring places but relaxed and friendly settings for a social drink and conversation. If staying in the city for more than a few hours, you'll almost certainly find yourself in one eventually, so take it in and don't worry too much about the title.

OUDE ZIJD

Both **Zeedijk** and **Nieuwmarkt** are lined with bars, so you certainly won't be at a loss for options when you head out to grab a drink in the evening. The watering holes on Zeedijk tend to be more popular with tourists, while Nieuwmarkt's crowd is mixed. If you head east toward Jodenbuurt, you will find more locals. Heading west will bring you to the Red Light District in all its glory. Though some overflow energy from the busier neighborhoods to the west spills into the Oude Zijd, things are generally a bit tamer at night. It's telling that most of the establishments listed here have "cafe" in their name. The northern part of Zeedijk, near Centraal Station, has a smattering of ☑**GLBT** bars, identified by their rainbow flags.

▨ **HET ELFDE GEBOD**　　　　　　　　　　　　　　　　　⊛⊗♈ BAR
Zeedijk 5　　　　　　　　　　　　　☎062 235 77 ▤www.hetelfdegebod.com
Named "The Eleventh Commandment" after a now nonexistent Belgian beer, this bar sets itself apart from the endless row of pubs along the street with its

incredible beer selection. The completely Belgian and incredibly delicious brew menu includes seven beers on tap and over 50 more in bottles (many of which come served in their own special glasses). Don't worry if you're overwhelmed by the choices: the knowledgeable bartenders are happy to recommend something. Gets crowded on weekend nights with jolly locals.

 # At the beginning of Zeedijk, near Centraal Station. $ Beer from €3. ⏰ Open M 5pm-1am, W-Su 3pm-1am.

👍 CAFE DE JAREN

💳⊗🍸⛅ BAR

Nieuwe Doelenstraat 20-22 ☎062 557 71 💻www.cafedejaren.nl

Incredibly popular with locals and tourists of all ages, Cafe de Jaren has an expansive interior and a two-tiered terrace overlooking the Amstel, making it one of the nicest spots to sit in Amsterdam. Thanks to its size and elegance, it looks a lot more expensive than it is. It also serves a diverse lunch and dinner menu.

 # Tram #4, 9, 16, 24, or 25 to Muntplein. Cross the Amstel and walk a ½-block. $ Beer from €2.50. Wine from €3. ⏰ Open M-Th 9:30am-1am, F-Sa 9:30am-2am, Su 9:30am-1am.

COTTON CLUB

⊘♿🍸⛅ JAZZ CLUB

Nieuwmarkt 5 ☎062 661 92 💻www.cottonclubmusic.nl

An old and storied jazz club on the edge of Nieuwmarkt. Legendary musicians have played here, and every Saturday 5-8pm, you can hear the talented house musicians play, often with special guests. The rest of the week this is still a tuneful and relaxed place to enjoy a drink.

 # ⓂNieuwmarkt. $ Beer from €2.50. Weekly concerts are free. ⏰ Open M-Th noon-1am, F-Sa noon-2am, Su noon-1am.

CAFE NAGEL

⊘♿🍸 BAR

Krom Boomssloot 47 ☎051 684 93

Cafe Nagel is a truly local spot that feels miles away from tourist-filled Nieuwmarkt (though it's just a 2min. walk). It's packed with a regular crowd of locals in their 20s and early 30s on weekend nights. The good selection of beers and spirits (at some of the cheapest prices in town) should be enjoyed at the cafe's simple wooden tables or bustling bar.

 # ⓂNieuwmarkt. Walk down Keizersstraat; it's across the canal. $ Beer from €2.50. Spirits from €3. ⏰ Open M-Th 11am-1am, F-Sa 11am-3am, Su 11am-1am.

CAFE DE ENGELBEWAARDER

⊘⊗🍸⛅ BAR

Kloveniersburgwal 59 ☎062 537 72 💻www.cafe-de-engelbewaarder.nl

This "literary cafe" with a fine selection of Belgian beers is located on the first floor of a canal house and has a seating area by the water. It's an artistically hip place more conducive to conversation than cruising but without an ounce of pretension, and the wall full of posters advertising local goings-on will bring you up to speed on all that's, well, going on.

 # ⓂNieuwmarkt. i Live jazz Su 4:30pm. $ Beer from €3. ⏰ Open M-Th 11am-1am, F-Sa 11am-3am, Su 11am-1am.

TEMPLE BAR

💳♿🍸⛅ BAR

Kloveniersburgwal 59 ☎042 744 00

This glossy pseudo-Irish pub attracts a diverse crowd of tourists. A large interior and canalside patio also mean that you won't be jostling for space, unlike at most nearby establishments. Helpful bartenders keep the Guinness flowing and the music fun.

 # ⓂNieuwmarkt. $ Beer from €3. ⏰ Open M-Th 11am-1am, F-Sa 11am-3am, Su 11am-1am.

CAFE "OOST-WEST"

⊘⊗🍸 BAR

Zeedijk 85 ☎042 270 80

The painting on Cafe "Oost-West"'s outer wall and the strains of Dutch pop wafting from the door call out to be noticed. The music is unabashedly cheesy and often hilarious (we particularly enjoyed the Dutch techno cover of "Sweet Caroline"), which is just how the slightly rowdy crowd of older locals—along with a few bemused backpackers—likes it.

✱ Ⓜ Nieuwmarkt. Ⓢ Beer from €2.50. ☑ Open M-Th 11am-1am, F-Sa 11am-3am, Su 11am-1am.

RED LIGHT DISTRICT

Ah, the Red Light District at night. Most of the neon glow bathes **Oudezijds Achterburgwal** and the nearby alleyways. Farther over on **Warmoesstraat,** you can still get a tinge of the lascivious luminescence but will find far more non-sex-related establishments. Especially on weekends, the whole area is filled with crowds of predominantly male tourists. Despite getting very busy, the hotel bars on Warmoesstraat and Oudezijds Voorburgwal can be fun places to mingle with fellow backpackers.

▨ CLUB WINSTON
♣♿☕ CLUB

Warmoesstraat 129 ☎062 539 12 ▣www.winston.nl

A surprisingly large spectrum of musical genres fills this club each night with young locals and tourists. Live bands often play earlier in the evening, while DJs take over after 11pm. Once the bands clear out, the stage is free for intrepid dancers. There's also a lounge area across the dance floor, but people tend to stay on their feet. You can hear everything from rock, metal, and drum 'n bass to electronica, indie pop, or hip hop. Check the website for the schedule and to see a long list of previous musicians who have played here. A very popular bar sits next door.

✱ From Centraal Station, go south on Damrak, turn right onto Brugsteeg, and veer left onto Warmoesstraat. Ⓢ Cover varies by event, usually around €5. Beer from €2.50. ☑ Hours vary by event but usually 9pm-4am.

▨ WYNAND FOCKINK
●♿☕ BAR

Pijlsteeg 31 ☎063 926 95 ▣www.wynand-fockink.nl

Many people avoid the small alleyways of the Red Light District, but this one holds a unique draw—an over-300-year-old distillery and tasting room that makes the best *jenever* in the city in addition to other delightfully flavored liquors. Perfect for day-drinking (it closes at 9pm), there's no music, no flatscreen TV, and not even any chairs: just rows of bottles on creaking shelves behind the small bar. Dozens of liquors are available with flavorings like cinnamon, rose petals, bergamot, or strawberry. Most are complex blends with names like "Forget Me Not" or "The Bride's Tears" that come with often humorous histories. Make sure to try the fruit-flavored Brandywines.

✱ From Dam Square, walk down Dam to Oudezijds Voorburgwal; make a left and then the next left onto Pijlsteeg. Ⓢ Spirits from €2.50. ☑ Open daily 3-9pm.

GETTO
●⊗☕▼ BAR

Warmoesstraat 51 ☎042 151 51 ▣www.getto.nl

A fun, everyone's-welcome-here cocktail bar crossed with a diner, Getto offers a phenomenal cocktail menu as well as their very own homemade infused vodka (flavors range from vanilla to cucumber). Though the bar's considered a GLBT establishment, the crowd is really as diverse as they come. It also serves a mean BBQ burger alongside a rotating selection of other good food.

✱ From Centraal Station, go south on Damrak, turn right onto Brugsteeg, and veer left onto Warmoesstraat. ℹ €4.50 cocktails during happy hour. Su DJ party from 5pm with special cocktail deals. Ⓢ Cocktails from €6. ☑ Open Tu-Th 4pm-1am, F-Sa 4pm-2am, Su 4pm-midnight. Happy hour Tu-Sa 5-7pm.

CAFE AEN'T WATER
●⊗☕♨ BAR

Oudezijds Vorburgwaal 2a ☎065 206 18

Smack in the middle of the two busiest Red Light District drags, you'll be surprised by how relaxed you feel and how much Dutch you hear. The star attraction is the large outdoor patio that hugs a bend in the canal, but if you choose to sit inside, you'll be able to enjoy the soundtrack of quality rock and indie music.

➔ From Centraal Station, turn left onto Prins Hendrikkade and then bear right onto Nieuwebrugsteeg; continue straight as it becomes Oudezijds Vorburgwaal. $ Beer from €2. ⏰ Open M-Th noon-1am, F-Sa noon-3am, Su noon-1am.

DURTY NELLY'S PUB

⊛♿🍸 IRISH PUB

Warmoesstraat 115-117 ☎063 801 25 💻www.durtynellys.nl

Right underneath **Durty Nelly's Hostel,** this pub attracts backpackers from upstairs, students from around the world, and drunkards from the official Red Light District pub crawl. With pool, foosball, darts, and all kinds of international sports playing on the TVs, there's plenty here to keep you entertained. The atmosphere is about as fun-loving and rowdy as you would expect, making it a great place for a pint or six. it also serves standard pub food, including full Irish breakfast (which, big surprise, includes Guinness).

➔ From Centraal Station, go south on Damrak, turn right onto Brugsteeg, and veer right onto Warmoesstraat. $ Beer from €2. ⏰ Open M-Th 8am-1am, F-Sa 8am-3am, Su 8am-1am.

ROCK PLANET

⊛♿🍸⛅ BAR

Oudezijds Voorburgwal 246 ☎042 164 00

This bar serves as an appropriate reminder that though some in the Red Light District may try, no one does debauchery like a rock star. The staff happily takes any music requests (as long as they're for rock), but you can also select from a vast collection of live concert DVDs and watch the performances while you drink. Reasonably mellow on weekdays (despite the high decibels); Rock Planet really fills up on weekend nights.

➔ From Dam Square, walk east on Dam and make a right onto Oudezijds Voorburgwal. $ Beer from €2. ⏰ Open M-Th 9am-1am, F-Sa 9am-3am, Su 9am-1am.

THE END

💳♿🍸 BAR, KARAOKE

Nieuwebrugsteeg 32 ☎06 49 048 839 💻www.theendkaraoke.nl

If you want to try something a little different on your night out (assuming that being in Amsterdam's Red Light District isn't different enough from your average outing), head to this karaoke emporium at the neighborhood's tip. Its popularity varies from night to night, so you may want to bring a group of friends unless you feel like performing for just the bartenders. With tens of thousands of songs in English, Dutch, French, Italian, and more at your fingertips, you'll be all set once you get up the courage to sing.

➔ From Centraal Station, turn left onto Prins Hendrikkade and then bear right onto Nieuwebrugsteeg. $ Beer from €2.50. ⏰ Open daily 9pm-4am.

THE BULLDOG MACK

⊛⊗📶🍸⛅ BAR

Oudezijds Voorburgwal 132 💻www.thebulldog.com

An offshoot of the vast Bulldog empire (you can see their logo on buildings from three blocks down the canal), this is one of the busiest hotel bars in the Red Light District. A pool table and TVs with international sports keep patrons entertained under the bar's neon glow and slightly tropical decor. Large outdoor patio by the canal.

*➔ From Dam Square, walk east on Dam and make a left onto Oudezijds Voorburgwal. **i** Free Wi-Fi. $ Beer from €2.50. ⏰ Open M-Th 9am-1am, F-Sa 9am-3am, Su 9am-1am. Kitchen open 9am-3pm.*

HEFFER

💳⊗🍸⛅ BAR

Oudebrugsteeg 7 ☎042 844 88 💻www.heffer.nl

Bigger and less pub-y than most places in the area, this bar is located in the old home of the city tax collector. Despite its history, Heffer's not so grand that you can't come just to enjoy a pint from their good beer menu and watch the game. On sunny days, the large patio is especially nice.

✈ *From Centraal Station, walk down Damrak and make a left onto Oudebrugsteeg.* ⑤ *Beer from €2.50.* ☑ *Open M-Th 10am-1am, F-Sa 10am-3am, Su 10am-1am.*

NIEUWE ZIJD

Though not very concentrated, nightlife in the Nieuwe Zijd is diverse. **Spuistraat** is the place to go for artsier cafes and bars, while **Dam Square** and **Rokin** are lined with larger, rowdier pubs. The small streets in the southern part of the neighborhood are home to quite a few good beer bars and a couple of energetic clubs as well.

PRIK
●&♀⊙▼ BAR, CLUB

☎032 000 02 ▣www.prikamsterdam.nl

Spuistraat 109

Voted both best bar and best gay bar in Amsterdam on multiple occasions, Prik attracts pretty much everyone—locals and tourists, gay and straight people, men and women—though the majority of patrons tend to be men. It's a place that is as light and fun as its name ("bubble" in Dutch). Serves great inventive cocktails and tasty bar snacks. Come for cocktail specials all day Thursday and Sunday evenings. On weekends, DJs spin pop, house, and disco classics.

✈ *Tram #1, 2, 5, or 14 to Dam/Paleisstraat. Walk down Paleisstraat and right onto Spuistraat.* ⑤ *Beer from €2. Mixed drinks from €6.* ☑ *Open M-Th 4pm-1am, F-Sa 4pm-3am, Su 4pm-1am. Kitchen open until 11pm.*

DANSEN BIJ JANSEN
●⊗♀ CLUB

☎062 017 79 ▣www.dansenbijjansen.nl

Handboogstraat 11-13

A student-only club (must have ID or be accompanied by someone who does), Dansen bij Jansen attracts those from both the nearby University of Amsterdam and local hostels. The music in the crowded main dance floor may feel a bit three-years-ago, with a slightly cheesy mix of Top 40, R and B, and disco, but it certainly gets people dancing. Upstairs, another bar offers a range of more ambient electronic music.

✈ *Tram #1, 2, or 5 to Koningsplein. Cross the canal, walk up Heiligeweg, and turn left onto Handboogstraat.* ℹ *Students only.* ⑤ *Cover M-W €2; Th-Sa €5. Beer from €2.* ☑ *Open M-Th 11pm-4am, F-Sa 11pm-5am.*

CLUB NL
●&♀ CLUB

☎062 275 10 ▣www.clubnl.nl

Nieuwezijds Voorburgwal 169

This is a swanky lounge club with surprisingly low cover charges. Patrons are slinkily dressed, and you'd be advised to spruce up a bit before trying to get in, especially later on a weekend night. Music goes from ambient house to more energetic dance tunes; check website for guest DJ appearances. The carefully crafted cocktail menu is just as image-conscious as the club itself, with delicious results.

✈ *Tram #1, 2, 5 or 14 to Dam/Paleisstraat. Just south of the stop on Nieuwezijds Voorburgwal.* ⑤ *Cover F-Sa €5. Beer from €2.50. Mixed drinks from €8.* ☑ *Open M-Th 10pm-3am, F-Sa 10pm-4am, Su 10pm-3am.*

BITTERZOET
●⊗♀ BAR, CLUB

☎042 123 18 ▣www.bitterzoet.nl

Spuistraat 2

A young (though not necessarily student) urban crowd enjoys drinks and music at this funky bar and club with an upstairs lounge. The musical events are terrifically diverse—there could be bouncy house one night, smooth reggae the next, and a live rock band after that.

✈ *From Centraal Station, walk down Martelaarsgracht, which will become Hekelweg and then Spuistraat.* ⑤ *Cover €5-8. Beer from €2.* ☑ *Open M-Th 8pm-3am, F-Sa 8pm-4am, Su 8pm-3am.*

GOLLEM

Raamsteeg 4

BAR

☎067 671 17 www.cafegollem.nl

This is not a bar for the indecisive. Beer aficionados from all across the city (and the world) flock to Gollem's slightly Gothic interior for the brews: this was one of the first cafes in Amsterdam to serve specialty Belgian beers way back in the '70s, and now the bar sells over 200 different kinds, with eight on tap. You can find Trappist ales, fruit lambics, double beers, triple beers—pretty much anything you can do with yeast and some hops. They even have the famed **Westvleteren,** made by reclusive monks in incredibly small batches to prevent it from becoming commercialized.

Tram #1, 2, or 5 to Spui/Nieuwezijds Voorburgwal. Walk up Spui and make a left onto Raamsteeg. $ Beer from €2.50. Open M-F 4pm-1am, Sa-Su 2pm-2am.

BELGIQUE

Gravenstraat 2

BAR

☎062 519 74 www.cafe-belgique.nl

If you can muscle your way through to the bar—it tends to be packed in here, even on weekday nights—you'll be rewarded by a choice of eight draft beers and dozens more in bottles, all high-quality Belgian brews with a few Dutch offerings mixed in. "But I'm in Holland," you say. "Should I really be at a bar called 'Belgium'?" Be quiet and enjoy your beer. Now you have a great excuse to add Brussels to your itinerary.

From Dam, walk down Zoutsteeg; the bar is behind the Nieuwe Kerk, in between Nieuwendijk and Nieuwezijds Voorburgwal. $ Beer from €2.50. Open daily 3pm-1am.

CAFE'T SPUI-TJE

Spuistraat 318

BAR

☎062 676 84 www.cafehetspui-tje.nl

This is the place to come when you need a stiff drink. With dozens upon dozens of kinds of whiskeys, bourbons, rums, vodkas, and other spirits crammed onto the shelves behind the bar, Cafe't Spui-tje is sure to stock something you like. The red and burnished brass interior gives it a decidedly old-fashioned feel that is only enhanced by the soul, blues, and classic crooners on the speakers. Your fellow drinkers will likely be of a similar era, though some younger tourists do wander in from time to time.

Tram #1, 2, or 5 to Spui/Nieuwezijds Voorburgwal. $ Beer from €2.30. Liquor from €4. Open M-Th 10am-1am, F-Sa 10am-3am, Su 10am-1am.

DE BARONESSE

Torensteeg 2

BAR

☎043 95 45 51

This unfussy, under-the-radar cafe is a great spot to take a breather from the rest of the night. You'll be sharing the candlelit bar with a few travelers, a few regulars, and a few members of the frank and funny staff. A good, eclectic selection of music (rock, blues covers, indie) plays over the sound system. Sometimes events are hosted here, but you'll more likely find action on the flyers for local parties posted on the tables and walls.

Tram #1, 2, 5, or 14 to Dam/Paleisstraat. Walk down Paleisstraat toward Singel and make a right onto Spuistraat. $ Beer from €2. Open M-Th 11am-1am, F-Sa 11am-3am, Su 11am-1am.

THE TARA

Rokin 85-89

IRISH PUB

☎042 126 54 www.thetara.com

An Irish bar that's one of the largest pub complexes in the city, The Tara keeps multiple bars running, so the Guinness flows all night long. Different parts of the building have different themes—go from a hunting lodge to a downtowny lounge without even stepping outside. Most patrons are tourists, with a liberal sprinkling of expat regulars mixed in. Live music some Saturday nights.

Tram #4, 9, 14, 16, 24, or 25 to the Spui/Rokin stop. Walk a few blocks up Rokin; Tara's on the right. $ Beer from €2.70. Open M-Th 10am-1am, F-Sa 10am-3am, Su 10am-1am.

SCHEEPVAARTBUURT

Nightlife in Scheepvaartbuurt is not exactly what one would call happening. After dark, those who do stick around tend to congregate in the coffeeshops on **Haarlemmerstraat.** However, a few places are enjoyable stops for a quiet drink and draw small weekend crowds.

💳♿⃠🍸⛅ BAR

👍 DULAC

Haarlemmerstraat 118 ☎062 442 65 💻www.restaurantdulac.nl

This bar is a popular place with local and foreign-exchange students. (There's a 50% student discount on the food served by the restaurant within.) The interior presents a fantastical mix of vintage designs, crazy sculptures, and found objects, including a pair of antlers and an antique saxophone. The four beers on tap taste extra good when sipped to the soundtrack of relaxed Spanish music in the background. A garden terrace is in the back, and a pool table is inside.

🧭 From Centraal Station, make a right, cross the Singel, and walk down Haarlemmerstraat. $ Beer from €2.50. Entrees €10-18. ⏰ Open M-Tu 4pm-1am, W-Th 1pm-1am, F-Sa 1pm-3am, Su 1pm-1am.

💳♿⃠🍸 BAR

BARNEY'S UPTOWN

Haarlemmerstraat 105 ☎061 242 21 💻www.barneys-amsterdam.com

Under the same hospitable umbrella as the ever-popular coffeeshop across the street, Barney's Uptown is about as close as you'll get to a cocktail bar in Scheepvaartbuurt. Paintings of musical greats overlook sleek leather couches and wood tables: everything feels very, well, uptown. There are options aplenty here, as the bar is extremely well stocked and food is available from breakfast until dinner.

🧭 From Centraal Station, make a right, cross the Singel, and walk down Haarlemmerstraat. $ Beer €2.60-3.40. Liquor €5.40-7.80. Cocktails €7.80. ⏰ Open M-Th 8:30am-1am, F-Sa 7:30am-3am, Su 8:30am-1am. Kitchen closes 10pm.

CANAL RING WEST

The Canal Ring West doesn't go wild after sunset, but the pubs along the water are great places to grab a cheap beer and make friends with some locals.

💳⃠♿⃠🍸⛅ BAR

👍 DE PRINS

Prinsengracht 124 ☎062 493 82 💻www.deprins.nl

One of the few unassuming bar-and-cafes in town, De Prins serves a variety of beers on tap (five, to be precise). Enjoy your brew in the wooden interior that inexplicably has pictures of the queen facing portraits of Al Pacino and Humphrey Bogart or at the canalside seating outside. Music ranges from country blues to indie rock at this favorite haunt of young locals.

🧭 Tram #13, 14, or 17 to Westermarkt. 2 blocks up Prinsengracht, on the far side. $ Beer €2.10-3.40. Liquor €3.50-5. ⏰ Open M-Th 10am-1am, F-Sa 10am-2am.

💳⃠♿⃠🍸⛅ BAR

THIRSTY DOGG

Oude Leliestraat 9

Small bar in the Nine Streets that shares the neighborhood's urban, alternative charm. Excellent selection of liquor, including a half-dozen types of absinthe. During the week the bartender dictates the sound, which tends toward heavy hip hop; on some weekend nights a live DJ brings in trip hop and dubstep. Some travelers consider Thirsty Dogg a marijuana-friendly environment.

🧭 Tram #13, 14, or 17 to Westermarkt. Walk down Raadhuisstraat, make a left onto Herengracht, and then a right onto Oude Leliestraat. $ Beer €2.50. Wine €3. Absinthe €4. ⏰ Open M-Th 4pm-1am, F 4pm-3am, Sa noon-3am, Su noon-1am.

CAFE BRANDON

Keizersgracht 157

●✖⊗♀☕ BAR

☎065 434 7136

The owners of this bar took an 18-year hiatus when they won the lottery—twice in one year. Now Cafe Brandon is reopened, much to the joy of the locals who pack the tiny place to the brim on weekend nights. Enjoy the Dutch memorabilia on the walls, the pool table in the slightly larger back room, or the reliable soundtrack of classic rock and disco to which you can rock out wherever you want. Comfy outdoor seating includes benches with large cushions and one tiny table overlooking the water.

� *Tram #13, 14, or 17 to Westermarkt. 1 block up Keizersgracht, on the corner with Leliegracht.* ⑤ *Beer €2.40.* ⌚ *Open M-Th 11am-1am, F-Sa 11am-3am, Su 11am-1am.*

CENTRAL CANAL RING

With the meccas of Leidseplein and Rembrandtplein at its corners, the Central Canal Ring doesn't have much in the way of large-scale nightlife. Given their proximity to the larger squares, **Spiegelgracht** and **Utrechtsestraat** house most of the neighborhood bars.

MANKIND

Weteringstraat 60

●✖♿(((•)))♀☕▼ BAR

☎063 847 55 ◼www.mankind.nl

In a surprisingly quiet spot just a few blocks from Leidseplein and the **Rijksmuseum**, Mankind is an ideal bar to grab an afternoon or evening beer. Two outdoor patios, one facing Weteringstraat and the other adjacent to the canal, allow you to people-watch by land or by sea. Draws loyal regulars and diverse tourists for after-work drinks. Serves the usual menu of Dutch bar snacks (*bitterballen*, *tostis*, etc.). Advertised as GLBT-friendly but doesn't feel like an exclusively gay crowd.

✎ *Tram #7 or 10 to Spiegelgracht. Walk down Weteringschans and make a left.* ⑤ *Beer from €2.* ⌚ *Open M-Sa noon-11pm. Kitchen closes at 8pm.*

CAFE KROM

Utrechtsestraat 76

●✖♿♀☕ BAR, BRUIN CAFE

☎062 453 43

At night, this place fills up with locals of all ages, some parking here for the night and others slowly making their way up to Rembrandtplein. During the day, the atmosphere better fits the vintage cafe surroundings, where people might sip coffee inside or on one of the benches along the sidewalk. Either way, it's classic *bruin cafe.*

✎ *Tram #4, 16, 24, or 25 to Keizersgracht. Walk east on Keizersgracht and make a right onto Utrechtsestraat.* ⑤ *Beer from €2.* ⌚ *Open M-Th 9am-1am, F-Sa 10am-2am, Su 10am-1am.*

TWSTD

Weteringschans 157

●✖⊗♀ CLUB

☎032 070 30 ◼www.twstd.nl

This is a teeny-tiny club with a big sound. The TWSTD team makes a point of nurturing up-and-coming DJ talent, through both regular club nights and their yearly DJ contest. It calls itself Holland's smallest club, and while we don't know if that's true, when you're getting bumped around by the clubbers who dance here in any space they can eke out, you'll probably believe it.

✎ *Tram #4, 7, 10, 16, 24, or 25 to Weteringcircuit. Walk down Weteringschans toward Leidseplein.* ⑤ *Beer from €2.* ⌚ *Open M-Th 9pm-1am, F-Sa 9pm-3am, Su 9pm-1am.*

LEIDSEPLEIN

"Leidseplein" translates to "more diverse nightlife per square foot than anywhere else in the city" (don't listen to anyone who feeds you a story about how it means something to do with a road to the city of Leiden). Some native Amsterdammers scoff at this area, considering it a sea of drunken British and American tourists, but the bars that cater to the liquored-up crowd are primarily confined to the Korte and

Lange Leidsedwarsstraats. The rest of the area, a bit to the south, plays host to some very hip and friendly bars as well as a few terrific nightclubs. Scattered within the whole of the neighborhood are several bastions of incredible live music (including the aforementioned nightclubs). Unless you are going to a big-name event at **Paradiso** or **Melkweg,** prices in the neighborhood are extremely reasonable. Many establishments are just as full of locals, young and old, as they are with tourists. And if you want to be one of the revelers that gives the Leidseplein its bad name, check out the Leidseplein Pub Crawl (promoters lurk in the main square all day long).

PARADISO
CLUB, CONCERT VENUE

Weteringschans 6-8 ☎062 645 21 🖥www.paradiso.nl

You can have a *very* good Friday in this ex-church, now converted into a club and concert hall. It began in 1968 as the "Cosmic Relaxation Center Paradiso," and its laid-back vibe keeps the establishment true to its roots. Hosts an infinity of live music performances (generally less well-known artists than nearby Melkweg, though it has played host to some big names like Wu-Tang Clan and Lady Gaga) every day and club nights five nights a week—including *Noodlanding!* ("emergency landing"), a party with "alternative dance hits" on Thursdays.

✣ Tram #1, 2, 5, 6, 7, or 10 to Leidseplein. Take a left onto Weteringschans. ⓢ Prices vary by event; tickets are usually €5-20 plus a €3 monthly membership fee. ☒ Hours vary by event; check website for details.

MELKWEG
CLUB, CONCERT VENUE

Lijnbaansgracht 234A ☎053 181 81 🖥www.melkweg.nl

The name translates to "milky way"—a pun on the fact that this cultural center is housed in an old milk factory. One of Amsterdam's legendary night spots and concert venues, Melkweg hosts rock, punk, pop, indie, reggae, electronic...basically, any type of music that exists in the big Milky Way has probably been played in this little one. Popular events sell out quickly, so keep an eye on the website if you're planning a visit. After the concerts on Friday and Saturday, there are club nights with techno, house, and alternative music. The building is also home to theater performances, photography exhibits, and a restaurant.

✣ Tram #1, 2, 5, 6, 7, or 10 to Leidseplein. Turn down the small street to the left of the Stadsschouwburg theater. ⓢ Tickets vary depending on event; generally €10-30 plus €3.50 monthly membership fee. ☒ Hours vary depending on event, but concerts usually start around 8 or 9pm, with clubbing getting going around 11pm or midnight.

SUGAR FACTORY

⊛⊗⫏ CLUB

Lijnbaansgracht 238 ☎062 650 06 █www.sugarfactory.nl

Billing itself as a *nachttheater*, Sugar Factory is, at its core, just a very cool place to dance. Live music and DJs are often accompanied by mind-bending video displays, dancers, and other performers. Music tends toward house, electro, and "club jazz." The sizeable dance floor fills with a mix of young Dutch hipsters, older locals, and a smattering of tourists. The cocktail balcony provides the perfect spot to people watch, while the smoking lounge upstairs is the perfect place to...smoke. Check the website for upcoming events; it's a safe assumption that there will be something going on Friday and Saturday nights midnight-5am.

🚋 *Tram #1, 2, 5, 6, 7, or 10 to Leidseplein. Turn down the small street to the left of the Stadsschouwburg theater.* Ⓢ *Cover varies depending on event; usually €8-12. Beer from €3. Mixed drinks €6.50.* Ⓣ *Hours vary depending on event; check website for details.*

WEBER

⊛⊗⫏ BAR

Marnixstraat 397 ☎062 299 10

A bar that's tremendously popular with young locals and a few stylish tourists alike, Weber is the place to be. Come early or late (once people have departed for the clubs) if you want to get a seat on a weekend night. Tiny, frilly red lampshades and vintage pornographic art give the place a cheeky bordello feel, which is complemented by jazzy French pop. But don't be fooled: this bar steers clear of the tawdriness that plagues so much Amsterdam nightlife. Small balcony seating raised above the bar area and a large downstairs room are great spots to grab a drink and chat with friends.

🚋 *Tram #1, 2, 5, 6, 7, or 10 to Leidseplein. Walk south of the main square and make a right onto Marnixstraat.* Ⓢ *Beer €2.50. Spirits from €4.* Ⓣ *Open M-Th 8pm-3am, F-Sa 8pm-4am, Su 8pm-3am.*

DE PIEPER

⊛⊗⫏⫐ BRUIN CAFE

Prinsengracht 424 ☎062 647 75

One of Amsterdam's oldest cafes, De Pieper calls a building that's been around since the 17th century its home. The interior reflects the building's age, with low ceilings, dark wood paneling, and Delft mugs hanging behind the bar, but De Pieper also makes a quirky nod to modernity, with strings of fairy lights and posters from performances at nearby venues. This is the perfect place to escape from the internationalism of the Leidseplein and just have a good *bier* like a local. It has a jovial and loyal following, especially on weekend nights.

🚋 *Tram #1, 2, or 5 to Prinsengracht or #7 or 10 to Raamplein. At the corner of Prinsengracht and Leidsegracht.* Ⓢ *Beer from €2.50.* Ⓣ *Open M-Th 11am-1am, F-Sa 11am-3am.*

LUX

⊛⊗⫏ BAR

Marnixstraat 403 ☎042 214 12

Shares the same three-tiered structure and extreme popularity of its sister bar, Weber. The decor here is a bit more exotic, with wood paneling and brassy metal sculptures that create a modern-chic air. Electro-indie pop dominates the sound over the speakers.

🚋 *Tram #1, 2, 5, 6, 7, or 10 to Leidseplein. Walk south of the main square and make a right onto Marnixstraat.* Ⓢ *Beer €2.50. Spirits from €3.* Ⓣ *Open M-Th 8pm-3am, F-Sa 8pm-4am, Su 8pm-3am.*

BOURBON STREET

⊛⊗⫏ BLUES CLUB

Leidsekruisstraat 6-8 ☎062 334 40

This is a jovial and bustling home of nightly live blues, soul, and funk. Walls are packed with memorabilia and photos from past events. At the jam nights on Monday, Tuesday, and Sunday, all are welcome to bring their own instruments and play along. (We assume that this works, because if you're willing to haul your gear to the Leidseplein, then you're hopefully pretty good.) Bourbon attracts large crowds of locals and tourists alike.

 # Tram #1, 2, 5, 6, 7, or 10 to Leidseplein. Make a right onto Korte Leidsedwarsstraat and Leidsekruisstraat will be on your left. i Music starts M-Th at 10:30pm, F-Sa at 11pm, Su at 10:30pm. $ Beer from €3. ⏰ Open M-Th 10pm-4am, F-Sa 10pm-5am, Su 10pm-4am.

PIRATES BAR ♿🍸 BAR

Korte Leidsedwarsstraat 129

Belly up to the bar here for some cheap grog; weekly deals have beer going for as little as €1.50. The atmosphere is perhaps a bit more frat boy than salty sea dog (though ship accoutrements abound); if you end up intersecting the Leidseplein Pub Crawl as it makes its way through this watering hole, be prepared for a lot of crowded, sweaty bumping and grinding to the Top 40, hip hop, and dance music. It's a great place to get yourself ready for an evening of debauchery on the town.

 # Tram #1, 2, 5, 6, 7, or 10 to Leidseplein. $ Cover €2.50 for men, includes one drink. Beers around €2.50, but price changes depending on the night. Shots €3.50. ⏰ Open M-Th 6pm-3am, F-Sa 6pm-4am, Su 6pm-3am.

from the road

Everyone knows that the Dutch have a thing for **bicycles.** I have seen people do everything while riding their two-wheelers around town—they eat, talk on cell phones, smoke cigarettes, and apply makeup. Bikes really are an excellent way to get around the city, but because Amsterdam is also so easily traversed on foot, I never got around to renting one. Part of me felt, though, that in not pedaling around the city, I was missing out on an important aspect of local culture.

At least, that was the case until I went to research the Leidseplein. This square is renowned for its nightlife, so to make the best use of my time and the biggest dent in my list of establishments, I decided to try and research as many bars and clubs as possible in one night. My last stop was the Sugar Factory. I didn't get there until after 1am, and the music was so good and the people so friendly that I ended up staying until closing. Exiting to the disconcertingly bright morning (it seems that during the Dutch summer it's only really dark from 11pm-3am), my newfound Dutch pals asked me how I planned on getting home. "The tram," I replied. They all looked at me in astonishment. "You don't have a bike?" they asked. Somehow, in my foreign naïveté, I had assumed that people surely didn't bring their bicycles when they went out for a night on the town. What if you get drunk? Or are wearing high heels? Or are just tired from dancing all night?

Such things, while obstacles to an ungainly and inexperienced cyclist like myself, are barely even considerations for a native Amsterdammer. Sure enough, the phalanx of people pouring out from the clubs on the Leidseplein were all headed toward the bicycle racks outside. I think that my new friends must have seen a certain wistfulness in my eyes, and they kindly offered to give me a ride home. So I perched on the back of a bike, and we zipped off along the canals in the 5am sunshine. Only if I had been eating some Gouda at the same time could I have felt more Dutch.

—Beatrice Franklin

THE CAVE BAR

Prinsengracht 472 ☎062 689 39 💻www.thecave.nl

THE place to be if you're into bands named after Ostrogoth warlords or head-banging Vikings—by which we mean this is a bar that rocks. Hard. Dark and smoky with gothic graffiti on the walls, the space lives up to its name, which seems to suit its patrons just fine. All kidding aside, this is a welcome and unique break from the Top 40 tunes and lechery of Leidseplein's main drag. Live music every Friday, drawing bands from across the world.

🚊 Tram #1, 2, or 5 to Prinsengracht. $ Cover F €5. 🕐 Open M-Th 8pm-3am, F-Sa 8pm-4am, Su 8pm-3am.

PUNTO LATINO CLUB, SALSA

Lange Leidsedwarsstraat 35 ☎042 022 35

Punto Latino is a small club that remains popular on weekends, boasting fiery Latin music and dancing to match. Attracts a crowd of young tourists and older locals (many of Spanish or Latin origin) alike.

🚊 Tram #1, 2, 5, 6, 7, or 10 to Leidseplein. $ Beer €2.50. 🕐 Open daily 11pm-4am.

REMBRANDTPLEIN

Rembrandtplein *is* its nightlife. Yeah, there's a pretty sweet statue of Rembrandt in the middle of this square, but if you were interested in the man himself, then you would be at one of Amsterdam's many fine museums—none of which can be found here. This is home to the art of looking good and getting down, not the art of the Dutch Renaissance. The square itself is lined with massive bars and clubs, while the streets that fan out from it are home to smaller establishments. **Reguliersdwarstraat,** particularly once you cross Vijzelstraat, is well known as **"the gayest street in Amsterdam,"** lined with a diverse array of gay bars and clubs, though many more are to be found on other neighboring streets as well. Whatever (or whomever) you're looking for in terms of nightlife, you can find it here: Irish pub, sleek bar, chic club, grungy dive, gay cafe, tourist dance party. Just shop around until you hear some music that you like.

Rembrandtplein is conveniently serviced by night buses #355, 357, 359, 361, and 363; taxis also loiter around the main square at all hours.

ESCAPE CLUB

Rembrandtplein 11 ☎062 211 11 💻www.escape.nl

This is Amsterdam's biggest club, with a capacity for thousands. Although it may no longer be considered the hottest spot in town, it still reliably draws large crowds and excellent DJs. The main dance floor is a glam space with a massive stage (VIP area behind the DJ) and platforms strewn throughout for those brave enough to take the dancing spotlight. A lounge, another dance space, and a balcony from which to observe the bacchanalia below can all be found upstairs. Futuristic white bars are scattered throughout. Music varies depending on the DJ but generally tends toward house, electro, and trance. The crowd is a mix of large groups of tourists and chic young Dutch. On weekends lines can grow long after 1am, and some suggest that upping your style will increase your chances of getting in.

🚊 Tram #9 or 14 to Rembrandtplein. $ Cover €5-10, students €6 on most Th. Beer from €2.60. Spirits €3.80-5.80. 🕐 Open Th 11pm-4am, F-Sa 11pm-5am, Su 11pm-4am.

STUDIO 80 CLUB

Rembrandtplein 17 💻www.studio-80.nl

A grungier alternative to the more polished clubs around Rembrandtplein, Studio 80 is extremely popular with the young student crowd. The emphasis is on dancing and music at this club, where you'll be rocking out on plywood planked floors. Sound varies from minimal electro to deep house to hip hop. Be prepared for a thorough pat down by bouncers at the door.

🚋 *Tram #9 or 14 to Rembrandtplein. The entrance is next to Escape (see above), under the large balcony.* [$] *Cover depends on the night, usually €6-10. Beer €2.50.* ⏰ *Open W-Th 11pm-4am, F-Sa 11pm-5am, Su 11pm-4am.*

LELLEBEL 🍸 ▼ BAR

Utrechtstraat 4 ☎042 751 39 💻www.lellebel.nl

A terrifically fun and welcoming bar presided over by outrageous drag queens. With decor that's as campy as the costumes, Lellebel is all the more ready to help you make friends with your fellow drinkers. While it attracts a primarily gay male crowd, absolutely all genders and sexualities will feel comfortable here, as the ladies behind the bar are eager to assert. It plays host to a variety of theme nights—karaoke, Transgender Cafe, and Salsa Night, to name a few—and events such as the frequent Miss Lellebel contests and a Eurovision party.

🚋 *Tram #9 or 14 to Rembrandtplein. Just off the southeast corner of the square. Karaoke on Tu. Transgender Cafe on W. Red Hot Salsa Night on Th.* [$] *Beer €2.50.* ⏰ *Open M-Th 8pm-3am, F-Sa 8pm-4am, Su 8pm-3am.*

MONTMARTRE 🍸 ▼ BAR

Halvemaansteeg 17 ☎062 076 22 💻www.cafemontmartre.nl

A sinfully luxurious **Garden of Eden** inspired interior provides the backdrop for this popular spot, regularly voted the best gay bar in Amsterdam. The crowd is dominated by gay men, but all are welcome. As the night wears on, the dancing heats up to Euro and American pop and bouncy disco. Special theme nights spice up each day of the week.

🚋 *Tram #9 or 14 to Rembrandtplein. Off of the northwest corner of the square.* [$] *Beer from €2.50. Liquor from €3.50.* ⏰ *Open M-Th 5pm-1am, F-Sa 5pm-3am, Su 5pm-1am.*

ARC ♿ 🍸 BAR

Reguliersdwarsstraat 44 ☎068 970 70 💻www.bararc.eu

Dim, red lighting and leather couches complement one of the hipper bars in the area. The crowd is trendy, and the music goes from nouveau disco to R and B, getting you ready for a night spent dancing nearby. Arc's real draw is its exquisite and inventive mixed drinks menu; Wednesday and Sunday are mixed drink nights when selected libations are only €6. Arc also serves a varied menu of tapas and other European dishes.

🚋 *Tram #9 or 14 to Rembrandtplein. On the stretch of Reguliersdwarsstraat that is across Vijzelstraat from the main square.* [$] *Beer from €2.50. Mixed drinks €8-10.* ⏰ *Open M-Th 4pm-1am, F-Sa 4pm-3am, Su 4pm-1am. Kitchen closes at 11pm.*

DE DUIVEL 🍸 BAR

Reguliersdwarsstraat 87 ☎062 661 84 💻www.deduivel.nl

Amsterdam's premier hip-hop joint, visited by top names from Cypress Hill to Ghostface. Even without famous guests, De Duivel remains a nighttime favorite, with DJs who spin a terrific mix drawing a diverse crowd of patrons. A small space overlooked by an intimidating stained-glass devil that gives the bar its name is provided for dancing, but most visitors line the walls and bar and chat over their beers.

🚋 *Tram #9 or 14 to Rembrandtplein.* [$] *Beer €2.50.* ⏰ *Open M-Th 10pm-3am, F-Sa 10pm-4am, Su 10pm-3am.*

PARTY CREW CAFE ♿ 🍸 BAR, CLUB

Rembrandtplein 31 ☎062 337 40 💻www.partycrewcafe.nl

An energetic atmosphere fills this bar even when patrons are few and far between, largely due to some of the friendliest bartenders in town. Smaller (although a whole second bar opens on weekends) and less pretentious than many neighboring clubs, the music—top 40, house, and hip hop—makes for fun dancing. Attracts a mix of tourists and some local students with theme nights once a month as well as an after-party a few times a year that goes until 9am.

🚊 Tram #9 or 14 to Rembrandtplein. ℹ Happy hour 2-for-1 drinks. $ Cover €5 on Sa; some travelers report that speaking Dutch increases your chances of free entry. Beer from €2.50. ⏰ Open M-Th 10pm-4am, F-Sa 10pm-5am, Su 10pm-4am. Happy hour daily 10pm-midnight.

VIVE LA VIE ♿🍸 BAR

Amstelstraat 7 ☎062 401 14 💻www.vivelavie.net

This long-established lesbian bar draws a diverse crowd of women and a few of their male friends thanks to its unpretentious atmosphere focused on having a fun time. Excellent drink selection includes the **Clit on Fire** shot *(€4)*, whose ingredients are a closely guarded secret. Music goes from indie rock and bluesy country in the early evening toward dancier tunes as the night progresses.

🚊 Tram #9 or 14 to Rembrandtplein. $ Beer from €2.50. Spirits from €4. ⏰ Open M-Th 3pm-3am, F-Sa 3pm-4am, Su 3pm-3am.

JORDAAN

Nightlife in the Jordaan is much more relaxed than in Leidseplein or the Nieuwe Zijd, but that doesn't mean it's not popular or busy. Establishments tend more toward cafe-bars or local pubs than clubs, though some excellent music can be found in the neighborhood's southern stretches. If you're looking to seriously mingle with the locals, try one of the places along **Lijnbaansgracht** and **Noordermarkt** that really get going on weekends.

FESTINA LENTE ♿🍸 BAR

Looiersgracht 40b ☎063 814 12 💻www.cafefestinalente.nl

Looking something like what you would get if you stuck a bar in the middle of an elegant vintage living room, this spot is enduringly popular with fun and cultured young Amsterdammers. Bookshelves line the walls, and games of chess and checkers are readily available for use—just try to find a free spot to play. Poetry contests and live concerts are held often: check the website for details. The kitchen serves a menu of *lentini*, small Mediterranean dishes, and an astonishing selection of bruschettas (on homemade bread!). No wonder it's always so crowded.

🚊 Tram #7, 10, or 17 to Elandsgracht. Go straight on Elandsgracht and make a right onto Hazenstraat; the bar is 2 blocks down on the corner. $ Beer from €2. Wine from €3.30 per glass. ⏰ Open M noon-1am, Tu-Th 10:30am-1am, F-Sa 10:30am-3am, Su noon-1am. Kitchen closes at 10:30pm.

'T SMALLE ♿🍸 CAFE, BRUIN CAFE

Egelantiersgracht 12 ☎062 396 17

One of the most revered and popular *bruin cafes* in the city, 't Smalle was founded in 1780 as a spot to taste the products of a nearby *jenever* distillery. Today, the interior is appropriately old-fashioned and classic, but the real place to be is outside at one of the many tables lining Egelantiersgracht, for our money one of the prettiest canals in Amsterdam. Be warned, though: on nice days, you may have to get here very early or very late to claim a chair. An alternative location—in Nagasaki, Japan—features a replica of the cafe that stands in the model "Holland Village." *(🚊 Head east about 9200km. The bar is on your right.)*

🚊 Tram #13, 14, or 17 to Westermarkt. Cross Prinsengracht, make a right, and walk a few blocks. $ Beer from €2. ⏰ Open M-Th 10am-1am, F-Sa 10am-2am, Su 10am-1am.

CAFE CHRIS ♿🍸 BAR

Bloemstraat 42 ☎062 459 42 💻www.cafechris.nl

Workers building the tower of the nearby Westerkerk used to stop here to pick up (and then probably spend) their paychecks—the bar first opened its doors in 1624, making it the oldest in the Jordaan. Today, it is just as popular with the local after-work crowd as it was with the construction dudes, and the antique interior of deep wood and stained glass keeps history at the forefront. Pool table inside, though it tends to be occupied by regulars.

 # Tram #13, 14, or 17 to Westermarkt. Cross Prinsengracht, make a right, and walk 1 block. $ Beer €3-5. ⏰ Open M-Th 3pm-1am, F-Sa 3pm-2am, Su 3-9pm.

SAAREIN ◉🚭📶🍸▼ BAR, BRUIN CAFE

Elandsstraat 119 ☎062 349 01 💻www.saarein.info

A *bruin cafe* very much in the tradition of the Jordaan but with a GLBT focus, Saarein attracts mainly older lesbians, though all genders and orientations are heartily welcome. Hosts a variety of events, from a pool competition every Tuesday to discussion groups about issues of gender and sexuality.

 # Tram #7, 10, or 17 to Elandsgracht. Make a left onto Lijnbaansgracht and walk 2 blocks. i Free Wi-Fi as well as a computer available for customers' use. $ Beer from €2. ⏰ Open Tu-Th 4pm-1am, F 4pm-2am, Sa noon-2am, Su noon-1am.

WESTERPARK AND OUD-WEST

Large swathes of these neighborhoods are dead at night, but you can also find some of the most up-and-coming nightlife in the city if you know where to look. Prices are cheap, and locals abound. Look for posters advertising weekend parties; many of the nightspots are open only irregularly.

OT301 ◉🚭🍸 CLUB

Overtoom 301 💻www.ot301.nl

This establishment plays home to everything even remotely entertaining—a temporary handicrafts store, a cinema, live music, yoga and acrobatic classes, a vegan restaurant, and excellent DJ parties on most weekend nights make some strange bedfellows. The building was a squat inhabited by artists in the late '90s who brought in art and music, causing the city to consider it a cultural breeding ground. Check the website for upcoming events; the parties have music that ranges from electro house to soul and funk. The crowds who come to dance are as diverse and laid-back as one would expect from the surroundings.

 # Tram #1 to J. Pieter Heijestraat. $ Cover €3-5 most nights. ⏰ Hours vary depending on programming; check website for details.

PACIFIC PARC ◉♿🍸🎸 BAR, CONCERT VENUE

Polonceaukade 23 ☎062 493 79 💻www.pacificparc.nl

"Industrial honky-tonk" is the best phrase we can think of to describe this large bar on the end of the Westergasfabriek. Iron staircases and a massive stove in one corner recall the building's factory roots, but cowhide coverings on the window shades will make you feel as if you're home, home on the range. The who-knows-what-the-hell-it's-made-of chandelier has to be seen to be believed. Plenty of tables and benches with cushions for lounging and enjoying a drink proliferate amid a local, late-20s crowd. There's also space for dancing to the blues and old-school country rock on the speakers. Live music plays some nights as well, beginning at 11pm. Pacific Parc doubles as a restaurant during the day.

 # Tram #10 to Van Limburg Stirumstraat or Van Hallstraat. Either way, walk to the Haarlemmerweg and cross over; it's at the corner of the Westergasfabriek that is farthest from Westerpark. $ Beer from €2.50, spirits from €3. ⏰ Open M-Th 11am-1am, F-Sa 11am-3am, Su 11am-11pm.

CAFE KAMERZ ◉♿🍸🎸 BAR, CONCERT VENUE

Van der Hoopstraat 29W ☎068 891 88 💻www.cafekamerz.nl

This cafe-restaurant hosts a number of interesting nightlife events, from an evening of Doors covers to live salsa and jazz. Check their website for listings. A colorful and well-stocked bar makes it a great place to mingle with Westerpark locals, fiercely proud of their neighborhood, any time of the week.

 # Tram #10 to Van Limburg Stirumstraat. i Smoking room in the back. $ Beer from €2. ⏰ Open M-Th 4pm-1am, F-Sa 4pm-3am, Su 4pm-1am.

MUSEUMPLEIN AND VONDELPARK

Museums don't often stay open past 6pm, which means there's not much bringing you to Museumplein post-dinner. Vondelpark has a few choice spots for grabbing a drink and enjoying the scenery, but for a livelier night out, you'd best head across the canal to Leidseplein.

'T BLAUWE THEEHUIS

⊛⅄⅋⊘ BAR

Vondelpark 5   ☎066 202 54 📧www.blauwetheehuis.nl

Surrounded by the Vondelpark greenery, 't Blauwe Theehuis looks a bit like a UFO that's just crash-landed on Earth. But here it is, and alien or not, it's probably the only place in the city center where you can drink and at least feel somewhat close to nature. Enjoy the view from the large circular patio outside, the terrace above, or inside if the weather is so bad that you really have to head indoors. DJs spin tunes on Friday nights.

✴ *Tram #2 to Jacob Obrechtstraat. Enter Vondelpark, walk straight and over the footbridge, and you should see the building ahead.* ⑤ *Beer from €2.30. Spirits from €2.40. Wine from €3.* ② *Open M-Th 9am-midnight, F-Sa 9am-2am, Su 9am-midnight.*

CAFE GRUTER

⊛⅄⅋⊘ BAR

Willemsparkweg 73   ☎067 962 52

This simple pub-cafe fills with tourists during the day and locals from nearby neighborhoods at night. A cheerful selection of world music plays over the speakers. Outside seating on the sidewalk makes for some great people-watching.

✴ *Tram #2 to Jacob Obrechtstraat. The bar is on the corner.* ⑤ *Beer from €2.40.* ② *Open M-Th 11am-1am, F-Sa 11am-3am, Su 11am-1am.*

DE PIJP

What De Pijp does—laid-back hipster bars with good beer, good food, and good company—it does very well.

🔖 CHOCOLATE BAR

⅌⅄⅋⊘ BAR

1e Van Der Helststraat 62A   ☎067 576 72 📧www.chocolate-bar.nl

While most bars in the neighborhood have a cafe-like vibe, this place veers more toward cocktail lounge. It's certainly not a dressy affair, but the long, glossy bar and seating area peppered with small, chic tables up the cool factor. The outdoor patio is a special place, with couches and picnic tables—a prime place to survey the De Pijp scene. On weekends, DJs spin laid-back dance tunes inside.

✴ *Tram #16 or 24 to Albert Cuypstraat. Walk 1 block down Albert Cuypstraat and make a right.* ⑤ *Beer from €2. Cocktails €7.* ② *Open M-Th 10am-1am, F-Sa 10am-3am, Su 11am-1am.*

TROUW AMSTERDAM

⊛⊗⅄ CLUB

Wibautstraat 127   ☎046 377 88 📧www.trouwamsterdam.nl

This club's not strictly in De Pijp, but just across the Amstel. Housed in the former office building of the newspaper *Trouw*, this complex includes a restaurant, exhibition space, and club. It's a rather gritty, industrial-feeling space that's extremely popular with local students. The music ranges from dubstep to electronic to house and more; check the website for specific events. It occasionally hosts after-parties that begin at 6am.

✴ Ⓜ*Wibautstraat. The stop is right next to the building. Or tram #3 to Wibautstraat. Walk a few blocks south on Wibautstraat. You're looking for a giant white office building that says "Trouw" on the upper corner.* ⑤ *Cover €10-17.* ② *Club generally open F-Sa 10:30pm-5am. Check website for specifics.*

KINGFISHER

⊛⅄⅋⊘ BAR

Ferdinand Bolstraat 24   ☎067 123 95

One of the original bars that set the stage for the rise of cool in De Pijp, Kingfisher hasn't let the popularity go to its head, and it remains a wonderful spot to enjoy one of their international beers and a chat in the spacious wood interior. The place is filled to the gills on weekend nights, but on a sunny afternoon, you should still be able to grab a coveted table outside.

🚊 Tram #16 or 24 to Stadhouderskade. Walk 1 block down Ferdinand Bolstraat. $ Beer from €2. ⏰ Open M-Th 11am-1am, F-Sa 11am-3am, Su noon-1am.

CAFE KRULL

🍸 BAR

Sarphatipark 2 ☎062 202 14

Just across from Sarphatipark's leafy expanse, this spot feels well removed from the crowds surrounding the market, though in reality, it's just a few blocks away. The clientele shifts from families and older regulars to local young'uns as the day turns into night. Enjoy a wide selection of beers on tap.

🚊 Tram #3 or 25 to 2e Van der Helststraat. Walk 1 block up the length of the park. $ Beer from €2. ⏰ Open M-Th 9am-1am, F-Sa 9am-3am, Su 9am-1am.

CAFE DE GROENE VLINDER

♿🍸 BAR

Albert Cuypstraat 130 ☎047 025 00 🖥www.cafedegroenevlinder.nl

At the corner with 1e Van der Helststraat, this bar is full of the young hipsters and students that roam the area. An extremely well-kept bar graces the lovely interior, but drinks can also be enjoyed at the plentiful alfresco seating. The menu of sandwiches, tapas, and dinner entrees here is more extensive than those of other area cafe-bars.

🚊 Tram #16 or 24 to Albert Cuypstraat. $ Beer from €2. ⏰ Open M-Th 10am-1am, F-Sa 10am-3am, Su 10am-1am.

JODENBUURT AND PLANTAGE

This is not the neighborhood for rowdy nightlife. If you're looking for a big night out, you'd do better to head to nearby **Rembrandtplein** or **Nieuwmarkt.** However, there are a few excellent laid-back local bars in the neighborhood, befitting its overall character.

DE SLUYSWACHT

♿🍸 BAR

Jodenbreestraat 1 ☎062 576 11 🖥www.sluyswacht.nl

This tiny, tilting 17th-century building houses the kind of bar you would expect to find on a lone seacoast, not a bustling street. The outdoor patio sits right above the canal, with giant umbrellas ready in case the weather should turn rainy. When it gets really inclement, the plain wooden interior is invitingly snug. A good selection of draft and bottled beers is available.

🚊 Tram #9 or 14 or Ⓜ Waterlooplein. $ Beer €2.10-4. ⏰ Open M-Th 11:30am-1am, F-Sa 11:30am-3am, Su 11:30am-7pm.

HET GENOT VAN RAPENBURG

🍸 BAR

Rapenburg 16-18 ☎062 231 50 🖥www.hetgenotvanrapenburg.nl

A welcoming, quality bar tucked away on an out-of-the-way corner of Plantage, this watering hole is populated mostly by locals from the nearby offices. Four beers on tap, a full bar, and music at the bartender's discretion that usually leans toward relaxed British and American indie rock add to this unfussy watering hole's charm. Enjoy Indonesian cuisine upstairs.

🚊 Tram #9 or 14 or Ⓜ Waterlooplein. Walk along Nieuwe Uilenburgerstraat until it becomes Peperstraat; the bar is at the corner. $ Beer €2.20-4 ⏰ Open M-Th 5pm-1am, F-Sa 5pm-2am, Su 5pm-1am.

arts and culture

Besides its stunning collection of visual arts, Amsterdam offers a whole host of cultural attractions to travelers and locals alike. The music and film scenes here rival those of any other city in Europe, and many argue that the **Concertgebouw** concert hall has the best acoustics in the world. Comedy shows have been increasing in popularity, and with large summer festivals held each year, you can see some wonderfully innovative theater and dance if you time your visit right. As befits a city where the most cutting-edge photography exhibits are held in a 17th-century canal house, the performing arts in Amsterdam run the gamut from high-quality traditional performances to some of the weirdest (and quite brilliant) new art you might ever see. Many troupes and establishments make an effort to provide significant student discounts or rush tickets so that you can take a trip to the theater or opera without having to miss out on Amsterdam's other delights.

CLASSICAL MUSIC, OPERA, AND DANCE

For a city of its size, Amsterdam has a bounty of performing arts venues. Classical music is a particularly strong presence here, thanks to high-caliber orchestras and innovative chamber ensembles. Use this guide to begin your exploration of Amsterdam's arts scene, but as with nightlife, keep an eye out for posters around the city that advertise upcoming events. Churches (especially the **Oude Kerk**) also hold many organ and choral concerts—they're particularly nice venues in the summer when a lot of the concert halls close.

CONCERTGEBOUW ✈& MUSEUMPLEIN

Concertgebouwplein 2-6 ☎057 305 73 ▣www.concertgebouw.nl

Even if you don't catch a concert here, it's worth taking a look at this magnificent 1888 building when you're in Museumplein. However, with some of the best acoustics in the world and a highly renowned classical ensemble, the **Royal Concertgebouw Orchestra,** this performance space is more than just a pretty sight. Some 900 concerts, primarily classical but also programs of jazz and world music, are held here each year. Free lunch concerts are held Wednesdays in the small concert hall, while even performances in the main hall have some tickets in the €20 range. If you plan on attending multiple events here, consider joining the **Entrée society** for €10, which, if you are under 30, gives you access to over 200 concerts per season for tickets of only €8.

✴ Tram #3, 5, 12, 16, or 24 to Museumplein. Ⓢ Varies by concert; main events generally €20-100. ⍟ Ticket office open M-F 1-7pm, Sa-Su 10am-7pm.

MUZIEKTHEATER ✈& JODENBUURT

Waterlooplein 22 ☎062 554 55 ▣www.het-muziektheater.nl

A somewhat controversial building when it was constructed (it incited riots and protests from squatters and left-wing groups in the 1980s), this large complex is now the best place in Amsterdam to see opera and classical ballet—it's the home turf of both the **Netherlands Opera** and the **Dutch National Ballet.** Also hosts performances by visiting companies and some more modern works. Rush tickets are available for students 90min. before curtain for the ballet *(€10)* and for the opera *(€15).*

✴ Ⓜ Waterlooplein. Ⓢ Most tickets €15-100, depending on seating area. ⍟ Open early Sept-mid-July. Box office open M-Sa 10am-6pm, Su 11:30am-2:30pm, and before curtain on performance days.

BETHANIENKLOOSTER ✈⊗ OUDE ZIJD

Barndesteeg 6b ☎062 500 78 ▣www.bethanienklooster.nl

Small classical performances are held in this intimate venue for chamber music, once a convent. Talented music students play free concerts here, and you can also catch members of the Royal Concertgebouw Orchestra for far less than at the Concertgebouw itself. Concert series passes are available.

✦ Ⓜ*Nieuwmarkt. Cross the square and go down the street at the corner with Kloveniersburgwal.* Ⓢ *Most concerts free-€15.* ☒ *Hours vary; check website for details. Open fall-spring.*

MUZIEKGEBOUW AAN'T IJ
✦♿ PLANTAGE

Piet Heinkade 1   ☎078 820 00 ▣www.muziekgebouw.nl

This is Amsterdam's prime spot for hearing modern, cutting-edge classical music. In addition to their main concert hall, they perform in a smaller hall that houses the newly-renovated 31-tone Fokker organ. For every concert, a certain number of "Early Bird" tickets (€10) are set aside for those under 30. If you miss out on those, you can still try to get under-30 rush tickets (also €10) 30min. before the performance.

✦ *Tram #25 or 26 to Muziekgebouw Bimhuis. Make a hairpin turn around the small inlet of water to get to the theater.* Ⓢ *Most tickets free-€18.* ☒ *Open mid-Aug-June. Box office open M-Sa noon-6pm.*

LIVE MUSIC

There is a dizzying array of awesome music to hear in Amsterdam. Some of the major venues are all-purpose entertainment spaces where you could hear a Snoop Dogg concert in the evening and then stick around to dance to some house from a live DJ. Small, character-filled jazz joints have also proliferated in the city, so you can get your fix of cool swing or hot bebop every night of the week. In the summer, festivals explode in Amsterdam and the surrounding cities. Check the websites of major venues, look for posters around the city, and consult *NL20* or *Time Out Amsterdam* once you've exhausted our suggestions.

▧ MELKWEG
✦⊗♉ LEIDSEPLEIN

Lijnbaansgracht 234A   ☎053 181 81 ▣www.melkweg.nl

A legendary venue for all kinds of live music as well as clubbing. See listing in **Nightlife.**

✦ *Tram #1, 2, 5, 6, 7, or 10 to Leidseplein. Turn down the small street to the left of the Stadsschouwburg theater.* Ⓢ *Ticket prices vary depending on event; generally €10-30, with €3.50 monthly membership fee.* ☒ *Hours vary depending on event, but concerts usually start around 8pm or 9pm.*

▧ PARADISO
✦⊗♉ LEIDSEPLEIN

Weteringschans 6-8   ☎062 645 21 ▣www.paradiso.nl

Everything from big-name pop acts to experimental DJs. See listing in **Nightlife.**

✦ *Tram #1, 2, 5, 6, 7, or 10 to Leidseplein. Take a left onto Weteringschans.* Ⓢ *Prices vary by event; tickets usually €5-20 plus a €3 monthly membership fee.* ☒ *Hours vary by event; check website for details.*

▧ ALTO
✦⊗♉ LEIDSEPLEIN

Korte Leidsedwarsstraat 115   ☎062 632 49 ▣www.jazz-cafe-alto.nl

Amsterdam's most respected jazz joint, Alto is small, dark, and cozy—as any such place should be. Look for the giant saxophone outside marking the location. With live performances every night by renowned artists, the place fills up quickly, so come early to get a seat.

✦ *Tram #1, 2, 5, 6, 7, or 10 to Leidseplein.* ☒ *Open M-Th 9pm-3am, F-Sa 9pm-4am, Su 9pm-3am. Music starts daily at 10pm.*

MALOE MELO
⊗⊗♉ JORDAAN

Lijnbaansgracht 163   ☎042 045 92 ▣www.maloemelo.nl

One of the best spots in the city for intimate live music, especially blues with a smattering of jazz and country. The cozy bar in the front and a simple stage in back are exactly what you imagine a blues bar to be. Maloe Melo is run by a father and son team—the dad sometimes joins performers on the accordion. Concerts held every night, with jam sessions frequently throughout the week. Check website for details.

🚋 Tram #7, 10, or 17 to Elandsgracht. Walk up the Jordaan side of Lijnbaansgracht a few blocks. [S] €5 cover to music room on weekends; as high as €7.50 depending on the performer. Beer from €2. ⏰ Open M-Th 9pm-3am, F-Sa 9pm-4am, Su 9pm-3am. Music room opens 10:30pm.

THEATER AND COMEDY

Traditional theater and showy musicals don't have the same presence here as they do in other cities, leaving room for more modern pieces in Dutch or English. The comedy scene is perhaps more varied and is certainly vibrant, with shows every night at pretty reasonable prices. We highly recommended trying to catch some sketch comedy or a stand-up performance while you're in town.

👍 BOOM CHICAGO — 🎟♿🍸 LEIDSEPLEIN

Leidseplein 12 — ☎042 301 01 💻www.boomchicago.nl

Boom Chicago is the place for extremely popular English-language improv comedy shows with plenty of audience participation, every night of the week. Dinner can be enjoyed at the theater before the show; a bar and lounge is located upstairs. It hosts special events with a comedy twist as well, such as the beer pong tournament on the last Thursday of every month.

🚋 Tram #1, 2, 5, 7, or 10 to Leidseplein. At the far corner of the square. [S] Tickets €20-25. ⏰ Most shows begin 8-9pm; check website for details.

COMEDY THEATER — 🎟⊗ RED LIGHT DISTRICT

Nes 110 — ☎042 227 77 💻www.comedytheater.nl

Standup comedy in both Dutch and English; hosts international guests as well as three comedy troupes based here. Open-mike nights are also held here a few times a month.

🚋 Tram #4, 9, 14, 16, 24, or 25 to Spui/Rokin. Cross the canal and make a left onto Nes. [S] Most tickets free-€20. ⏰ Shows start 7:30-9pm. Box office open W-Th 5:30-8:30pm, F-Sa 5:30-11:30pm.

COMEDY CAFE AMSTERDAM — 🎟♿ LEIDSEPLEIN

Max Euweplein 43-45 — ☎063 839 71 💻www.comedycafe.nl

A mix of stand-up, open-mike comedy, and improv, often in Dutch with some English mixed in. Every Sunday, Comedy Cafe Amsterdam runs a guaranteed English-language improv show called "Hole in the Boat." Dinner is available for an extra €20.

🚋 Tram #1, 2, 5, 7, or 10 to Leidseplein. Walk down Weteringschans and then right through the colonnade. ℹ Reserve ahead. [S] Tickets €3-16. ⏰ Shows M-F 9pm, Sa 9pm and 11pm, Su 8pm. Box office open M-F 9am-5pm.

STADSSCHOUWBURG — 🎟♿ LEIDSEPLEIN

Leidseplein 26 — ☎062 423 11 💻www.ssba.nl

A prime spot for catching Dutch-language theater in Amsterdam and the base for the **Holland Festival** in June, it also hosts opera and dance performances. The cafe that spills out onto the Leidseplein is almost as popular as the theater itself.

🚋 Tram #1, 2, 5, 7, or 10 to Leidseplein. You can't miss it. [S] Tickets €10-20. ⏰ Box office open M-Sa noon-6pm.

THEATER DE CAMELEON — 🎟♿ OUD-WEST

3e Kostverlorenkade 35 — ☎048 946 56 💻www.decameleon.nl

This theater may be a ways outside of town, but they put on a variety of interesting modern pieces, some in English. They also hold voice and acting workshops.

🚋 Tram #1 to Overtoomsesluis. Continue on a bit down Overtoom and then right on 3e Kostverlorenkade. [S] Tickets €8-10. ⏰ Box office open daily noon-6pm.

DE KLEINE KOMEDIE

Amstel 56-58   ☎062 405 34 🖳www.dekleinekomedie.nl

A theater since 1786, this has long been a favorite spot for cabaret performances. Today, it hosts a huge variety of drama and musical theater, from the traditional to the modern. Shows are mostly in Dutch, but the colorful atmosphere can be enjoyable even if you don't quite understand what's going on.

🌿 *Tram #9 or 14 to Rembrandtplein. Walk down Halvemaansteeg to Amstel.* Ⓢ *Tickets €9-20.* Ⓩ *Box office open M-Sa noon-5pm.*

FILM

The Amsterdam film scene benefits not only from screenings of a wide variety of old, new, and totally out-there cinema, but also from its character-filled theaters, many of which are in old Art Deco buildings or repurposed squats. Most films originally in English remain so, with Dutch subtitles added.

▧ EYE INSTITUTE

Vondelpark 3   ☎058 914 00 🖳www.eyefilm.nl

At the beginning of 2010, a number of Dutch film organizations (including the Filmmuseum, the organization that used to occupy this space) merged to form the **EYE Institute.** Now, this elegant building on the edge of Vondelpark is used primarily for film screenings—mostly new, international indies—but they also play classics and organize retrospectives on important actors and directors. Occasional exhibitions are held on specific, film-related topics. Across the street *(Vondelstraat 69),* the Institute's library houses thousands of movies stretching back to 1898 as well as the Netherlands's largest collection of books and periodicals on film. An excellent cafe is also located within the same pavilion at Vondelpark 3.

🌿 *Tram #1, 3, or 12 to 1e Constantijn Huygensstraat/Overtoom. Walk down 1e C. Huygensstraat, make a right onto Vondelstraat, and enter the park about a block down; the Institute is on your left.* Ⓢ *Screening tickets €7.80, students €6.50.* Ⓩ *Open M-F 9am-10:15pm, Sa-Su 1hr. before the 1st show-10:15pm. Library open M-Tu 1-5pm and Th-F 1-5pm.*

▧ PATHE TUSCHINSKI

Reguliersbreestraat 26-28   ☎062 626 33 🖳www.tuschinski.nl

One of Europe's first experiments with Art Deco design, this 1921 building still has all of its original luxurious style (but now with better technology). Screens current Hollywood films on its main screens and artsier fare on the screens at its **Tuschinski Arthouse** next door.

🌿 *Tram #9 or 14 to Rembrandtplein. Walk down Reguliersdwarsstraat, and you'll see the cinema on your right.* Ⓢ *Tickets €7.80-9.30.* Ⓩ *Open daily from 11:30am.*

▧ THE MOVIES

Haarlemmerdijk 161-163   ☎063 860 16 🖳www.themovies.nl

Amsterdam's oldest still-functioning theater—it's been around since 1912—is less grandiose than the Tuschinski, but provides the same feeling of slightly stepping back in time. Most of the movies shown here are current films, but classics like *Casablanca* are also screened. Dinner packages are available.

🌿 *Tram #3 to Haarlemmerplein. Walk across the square away from the large arch to Haarlemmerdijk.* Ⓢ *Tickets €7-9.* Ⓩ *Box office open daily from 3pm.*

RECREATION AND GAMBLING

Sometimes the endless stream of interesting art, cozy *bruin cafes,* and picturesque canals can get overwhelming. When this happens, you may feel the need to blow off some steam. Amsterdam can make that happen, whether you let it out by furiously hitting a small ball in a squash court, cranking a slot machine, or living vicariously through the athletes of Ajax.

☑ SQUASH CITY — 💳🚭 SCHEEPVAARTBUURT

Ketelmakerstraat 6 — ☎062 678 83 💻www.squashcity.com

This large gym complex on the IJ near Centraal Station has squash courts, two floors of fitness equipment, group lessons (spinning, Pilates, yoga, and more), and personal trainers. It also offers a sauna (free for members), restaurant, and bar.

➤ Bus #18, 21, or 22 to Buiten Oranjestraat. You'll see Squash City across the road from there. $ Monthly memberships from €35, single visits from €10.50. ⏰ Open M-Th 7:30am-midnight, F 7:30am-11:30pm, Sa-Su 8:45am-8pm.

HET MARNIX — 💳♿ JORDAAN

Marnixplein 1 — ☎052 460 00 💻www.hetmarnix.nl

In the site of a former bathhouse, this highly modern large sports complex has a great view of the old Jordaan. Marnix holds two swimming pools, courts for all kinds of sports, and a luxurious spa. Group classes for aerobics by land and by sea are available.

➤ Tram #3 or 10 to Marnixplein. $ Prices vary by subscription; single visit to pools €3.70. Make sure to bring your own towel. ⏰ Open M-F 7am-10pm, Sa-Su 7am-7pm. Check website for specific schedules, as classes sometimes interfere with public use.

HOLLAND CASINO AMSTERDAM — 💳♿🍸 LEIDSEPLEIN

Max Euweplein 62 — ☎052 111 11 💻www.hollandcasino.nl

If the rest of Leidseplein doesn't provide enough debauchery for you, head into this stylish casino to try your hand at slots, blackjack, roulette, and poker. All of the casino's profits go to the Dutch treasury, but that doesn't mean it's any easier to hang onto your money. There's another branch at Schiphol Airport if you have some time to kill before your flight. Another dozen are scattered throughout Amsterdam.

➤ Tram #1, 2, 5, 7, or 10 to Leidseplein. Walk down Weteringschans and make a right under the colonnade into Max Euweplein. ℹ 18+. $ Admission €5. After that, good luck. ⏰ Open daily noon-3am.

AMSTERDAM ARENA — 💳♿ OUTSKIRTS

ArenA Bld. 1 — ☎031 113 33 💻www.amsterdamarena.nl

This stadium is the home turf of Amsterdam's beloved Ajax football (soccer) team. Unfortunately, the only way to get tickets to a game when you're outside of the Netherlands is to buy a fairly expensive hospitality package through the Ajax website; it includes a tour of the stadium, food and drink, a souvenir, etc. If you are in the country, however, you can either buy tickets at the stadium on game day (keeping in mind that the games, especially those against the larger Dutch city teams, often sell out) or call to find out when ticket pre-sales will begin, then buy the tickets at any shop in the city that is part of the TicketBox network. There are a number of rules for who can buy tickets and when those tickets can be purchased depending on the game, so it's advised that you call and figure out the specifics for the game you want to attend. If you'd like to get a taste of Ajax outside of football season, tours introducing you to the "World of Ajax" are given daily at the stadium.

➤ In the city's southern suburbs. ⓂBijlmer Arena. Follow signs for stadium. $ Game tickets from €30. Tour €12. ⏰ Open daily 11am-4:30pm. Tours offered daily 4-7pm, depending on season. Check website for specific times.

SAUNAS AND SPAS

Saunas and spas fall into two categories: those intended for some indulgent pampering, and gay saunas where men go to indulge in the other pleasures of the flesh. It should be fairly obvious which are which, but if you want to be sure, you can just stick to the listings that follow.

THERMOS

📧⊗(((•)))⚓♥ ▼ LEIDSEPLEIN

Raamstraat 33

☎062 391 58 🖳www.thermos.nl

Thermos is one of the oldest and largest gay saunas in Europe; its day and night branches were recently fused together into one complex that is open almost all day. It has a Finnish sauna, Turkish steam bath, whirlpool, swimming pool, video room, private rooms, beauty salon, bar, and restaurant. Popular with a diverse crowd of men; depending on the season, there may be a lot of tourists, but tends to attract a slightly older clientele.

🚋 *Tram #7 or 10 to Raamplein.* 🛈 *Men only. 18+.* Ⓢ *€18, under 24 and over 65 €14.* 🕘 *Open daily noon-8am.*

SAUNA DECO

📧⊗⊘ ⛱ CANAL RING WEST

Herengracht 115

☎062 382 15 🖳www.saunadeco.nl

In a stunning Art Deco interior (with ornaments from the original Le Bon Marché store on rue des Sevres in Paris), you can enjoy a sauna and steam room, plunge bath, and spa with a full range of services, from massages to facials. Patio garden and lounge beds make it the perfect place to relax even on dry land. All bathing is unisex.

🚋 *Tram #1, 2, 5, 14, or 17 to Nieuwezijds Kolk. Walk east, cross the Singel, and make a left onto Herengracht.* Ⓢ *€20 for use of sauna area, €2 towel rental; €55 for 55min. massage, €30 for 25min.* 🕘 *Open M noon-11pm, Tu 3-11pm, W-Sa noon-11pm, Su 1-7pm.*

shopping 🛍️

With shopping, as with pretty much every other aspect of life in Amsterdam, a wide range of options is at your fingertips. The **Nine Streets** just south of Westerkerk are packed with vintage stores and interesting boutiques. **Haarlemmerstraat,** in Scheepvaartbuurt, is also an up-and-coming neighborhood in terms of clothing design. For more established brands, look to **Kalverstraat,** with its string of international chains and large department stores. If you're looking for something really pricey, **P. C. Hooftstraat,** near Museumplein, is the part of town with the big-name designers. On the other end of the spectrum, markets like **Albert Cuypmarkt** and **Waterlooplein** offer dirt-cheap and, at times, flat-out bizarre clothing and other wares.

CLOTHING AND JEWELRY

STUDIO 88

📧♿ DE PIJP

Gerard Douplein 88

☎077 065 84 🖳www.fashionstudio88.nl

Sometimes, it feels like no matter how cheap they might be, most of the clothes in **Albert Cuypmarkt** are never going to be a good deal because you'd never actually wear them. The clothes at Studio 88 might not be at the same rock-bottom prices, but for an overstock and sample store, it sells some very nice high-end pieces for a fraction of what they would ordinarily cost. It carries mostly women's clothes with a few racks of men's things in the back.

🚋 *Tram #16 or 24 to Albert Cuypstraat. Walk 1 block up and make a right onto Gerard Doustraat; the store is up ahead on the right.* Ⓢ *Prices vary by brand. Most shirts average around €20. Dresses around €40.* 🕘 *Open M 1-6pm, Tu-F 11am-6pm, Sa 10am-6pm.*

SPRMRKT

📧♿ JORDAAN

Rozengracht 191-193

☎033 056 01 🖳www.sprmrkt.nl

Too cool for school (or for vowels, at least), this very large store in the Jordaan sells excruciatingly hip street-wear—think lots of black, well-cut bright shirts, etc. The store-within-the-store, SPR+, sells even nicer designer pieces. It stocks clothing for both men and women.

⚡ *Tram #10, 13, 14, or 17 to Rozengracht/Marnixstraat. Walk a few blocks on Rozengracht; the store is on the right.* ⏰ *Open Tu-W 10am-6pm, Th 10am-8pm, F-Sa 10am-6pm, Su noon-6pm.*

VEZJUN
Rozengracht 110

🚶♿ JORDAAN
🖥 www.vezjun.nl

A small store that only sells clothing from independent, young Dutch designers. The clothes can occasionally be a little out there, but for the most part, they are well constructed, fresh, and modern—and you can be sure that no one else will be wearing the same thing at your next party.

⚡ *Tram #10, 13, 14, or 17 to Rozengracht/Marnixstraat. Walk a few blocks on Rozengracht; the store is on the left.* 💲 *Dresses €70-90.* ⏰ *Open Tu-W noon-7pm, Th noon-8pm, F noon-7pm, Sa 11am-6pm.*

THE DARLING
Runstraat 4

🚶⊘ CANAL RING WEST
☎042 231 42 🖥 www.thedarling.nl

A girly, white-and-pastel store that sells well-priced dresses and other women's clothes by boutique European brands. Some are dreamy and lacy, others are more mod. Vintage pieces are available as well, plus some jewelry items. The store also sells cupcakes, the cherry on top of any shopping experience.

⚡ *Tram #13, 14, or 17 to Westermarkt. Make a right down Keizersgracht and then a right onto Runstraat.* 💲 *Dresses €30-40.* ⏰ *Open M noon-6pm, Tu-W 10am-6pm, Th 10am-7pm, F-Sa 10am-6pm.*

SPOILED
Wolvenstraat 19

🚶♿ CANAL RING WEST
☎062 638 18 🖥 www.spoiled.nl

Large, ultramodern space packed with men's and women's chic urban wear. The real draw is the massive denim bar, with dozens of brands of American and European designer jeans. You can browse through their denim menu or have the knowledgeable staff help you find your perfect pair.

⚡ *Tram #1, 2, or 5 to Spui/Nieuwezijds Voorburgwal. Walk west to the far side of Herengracht, make a right, and then a left onto Wolvenstraat.* 💲 *Jeans from €80.* ⏰ *Open M noon-6pm, Tu-W 10am-6pm, Th 10am-7pm, F-Sa 10am-6pm.*

V AND D DEPARTMENT STORE
Kalverstraat 203

🚶♿ NIEUWE ZIJD
☎0900 235 8363 🖥 www.vd.nl

One of the large department stores in the Nieuwe Zijd, with a good selection of interesting, affordable brands. Excellent summer sales. Also sells house-wares, electronics, CDs/DVDs, etc. If you get peckish while shopping, pop into the store's amazing cafeteria, **La Place.**

⚡ *Tram #4, 9, 14, 16, 24, or 25 to Muntplein. You'll see the store from there.* 💲 *Prices vary by brand.* ⏰ *Open M 11:30am-7:30pm, Tu-W 10:30am-7:30pm, Th 10:30am-9pm, F-Sa 10am-8pm, Su noon-6:30pm.*

BOOKS

📕 THE BOOK EXCHANGE
Kloveniersburgwal 58

🚶⊘ OUDE ZIJD
☎062 66 266 🖥 www.bookexchange.nl

A tremendous selection of hardcover and paperback secondhand English books, ranging from New Age philosophy to poetry and beyond. Largest choice is with paperback fiction. Knowledgeable expat owner is more than happy to chat at length with customers. Store also buys and trades books.

⚡ *From Nieuwmarkt, cross to the far side of Kloveniersburgwal and make a left.* ⏰ *Open M-Sa 10am-4pm, Su 11:30am-4pm.*

AMERICAN BOOK CENTER
Spui 2

🚶⊘ NIEUWE ZIJD
☎062 555 37 🖥 www.abc.nl

An independently run English-language bookstore with a wide range of new and classic titles, American Book Center also has an excellent selection of maps of the city, from the simple to the vastly detailed.

Tram #1, 2, or 5 to Spui/Nieuwezijds Voorburgwal. It's on the northern edge of the square. i 10% discount for students and teachers. Open M-W 10am-8pm, Th 10am-9pm, F-Sa 10am-8pm, Su 11am-6:30pm.

THE ENGLISH BOOKSHOP JORDAAN

Lauriergracht 71 ☎062 642 30 www.englishbookshop.nl

This small, cozy shop in the Jordaan has a vibrant community of regulars who enjoy coffee or tea (and fresh pastries!) while browsing the good selection of English-language books. The store hosts events like writing workshops, a monthly book club, and quirkier nights like literary Trivial Pursuit.

Tram #10, 13, 14, or 17 to Rozengracht/Marnixstraat. Cross Lijnbaansgracht, make a right, and then a left onto Lauriergracht. Open Tu-Sa 11am-6pm.

ANTIQUES AND VINTAGE CLOTHING

The **Nine Streets** area in Canal Ring West is your best destination for finding quirky stores that sell a delightful and surprising array of somewhat practical objects.

LAURA DOLS CANAL RING WEST

Wolvenstraat 7 ☎062 490 66 www.lauradols.nl

An amazing collection of vintage gowns includes taffeta prom dresses, fluffy shepherdess-y numbers, and things you could actually get away with wearing outside of the house. Also sells shoes, bags, and old-school lingerie (including some awesome metallic bras).

Tram #1, 2, or 5 to Spui/Nieuwezijds Voorburgwal. Walk west to the far side of Herengracht, make a right, and then a left onto Wolvenstraat. $ Most dresses €30-60, though some go up into the hundreds. Open M 1-6pm, Tu-W 11am-6pm, Th 11am-7pm, Sa 11am-6pm, Su 1-6pm.

NIC NIC CANAL RING WEST

Gasthuismolensteeg 5 ☎062 285 23 www.nicnicdesign.com

Everything you could possibly think of can be found in this antique store, from Art Deco furniture to plastic jewelry. A remarkable diversity of dishware and glasses. Have fun trying on the many wigs perched on vintage lamps.

Tram #1, 2, 5, or 14 to Dam/Paleisstraat. Walk down Paleisstraat, cross the Singel, and you'll be on Gasthuismolensteeg. $ Set of vintage martini glasses €65. Everything else from €0.50 to, well, a lot more. Open M-F noon-6pm, Sa 11am-5pm.

LADY DAY CANAL RING WEST

Hartenstraat 9 ☎062 358 20 www.theninestreets.com/ladyday

An established go-to spot for '50s, '60s, and '70s vintage style, Lady Day has a massive sampling of men's and women's clothes: tweed jackets, cocktail dresses, bathing suits, sweaters, tops, scarves, and so on. Most of the stuff is still quite fashionable, and the things that aren't are still really cheap.

Tram #13, 14, or 17 to Westermarkt. Walk down Radhuisstraat to the far side of Keizersgracht, make a right, and then a left onto Hartenstraat. $ Dresses around €25; sweaters €20; tops €15; scarves €1. Open M-W 11am-6pm, Th 11am-9pm, F-Sa 11am-6pm, Su 1-6pm.

PETTICOAT ♿ JORDAAN

Lindengracht 99 ☎062 330 65

A good selection of secondhand men's and women's clothing, some from fairly upscale brands, can be found here.

Tram #3 to Nieuwe Willemstraat. Cross Lijnbaansgracht, make a right, and then a left onto Lindengracht. $ Tops from €10; bottoms from €15. Open M 11am-6pm, W-F 11am-6pm, Sa 11am-5pm.

GIFTS

★ WYNAND FOCKINK ◉♿🍸 RED LIGHT DISTRICT

Pijlsteeg 31 ☎063 926 95 💻www.wynand-fockink.nl

Sells bottles of the distillery's Brandywines and *jenevers*. See listing in **Nightlife.**

⇆ From Dam Square, walk down Dam to Oudezijds Voorburgwal, make a left, and then the next left onto Pijlsteeg. $ Bottles from €18. ⏰ Open daily 3-9pm.

CONDOMERIE HET GULDEN VLIES 🏷♿ RED LIGHT DISTRICT

Warmoesstraat 141 ☎062 741 74 💻www.condomerie.com

According to their website, the "Condomerie of the Golden Fleece" is the world's first specialized shop for condoms. Regardless of whether they're right about being the first to come up with the idea of a condom store, they certainly do have one remarkable collection of prophylactics. You'll find an immense variety of male condoms in different materials (including vegan-friendly) and sizes, female condoms, lubes, and sex toys. The store also sells "novelty" condoms, which might come with terrifying-looking spiky appendages or be painted like cute frogs.

⇆ Tram #4, 9, 16, 24, or 25 to Dam. Cross the square and make a left up Warmoesstraat. ⏰ Open M-Sa 10am-6pm.

MOONLIGHT GIFTS ◉♿ SCHEEPVAARTBUURT

Haarlemmerstraat 20 ☎077 220 13

Small store with an inexplicable and eclectic collection of painted cow figurines, cow clocks, and other bovine paraphernalia. There are some more traditional Dutch souvenirs as well—posters, postcards, Delft, and the like.

⇆ From Centraal Station, make a right, cross the Singel, and go down Haarlemmerstraat. ⏰ Open daily 10am-6pm.

DE EMAILLEKEIZER ◉⊘ DE PIJP

1e Sweelinckstraat 15 ☎066 418 47 💻www.emaillekeizer.nl

Sells all kinds of imported and West African inspired items: woven baskets, pots, cloth, jewelry, enameled items, and more. A really good selection of bright dishware is here as well as some interesting vintage postcards and "nostalgic enamel signs."

⇆ Tram #16 or 24 to Albert Cuypstraat. Walk a few blocks through the market and make a right onto 1e Sweelinckstraat. $ Most things from €4. ⏰ Open M-Sa 10:30am-6:30pm.

DAM SQUARE SOUVENIRS 🏷♿ NIEUWE ZIJD

Dam 19 ☎062 034 32 💻www.dutchsouvenirs.com

The largest collection of cheesy Dutch souvenirs in town. You can get clogs, windmills, Delft, Amsterdam T-shirts, and just about any other kitschy thing. The store is a sight in and of itself, with a boat-sized clog outside and a massive cow hanging from the ceiling indoors.

⇆ Tram #4, 9, 16, 24, or 25 to Dam. The store is on the south side of the square. ℹ 10% off coupon on store website. ⏰ Open daily 9am-10pm.

MARKETS

★ ALBERT CUYPMARKT ◉♿ DE PIJP

Albert Cuypstraat

Stretching almost half a mile along the length of Albert Cuypstraat, this is the most famous market in Amsterdam. Need a motorcycle helmet, sundress, and cinnamon all in one afternoon? This is the place to go. The clothes are certainly hit-or-miss, but for produce or knick-knacks, it's a great option. On both sides of the street just behind the market, rows of stores sell similar items at slightly higher prices (though some of the stuff is quite a bit more wearable).

⇆ Tram #16 or 24 to Albert Cuypstraat. ⏰ Open M-Sa 9am-6pm.

⬛ NOORDERMARKT

Noordermarkt

🏢♿ JORDAAN
💻www.boerenmarktamsterdam.nl

In the picturesque northern corner of the Jordaan, an organic market pops up every Saturday selling produce, cheese, baked goods, herbs, homeopathic remedies, and some hippie-esque clothes.

🚋 *Tram #3 to Nieuwe Willemstraat. Cross Lijnbaansgracht, walk up Willemstraat, make a right onto Brouwersgracht, and then another right onto Prinsengracht; the market is about a block down.* 🕐 *Open Sa 9am-4pm.*

DAPPERMARKT

Dapperstraat

🏢♿ OUTSKIRTS
💻www.dappermarkt.nl

A market that really exudes local flavor, this also blends old Amsterdam charm with the newer North African and Middle Eastern immigrant communities. Come to find vegetables, spices, cloth, furniture, clothes, and more—at prices that tend to be much cheaper than the more touristy markets in the center. It's near Oosterpark, just south of Plantage.

🚋 *Tram #3 or 7 to Dapperstraat.* 🕐 *Open M-Sa 9am-5pm.*

NIEUWMARKT

Nieuwmarkt

🏢♿ OUDE ZIJD

You can find a few stalls selling everything from souvenirs to clothes here daily, but the main markets are the organic food market on Saturdays and an antiques and book market on Sundays in the summer.

🚋 *Ⓜ️Nieuwmarkt.* 🕐 *Open daily 9am-4pm.*

SPUI

Spui

🏢♿ NIEUWE ZIJD

In the warmer months of the year, local and international artists flock here to sell their paintings, sculptures, etchings, and photographs. Even if you're not looking to buy, wandering through this marketplace is just like visiting an art gallery.

🚋 *Tram #1, 2, or 5 to Spui/Niuwezijds Voorburgwal. Walk just a tad south on Nieuwezijds Voorburgwal to get to the square.* 🕐 *Open daily Mar-Oct 10am-3pm.*

SMOKING ACCESSORIES AND MUSIC

Smartshops and the larger coffeeshops often have very good selections of mechanisms that can be used to help get THC into your system. If you want something specific to listen to while you're high (or sober), Amsterdam has many excellent music stores. Quirky secondhand music can also be found at some of the **markets.**

⬛ CONCERTO

Utrechtsestraat 52-60

🏢♿ CENTRAL CANAL RING
☎062 352 28 💻www.platomania.eu

Multiple storefronts make up a huge complex with the best music selection in Amsterdam. Sells every kind of music imaginable and has a good amount of records, DVDs, and secondhand CDs. It's also a great place to check out flyers and posters for upcoming concerts and festivals. Tickets for some performances can be purchased here.

🚋 *Tram #4, 7, 10, or 25 to Frederiksplein. Walk diagonally across the square and up Utrechtsestraat.* 🕐 *Open M-W 10am-6pm, Th 10am-9pm, F-Sa 10am-6pm, Su noon-6pm.*

SOUTH MIAMI PLAZA

Albert Cuypstraat 116

🏢♿ DE PIJP
☎066 228 17 💻www.southmiamiplaza.nl

A fine selection of pop, blues, reggae, R and B, world music, and a special section of Dutch classics. Plenty of DVDs, music-related and otherwise, can also be found. Bargain bins hold an eclectic mix of CDs starting from just €1.

🚋 *Tram #16 or 24 to Albert Cuypstraat. Walk through the market; the store is on the right.* 🕐 *Open M-Sa 10am-6pm.*

THE OLD MAN

Damstraat 16

🖐♿ NIEUWE ZIJD

☎062 700 43 🖥www.theoldman.com

Large store near Dam Square that sells smoking accessories, board-sport equipment, and knives—hopefully no one will be using all three at once. Has a collection of smoking tools that range from tiny pipes to bongs and hookahs to grinders, scales, and the like. Not necessarily a better selection than what you'd find at a smartshop or some coffeeshops but definitely a wider variety. Check out the bong in the shape of a clog, clearly the Dutch souvenir your mom is hoping for.

⚓ Tram #4, 9, 16, 24, or 25 to Dam. Walk to the end of the square and make a left. ☒ Open daily 10am-6pm.

VELVET MUSIC

Rozengracht 40

🖐♿ JORDAAN

☎042 287 77 🖥www.velvetmusic.nl

Carries both the latest releases (their handy board of upcoming titles in the window will let you know what to look forward to) and older music in virtually all genres. Not as large as a place like Concerto, but perhaps less overwhelming to navigate. Strong selection of vinyl in the back.

⚓ Tram #13, 14, or 17 to Westermarkt. Cross Prinsengracht and walk down Rozengracht. ☒ Open M noon-6pm, Tu-Sa 10am-6pm.

essentials 🟨

PRACTICALITIES

- **TOURIST OFFICES: VVV** provides information on sights, museums, performances, and accommodations; you can buy maps and guidebooks (not that you'd need another one) here too. They also heavily advertise and sell the **I Amsterdam** card, which gives you unlimited transport and free admission to many museums within a certain number of days. For other transportation information, you're better off going to the **GVB office** next door. The lines at the office by Centraal Station can be pretty unbearable, so unless you need information right after you step off the train, you're better off going to the one in Leidseplein. (Stationsplein 10 ☎020 188 00 🖥www.iamsterdam.com ⚓ Across from the eastern part of Centraal Station, near tram stops 1-4. ☒ Open M-W 9am-6pm, Th-F 9am-9pm, Sa-Su 9am-6pm.) Other locations at: **Schiphol Airport** (Aankomstpassage 40, in Arrival Hall 2 ☒ Open daily 7am-10pm.) and **Leidseplein 26.** (☒ Open M-Sa 10am-7:30pm, Su noon-7:30pm.) **GAYtic** is a tourist info office authorized by the VVV that specializes in GLBT tourist info. (Spuistraat 44 🖥www.gaytic.nl ⚓ Tram #1, 2, 5, 13, or 17 to Nieuwezijds Kolk. Walk 1 block west to Spuistraat; the office is inside the Gays and Gadgets store. ☒ Open M-Sa 11am-8pm, Su noon-8pm.)

- **GLBT RESOURCES: Pink Point** provides information on GLBT issues, events, and attractions in the city, and sells all kinds of GLBT souvenirs. (Westermarkt, by the Homomonument ☎042 810 70 🖥www.pinkpoint.org ⚓ Tram #13, 14, or 17 to Westermarkt. ☒ Open daily 10am-6pm.) **GAYtic** (see **Tourist Offices**). **Gay and Lesbian Switchboard** takes anonymous calls with any GLBT-related questions or concerns. (☎062 365 65 🖥www.switchboard.nl ☒ Operates M-F noon-6pm.)

- **LAUNDROMATS: Rozengracht Wasserette** sells detergent and provides self-service as well as next-day laundry options. (🏧 Rozengracht 59 ☎063 859 75 ⚓ Tram #13, 14, or 17 to Westermarkt. Cross Prinsengracht and walk a few blocks down on Rozengracht. 💲 Wash €6, dry €7. Overnight service €10. ☒ Open daily 9am-9pm.) **Powders Laundrette.** (🏧 Kerkstraat 56 ☎062 630 6057 🖥www.powders.nl ⚓

Tram #1, 2, 5, 7, or 10 to Leidseplein. Walk up Leidsestraat and make a right. [i] *Detergent for sale. Internet available to kill time while you wait.* $ *Self-service wash €4 per hr., dry €0.50 per 12min. €10 for 5kg wash, dry, and fold.* ⏰ *Self-service open daily 7am-10pm; full service open M-F 8am-5pm, Sa-Su 9am-3pm.)*

- **INTERNET: Openbare Bibliotheek Amsterdam** provides free Wi-Fi and free use of computers that can be reserved through the information desk. *(Oosterdokskade 143 ☎052 309 00 💻www.oba.nl 🚏 From Centraal Station, walk straight east, sticking close to the latitude of the station building. You'll cross a canal, and the street will become Oosterdokskade.* ⏰ *Open daily 10am-10pm.)* **The Mad Processor** is extremely popular with gamers. *(Kinkerstraat 11-13 ☎061 218 18 💻www.madprocessor.nl 🚏 Tram #7, 10, or 17 to Elandsgracht. Cross Nassaukade onto Kinkerstraat.* [i] *Computers with Skype capabilities. Fax machines and scanners available.* $ *Internet €1 per 30min. Printing €0.20 per page.* ⏰ *Open daily noon-2am.)* **Internet Cafe** provides high-speed internet. All computers have webcams; some have specific programs like Microsoft Word. Has a bar with lots of drink options too. *(Martelaarsgracht 11 ☎062 710 52 💻www.internetcafe.nl 🚏 Centraal Station. Cross the canal on the western end of the station and walk down Martelaarsgracht.* $ *€1 per 30min.* ⏰ *Open M-Th 10am-1am, F-Sa 10am-3am, Su 10am-1am.)*
- **POST OFFICES: Main branch** deals with all of your mailing needs, plus has banking services and sells phone cards. *(Singel 250 ☎055 633 11 💻www.tntpost.nl 🚏 Tram #1, 2, 5, or 14 to Dam/Paleisstraat. Walk 1 block north and make a left onto Raadhuisstraat.* ⏰ *Open M-F 9am-6pm, Sa 10am-1:30pm.)* Besides the main office, you can get stamps and send packages at any store that has the orange and white TNT sign (mostly grocery stores and tobacco shops).
- **POSTAL CODES:** Range from 1000 AA to 1099 ZZ. Check the TNT website or 💻maps.google.nl to find out the code for a specific address.

EMERGENCY!

- **POLICE: Politie Amsterdam-Amstelland** is the city's police department. The following are the most convenient bureaus to central Amsterdam. All can be reached at ☎0900 8844, where you will be connected to the nearest station or rape crisis center. **Lijnbaansgracht.** *(Lijnbaansgracht 219 🚏 Tram #7 or 10 to Raamplein. Walk 1 block south and make a left onto Leidsegracht.* ⏰ *Open 24hr.)* **Nieuwezijds Voorburgwal.** *(Nieuwezijds Voorburgwal 104-108 🚏 Tram #1, 2, 5, 13, or 17 to Nieuwezijds Kolk. Walk 1 block down Nieuwezijds Voorburgwal.* ⏰ *Open 24hr.)* **Prinsengracht.** *(Prinsengracht 1109 🚏 Tram #3, 4, 7, 10, or 25 to Fredericksplein. Walk diagonally through the square, up Utrechtsestraat, and make a right onto Prinsengracht.* ⏰ *Open 24hr.)*
- **CRISIS HOTLINES: Telephone Helpline** provides general counseling services. *(☎067 575 75* ⏰ *Available 24hr.)* **Amsterdam Tourist Assistance Service** provides help for victimized tourists in Amsterdam, generally those who have been robbed. Gives emotional support, use of phone and fax, and assistance with practical matters like money transfers, replacing documents, and finding temporary accommodations. *(Nieuwezijds Voorburgwal 104-08 ☎062 532 46 💻www.stichtingatas.nl 🚏 Tram #1, 2, 5, 13, or 17 to Nieuwezijds Kolk. Walk 1 block down Nieuwezijds Voorburgwal. It's inside the police station.* ⏰ *Open daily 10am-10pm.)* **Rape Crisis Hotline** provides assistance to those who have been victims of rape. *(☎061 202 45* ⏰ *Staffed M-F 10:30am-11pm, Sa-Su 3:30-11pm.)* **Jellinek Clinic** provides counseling and information about drugs, alcohol, and smoking. *(☎059 050 00 💻www.jellinek.nl* ⏰ *Operates M-F 9am-5pm.)*
- **LATE-NIGHT PHARMACIES: Afdeling Inlichtingen Apotheken hotline** provides

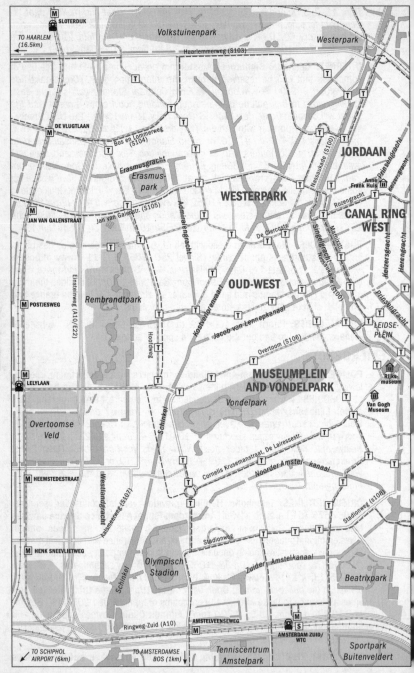

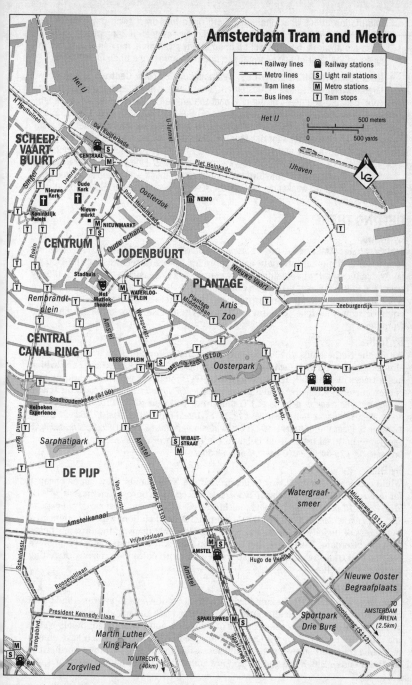

Amsterdam Tram and Metro

······ Railway lines	🚉 Railway stations
▭▭▭ Metro lines	S Light rail stations
▨▨▨ Tram lines	M Metro stations
- - - Bus lines	T Tram stops

Het IJ

0 ⊢─────┤ 500 meters
0 ⊢─────┤ 500 yards

N

Het IJ

Het IJ

't Houttuinen

De Ruijterkade

U-Tunnel

Piet Heinkade

IJhaven

SCHEEP-VAART-BUURT

Singel

CENTRAAL S M

Damrak

Nieuwe Kerk

Oude Kerk

Nieuw-markt

NIEUWMARKT

Koninklijk Paleis

CENTRUM

Rokin

Oosterdok

Prins Hendrikkade

NEMO

Oude Schans

JODENBUURT

Nieuwe Vaart

Stadhuis

Het Muziek-theater

WATERLOO-PLEIN

PLANTAGE

Plantage Middenlaan

Artis Zoo

Zeeburgerdijk

Rembrandt-plein

Amstel

Weesperstr.

CENTRAL CANAL RING

WEESPERPLEIN S M

Mauritskade (S100)

Oosterpark

Stadhouderskade (S100)

Linnaeus-str.

MUIDERPOORT

Ferdinand Bolstr.

Heineken Experience

Amstel

Sarphatipark

WIBAUT-STRAAT S M

DE PIJP

Van Woustr.

Amsteldijk (S110)

Watergraaf-smeer

Middenweg (S113)

Amstelkanaal

Vrijheidslaan

AMSTEL M S

Hugo de Vrieslaan

Nieuwe Ooster Begraafplaats

Scheldestr.

Roosevelt-laan

President Kennedy-laan

Gooiseweg (S112)

Sportpark Drie Burg

TO AMSTERDAM ARENA (2.5km)

Europablvd.

M S RAI

Martin Luther King Park

Zorgvlied

SPAKLERWEG M S

Spaklerweg

TO UTRECHT (40km)

essentials · emergency!

www.letsgo.com ℘ 115

information about what pharmacies are open late on a given day. *(☎069 487 09 ⏰ Available 24hr.)* There are no specifically designated 24hr. pharmacies, but there are always a few that will be open at any given time. You can also check the signs on the door of any pharmacy to find the nearest one open in the area.

- **HOSPITALS/MEDICAL SERVICES: Academisch Meidsch Centrum** is one of two large university hospitals in Amsterdam, providing excellent general and specialized care. Located southeast of the city, past the Amsterdam ArenA stadium. *(Meibergdreef 9 ☎056 691 11 💻www.amc.uva.nl ➡ Bus #45, 47, 120, 126, 153, 155, 158 or night bus #375, 376, 377, 378, and 379 to Paasheuvelweg. Hospital is directly across. ⏰ Open 24hr.)* **Tourist Medical Service** provides doctor's visits for guests at registered hotels and runs a 24hr. line to connect tourists to non-emergency medical care. *(☎059 233 55 💻www.tmsdoctor.nl ⏰ Line staffed 24hr.)* **Doctors Service Foundation of Amsterdam** will put you in touch with a doctor's clinic open after hours or on weekends. *(☎088 00 30 600 💻www.shda.nl ⏰ Line open daily 5pm-8am.)*

GETTING THERE

By Plane

Schiphol Airport (AMS) *(☎090 001 41 inside the Netherlands; 31 207 940 800 outside 💻www.schiphol.nl)* is the main international airport for both Amsterdam and the Netherlands. It's located 18km outside the city center, and the easiest way to reach it is by **train** *($ €4.20. ⏰ 15 min., 4-10 per hr. 6am-1am, then 1 night train per hr.)* The train station is located just below the airport; you can buy tickets at machines with cards or coins or from the ticket counter with cash. Trains also go to other Dutch cities from here.

By Train

Within the Netherlands, the easiest way to reach Amsterdam is by train, which will almost certainly run into **Centraal Station** *(Stationsplein 1 ☎0900 9292 💻www.ns.nl)*, which has services like the VVV Tourist Info Office, GVB public transportation information center, currency exchange, and luggage storage. *(➡ Toward the eastern end of the station. **i** Only accepts credit or debit cards.)* Trains from **The Hague** *($ €10.10. ⏰ 1 hr., 3-6 per hr., 4:45am-12:45am.)*, **Rotterdam** *($ €13.30. ⏰ 1hr., 3-8 per hr. 5:30am-12:45am, 1 per hr. 12:45am-5:30am.)*, and **Utrecht.** *($ €6.70. ⏰ 30min., 4 per hr. 6am-midnight, 1 per hr. midnight-6am.)* International trains from Belgium run by **Thalys** *(💻www.thalys.com)*. Trains from **Brussels.** *($ €25-64. ⏰ 2hr., 1 per hr. 7:50am-8:50pm.)*

By Bus

While buses aren't a great way to get around the Netherlands, they can be cheaper for international travel. **Eurolines** *(💻www.eurolines.com)* runs buses from **Brussels** *($ €15. ⏰ 3-4½hr., 10 per day 6am-8:30pm.)* and **Bruges** *($ €15. ⏰ 5hr., 1 per day from Bruges at 3pm, from Amsterdam at 11am.)* to the Amsterdam Amstel station, which is connected to the rest of the city by Metro and tram #12. Note that many of the Brussels buses stop in Rotterdam, The Hague, and Utrecht on their way to Amsterdam, although we recommend trains as an equally expensive and more convenient means of getting between these cities.

GETTING AROUND

Tram, bus, and Metro lines extend from Centraal Station, and more trams and buses cross those routes perpendicularly or circumnavigate the canal rings. Trams are generally the fastest and easiest modes of transport, going to all major points within the city center (except for the Oude Zijd and Red Light District, which have almost no public transport stops but are easily accessible by the stops on their northern or southern ends). Buses are good if you are going to more residential areas or spots outside of the center, though trams extend to farther distances as well. The Metro is rarely useful, as it only goes down the eastern side of the city and has few stops within the center.

Tickets and information can be found at **GVB,** on Stationsplein across from the eastern end of Centraal Station next to the VVV tourist office. *(☎046 060 60 💻www.gvb.nl 🕐 Open M-F 7am-9pm, Sa-Su 10am-6pm.)* The lines here can be long, but it's the easiest place to buy transport tickets. The **OV-chipkaart** has replaced the strippenkaart as the only type of ticket used on Amsterdam public transport. One-hour tickets can be purchased directly on trams and buses for €2.60. One- to seven-day tickets (valid also on night buses) cost €7-29. Otherwise, you can purchase an OV-chipkaart for €5 and add money to it as you need. (To add money with cash, you have to go to the GVB center; otherwise, there are many points throughout the city where you can add money with cards.) With the chipkaart, a ride on the bus, tram, or Metro costs €0.78 plus €0.10 per km. A ride pretty much anywhere in the city center will only cost you around €1. Most transport runs from about 5am-midnight; after that, there are 12 night bus lines that run once an hour (twice an hour on weekend nights). An ordinary chipkaart does not work on night buses; you have to buy special tickets, which cost €3.50 per ride or 12 for €25. Daily tickets (the one- to seven-day ones) do work on night buses without having to buy extra tickets. Make sure to both tap in *and* tap out with your chipkaart to avoid being charged for more than you actually travel.

Bike Rentals

👍 FREDERIC RENT-A-BIKE — SCHEEPVAARTBUURT

Brouwersgracht 78 — ☎062 455 09 💻www.frederic.nl

In addition to his position as room-renter and general guru of all things Amsterdam (see **Accommodations**), Frederic rents bikes.

➥ From Centraal Station, cross the canal, make a right on Prins Hendrikkade, cross the Singel, make a left, and then a right onto Brouwersgracht. i Prices include lock and insurance. No deposit required, just a copy of a credit card or passport. [S] Bikes €10 per day. 🕐 Open daily 9am-6pm.

BIKE CITY — JORDAAN

Bloemgracht 68-70 — ☎062 637 21 💻www.bikecity.nl

Rents a few different kinds of bikes.

➥ Tram #13, 14, or 17 to Westermarkt. Cross Prinsengracht, make a right, and then a left onto Bloemgracht. i Deposit of either a credit card or €50 required. [S] Bikes from €10 per 4 hr., €13.50 per 24hr., up to €43.50 per 5 days. Insurance €2.50 per day. 🕐 Open daily 9am-6pm.

DAMSTRAAT RENT-A-BIKE — RED LIGHT DISTRICT

Damstraat 22 — ☎062 550 29 💻www.bikes.nl

Rents multiple kinds of bikes, including tandems. Also sells new and second-hand bikes.

➥ Tram #4, 9, 16, 24, or 25 to Dam. Walk to the end of the square and make a left onto Damstraat. i Deposit requires copy of credit card or ID and €25. [S] From €6.50 per 3hr., €9.50 per 24hr., €30.55 per 6 days. Sells bikes from €160. 🕐 Open daily 9am-6pm.

amsterdam 101

facts and figures

- **POPULATION:** 1,360,000
- **AGE:** 736 years old in 2011
- **SIZE:** 219.4 sq. km
- **LAND RESERVED FOR PARKS:** 12%
- **INHABITANTS PER SQ. KM:** 4457
- **ETHNIC GROUPS:** 173
- **CANALS:** 165
- **BRIDGES:** 1281
- **POT SMOKERS:** 5.2% of *Nederlanders* in any given year (compared with 12.5% of Americans)
- **COFFEESHOPS IN 1960, THE FIRST TIME LET'S GO WENT TO AMSTERDAM:** 5
- **COFFEESHOPS TODAY:** 241
- **TOURISTS THAT VISIT A COFFEESHOP:** 30%
- **BICYCLE THEFTS:** 80,000

Too many people demonize—or worship—Amsterdam as a world of sex, drugs, and rock 'n' roll. Yes, it has all of those things, but the Dutch legacy is rooted in two more profound pillars: innovation and internationalism. From superiority on the seas to expertise on the easel, the Dutch have blazed their own unique path. They applied their ingenuity to literally cover new ground, claiming 2745 sq. mi. of land from the North Sea with an intricate network of ocean-conquering dikes, canals, and pumps— land that was, in turn, quickly settled by international newcomers. Even with this outside influence, some credence must be given to the local adage, "God created the world, but the Dutch created the Netherlands." Thank this geopolitical black sheep with its fiercely independent attitude for giving birth to a city like Amsterdam, where international flavors are combined with innovative liberality to create a captivating mix of multi-ethnic sophistication and come-one, come-all openness.

HISTORY

Amsterdam took root by a natural harbor at the mouth of the river Amstel, immediately setting itself up for importance in trade. The city grew rapidly after imposing a beer tax on exports to the Baltic Sea and becoming an important pilgrimage town for Roman Catholics. (For the record, we're not suggesting the two events are related.)

By the 16th century, the city had begun to resent the religious intolerance imposed on the Dutch people by its tyrannical Spanish monarchs. This discontent inspired the Eighty Years' War, Dutch independence, and the establishment of the city's status as a refuge for all of Europe's religiously persecuted. The 17th century was Amsterdam's golden age, when the city was the center for world-wide trade in an unchecked era of exploration and colonization. Yet though merchants brought Amsterdam wealth, they also introduced the **Bubonic Plague** (1663-1666) to the city. This epidemic would eventually kill 10% of the population. Amsterdam's mayors, exhibiting all the effectiveness and usefulness we've come to associate with local government, advised strongly against the consumption of salad, spinach, or prunes and instead recommended increased consumption of tobacco to protect against the plague.

In the European tradition, Amsterdam's self-destructive tendency toward war led to it's downfall in the 18th and 19th centuries. After decades of fighting economic rivals England and France, however, Amsterdam rebuilt itself during the **Industrial Revolution.** This development wasn't without growing pains, though, as new jobs in the city attracted peasants from the countryside who soon made up a militant socialist base. Violence between protesters and police became something of a weekly affair, with all the old crowd showing up in the all old places for some good old-fashioned face-offs between the Proletariat and The Man.

Perhaps having had its fill of violent conflict, the Netherlands remained neutral during WWI, though it couldn't escape the effects of the war when food became scarce. During WWII, Amsterdam was occupied by the Germans, who deported more than 100,000 Jews, including, famously, **Anne Frank.** The formerly robust diamond trade, which had been run mostly by Jewish business and craftspeople, dissolved after the Jewish community disappeared.

Amsterdam was reborn in the 1960s and '70s during its cultural revolution. Soft drugs became legal (yes, we got there in the end), anarchists and squatters laid claim to the streets, and yuppies took over neighborhoods previously home to the working class. This last development marked an important transition in Amsterdam's economy from industry to service and sparked the growth of wealth and finance in the city.

Demographics in Amsterdam have also changed remarkably in the past century. Now, nearly a third of residents are from non-Western countries, predominantly those of the Middle East and Northern Africa. Cultural tensions accompanied the early days of immigration but have been mollified, largely successfully, with the imposition of strict and far-reaching social tolerance laws and harsh measures against those that disturb the peace.

CUSTOMS AND ETIQUETTE

We know you're expecting some culture shock in the Red Light District, but there's plenty to be aware of in (ahem) your slightly more "professional" encounters with Amsterdam natives.

Upon being introduced to someone, a firm handshake is customary, though close friends greet each other with three kisses, *comme le style français.* When sharing a meal, it is still common for men to wait for women to be seated. Soft drugs and prostitution may be legal in Amsterdam, but abusers and law-breakers are punished harshly.

HOLIDAYS AND FESTIVALS

HOLIDAY OR FESTIVAL	DESCRIPTION	DATE
Queen's Birthday	A day of national pride. Orange clothing and street parties everywhere. Not the queen's real birthday.	April 30
WWII Remembrance Day	A solemn day to remember the Netherlands's WWII dead. A moment of silence is observed.	May 4
Liberation Day	A day of public *fêtes* to celebrate the country's liberation from Nazi occupation. Controversy often erupts over Dutch appeasement of their conquerors.	May 5
National Windmill Day	Windmills throw open their doors, and many have special (often educational) events.	2nd Tuesday in May
Amsterdam Gay Pride	Three days of tolerance and partying, with a parade and street festivals for all sexual orientations.	Early August
Aalsmeer Flower Parade	Flower floats, flower art, and flowery music in the world's flower capital.	Early September

HOLIDAY OR FESTIVAL	DESCRIPTION	DATE
High Times Cannabis Cup	One long tokefest. At the end of the festival, awards are given to the best hash and marijuana.	November
Amsterdam Leather Pride	The premier gathering for "leather men." Features fetish parties and a lot of leather outfits.	November
Sinterklaas Eve	Dutch Santa Claus delivers candy and gifts to nice Dutch children. The naughty ones are kidnapped (hope you're on the nice list).	December 5

ART

Amsterdam is world-renowned for its art, and with good reason. Dutch painters were responsible for the departure from the International Gothic style, the development of the Northern Renaissance, the perfection of oil painting, and the solution to global hunger (well, maybe not yet, but give them time).

Van Eyck is one of Amsterdam's most well known painters. He was among the first to effectively utilize oil paint as a medium, impressing the art world with his attention to architectural details. Perhaps at times one to lose the forest for the trees, Van Eyck's work often neglected perspective. His paintings are featured in Amsterdam's Rijksmuseum.

Bosch's departure from the Flemish painting style prevalnt in Van Eyck's work seems to have carried him toward surrealism, 400 years before the Surrealist movement is recognized as beginning. Though his paintings are inspirational in their revolutionary technique, Bosch often featured fantastical demons and gruesome depictions of humanity without morality.

When the Church ended its tradition of funding religious paintings during the Reformation of the 17th century, Dutch painters began to experiment with other kinds of subject matter, capturing images of daily life and everyday people on canvas. These paintings are generally surprisingly small in size, as they needed to be marketed to wealthy patrons for display in their homes rather than large church alters.

Of course, the Golden Boy of Amsterdam's Golden Age had to be **Rembrandt.** Initially celebrated by his compatriots, when Rembrant's art took an experimental turn, he was alienated by his clientele. By the mid-1600s he had declared bankruptcy and was living in poverty. Though his style evolved, all of Rembrant's paintings are marked by their masterful realism as well as their attention to elements of light and dark that add interest and emotion to his scenes. Most of Rembrant's work is displayed in the Rijksmuseum.

Vermeer, Rembrant's extraordinary contemporary, is celebrated for his attention to detail, which adds life and refreshing honesty to otherwise ordinary scenes of 17th-century Dutch life. Among Vermeer's most renowned works is *Girl with a Pearl Earring.* Sometimes hailed as the *Mona Lisa* of the north, this remarkable canvas deserves to be valued on its own terms and can be viewed at the Mauritshuis.

ARCHITECTURE

Amsterdam itself is something of an architectural miracle. The city's proximity to water forced architects to be creative—canalside houses were built with many large windows to help reduce the weight of the buildings constructed on top of unstable topsoil and were designed to be exceptionally narrow because of lack of space. Homes were often built at frightening angles to allow large pieces of furniture to be hoisted through windows without hitting the buildings. The hooks that served as pulleys still stick out from just about every canal house, and some are still used today.

BRUSSELS

After cavorting with hash and hookers in Amsterdam, most students see Brussels as a dull hub of Eurocrats, a place to go hole up and detox from Holland just long enough to pass the parents' drug test. That's a mistake. Scratch beneath this city's surface, and you'll uncover an endearingly odd local culture and increasingly relevant sociopolitical scene. Not every city in Europe is collectively enamored with not one, not two, but *three* centrally located statues preoccupied with urinary expulsions (we're obsessed with you too, oh Manneken Pis). Not every city in Europe is purportedly home to the world's best beer, chocolate, waffles, *and* fries. And not every city in Europe can be its capital—there can only be one, and it's Brussels. So find a cure for that Holland hangover fast, because this city's a lot more than a parliamentary pit stop.

Brussels is admittedly a small city, and many visitors only spend a few days exploring its cobbled streets and quirky museums. You should certainly visit the "classics," such as the **Manneken Pis** and the **Grand Place,** but we also urge you to head farther afield. Get lost in the eclectic **Marolles flea market** or the utterly brilliant **Magritte Museum**. We hope you're not actually coming here to cool down after Amsterdam, because with all its Belgian beers and bangin' bars, Brussels is bound to up the ante and your alcohol tolerance.

greatest hits

- **WAX PHILOSOPHIC** Grab a glass of strawberry wine and talk philosophy at Goupil le Fol (p. 152).

- **YOU CAN HAZ CHOCOLATE?** Belgian chocolate is famous for a reason. Head on down to the Musée du Cacao et du Chocolat (p. 131) in the Grand Place to debunk some of those myths you've heard about your favorite guilty pleasure.

- **TIME TO GET SURREAL** Feed your inner art enthusiast with the works on display at the Magritte Museum (p. 135).

- **THE HORROR, THE HORROR.** Examine Belgium's legacy of colonialism, war crimes, and human rights activism in the Musée Royal de l'Afrique Centrale (p. 139).

orientation

LOWER TOWN

Most visitors to Brussels stick around the **Grand Place,** drawn to the dozens of beer and jazz bars in its environs. But the Lower Town has more to offer you than tourist traps and cheap booze—with local markets and museums, independent bookstores, bars, restaurants, and important sights, this area's bubbling with activity from the side streets to **Ste.-Catherine.**

That being said, the neighborhood's still centered around the Grand Place. The main Metro stop here is Ⓜ**Bourse,** which is within walking distance of the historic center. To the north is **rue Neuve,** a central shopping district filled with clothing outlets and fast food. East of the Bourse is **Place St. Géry,** where you will find some of Brussels's trendy terrace bars. A walk from the Place down **rue St.-Christophe** will take you to the seafood-heavy area of Ste.-Catherine. **Boulevard Anspach** runs directly past the Bourse, and can be used to reach the Marolles area in the Upper Town to the south, or Place Rogier and Le Botanique to the north.

UPPER TOWN

The Upper Town stretches to the north, east, and south of the Grand Place and Lower Town. Renowned for its museums, refined shopping districts, and expensive restaurants, this area was bound to have less nightlife than the Lower Town. Though it's still home to some of Brussels's bigger clubs, they're not necessarily Brussels's best, so travelers should stay closer to the Grand Place for a decent bar scene. Fortunately, the Upper Town is within walking distance of the center, and you can swing by the Lower Town for drinks after a visit the Upper Town's churches and galleries without too much trouble.

The Upper Town is quite spread out, splits into additional neighborhoods, and is difficult to navigate on foot. **Rue Royale** runs parallel to **rue Anspach** from Ⓜ**Botanique** past the **Parc de Bruxelles,** and into the historic neighborhood known as **Beaux-Arts.** The neighborhood is chock full of museums, galleries, and grand palaces—not to mention home of the **Belgian Parliament.** Farther east is the **Avenue des Arts** and **Boulevard**

brussels

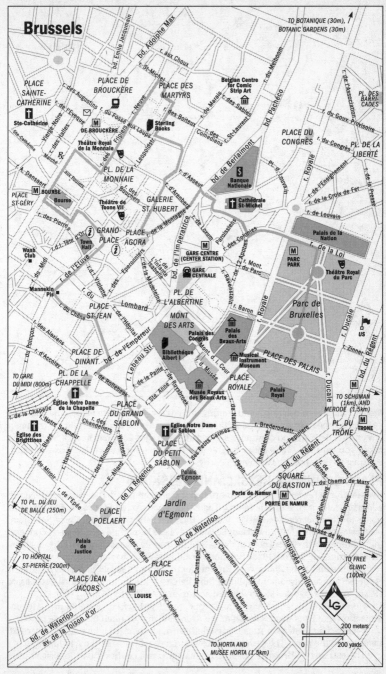

Brussels

PLACE SAINTE-CATHERINE
Ste-Catherine
PLACE DE BROUCKÈRE
PLACE DES MARTYRS
Belgian Centre for Comic Strip Art
PL. DES BARRI-CADES
r. du Gouv. Provisoire
PLACE DU CONGRÈS
PL. DE LA LIBERTÉ
DE BROUCKÈRE
Sterling Books
Théâtre Royal de la Monnaie
PL. DE LA MONNAIE
Banque Nationale
Cathédrale St-Michel
PLACE ST-GÉRY
BOURSE
Bourse
GALERIE ST. HUBERT
Théâtre de Toone VII
Palais de la Nation
Wash Club
GRAND-PLACE
PLACE AGORA
Town Hall
GARE CENTRE (CENTER STATION)
GARE CENTRALE
PARC PARK
Théâtre Royal du Parc
Mannekin Pis
PLACE ST-JEAN
PL. DE L'ALBERTINE
Parc de Bruxelles
US
PLACE DE DINANT
MONT DES ARTS
Palais des Congrès
Palais des Beaux-Arts
PLACE DES PALAIS
TO GARE DU MIDI (800m)
PL. DE LA CHAPPELLE
Bibliothèque Albert I
Musical Instrument Museum
PLACE ROYALE
Palais Royal
TO SCHUMAN (1km), AND MERODE (1.5km)
Église Notre Dame de la Chapelle
Musée Royaux des Beaux-Arts
Église des Brigittines
PLACE DU GRAND SABLON
Église Notre Dame du Sablon
PL. DU TRÔNE
TRONE
PLACE DU PETIT SABLON
Palais d'Egmont
Porte de Namur
PORTE DE NAMUR
SQUARE DU BASTION
TO PL. DU JEU DE BALLE (250m)
PLACE POELAERT
Jardin d'Egmont
Chaussée de Wavre
TO HÔPITAL ST-PIERRE (200m)
Palais de Justice
PLACE JEAN JACOBS
PLACE LOUISE
TO FREE CLINIC (100m)
LOUISE
TO HORTA AND MUSEE HORTA (1.5km)

TO BOTANIQUE (30m), BOTANIC GARDENS (30m)

0   200 meters
0   200 yards

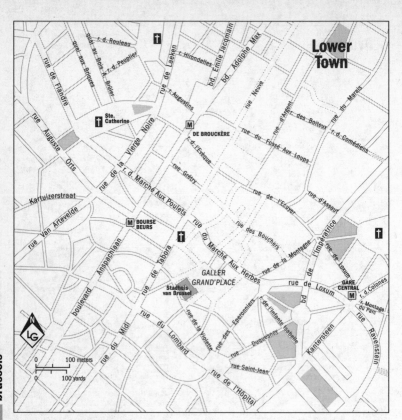

Régent, which also run north and south. South of the Beaux-Arts area is the **Boulevard de Waterloo** and **Avenue de la Toison d'Or;** the lucrative **Avenue Louise** is right off the main street. Bld. de Waterloo continues around and becomes **Boulevard du Midi,** which then takes you through the **Marolles** neighborhood, a run-down area that poses a sharp contrast to the opulent Av. Louise nearby.

PLACE SCHUMAN, HEYSEL, AND OUTSKIRTS

Brussels has a few areas worth exploring that aren't directly in the center and require a longer walk or ride on the Metro. The EU centers around **Place Schuman,** which is home to the **European Commission** and the **European Parliament.** From Place Schuman, **rue Archimède** runs north to **Ambiorix Square** and **rue de la Loi** runs east to west, connecting Schuman with ⓂArts-Loi to the west and the **Parc du Cinquantenaire** to the east. **Rue Froissart** runs south from Place Schuman, leading to **Place Jourdan,** a square with a few restaurants and pubs and a very European crowd. **Parc Léopold** is nearby; behind it is the European Parliament building, and behind Parliament is **Place du Luxembourg** (PLux to the EU workers), the busiest square in the EU area.

Home to the Atomium and Mini-Europe, the **Heysel** area consists of one large intersection that runs from ⓂHeysel to the Atomium, and through into **Parc de Laeken.**

Boulevard du Centenaire runs north-south through the Atomium and into **Place St. Lambert** and the park. The **Avenue de l'Atomium** runs east towards the A12 highway.

The **outskirts** of Brussels covered in this guide are centered on the **Simonis** area

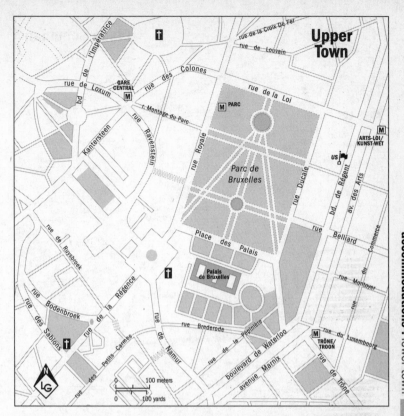

and the **Basilica** located there. From ⓜ**Simonis, Boulevard Léopold II** runs westwards towards the Basilica, and features a large green park area. If you continue east along the road, you will head back toward Rogier and the center of Brussels.

accommodations

Accommodations in Brussels fill up quickly, especially during the week. Thanks to the EU Parliament, expensive and lucrative hotels have sprung up throughout the city, making a cheap hotel even harder to find. Most student-friendly accommodations are slightly north of the **Grand Place**; five of the city's most prominent hostels are within walking distance of the Lower Town. Rooms in the Upper Town get much more expensive, especially if you don't stay in a hostel. Many hotels offer cheap weekend rates, and prices are slashed by nearly 50% when the EU Parliament isn't in session in July and August. Book in advance, especially when Parliament's in session.

LOWER TOWN

🏨 SLEEP WELL ⬥♿(ⁱ)⌇ HOSTEL ❶
23 rue du Damier ☎02 218 50 50 🖳www.sleepwell.be
Sleep Well has two options: hostel or hotel. Both are bright, cheerful, and cheap,

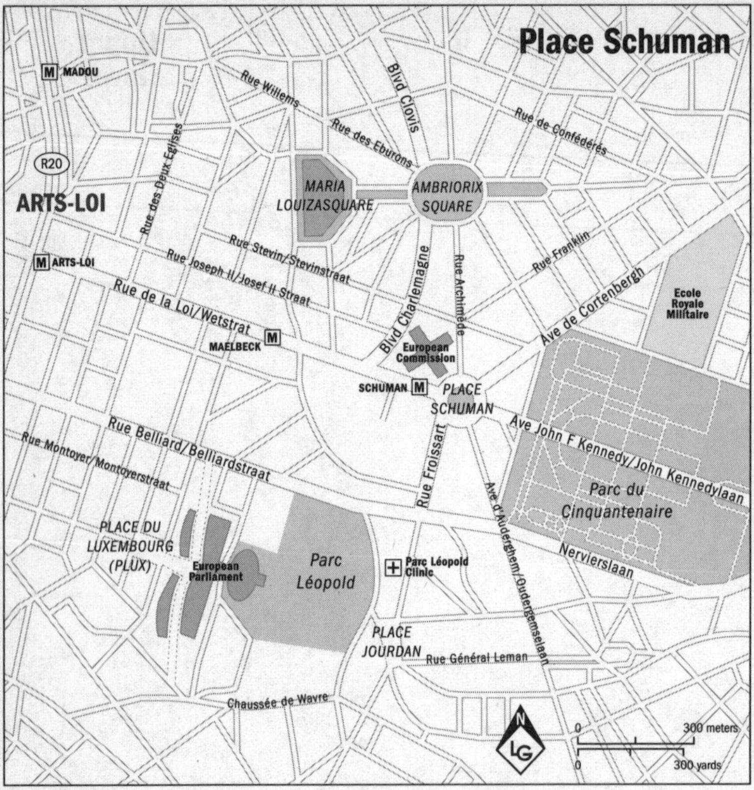

though the hotel option has a few extra perks, including no lockout and ensuite bathrooms. But you might as well save the money and head to the hostel; an ensuite really isn't worth an extra €20. In keeping with Brussels tradition, the hostel is covered in murals and caters to families, groups, and the lone traveler. The bar downstairs stays busy until closing, so even if you're returning from a night's bar crawl in the center you can continue to sample the local beer until the wee hours.
*⇞ [M]Rogier. Follow rue Neuve and take a left onto rue de la Blanchisserie. Rue du Damier is on your right. **i** Breakfast included. Sheets provided; towels available for rent. Wi-Fi €1.50 per 15min. [$] Dorms €19-23; singles €35; doubles €52. 🕐 Reception 24hr. Lockout 11am-3pm.*

2G04 HOSTEL — HOSTEL [1]

99 Bld. Emile Jacqmain ☎02 219 30 19 www.2go4.be

2go4 doesn't really look or feel like your typical European hostel. Its strict no-large-groups policy has made it a haven for young solo travelers and students. Shared spaces like the funky common room and the well-trafficked communal kitchen are great places to meet other travelers. Head out with your new friends for a night in Brussels's main town, only a short walk away.
*⇞ [M]Rogier. Follow Bld. d'Anvers and take a left onto Bld. Emile Jacqmain. **i** Sheets provided; towels available for rent. Max. 6 people per group. No school groups allowed. Rooms have either ensuite or communal bathrooms. Free tea and coffee. Wi-Fi and free internet corner available. [$] Dorms €21-29; singles €50-55. 🕐 Reception 7am-1pm and 4-10pm.*

GENERATION EUROPE

🛏🛜 HOSTEL ❶

4 rue de l'Eléphant   ☎02 410 38 58 💻www.aubergesdejeunesse.be

Located in a thriving immigrant neighborhood, Generation Europe is a 10-15min. Metro ride or a 20min. walk outside the Lower Town, but the hostel's stunningly low prices more than make up for the inconvenience. Rooms are big and spacious, and the dorms come with desks, lockers, and shelves. The lounge areas and communal kitchen provide travelers with numerous opportunities to meet other guests. The area isn't especially dangerous at night, but it's probably best not to walk alone.

🚇 ⓂComte de Flandre. Head east, past the police station, and turn left onto rue de l'ecole. Keep walking along this road and turn right onto rue Chaussée de Grand. Take the first left, which leads onto rue de l'Eléphant. *i* Breakfast included. Sheets included; towels available for rent. Wi-Fi €1.50 per 1hr. Ⓢ Dorms €16-20; singles €32-34. 🕐 Reception 24hr. Lockout between 11am-2:30pm.

ROYAL HOTEL

🛏🛜 HOTEL ❸

8 Bld. Jardin Botanique   ☎02 218 32 18 💻www.royal-hotel.be

This small hotel slightly north of the Grand Place offers simple rooms for a lower price than many of the big chains around the Rogier area. The rooms feel a bit worn down and are in need of a new paint job, but the price and location make up for the faded decor. The bathrooms look modern and are a decent size. There are only a few rooms, so be sure to reserve in advance.

🚇 ⓂRogier. *i* Wi-Fi available. Ⓢ Singles €45-50; doubles €60. 🕐 Reception 24hr.

HOTEL LE GRAND COLOMBIER

🛏🛜 HOTEL ❸

10 rue du Colombier   ☎02 223 25 58 💻www.hotelseurop.com

With a fantastic graffiti mural across the street from the entrance, Hotel Colombier is the better of the two adjoining hotels on this little side street. Although the walls are a bit faded, and the winding staircase will likely give you a headache, the rooms are some of the largest you will find in this price bracket. Many even come with (non-functioning) marble fireplaces. The colorful interior makes up for the building's drab exterior, and the rooms facing the street have a brilliant view of the graffiti mural.

🚇 ⓂRogier. Just off of rue Neuve. *i* Breakfast €5. Wi-Fi available. Ⓢ Singles €55-65; doubles €59. 🕐 Reception 24hr.

HOTEL ABERDEEN

🛏🍴 HOTEL ❸

4 rue du Colombier   ☎02 223 52 58 💻www.hotelseurop.com

Hidden down a tiny side street, Hotel Aberdeen neighbors Hotel Colombier, and also boasts a great view of the tasteful and artistic graffiti mural that covers the wall opposite the hotels. The hotel has less character than Hotel Colombier (read: no defunct marble fireplaces), but provides good value rooms with plush beds and a view of the street. Cheaper rooms with a little less comfort are available for a reduced price. The location puts you right next to Brussels's busy shopping district.

🚇 ⓂRogier. Just off of rue Neuve. Ⓢ Singles €55; doubles €65. 🕐 Reception 9am-6pm.

RÉSIDENCE LES ECRINS

🛏🛜 HOTEL ❹

15 rue du Rouleau   ☎02 219 36 57 💻www.lesecrins.com

The extremely friendly Dutch owner of this hotel will welcome you into his home with pride and a large smile. One building offers studio apartments, complete with a bathroom, kitchen, and lounge area; the other seven rooms provide more conventional hotel accommodations, and are both spacious and creatively decorated. The Tintin posters on the wall and the local artwork for sale in the dining room really give this place a homey feel, helped along by the very lively, English-speaking owner.

accommodations • lower town

⋕ Ⓜ Ste.-Catherine. *i* Breakfast included. Wi-Fi available. Ⓢ Singles €80; doubles €90; triples
€125. Apartments €125 per day. Ⓩ Reception M-F 7:30am-10pm, Sa-Su 8am-10pm.

HOTEL ESPERANCE

⦁(φ) HOTEL ❹

1-3 rue du Finistère   ☎02 219 10 28 ✉www.hotel-esperance.be

Concealed above a French-style brasserie, the Hotel Esperance is in a sense a bit
of a crap shoot; each of its 11 rooms has been individually decorated with bright
blocks of color, and you could either find yourself in a very calming blue room
or a room with garish purple walls. Each room is furnished with grand chairs or
desks, and the beds come with enough pillows to keep a family of 20 comfortable.
The standard rooms, although a little less lavish than their superior counterparts,
will still provide some comfort at a lower price. Breakfast can be enjoyed in the
very quaint dining area that also serves as a restaurant in the evening.

⋕ Ⓜ De Brouckère. *i* Breakfast €10. Free Wi-Fi. Ⓢ Singles €80; doubles €110. Ⓩ Reception 24hr.

WELCOME HOTEL

⦁(φ) HOTEL ❹

23 quai Bois à Brûler   ☎02 219 95 46 ✉www.hotelwelcome.com

Welcome to the Welcome Hotel, a doorway to the rest of the world. The hotel
was once the "smallest hotel in Brussels," and although that is no longer the
case, it is certainly the most interesting hotel Brussels has to offer. Every room
is named after a country of the world, and the decor is designed to reflect that
country. The oriental Japanese room or the lavish Zanzibar suite will provide you
with a bedroom and bathroom experience like no other hotel you have stayed in.
Such a quirky residential experience comes at a price, and Hotel Welcome will
stretch many budgets, but if you're planning to shell out some cash, it ought to
be for something special.

⋕ Ⓜ Ste.-Catherine. Ⓢ Doubles €135, on the weekend €100. Ⓩ Reception 7am-11pm.

HOTEL OPERA

⦁(φ) HOTEL ❹

53 rue St. Grétry   ☎02 219 43 43 ✉www.hotel-opera.eu

This peaceful little hotel will make you forget that the busy Grand Place is a
stone's throw away from your front door. The rooms are simply furnished, and
some have a view of the little streets below. The friendly gentleman at the reception will help you with restaurant suggestions and maybe even a recommenda-
tion for a show at the opera house down the road—after all, what else would you
expect from Hotel Opera?

⋕ Ⓜ Bourse. Ⓢ Singles €75-85; doubles €95-110. Ⓩ Reception 24hr.

HOTEL ST. MICHEL

⦁(φ) HOTEL ❹

15 Grand Place   ☎02 511 09 56 ✉www.hotelsaintmichel.be

Talk about being right in the center of the action. Hotel St. Michel is smack dab
in the middle of the Grand Place and boasts some beautiful views of this busy
square—for a price. Cheaper rooms at the back of the hotel have less enticing
views, but they'll still put you right in the heart of Brussels's sights and nightlife—
even if you can't see them.

⋕ Ⓜ Bourse. Directly in the Grand Place. *i* Breakfast included. Free Wi-Fi. Ⓢ Rooms €65-105,
with view €120-150. Ⓩ Reception 24hr.

APRT'HOTEL CITADINES

⦁(φ) APARTMENT BUILDING ❹

51 quai Bois à Brûler   ☎02 221 14 11 ✉www.citadines.com

If you're preparing for a long stay in Brussels, or maybe just looking to stay in an
apartment rather than a hostel or a hotel, Citadines will sort you out. Each of the
three areas of the building—aptly named Brussels, Strasbourg, and Luxembourg—
provide standard and superior apartment suites. The longer your stay, the cheaper
your daily rate, so these accommodations are really only ideal for long-term travel-
lers. The apartments are large and spacious with a kitchen, television, and sofa.
The cheaper apartments substitute a bed for sofa-bed to save on space.

♯ ⓂSte.-Catherine. *i* Breakfast €13. ⓈApartments for up to 4 people €85-170 per day; studio for up to 2 people €68-135. Rates depend on length of stay. ⓏReception 24hr.

HOTEL CHANTECLER
♥♦(ɸ) HOTEL ❸

26 rue de la Grande Ile   ☎02 512 11 52 ■www.hotel-chantecler.be

When checking into this hotel, you'll be surprised by the big size of some of the rooms on offer, but the location and the facilities mean that you'll pay a little more. Though nothing special beyond its size, the hotel puts you in walking distance of the busy Place St. Géry, where Brussels's best bars can be found. Like many hotels in Brussels, special rates can be applied if you call to enquire.

♯ ⓂBourse. Just off of Place St. Géry. *i* Breakfast €9. Wi-Fi €4 per hr. Ⓢ Singles €90-100; doubles €100-120. Ⓩ Reception 24hr.

UPPER TOWN

▨ JACQUES BREL
♥♦(ɸ)⚲ HOSTEL ❶

30 rue de la Sablonnière   ☎02 218 01 87 ■www.laj.be

Surprisingly lively, Jacques Brel provides a modern bar and lounge in its reception area. Although the stairwell is a bit drab, the rooms are comfortable, priced for the student traveler, and not nearly as boring as the exterior suggests. Some of the rooms come with well-furnished ensuite baths, but be warned that some of the bigger dormitories may not be worth those couple of euros you'll save. It's located right next to Le Botanique, one of Brussels's most diverse concert spaces, and a 20min. walk from the Grand Place.

♯ ⓂBotanique. Head south down rue Royale (away from Botanique) and take the first left. *i* Breakfast and sheets included. Free Wi-Fi and computer units in reception. Booking at least 4 weeks in advance is recommended. Ⓢ 6- to 14-bed dorms €16.40; 3- to 4-bed dorms €18.50. Singles €32; doubles €45. €2 extra for ages 26 and older. Ⓩ Reception daily 7am-midnight. Lockout noon-3pm. Code access after 1am.

▨ BRUEGEL
♥♦(ɸ)⚲ HOSTEL ❶

Heilige Geeststraat 2   ☎02 522 04 36 ■www.youthhostels.be

Bruegel has one of the most important amenities a hostel can have: a ■**brilliant bar.** This hostel hangout looks like a watering hole you would find in the city center, and stays open until all the guests have gone to bed. Finish out your night with some dancing and karaoke. The rooms here are basic and decent-sized. Only some have ensuite bathrooms, but the communal bathrooms really aren't that bad. Each of the three floors has a lounge or seating area with free Wi-Fi.

♯ ⓂGare Centrale. Head west along Bld. de l'Empereur. Bruegel is opposite the skate park. *i* Sheets included. Free Wi-Fi. Some wheelchair-accessible rooms available upon request. Ⓢ 3- to 4-bed dorms €18.90. Singles €31; doubles €46. €1.20-4 extra for ages 26 and older. Ⓩ Reception 7-10am and 2pm-1am. Lockout 10am-2pm.

VINCENT VAN GOGH CENTER—CHAB
♥♦(ɸ) HOSTEL ❶

8 rue Traversière   ☎02 217 01 58 ■www.chab.be

Between the lack of light, drab exterior, and rickety and uncomfortable beds in the dorms, this hostel feels a little like a prison. Compared to most hostels, though, the communal bathrooms are clean and modern, and you're free to come and go as you please—Van Gogh doesn't feel the need to put a curfew on its residents. The location situates you near some awesome museums and Le Botanique, a brilliant local concert venue, so there is some light at the end of the tunnel. When you really do feel like you're behind bars, go outside and take in the beautiful sights of the Botanic Gardens.

♯ ⓂBotanique. Head north along rue Royale, past La Botanique, then turn right onto rue Traversière. *i* Breakfast and sheets included. Ages 18-35 only. Wi-Fi €2 per hr. Ⓢ 8- to 10-bed dorms €18.50; 6-bed €20.50; 4-bed €21.50; 3-bed €27.50. Singles €33.50; doubles €53. Ⓩ Reception 24hr.

HOTEL SABINA
78 rue du Nord

📶(𝗉) HOTEL ❸

☎02 218 26 37 🖥www.hotelsabina.be

This quaint little guest house isn't your typically bland budget Brussels hotel, nor is it your average sickeningly bright youth hostel. Hotel Sabina's classy ornamented hallways and simple stairwell will keep you comfortable and well-rested. The singles here aren't too big, but the simple furnishings and clean bathrooms will make you feel at home during your stay in the city. Doubles are slightly bigger and just as pretty.

✛ Ⓜ️Botanique. Head south along rue Royale. Turn left up rue de la Sablonnière, which leads to rue du Nord on your right. *i* Breakfast included. Free Wi-Fi. Ⓢ July-Aug singles €45; doubles €55. Sept-June singles €70; doubles €80. 🕐 Reception 7am-11pm. Code access after 11pm.

HOTEL GALIA
15-16 Place du Jeu de Balle

📶(𝗉) HOTEL ❸

☎02 502 42 43 🖥www.hotelgalia.com

This hotel is perfect for bargain hunters, but not necessarily because of the prices or the hotel itself. Hotel Galia is ideally situated near the daily Marolles flea market, which starts up around 4am—when the best bargains in the city can be found. Once you've snagged that €3 antique necklace, you can take your pre-sunrise purchase back inside the hotel and catch up on sleep in the small but well-furnished rooms. The open terrace area is also a great place to watch the hagglers in the market. Watch out for the rendition of Tintin that guards the reception desk.

✛ Ⓜ️Louise. Head along rue des Renards until you hit Place du Jeu de Balle. *i* Breakfast included. Free Wi-Fi. Ⓢ Singles €65; doubles €75. 🕐 Reception 24hr.

HOTEL ARISTOTE
5 Av. de Stalingrad

📶(𝗉) HOTEL ❷

☎02 513 13 10 🖥www.aristote-hotel.be

Come to Aristote to question your own existence, the meaning of "goodness," or why Belgians spell "Aristotle" without the "l," but the most important question you'll be asking yourself is how this hotel can afford to charge so little per night. Aristote finds itself at the lower price range without sacrificing quality of service. The small and simple rooms have a charming decor.

✛ Ⓜ️Anneseens. Head toward Place Rouppe, then head south down Av. de Stalingrad. *i* Wi-Fi €2 per hr. Free computer in reception. Ⓢ Singles €50; doubles €70. 🕐 Reception 24hr.

sights

LOWER TOWN

🏛 MANNEKEN PIS
STATUE

Intersection of rue de l'Étuve and rue du Chêne

Prepare to be pretty under whelmed but pretty amused by the icon of Brussels: a little boy taking a pee into a pond below. This little statue, whose real origins are not known, is one of Brussels's most famous monuments, and he is continually swamped with visitors who stand by his basin in various poses, one of the most popular being to cover his stonely manhood with a hand so that it does not show in the picture. The Manneken likes to celebrate certain national holidays and events, or even just indulge the weird happenings and habits of Brussels; hundreds of Elvis fans once congregated at his feet as he donned his blue suede shoes and classic white jacket. For true insight into the enigma that is the Manneken, start up a conversation with the souvenir vendor directly in front of the sight—he's been there for over 20 years and has some interesting stories to tell. Though, in his own words, the little boy doesn't cause much trouble. Despite his nudity, he is otherwise polite, well-mannered, and pleased to see the whole world coming to visit him.

public indecency

Fortunately or unfortunately, *Manneken Pis* is not one of those expressions in a foreign language that sounds hilarious but would be insensitive to mock—it means precisely what you might expect. Literally translated as "The Little Man Peeing," *Manneken Pis* is one of Brussels's most celebrated landmarks. The current bronze version of the *Manneken Pis,* which has been around since 1619, was designed by Jerome Duquesnoy, but it is commonly held that a stone version of the statue existed before the current bronze model, perhaps dating as far back as 1388.

There's a boatload of stories about how *Manneken Pis* came into being. One story recounts the exploits of the 2-year-old Belgian Lord Godfrey III of Leuven, whose troops were fighting against the Berthouts of Grimbergen; the precocious tot, who was hung from a tree in his cradle in order to inspire his troops, proceeded to pee on the Berthouts, who eventually lost the battle. Another version of the story involves a wealthy merchant who, on a visit to Brussels with his family, lost track of his son; miraculously, his son was found joyfully urinating in a small garden, and the wealthy merchant commissioned the sculpture in celebration of being reunited with his mischievous offspring.

Regardless of how it got there, *Manneken Pis* is absolutely worth seeing when traveling in Brussels. Located on the corner of rue de l'Étuve and rue du Chêne, the statue is often dressed in an elaborate costume, of which there are over 800. The costumes, which are changed multiple times a week, commemorate important dates in Belgian history, celebrate members of the Belgian working class, or represent the national dress of countries whose tourists regularly pass through the city. Unsurprisingly, there are times when water is not the only thing spouting forth from *Manneken Pis,* as the fountain is occasionally transformed into an elaborate beer-tap, much to the delight of passers-by (soon to be passers-out).

Due to the statue's high profile, it has been stolen 7 times, but has each time been returned safely to its fountain-top perch. For everyone's sake, make sure that *Manneken Pis* is the only one peeing into his fountain—control your intake of Belgian beer and ensure that you do not become the drunken tourist who defaces this important piece of Belgian heritage. It's only cute if you're bronze.

sights • lower town

▨ MUSÉE DU CACAO ET DU CHOCOLAT ⊛ MUSEUM
9-11 rue de la Tête d'or ☎02 514 20 48 ▣www.mucc.be

It is impossible to miss the smell of chocolate that flows out of this small museum just off of the Grand Place. Opened in 1998 by Jo Draps, the daughter of one of the founders of Godiva chocolate company, the Musée du Cacao et du Chocolat is a chocoholic's dream (or worst nightmare if it's Lent). Fresh milk chocolate is churned in the entrance, where you can taste both warm and cold chocolate before proceeding to watch the English-speaking chocolate chef work his magic (and of course taste the results). The museum also aims to promote the role of cacao in the development of chocolate, as so many people do not know about its origin or uses (did you know the Aztecs used cacao as a form of currency?). Although Godiva was sold to the Americans in the 1970s, the museum has been kept in the family and is currently run by Jo Drap's daughter. For those worried about the potential side effects of their chocolate consumption, head up to the third floor to bust some myths about your favorite foodstuff: chocolate does *not* cause acne! Well then, choc's away...

✦ ⓜBourse. Just south of Grand Place. ⓢ €5.50; students, seniors, and ages 12-16 €4.50; under 12 free with parent. ⌚ Open Tu-Su 10am-4:30pm.

GRAND PLACE   SQUARE
Grand Place

The historical center of Brussels is a very grand place known, naturally, as the Grand Place. Standing in the middle of the square, you'll find yourself surrounded by the breathtaking architecture. Soak up the grandeur in one of the square's many cafes, where you can sip coffee and watch the tourists plow on through with their cameras. Don't make the same mistake they often do—look *up* as well as around. The really interesting, intricate architecture is above you, not in front of you. Grand Place really lets down its hair at night, so you should definitely come back and explore once the sun goes down. The famous **Guildhall buildings,** including the **Hotel de Ville** and the **Maison de Roi,** are dramatically illuminated. During mid-August every year, the Grand Place is home to the "Flower Carpet," where green-thumbed Belgian gardeners create a design with colorful native fauna.

✦ ⓜBourse. Head straight down rue de la Bourse, which leads to the northeast corner of the square.

if they only had a brain...

In a city with traditions and festivals that are centuries old, the Scarecrow Festival's 10 years of existence seem relatively insignificant. But when Belgians host a festival, they host it right, and this annual event is no exception. Founded in 2001 as a way to draw more tourists and raise money for local charities, the **Scarecrow Festival** happens every October in the **Grand Place** in Brussels. If you thought that watching The Wizard of Oz was going to prepare you for this Belgian tradition, think again. Ranging from hilariously creative to incredibly frightening, past scarecrows have included Che Guevara, David and Goliath, and the Devil himself.

If you happen to be feeling particularly inspired, everyone is invited to participate. Simply pay your registration fee of €50 and you'll be provided with a 2m. by 2m. square in which to craft your masterpiece. As far as the rules go, anything goes—just make sure that your scarecrow is neither offensive nor a threat to you or those around you (except crows). If your scarecrow is deemed to be prize-worthy, you may even end up with a monetary award for your creativity.

SCIENTASTIC   ✦ MUSEUM
Bourse Metro Station   ☎02 732 13 36 🖳www.scientastic.be

Don't be put off by the location of this brilliant museum—although many of Brussels's homeless hang out in the Bourse Metro station, the museum's a load of fun. Head downstairs and follow the large, colorful signs to the Scientastic, which from the outside looks a bit like a fortune teller's tent. The museum's goal is to make science fun, interactive, and accessible for both kids and adults, and the curators have succeeded in making this more than just another science museum. Every visitor can try a "freebie" visit before deciding to pay for the entrance or not (!!). Make sure you try out the Manneken Pis recreation to discover how water actually flows, and experiment around with color shadows. The very comical ◙**"mirror performance"** demonstrates the magic of reflections, as the tour guide uses various illusions to appear to float, shrink, explode, and even stab himself. Young children and uncoordinated adults should take care not to try the tricks at home.

✤ Ⓜ*Bourse. Head toward the Anspach exit and follow the signs for Scientastic. ⓘ English-speaking tour guides and English walkthrough guide available. Ⓢ €7.70, under 26 and seniors €5.20. ☒ Open M-Tu 10am-5:30pm, W 2-5:30pm, Th-F 10am-5:30pm, Sa-Su 2-5:30pm.*

MUSÉE DE LA VILLE DE BRUXELLES (LA MAISON DU ROI)   ● MUSEUM
Grand Place   ☎02 279 43 55 ◙www.bruxelles.be

The dignified building that houses the Musée de la Ville de Bruxelles is arguably a bigger deal than the museum itself. La Maison du Roi (or King's House) was originally built in the 13th century both to demonstrate the power of the prince of Belgium and to serve as an economic center for the city, with a bustling meat hall, wool hall, and cloth hall. Since rebuilt and renovated, the building now houses exhibits on the history of the town, the renovation of Brussels, and even a special homage to the infamous **Manneken Pis.** Make sure to check out the stone remains from the original building on the first floor, which demonstrate the intricacies of the building's design. Climb staircases guarded by knights in shining armor to reach a room with model replicas of 13th-century Brussels, not to mention a series of small port windows, which provide a brilliant view of the Grand Place below. But the highlight of the grand museum has to be the display on the top floor of the numerous outfits that the Manneken Pis wears throughout the year. Look for a country of your choosing and prepare to be charmed (or horribly offended) by this little boy's attempt to represent the culture.

✤ *In the northeast corner of Grand Place. Ⓢ €3, students and seniors €2.50, ages 6-15 €1.50, under 6 free. ☒ Open Tu-Su 10am-5pm.*

FONDATION JACQUES BREL   ✎ MUSEUM
11 Place de la Vieille Halle aux Blés   ☎02 511 10 20 ◙www.jacquesbrel.be

If you love Belgian music, or just love the Belgian singer Jacques Brel, this exhibition at the Jacques Brel Foundation will make for a perfect afternoon out. If you are asking yourself, "Who is this guy?" better spend some more quality time with the Manneken Pis. But for those of you who *ne quitteriez pas* M. Brel will find themselves very much at home in this exhibition, which recreates the childhood home where Jacques recorded his albums, and even presents interviews with some of his closest friends and family. Diehard Brel fans can also take a walking tour of the city to visit some of the places where Jacques stayed, visited, or made an impact during his time in Brussels.

✤ *150m from the Manneken Pis, along rue du Chêne. ⓘ Audio tours in French only. Written guides available in English. Ⓢ Walk and audio tour €8, exhibition and audio tour €5. ☒ Open July-Aug daily 10am-6pm; Sept-June Tu-F 10am-6pm, Sa-Su noon-6pm.*

JEANNEKE PIS   STATUE
Off rue des Bouchers

The poor lonely sister of Manneken Pis is locked away behind bars down a tiny alley and not even listed by the Tourist Office in its official guides—where are women's rights activists when you need them? Jeanneke Pis shows no shame as she squats down to do her business in a small pond. Local lore has it that if you throw a coin into Jeanneke's puddle, the statue will bring you good luck in your personal relationships. Only in Brussels would these dots connect. This quirky alternative to Brussels's beloved Manneken was conceived by Denis Adrien Debourvrie in 1985 and actually aims to promote Cancer Research. Visitors to the sight are encouraged to donate to a cancer research charity if the Jeanneke Pis brought some happiness into their life. So throw a penny in the pond for good fortune and feminism, then dig a little deeper when donating to the cause this young girl promotes in the most eccentric of ways.

[M]Bourse. Just off rue des Bouchers. Take a right after Chez Léon.

HÔTEL DE VILLE HISTORIC BUILDING

Grand Place ☎02 279 20 10

Dating from the Middle Ages, the Hôtel de Ville's Gothic tower can be seen from anywhere in Brussels and is one of the city's most photographed sights. Be sure to get a look inside via one of the guided tours. The main courtyard features two grand fountains of Poseidon near the entrance, and the tour will take you around some of the building's most beautiful rooms. On weekends it is common to see weddings taking place at the Hôtel de Ville, so keep a look out for the bride and groom posing on the balcony for their wedding photos (then do the typical tourist thing and take your own photo of the happy couple). Throughout the year there are also expositions in the building that you can visit after your guided tour.

[M]Bourse. Next to Tourist Info. $ €3, students €2.50. ⏰ Tours Tu, W, Su afternoons.

ÉGLISE ST. NICOLAS CHURCH

1 rue au Beurre ☎02 513 80 22

This very grand church was built around 1000 years ago, when the city of Brussels was founded, but all that remain of the original edifice are some 12th-century archways and the main nave from the 13th century. The far transepts house three ornate altars. The first is dedicated to the Virgin Mary and encrusted in gold; the second is the High Altar, built in Louis XVI style, and the altar on the far right is dedicated to St. Nicolas himself. The most recent addition to the church was made during its last renovation in 1956, when Guy Chabrol designed a stunning stained glass window depicting the Assumption of the Virgin Mary.

[M]Bourse. Just behind the Bourse building. $ Free. ⏰ Open daily 10am-4pm. Mass in English Su 10am.

BOURSE HISTORIC BUILDING

Palais de la Bourse, Bld. Anspach

By the 19th century, Brussels was ready for an upgrade. And we're not talking the cell phone kind. As part of a commercial and architectural renewal plan, they traded their oh-so-glamorous butter market for a stock market, and today's Bourse is still home to the Belgian Stock Exchange. Designed by LP Suys, the Neo-Renaissance building lies on Brussels's busy commercial thoroughfare, **Boulevard Anspach.** Nowadays the steps to the Stock Exchange are often the sleeping place for some of Brussels's less desirable inhabitants, but Auguste Rodin's lion sculptures and impressive ornamentation are usually squatter-free.

[M]Bourse. i Not generally open to casual visitors.

ÉGLISE SAINTE CATHERINE CHURCH

Place Ste. Catherine ☎02 513 34 81

This beautiful church lies at the north end of Place Ste. Catherine, and it's the crowning jewel of this little Brussels neighborhood. The original 12th-century chapel went the way of the butter market (see Bourse) and was rebuilt and expanded upon in the 19th century. The current church was in turn threatened with demolition in the 1950s, when city officials wanted to replace it with a parking lot. Fortunately, the building was saved, but the renovations it so desperately needs have yet to be completed. Inside is a rather impressive 15th-century statue of the Virgin and Child, which locals rescued from the Seine in 1774 after Protestants chucked it away.

[M]Ste.-Catherine. $ Free. ⏰ Open M-Sa 10am-5pm, Su 10am-mid-afternoon.

L'ARCHANGE

MURAL

rue des Charteux

Elaborate murals and cartoons checker the walls of Brussels's winding streets. Some are intelligent designs painted by professional artists; others consist of SpongeBob SquarePants hastily scrawled on metal shutters. L'Archange is a less obvious example of the former. You'll only notice if you look up at the right place. The beautiful mural is hidden in the rooftops and, from afar, might be mistaken for an actual addition to the building.

✢ ⓜBourse. Head down rue Auguste Orts and take the first left onto rue des Charteux. Mural opposite building 42.

ZINNEKE

STATUE

rue des Charteux

Seriously, Brussels? This humorous addition to the city's peeing posse is, to say the least, a rather absurd sight to behold. At the intersection of rue des Charteux and rue du Vieux Marché, there's a bizarre statue of a dog doing his business on a post. Tom Frantzen, a Flemish sculptor, is the barking mad creator of the Zinneke, which is supposed to embody the irreverent spirit of the city. Perhaps it just means people (and dogs) in Brussels really just can't hold it in.

✢ ⓜBourse. Head down rue Auguste Orts and take the 1st left onto rue des Charteux. The Zinneke is on the corner of the street.

ÉGLISE NOTRE DAME DE FINISTÈRE

CHURCH

rue Neuve   ☎02 217 52 52

It's not every day that you find a delicately restored 18th-century church sandwiched between an H and M and a McDonald's, but this is Brussels, after all. Église Notre Dame de Finistère is situated in the center of Brussels's bustling commercial area and boasts a lavish Baroque interior. The church's grand altar portrays Moses holding the 10 Commandments, and artwork from the 16th-18th centuries depicts various religious moments. For those who enjoy organ music, the church offers free concerts on Mondays.

✢ ⓜDe Brouckère. Head east along rue du Fossé aux Loups and turn left onto rue Neuve. Ⓢ Free. Ⓒ Open daily 10am-5pm. Organ concerts M 12:45-1:30pm.

BREWER'S HOUSE

BREWERY, MUSEUM

10 Grand Place   ☎02 511 49 87 ▣www.beerparadise.be

This "museum" will take your money and leave you disappointed. The Brewer's House is only for the true beer fanatic, and even then you might get slightly annoyed. Even the tasting at the end can't salvage it. The exhibit that plays a video (in French) about beer would be interesting—if it wasn't spliced with random clips of chefs using beer. The rest of the museum consists of a few tanks that model how beer is distilled and an original 18th-century beer cellar. Save your €6 and spend it on the ☐final product instead.

✢ ⓜBourse. In the Grand Place. Ⓢ €6, students €5. Ⓒ Open daily 10am-5pm.

UPPER TOWN

🔲 MAGRITTE MUSEUM

✎ MUSEUM

3 rue de la Régence   ☎02 508 32 11 ▣www.musee-magritte-museum.be

The Magritte Museum will be one of the most enjoyable, educational and fascinating museum trips you make in Brussels, and maybe in Europe at all. The museum opened just last year, and until recently tickets had to be booked in advance to ensure you got a spot in line. Now that the crowds aren't as big, swing by and prepare to be amazed. Start your tour at the glass elevator; four Magritte paintings of a man, each at varying stages of completion, are mounted vertically on the opposite wall, and appear to eerily blur together as the elevator rushes by. Each of the museum's three floors conveys a period in the Belgian artist's life through a collection of paintings, drawings, and primary sources (translated into English) that convey the true genius of the man. Make sure you check out the collection of hand-drawn images, compiled by Magritte, Scutenaire, Hamoir and Nougé, in which each of the friends took turns drawing a different limb or cross-section of the human form—without looking at what their colleagues had drawn previously. The results are insightful and brilliant to look at. The audio tour is a very well-compiled and informative guide to this fascinating museum.

♯ ⓜParc. *i* *Audio tour in English €4. Combined ticket with Beaux-Arts €13.* ⓢ *€8, students €2, seniors and groups €5, 18 and under free.* ⌚ *Open Tu 10am-5pm, W 10am-8pm, Th-Su 10am-5pm.*

MUSÉES ROYAUX DES BEAUX-ARTS
MUSEUM

3 rue de la Régence   ☎02 508 32 11 ▣www.fine-arts-museum.be

Brussels's collection of fine art is split into two sections; ancient and modern. A ticket to the Musées Royaux des Beaux-Arts gets you access to both areas. Jan Fobre's massive globe towers over the museum's illustrious lobby; it is crawling with green and blue scarabs, providing a sample of the masterpieces showcased here. The museum's modern arts section displays some of the most mind-boggling works from the 19th-21st centuries, including provocative paintings and sculptures that will either fascinate you or make you wonder why you bought a ticket. The true highlight of the museum is the new ▧**Magritte Museum,** an homage to a modern master if ever there was one, which is housed in the same building complex. Head upstairs for the ancient arts, including a permanent collection called "Art and Finance," which examines historical figures and portraits. Before you head away from the area, make sure you visit the adjacent ▧**Garden of Sculptures,** filled with statues and sculptures watching over you as you eat your lunch.

♯ ⓜParc. *i* *Free first W every month after 1pm.* ⓢ *€8, students €2, under 18 free. Combined ticket with Magritte Museum €13.* ⌚ *Open Tu-Su 10am-5pm.*

CATHÉDRALE DES STS MICHEL ET GUDULE
CATHEDRAL

15 rue du Bois Sauvage   ☎02 217 85 45

Although the Cathedral was only granted status as such in 1962, the building before you has a marvelous history spanning over a millennium and several restorations. The original foundations of Cathédrale des Sts Michel et Gudule date back to the ninth century (more recent areas of the foundation can be seen in the crypt for €1). In the 11th century, the building was rebuilt over a 300-year period and heavily influenced by Gothic architecture. Beginning in the mid 1980s and ending in the late '90s, the Cathedral underwent extensive renovations again, restoring the stone work to its original splendor. As you wander through the cathedral, gaze up to the statues of the saints guarding the walls. Each holds an item symbolizing something from the Christian faith: St. Philippe, for example, holds the book of knowledge, while St. Peter possesses a set of golden keys.

♯ ⓜGare Centrale. ⓢ *Free. Crypt €1 Donation. Free choir concerts throughout the year.* ⌚ *Open M-F 7:30am-6pm, Sa-Su 8:30am-6pm. Mass in French Su 10am, 11:30am, and 12:30pm.*

MUSÉE DU JOUET
⊛ MUSEUM

24 rue de l'Association   ☎02 219 61 68 ▣www.museedujouet.eu

The slogan of this toy museum is *"un musée qui s'amuse"*—a museum which will amuse you. Although more valuable items are stored behind glass cabinets, this is a museum where you can let your inner child free. Children will have fun playing with the toys, while the adults (especially those older than 30) can nostalgically remember childhood classics. Many of the exhibits feature hands-on toys from days gone by, including marbles, dolls, teddy bears, and car sets. Some of the rooms are particularly brilliant, including the marionette puppet area, the teddy bear school, and toy robot section. Find the massive brown bear perched on top of a house.

⇄ Ⓜ Botanique. Just off of rue Royale. $ €5.50; students, children, and seniors €4.50. ⏰ Open daily 10am-noon and 2-6pm.

BOTANIQUE BOTANICAL GARDENS

Botanique

These beautiful gardens span 6 hectares of land and provide the ideal spot to catch a bit of sun or take a break during the summer. The numerous private enclaves are a welcome break from the touristy city center. Grab a drink at the cafe *(open daily 10am-8pm)* and sit on the terrace overlooking the gardens, or go for a stroll round the fountains and lake. The Botanic Gardens also has a concert venue on its terrace, where up-and-coming European and American artists entertain local students and concertgoers.

⇄ Ⓜ Botanique. $ Free. ⏰ Open daily Oct-Apr 8am-5pm; May-Sept 8am-8pm.

MUSICAL INSTRUMENTS MUSEUM (MIM) ★ MUSEUM

2 montagne de la Cour ☎02 545 01 30 🖥www.musicalinstrumentsmuseum.be

If you have the slightest interest in music, the history of instruments, or just cool art deco buildings, you should get yourself on down to the MIM. This museum just celebrated its 10th anniversary, and the 10 floors of its collection features impressive interactive exhibits, though not every floor has something to look at. A large glass elevator leads to the top floors and the rooftop restaurant, which boasts a panoramic view of the city. The main exhibits move from the fourth floor downward and host interactive displays on keyboards, strings, and western art music—there's even a sound lab. The most ingenious part of the museum is the audio tour, which, instead of being vocal, is just ♫**music.** The interactive headphones will pick up the music of the instrument you're looking at. Very cool.

⇄ Ⓜ Parc. $ €5, under 26 €4, under 13 free. ⏰ Open Tu-F 9:30am-4:45pm, Sa-Su 10am-4:45pm.

CENTRE BELGE DE LA BANDE DESINÉE ★ MUSEUM

20 rue des Sables ☎02 219 19 80 🖥www.cbbd.be

Don't expect to find Marvel or DC on the shelves of this comic book museum, dedicated to the likes of Tintin and Boulle and Bill. If these names mean nothing to you, then you might as well not bother. The Moomins currently rule the roost in this exhibition space.... OK, if that name's also drawing a blank for you, then this definitely isn't the museum for you. But if those names excite you to your international inner comic book nerd core, then the Centre Belge de la Bande Desinée may be your new home. With a Smurf statue, a bust of Tintin, and the famous red-and-white rocket from the Tintin series all just in the lobby, the comic book excitement begins before you even get into the permanent collection. The display is continually changing, but you can expect classic French and Belgian comic strips in both original and remastered form. Real comic book nerds head downstairs to the library, where you can read as many comics as you want, or pop next door to the bookshop where you can purchase your own to take home with you.

⇄ Ⓜ Rogier. $ €7.50, ISIC holders and ages 12-18 €6, under 12 €3. ⏰ Open Tu-Su 10am-6pm.

BOZAR ★ EXHIBITION SPACE

23 rue Ravenstein ☎02 507 82 00 🖥www.bozar.be

A center of innovation and discovery, Bozar puts on exhibitions ranging from art, to history, to geographical concerns. The modern arts space holds numerous exhibitions at once, as well as a cinema and different music festivals. Although the 2011 season had yet to be announced at time of printing, you can expect exhibits along the lines of this past year's "Visionary Africa," which celebrated the culture and heritage of African countries through its art. For a great view of the city, head up to the roof of the building once you exit, past the Bozar studios, and along the metal staircase.

✡ Ⓜ*Parc.* Ⓢ *Generally €5-10, but admission depends on event. Student rates available.* ☒ *Box office open July-Aug M-F 11am-5pm; Sept-June M-Sa 11am-7pm. Exhibits open Tu-W 10am-6pm, Th 10am-9pm, F-Su 10am-6pm.*

PARC DE BRUXELLES   PARK
Between Belgian Parliament and Royal Palace

Walk the perimeter of what is arguably Brussels's most beautiful park and view the **Palace of the Nation** and other beautiful monuments, or head inward for the trees and foliage. Joggers dominate the dirt tracks at all hours, so take care not to get mowed down. Luckily, there are plenty of places to escape the healthy crowd. The wide green patches, benches, and fountains make the park an ideal place to stop and have a picnic lunch, or just to rest your feet after a busy morning walking around the surrounding museums.

✡ Ⓜ*Parc.* ☒ *Open daily 7am-11pm.*

PALAIS DE LA NATION   GOVERNMENT BUILDING
16 rue de la Loi   ☎02 549 81 36

The line of very grand buildings opposite the **Parc de Bruxelles** is in fact the home of Belgium's most important political decision makers. During the week you can take a free guided tour around the rooms of the **Parliament**, but you must call in advance to ensure there is an English-speaking guide to accommodate you. The tour will take you through the many grand rooms of the palace, as well as explain the ins and outs of Belgian politics. You never know—you might just pass the Belgian Prime Minister walking through the grand corridors of the palace.

✡ Ⓜ*Parc.* ⓘ *Call in advance to arrange a tour.* Ⓢ *Free.* ☒ *Tours M-Sa 10am-4pm.*

BELVUE   ✒ MUSEUM
7 place des Palais   ☎070 22 04 92 ▣www.belvue.be

Through a selection of videos, artwork and even '60s clothing models, the BelVue's grand exhibits will better acquaint you with Belgian history, from its independence in the 19th century through to its current position as the "capital of Europe." Perhaps more for the history buffs amongst you, but the museum does have some interesting exhibits, especially the section on the recent developments of the European Union since WWII. The museum also houses a few free exhibits, ranging in media from artwork to photography.

✡ Ⓜ*Parc.* Ⓢ *€8, ages 18-25 €5, under 18 free.* ☒ *Open Tu-F 10am-5pm, Sa 10am-6pm.*

ROYAL LIBRARY   LIBRARY, PANORAMIC VIEW
4 Bld. de l'Empereur   ☎02 519 53 11 ▣www.kbr.be

The Royal Library not only houses a copy of every book published in Belgium but also boasts one of the best free views of the Upper Town area. Head into the library and straight for the elevators on the second floor. Once in the elevator, take it to the fifth floor. The cafeteria here will remind you of the one at your old high school, but the phenomenal view outside the wall-sized windows will be at least 12 times better than the view you had of your high school parking lot. Lots of local students hang out here and study for their exams or just read a book. It's a great place for photo ops or grabbing a cheap cup of tea and enjoy the view.

✡ Ⓜ*Gare Centrale.* Ⓢ *Free.* ☒ *Open July-Aug M-F 9am-5pm; Sept-July M-F 9am-7pm, Sa 9am-5pm.*

PARC ET PALAIS D'EGMONT   PARK
Bld. Waterloo

The grand Palace of Egmont is surrounded by beautiful gardens, ideal for a stroll after some heavy duty retail therapy in the fashionable Louise area. Now the home of Belgium's Ministry of Foreign Affairs, the palace is closed to the public, but the fountains and trails of the gardens are open daily for the public. This spot is off the main road and through a tunnel-like pathway, so many people miss it and walk straight by. Make sure you don't.

✣ ⓂLouise. Gardens just off of Bld. Waterloo. Palace on rue aux Laines. Ⓩ Park open daily 8am-9pm.

ÉGLISE ST. JACQUES

Place Royale

CHURCH
☎02 511 78 36

You would be forgiven for thinking that the facade of this church looks like a Greco-Roman Temple; Église St. Jacques's six Corinthian columns look more like a cross-section of the Parthenon than a Christian place of worship. Stepping inside, the columns continue throughout the church and the Corinthian columns surround the nave and transept. The church is filled with religious artwork, including two large pieces by Portaels: "Consummatum est" and "Venite ad Me Omnes." As you leave, look out for the two large statues of David and Moses in the peristyle.

✣ ⓂParc. ⑤ Free. Ⓩ Open Tu-Sa 1-5:45pm, Su 9am-5:45pm. Mass in French Su 9am.

PLACE SCHUMAN

🖾 MUSÉES ROYAUX D'ART ET D'HISTOIRE

10 parc Cinquantenaire

⚓ MUSEUM
☎02 741 72 11 🖳www.mrah.be

This exceptional museum covers a lot of historical ground, so be prepared to cover a lot of ground on foot through the endless exhibits. Immerse yourself in the civilizations of the Aztecs and Egyptians before moving on to the extensive Roman exhibits, which include a wide range of artwork, skeletal remains, and archaeological discoveries. Not all the signs in the museum are written in English, but the collection still lends great insight into the historical periods on display. Make sure to check out the Easter Island section, which showcases one of the island's famous and massive stone heads, before heading over to the medieval and Islamic art sections. The museum could take up a whole morning, and then some. Chances are you won't feel the time pass at all.

✣ ⓂSchuman. In the far southwest corner of Parc Cinquantenaire. ⑤ €5, students and under 18 €4. Ⓩ Open Tu-F 9:30am-5pm.

MUSÉE ROYAL DE L'AFRIQUE CENTRALE

13 Leuvensesteenweg

⚓ MUSEUM
☎02 769 52 11 🖳www.africamuseum.be

Although reaching this museum requires taking a 30min. tram ride from the city center, both the journey and the museum itself are well worth the trouble. The tram ride to the museum cuts through the suburbs of Brussels, and the view from the window provides a peaceful glimpse of the beautiful green forests that surround them. When you arrive at the Tervuren terminus, you walk through a luscious green park to reach the grand entrance of the museum. The walk itself is almost worth the price of admission. Built in 1910, the Musée Royal de l'Afrique Centrale was originally intended to celebrate the successes of Belgian expansion into the Congo. The systematic enslavement and mutilation of 20 million people has since become frowned upon (an estimated 50% of the Congo's population was killed under King Léopold II's reign), and today the museum works to showcase Africa's natural and cultural histories instead, as well as raise awareness about colonial exploitation. For a focused look at current African culture and concerns, make a stop at one of the temporary exhibits, which examine all aspects of the continent, including recent wars of independence. Make sure you try an African dish at the cafe.

✣ Line 1 to ⓂMontgomery or tram #44 to Tervuren. ⑤ €4, students and under 18 €1.50, under 13 free. Temporary exhibits €6-9; student discounts available. Ⓩ Open Tu-F 10am-5pm, Sa-Su 10am-6pm.

AUTOWORLD

◆ MUSEUM

Jubelpark 11   ☎02 736 41 65 ▣www.autoworld.be

Take a spin through Autoworld for a historical tour of the motor car and a large display of some of the world's oldest and newest cars. Racing cars, futuristic models and WWI jeeps sit side by side in what looks like a converted car warehouse. This is definitely one for car lovers, but if you don't know your Citron from your Clio then maybe sit this one out. Drive full speed ahead to the end of your visit, making sure you take in the ingenious car body made of wood and the plastic car shell.

✈ Ⓜ*Schuman. Head through the Arcade du Cinquantenaire and it's on your right.* ⑤ *€6, students €4.70, ages 6-13 €4, under 6 €2.25.* ☼ *Open daily 10am-6pm.*

ATOMIUM

◆ HISTORIC BUILDING

Square de l'Atomium   ☎02 475 47 77 ▣www.atomium.be

For many, it is the most horrific eyesore of the Brussels's skyline; for others, it is a stroke of architectural genius. Built for the World Expo in 1958, this structure was designed by André Waterkeyn to resemble the atom of an iron crystal—just 165 billion times bigger. The resulting structure is over 100m high, and one of the highlights of visiting the Atomium is a trip to the top in Europe's fastest elevator. As you ascend at 5m per second, you might feel your stomach do a little jump while you take in the panoramic view around you. But the Atomium isn't just a great place for a view of Brussels. Five of the nine spheres of the building are open for you to explore; collectively, they host a restaurant, permanent and temporary exhibits, and a cafe. The permanent collection is a walk through the history of Expo '58 and the Atomium's construction. Temporary exhibits often focus on science and European culture.

✈ *Take Line 6 to* Ⓜ*Heysel.* ⑤ *€11, students and ages 12-18 €8, ages 6-11 €4, under 6 free. Audio tour €2.* ☼ *Open daily 10am-6pm.*

MUSÉE ROYAL DE L'ARMÉE ET D'HISTOIRE MILITAIRE

MUSEUM

3 parc du Cinquantenaire   ☎02 737 78 33 ▣www.klm-mra.be

This grand museum is absolutely massive, and you can easily get lost among the weapons and swords on display. Make sure you step left, left, left, right, left as you march down the halls lined with busts of former army generals and commanders and explore battle strategies ranging from 19th-century tactics to modern warfare. Be sure to check out the old army airplanes hanging overhead. The museum is free, so even if you just spend 30min. wandering around its grand halls, it's worth the visit.

✈ Ⓜ*Schuman. Head through the Arcade du Cinquantenaire and it's on your left.* ⑤ *Free.* ☼ *Open Tu-Su 9am-4:30pm.*

PARC DU CINQUANTENAIRE

▣ PARK

This is one of Brussels's beautiful places, with long green lawns and benches for you to lounge on in the sun. The park is home to what you might mistake for the *Arch de Triomphe;* it is in fact Brussels's very own *Arcade Cinquantenaire*, complete with four stone horses drawing a chariot. A walk east along the park will bring you to Autoworld, the Musée Royal de l'Armée et d'Histoire Militaire, and the Musées Royaux d'Art et d'Histoire, which means that, even if it rains, you have somewhere to shelter (especially the *free* Military Museum). During the summer, bright green deck chairs are dotted round the park, making for a perfect picnic or sunbathing spot.

✈ Ⓜ*Schuman. At the bottom of rue de la Loi.*

NATURAL HISTORY MUSEUM

◆ MUSEUM

29 rue Vautier   ☎02 627 42 38 ▣www.natuurwetenschappen.be

If you're looking to keep the kids entertained, or if you just love dino-skeletons

brussels

140 ◗   www.letsgo.com

and fake **mammals,** then this museum should be on your list. Belgium has had a strong connection to dinosaurs since the very first fossilized skeleton was discovered in Belgium in the 19th century; it is now on display in the museum. The North and South Pole exhibitions are also entertaining, with stuffed polar bears and penguins ideally positioned for photo opps. Interactive and hands-on exhibits make visiting the museum even more enjoyable.

[M]Schuman. Head through Parc Léopold and follow the signs to rue Vautier. [S] €7, students €6, ages 6-17 €4.50, under 6 free. Open Tu-F 9:30am-5pm, Sa-Su 10am-6pm.

MINI-EUROPE — MINIATURE CITY

Bruparck ☎02 474 13 13 www.minieurope.eu

If you backpacked around Europe but never really got to all the countries, or if you like feeling extremely tall, then you should make a stop at Mini-Europe. Although the park is aimed more at families with small children, Mini-Europe still has something to offer the student traveler. Wander around and press the blue buttons, which play the national anthems of various countries, make cars and miniature people move, and even make bulls run around a stadium in the Spain display. Pose comically in front of famous landmarks such as the Eiffel Tower and Big Ben, and make sure you watch the miniature reenactment of the tearing down of the Berlin wall. The park is bright, fun, and cheerful—if you want to see the whole of Europe this summer, why not get it done in just one afternoon?

[M]Heysel. [S] €13.10, under 12 €9.80. Combination tickets with Atomium €22.40, under 18 €19.60, under 12 €12. Open daily July-Aug 9:30am-8pm; Sept 9:30am-6pm; Oct-Jan 10am-6pm; mid-Mar-June 9:30am-6pm.

EUROPEAN PARLIAMENT — GOVERNMENT BUILDING

60 rue Wiertz www.europa.eu

Although most of this tour involves watching a portable video explaining the inner workings of the EU and the Parliament, you might get **lucky** (or plan properly) and visit on a day when Parliament is actually in session and having full debates. If they are, make sure you sit in and grab a pair of headphones and witness the amazing skills of the institution's translators—all 24 official languages of the EU are readily available, and these people translate the debate more or less in real time. The tour itself can be a bit dull, especially if you're stuck looking at an empty room, but the architecture and artwork in the building are cool, and a trip to the capital of Europe is not complete without a visit to the room where all the decisions are made.

[M]Schuman. Walk through Parc Léopold and head to the northeast corner. Look for the visitor's entrance sign on rue Wiertz. [S] Free. Tours M-Th 10am and 3pm, F 10am, Sa-Su 10am and 3pm; arrive 15min. early.

BASILICA KOEKELBERG — BASILICA

1 parvis de la Basilique ☎02 421 16 67 www.basilique.be

The National Basilica of Brussels is the fifth-largest church in the world, and as you approach the building through its green park you will begin to realize just how stunning the Koekelberg really is. In fact, the Basilica is the largest Art Deco building ever constructed, and it gives a phenomenal panoramic view of the surrounding city. The church interior is grand but simple, and the real highlight of the visit is when you reach the top of the building and see Brussels below you.

[M]Rogier. [S] Panorama €4, students €3. Open daily in summer 9am-5pm; in winter 10am-4pm.

PARC LÉOPOLD — PARK

rue Belliard

Parc Léopold sits right at the foot of the European Parliament; pick a perch on the grassy banks and watch the Eurocrats rush by in their fine suits, scarfing down lunch on the way back to the office. The less manic local suits take to the grass to relax and snack, especially on *frites* bought from Place Jourdan a few meters away. The park was the location of Brussels Zoo until, in 1876, all the animals died; Brussels's historians appear to be fuzzy on the details. Now the only animals there are the pigeons who will try and share your lunch—and the stuffed animals in the Natural History Museum at the top of the hill.

➡ [M]Schuman. 🕐 Open daily until 10pm.

WIERTZ MUSEUM — ART GALLERY

62 rue Vautier — ☎02 508 33 33

Formerly the home of Antoine Wiertz himself, this small house is now a museum that honors his life and works, in conjunction with the Musée des Beaux Arts in the Upper Town. As you climb the steps to the entrance, you get the feeling this gallery isn't going to be too overwhelming, but a step into to the back room is enough to knock the wind out of you—the high ceiling allows some of Wiertz's most fantastic and apocalyptic work to tower formidably over visitors. A smaller room off of this exhibit houses some of his smaller pieces and sketches; many of these pieces are routinely sent off to temporary exhibits in Paris and the rest of the world, so it is not uncommon for some of his smaller works to be missing from the collection.

➡ [M]Schuman. Head through Parc Léopold and follow the signs to rue Vautier. $ Free. 🕐 Open Tu-F 10am-noon and 1-5pm.

PLACE SCHUMAN — GOVERNMENT BUILDINGS

Place Schuman

As you stand in the center of this horrific roundabout, you may wonder what's so special about it. Surprisingly, this hopelessly congested area is where all of the EU's important decisions are made. The European Commission, the governing body that must approve laws made by members of the European Parliament, is located in the cross-shaped building on the square. So is the European Council building, which locals say looks like a sandwich with glass in the middle. Take a moment to note the importance of this bizarre location before leaving to wander through the prettier parks and squares of the EU district.

➡ [M]Schuman.

food

Eating in Brussels can be cheap and inexpensive, which makes the city a student traveler's dream. Locals will even eat out once or twice a week thanks to the inexpensive cost, and Brussels prides itself on quality cuisine. In the Lower Town, *avoid* the tourist traps on **rue du Bouchers.** Cheap *friteries* and waffle stands can also be found all over the city, and supermarkets are plentiful on **rue Neuve.**

LOWER TOWN

👍 PUBLICO — 🥦🍸📶 BELGIAN ❷

32 rue des Chartreux — ☎02 503 04 30 🖥www.publico.be

The combination of cosmopolitan Brussels with traditional food works brilliantly in this spacious restaurant. The young and courteous owner happily guides travelers through a menu of classic Belgian dishes, including *stoemp* (sausage and mashed potatoes) and various meat stews. There are also some tasty vegetarian options available. The weekday *prix-fixe* menu is a ridiculously good deal: it includes *potage*, an entree choice from the menu, and a coffee, all for €11.50. The contemporary art that lines the walls adds a modern edge to this tasty, traditional dining experience.

➡ [M]Bourse. Just off of rue Orts. $ Lunch menu €11.50. Entrees €9-16. 🕐 Open daily 11am-

midnight. Kitchen open M-F noon-3pm and 6pm-midnight, Sa noon-midnight, Su noon-3pm and 6pm-midnight.

◾ IN'T SPINNEKOPKE

🍴 TRADITIONAL, BELGIAN ❸

1 Place du Jardin aux Fleurs　　　　　　　☎02 511 86 95 ▣ www.spinnekopke.be

Spinnekopke (that's "spider's head" in Flemish) might not sound like an appetizing name for a restaurant. But once you take in this rustic tavern's candlelit tables and crowds of locals, you'll know that you've stumbled across something very exciting. Green-aproned waiters will attend to your table with the utmost attention. For a really tasty meal, try one of the many sauces available for their steak *(steak €15.50, with sauce €3)*, including an exceptional cheese, limbic beer and cream sauce.

✝ Ⓜ*Bourse. Head down rue Orts and take a left onto rue des Charteux, which leads to Place du Jardin aux Fleurs. i English menus available. Ⓢ Entrees €12-25. ⏰ Open M-F noon-3pm and 6-11pm, Sa 6-11pm.*

◾ FIN DE SIÈCLE

🍴 BELGIAN ❸

9 rue des Charteux

With a mishmash of tables outside and no name above the door, this traditional Belgian restaurant may seem a little bizarre at first, and you could easily walk past it. But make sure you backtrack and take a step inside Fin de Siècle's airy interior, its walls lined with modern art by local artists. The antique cash register on the bar and the blue mosaic floor provide cutesy complements to the blackboard menu featuring largely traditional fare. Readers with peanut allergies beware, though—most menu items are cooked in or include a peanut oil, including the salad dressing.

✝ Ⓜ*Bourse. Head down rue Orts and then take a left onto rue des Charteux. Ⓢ Entrees €9-20. ⏰ Open daily 6pm-1am.*

CHEZ LÉON

🍴 FRITES ❸

18 rue des Bouchers　　　　　　　　　　☎02 511 14 15 ▣ www.chezleon.be

This popular restaurant spans several storefronts along the very busy *rue des Bouchers*, and it's always a safe option when choosing somewhere to dine. Although there is nothing too exciting or different about Chez Léon, the attentive staff will patiently refill you your water and bread basket while you choose from a menu of *moules frites*, fish, and traditional meat dishes. The restaurant hosts a varied clientele and is impressively family-friendly—with every adult meal you receive a free children's meal (ages 11 and under). The brightly colored walls are lined with photos and some very entertaining cartoons.

✝ Ⓜ*Bourse. Just northeast of the Grand Place. i Appetizers €6-20; entrees €9-25. ⏰ Open M-Th noon-11pm, F-Sa noon-11:30pm, Su noon-11pm.*

LA ROSE BLANCHE

TRADITIONAL ❸

11 Grand Place　　　　　　　　　　　　　　　　☎02 513 64 79

A window seat is a must in the two-story rustic house that hosts La Rose Blanche. Ogling out the window as the tourists pass through the Grand Place is the highlight of a trip to the old-fashioned restaurant, where traditional meat and fish dishes are cooked over a wood fire. The daily special plate will likely stuff you full of some sort of meaty goodness, including lamb or pork, and will be accompanied by an array of veggies, all for just €9.

✝ *In the far south corner of the Grand Place, just past the Tourist Office. Ⓢ Entrees €12-23. Daily special €9. ⏰ Open daily 10am-11pm.*

LE BOURGEOIS

🍴 TRADITIONAL, FRITES ❸

17 rue des Bouchers　　　　　　　　　　　　　　☎02 511 84 45

Though its name suggests otherwise, this cozy little restaurant sandwiched between local tourist traps is anything but pretentious. The doorway is decorated with small sailing ships and guarded by the naughty Manneken Pis; students and local seniors lunch side-by-side beside the burning log fire. Le Bourgeois' daily set menu *(€12)* is a great price for two courses and comes with a wide variety of choices. The restaurant also serves up the classic *moules frites (€12-19)*, which is an average price for this dish. The cheeky waiters will try to use their English to impress you and may even make a few jokes, fortunately not at your expense.

⚑ ⓂBourse. Just north of Grand Place. Ⓢ Set menu €12. Entrees €10-23. ⌚ Open daily noon-midnight.

MOKAFE
🍴♈ CAFE ❶
9 Galerie du Roi
☎02 511 78 70

If you're looking for a good, hearty snack in a grand setting, then the Galleries St. Hubert is your best bet. Lined with shops, cafes, and more expensive restaurants, it's hard to know where your money will go farthest. Skip the expensive restaurants and head for Mokafe, where the host will keep you happy and fed in a rather simple but stylish setting. The menu is full of random treats, like mushrooms on toast, which might be a welcome relief after all those *frites*, mussels, and waffles. Although the cafe is popular with students, pick the wrong time and you may be sharing a meal with some of Brussels older and more eccentric citizens. Sit outside in the evening and watch the shoppers pass by, gazing up in awe at St. Hubert's grand glass ceiling.

⚑ ⓂBourse. Head along rue du Marché aux Herbes, and the Galleries will be at the intersection with rue de la Montagne. Ⓢ Food €3-11. ⌚ Open daily 10am-11pm.

KASBAH
🍴♈ MOROCCAN ❶
20 rue Antoine Dansaert
☎02 502 40 26

Stepping inside the salon of the Kasbah restaurant is like stepping across the sea and into North Africa. The hundreds of lanterns that hang from the ceilings provide the only light in the interior; patrons lounge in the plush chairs at their tables or perch on wooden stools. The numerous teapots and spice jars surrounding the bar give a real Moroccan feel to the Kasbah, but the proof comes in the plentiful dishes. *Tajine* dishes (spicy meat stews) come in generous portions, while the couscous dishes (chicken, lamb, beef, or vegetarian) come complete with a boiling pot of vegetables. Kasbah offers a welcome break from the Belgian classics, and the portions will conquer even the most hungry of travelers.

⚑ ⓂBourse. Head along rue Orts, which leads onto rue A. Dansaert. *i* Couscous also available for takeout. Ⓢ Tajines €13. Couscous €12-17. ⌚ Open daily noon-1pm and 6pm-midnight.

L'ESTAMINET DU KELDERKE
🍴♈ BELGIAN, TRADITIONAL ❸
15 Grand Place
☎02 511 09 06 🖳www.atgp.be

A summer evening seat on the terrace may just be the highlight of L'Estaminet du Kelderke. You can watch the tourists trudging through the illuminated Grand Place while chowing down on the house's special *moules frites*, which come in a very large (and apparently bottomless) bucket. The waiters are dressed to the nines, and they'll give you quality service that won't cost a fortune. The vibes can get very romantic, so we suggest you treat that special someone (or maybe just that new friend at your hostel you've been crushing on) to indulge in night views of the Grand Place.

⚑ ⓂBourse. In the northwest corner of the Grand Place. Ⓢ Entrees €11-23. ⌚ Open daily noon-11pm.

AM TEASPOON
♈ TEA HOUSE, CHOCOLATIER ❶
4 rue des Chartreux
☎02 513 51 31

Situated on the bar-heavy rue des Charteux, this very cute chocolate shop also doubles as a tea house and serves as a welcome break from the beer-swigging and mojito-sipping establishments that surround it. The eccentric decor includes multiple chocolate sculptures of your favorite pissing Belgian boy.

➜ [M]Bourse. Head down rue Orts. $ Sweets €2-5. ⏰ Open T noon-6:30pm, W-Sa 9:30am-6:30pm.

CAFE METROPOLE 🍴🍸 CAFE, BRASSERIE [2]

31 Place de Brouckère ☎02 219 23 84

A night at the Metropole hotel would probably drain your college fund, but you can catch a glimpse of its beautiful interior by settling for its not-so-overpriced cafe instead. The Cafe Metropole really is the brasserie of Brussels's elite; businessmen, politicians, visiting entrepreneurs and the otherwise rich sit out on the street and discuss business, politics, and how to avoid getting paper cuts while making love in a pile of 💵**money.** Join their ranks temporarily by grabbing a coffee and watching the world go by. As an early evening drink, the Italiano cocktail goes down well *(€5.50).*

➜ [M]Brouckerie. $ Hot drinks €4-10. Beer €4-5. Food €5-16. ⏰ Open daily 9am-1am.

QUICK 💳📶 FAST FOOD [1]

101 rue du Marché aux Herbes ☎02 511 47 63 🖥www.quick.be

This French fast-food chain serves you up a burger, fries, and a shake quicker than you can say "What Golden Arches?" Belgium's alternative to good ol' Ronald features classic hamburgers, cheeseburgers, bacon burgers, and chicken meals to keep your stomach full of greasy goodness and your wallet full of hard-earned cash (to spend, of course, on Belgium's finest beers instead). This is the most centrally located Quick of the many in Brussels, and it has free Wi-Fi.

*➜ [M]Bourse. From Grand Place, take the northeast corner to rue du Marché aux Herbes. **i** Free Wi-Fi. $ Entrees €2-6. ⏰ Open M-F 7:30am-11pm, Sa-Su 8:30am-11pm.*

PANOS 🍴 BAKERY [1]

85 rue du Marché aux Herbes ☎02 513 14 43 🖥www.panos.be

Panos is a classic bakery that serves baked goodies to the hungry locals and tourists of Brussels's center. The pastries and baguettes will fill you up nicely, and those of you who want to pick up some daily rations can buy loaves of bread or baguettes from behind the counter. The bursting sandwiches are all under €3, and will keep both your stomach and your wallet full.

➜ [M]Bourse. From Grand Place, take the northeast corner to rue du Marché aux Herbes $ Filled baguettes €2.70-3. ⏰ Open M-F 6:30am-9pm, Sa 7:30am-8pm, Su 7:30am-9pm.

FRITERIE TABORA 🍴 FRITES [1]

4 rue de Tabora

If you're in Brussels, it'd be heresy not to eat *frites.* The famous fried potato is served on every street corner in Brussels, but finding a top-notch *friterie* can prove difficult. Tabora will double fry your *frites* and douse them in a sauce of your choice, from classic ketchup to Samurai sauce. The piping hot fries make for a perfect afternoon snack or, more likely, a brilliant way to end an evening sampling the beers of the local bars.

➜ [M]Bourse. Adjacent to Église St. Michel. $ Small €1.80; large €2.30. Sauce €0.50. ⏰ Open daily 10am-6am.

UPPER TOWN

★ LES SUPER FILLES DU TRAM 💳🍸 BURGERS, TARTINES [2]

22 rue Lesbroussart ☎02 648 46 60

With the tram line running outside and the crazy murals painted onto the walls, this little cafe specializing in burgers is far enough off the beaten track to avoid the tourists, but not so much that you get poor quality food. Make sure you look at the walls to get the full effect of the dream-like Brussels skyline being destroyed by monsters and a massive monkey, and look out for the Atomium blasting off from the disaster. All the burgers come stuffed with delicious fillings and a side of *frites* in a little flower pot. If you fancy a burger challenge, try finishing the Big Joe, which overflows with bacon, cheese, pickles, onions, BBQ sauce and a special house sauce *(€12)*.

 # [M]Louise. Off of Av. Louise, before you reach Place Flagey. $ Burgers and salads €10-14. Tartines €9-12. ⏰ Open M-Sa 10am-11pm, Su 11am-5pm. Kitchen open M-Sa noon-3pm and 6-11pm, Su 11am-5pm.

RESTAURATION NOUVELLE — 🍴 TRADITIONAL ❷

2 rue Montagne de la Cour ☎02 502 95 08 💻www.restauration-nouvelle.be

High atop the Museum for Musical Instruments is a modern-looking restaurant with one of the best views in Brussels. Ascend the 10 stories in the glass elevator, reminiscent of something out of *Charlie and the Chocolate Factory*, and be seated by penguin-like waiters. On a sunny day, make sure to request an outdoor seat, but if the weather doesn't permit, try to get a window seat inside this very expansive restaurant. The view of Brussels from above is breathtaking; you can see as far as the Atomium, the Grand Place, and the Palaces. The menu, considering the setting, is well-priced and has some traditional Belgian dishes as well as a fish dish of the day.

 # [M]Parc. Enter through museum and head up in the elevator. $ Appetizers €10-19. ⏰ Open M-W 10am-4pm, Th-Sa 10am-4pm and 7-11pm, Su 7-11pm.

LE PERROQUET — 🍴 CAFE ❶

31 rue Watteeu ☎02 512 99 22

A stained-glass window of a parrot sets the tone for this Art Deco cafe, popular with the locals and flying under the normal tourist's radar. Locals flock here for one reason: the stuffed pitas. With a menu of over 30 different pita fillings—traditional, vegetarian, adventurous, fruity—your every pita desire will be fulfilled. Why not try the Bangkok *(€7)* with chicken, rice, pineapple, and curry? Served up in small baskets and overflowing with fillings, these piping hot pocket snacks will fill you up for a day of exploring the fashion shops of the Sablon area.

 # [M]Parc. i Credit card min. €12. $ Pitas €6-7. ⏰ Open M noon-11:30pm, Tu noon-midnight, Th-Sa noon-1am, Su noon-11:30pm.

THE MERCEDES HOUSE — 🍴 BRASSERIE ❸

22-24 rue Bodenbroek ☎02 400 42 63

Looking for a way to combine your love for cars and Belgian fine dining? Then the Mercedes House Brasserie is the ideal location for a coffee or light lunch. Hot drinks are available *(€2-3)* and can be enjoyed on the terrace outside with shiny silver cars in the background. At lunchtime, you can sample traditional dishes which won't drive away with your money, but the upmarket setting will put you in the driving seat if you're trying to impress the opposite sex (this can work both ways given the car-heavy setting). If you want to really take a spin, order a bottle of champagne at €50 a pop.

 # [M]Parc. i Coffee still served when kitchen is closed. $ Entrees €14-24. Drinks €2-5. ⏰ Open M-Th 10am-5pm, F 10am-5pm and 7-11pm, Sa 10am-5pm. Kitchen open M-Th noon-3pm, F noon-3pm and 7-11pm, Sa noon-3pm.

LES BRASSINS — 🍴 TRADITIONAL, BRASSERIE ❷

36 rue Keyenveld ☎02 512 69 99 💻www.lesbrassins.com

Locals squash into the tightly stacked tables at this quaint Belgian brasserie for traditional dishes and plentiful salads. Turn to the daily specials, such as ribs or salmon salad, for an extra twist to your meal, or look to the old beer plates on the walls for advice on whether to drink a Duvel or down a Kriek. For a real taste of Brussels, give the *stoemp* a try—the massive sausage and mountain of potato will fill you right up.

 # [M]Porte de Namur. Head up rue des Chevaliers, which will lead to rue Keyenveld. $ Entrees

€11-20. ☏ *Open M-Th noon-2:30pm and 6pm-midnight, F noon-2:30pm and 6pm-1am, Sa noon-1am, Su noon-midnight.*

BELGA BELGE
✎❦ TRADITIONAL, BELGIAN ❷

20 rue de la Paix   ☎02 511 11 21 ▣www.belgobelge.be

This modern-looking restaurant serves filling lunches out of a large glass window to Eurocrats, businessmen, and expats. At night, enter into a very calm setting with artwork on the wall celebrating the Belgian heritage of Brussels (note the large three-paneled painting of babies holding the Belgian flag.). Behind the bar, a series of wines are stored on an amusing curved wine shelf.

✚ Ⓜ*Louise.* Ⓢ *Entrees €10-20.* ☏ *Open M-F noon-2:30pm and 6pm-midnight, Sa-Su noon-midnight.*

IL RINASCIMENTO
✎❦ ITALIAN ❸

14 rue Jourdan   ☎02 534 75 20

Just off of Av. Louise, rue Jourdan is full of cafes and eateries where ladies do lunch and businessmen spend 2hr. away from the office, but just because the area is full of the smell of money and fine perfumes doesn't mean the food is out of a budget price range. This traditional Italian restaurant, which still cooks its pizzas by stone oven, will stuff you full of large and well-topped pizzas for a sweet price. If you're in the market for something other than pizza or pasta, Il Rinascimento also has a range of seafood dishes which are slightly more expensive but are just as plentiful as their traditional Italian dishes.

✚ Ⓜ*Louise.* ⓘ *Credit card min. €15.* Ⓢ *Pizzas €8-12. Appetizers €12-22.* ☏ *Open Tu-Su noon-3pm and 6-11:30pm.*

L'AUBERGE ESPAGNOLE
✎❦ TAPAS, BAR ❸

10 Parvis la Trinité   ☎0473 31 59 79 ▣www.auberge-espagnole.be

Although this Tapas bar has the same name as a brilliant French film involving sex, debauchery, and rude English men, the Brussels restaurant version is classier but just as Spanish. Enter the candle lit room with cacti on the bar and a grand piano by the door and take a high seated table to enjoy the various warm and cold tapas available *(€3.60-7.90),* or try the very filling pot of beef chili *(€12).* The area, just off of Av. Louise, is definitely a place to take someone on a date; but be warned, this restaurant (and the area of Ixelles) is very much off of the Brussels beaten track.

✚ Ⓜ*Louise. Take tram #81 to Trinité, or follow Av. Louise, turn right onto Chaussée Charleroi, take a right onto rue de l'Aqueduc and then left onto Parvis de la Trinité.* Ⓢ *Tapas €3.60-7.90. Drinks €2-9. Jug of sangria €15.* ☏ *Open M-Sa 5:30pm-midnight.*

TITANIC
✎❦ SEAFOOD ❷

31 rue du Congres   ☎02 219 99 10 ▣www.titanicbrussels.be

Try not to go overboard in this boat-like restaurant, where the bar is the helm and the dining area resembles something you might find on a ship (though it isn't as grand as the dining room from the famous vessel, it's not as bad as where Jack was eating). Position yourself facing starboard on a table with a world map on it for you to stay oriented, and if you do feel like you might fall in there are life rings positioned around the bar for your safety. Specialties include *scampi martiniquais (€16.50)* and the *entrecôte argentine (Argentinian beef; €18).* Don't expect Celine Dion to be playing in the background and show some respect and refrain from asking for extra ice in your drink.

✚ Ⓜ*Arts-Loi.* Ⓢ *€12-18.* ☏ *Open M-F noon-10pm.*

DELIZ SPRL
✎⁽ᵗ⁾ DELI ❶

34 rue du Congrès   ☎02 203 93 13 ▣www.deliz.eu

This cheap and cheerful deli bar situated near the main museums in Brussels will be a welcome break from the expensive eateries and brasseries of the area.

If you don't want to pay for the overpriced sandwiches in the museum cafe, head a little farther along the street and tuck in to a sandwich, pasta, or omelette made fresh for you. The bright green interior will perk you up even on the most dismal day, and the cafe is one of the only places open on a Saturday afternoon in the area.

✠ ⓜArts-Loi. ⓢ Sandwiches €3.50. Omelettes €6-8. Salads €8. ⓩ Open M-F 9am-3pm, Sa 11am-3pm.

PIXEL
⬤❖ TAPAS ❶

39-41 rue Ernest Allard ☎02 502 20 84 💻www.pixelwinebar.be

This very tiny wine bar (likely named pixel due to its minute size), is a bright and colorful little bar where you can grab hot wraps at lunch time and return for tapas and wine in the evening. The small terrace area is a popular location to munch on your lunchtime snack, which includes both meat and vegetarian options. In the evening the small but sufficient tapas menus includes a variety of meats, wraps, and special delicacies. Considering the area you find yourself in, this is a tiny bargain worth the shot.

✠ ⓜParc. ⓢ Tapas and wraps €3-6. ⓩ Open daily noon-10pm.

L'OCÉAN
⬤ SEAFOOD ❸

94 Av. Stalingrad ☎02 513 30 38

This fish shop follows a simple business model: come in, choose the fish you want to eat, and they'll fry it up in front of you and serve it in the restaurant next door. They've got more than cod and scrod to choose from here, including five "rare fish" that will set you back a few more euros than normal. If you are after a rather hefty fish lunch you can pay by the kilo (€20), otherwise a plate for one (€3.50) or two (€7) is a better deal. For a real taste of some fine fish and to be able to see what you are eating before it is cooked, head under the sea and visit L'Océan.

✠ ⓜGare du Midi. ⓢ Entrees €3.50-7. €20 per kg; €35 for rare fish. ⓩ Open M-Th noon-2am, F 3pm-2am, Sa-Su noon-2am.

MANO À MANO
⬤❖ ITALIAN ❷

8 rue St. Boniface ☎02 502 08 01

The St. Boniface area has become popular lunch spot for young businesspeople and Brussels's younger crowd. Along this line of eateries, Mano à Mano whips up traditional Italian dishes that you can enjoy on its very pleasant wooden terrace with the church in the background. The setting is top-notch and the pizzas standard, but for the location you find yourself in, you can hardly scoff at the price. At lunchtime, especially in the summer, you may have to fight a man in a tie for the last available seat outdoors, so don't be too late.

✠ ⓜLouise. ⓢ Pizzas €8-12. Pasta €9-13. ⓩ Open M-F noon-2:30pm and 6:30pm-midnight, Sa-Su 6:30pm-midnight.

BIOLOUNGE
⬤❖ ORGANIC, VEGETARIAN ❶

116 rue de l'Enseignement ☎02 218 54 00 💻www.biolounge.be

BioLounge is great if you're looking for an organic or vegetarian lunch option, especially in the middle of the Upper Town. Lunches are available to eat in or takeout, and you can choose from soups, freshly made quiches, sandwiches, wraps, and other daily offerings. Although the prices are a little bit higher than you would normally pay for a sandwich at lunch, every product is made in-house using fine ingredients, so rest assured that you are getting a very healthy lunch indeed.

✠ ⓜMadou. Head down rue du Congrès and turn left onto rue de l'Enseignement ⓢ Lunch €3-7. ⓩ Open M-F noon-3pm.

PLACE SCHUMAN

⬛ CHEZ MOI
⬤ ♈ ⬠ PIZZERIA, BAR ❶

66 rue du Luxembourg ☎02 280 26 66

The innovative pizza bar has indoor, outdoor, and upstairs seating in which you can enjoy dirt-cheap slices of pizza (without any dirt in them). Avoid the expensive eateries in and around the EU area and just join the other young workers on the grass of Place du Luxembourg as they devour their slices. The daily menu changes regularly, but expect all the standards like mushroom, pepperoni, and vegetarian.

✠ Ⓜ*Maelbeek* *i* *Takeout and delivery also available.* Ⓢ *Slices €2-3.50.* Ⓩ *Open M-W 11am-11pm, Th-F 11am-midnight, Sa-Su 11am-11pm.*

⬛ ANTOINE'S
⬤ FRITES ❶

1 Place Jourdan

In Place Jourdan at lunch time, two long lines form of children, locals, businessmen, students, and tourists, all hoping to grab a cone of french fries from Brussels's oldest *friterie*. You may have passed out from hunger by the time you reach the counter to place your order, but tasting these *frites* will quickly restore you. Though they may not be Brussels's best *frites*, Antoine's piping hot potatoes are made with the city's oldest recipe and served in some of its biggest portions. Many people head to the grassy banks of Parc Léopold to enjoy their *frites* in the sun, instead of sitting on a dirty bench in Place Jourdan.

✠ Ⓜ*Schuman. Place Jourdan is just off rue Froissart* Ⓢ *Frites €2-2.20. Sauce €0.50.* Ⓩ *Open M-Th 11:30am-1am, F-Sa 11:30am-2am, Su 11:30am-1am.*

CAFÉ PARC AVENUE
⬤♦(( ))♈ CAFE ❸

50 Av. d'Auderghem ☎02 742 28 10 🖳www.parc-avenue.be

Eating out in the EU area can be expensive. Fortunately, this upscale cafe has a lunchtime option that will suit the budget traveler nicely—the "Business Lunch Menu," which includes the appetizer and entree of the day with tea or coffee (€10). Throw in the free Wi-Fi, the iPads available for patrons to play on, and the selection of international newspapers, and you'll be feeling as ritzy and savvy as the stuffed suits eating around you.

✠ Ⓜ*Schuman.* Ⓢ *Breakfast €7-17. Lunch €8-24. Lunch menu €10.* Ⓩ *Open M-F 7:30am-3:30pm.*

CAPOLINO'S
♦♈⬠ ITALIAN, PIZZA, PASTA ❸

69 Place Jourdan ☎02 230 37 51 🖳www.capolini.be

Among the expensive restaurants in this "lunching" square, Capolino's plentiful pizza and pasta are some of the best cheaper options. Make sure you grab a seat in the garden out back with wicker chairs and wooden tables. The eating area has a refreshingly earthy feel, but on colder days the indoor seating area also has some character. The welcoming staff will be keen to know where you're from, and will try to make you feel at home—this is one of those places where the pizza is made exactly how you want it, so don't be afraid to ask.

✠ Ⓜ*Schuman. Place Jourdan is just down rue Froissart.* *i* *8% discount for takeout.* Ⓢ *Pizzas €8.70-14. Pastas €10-16.* Ⓩ *Open M-Th noon-2:30pm and 6:30-11pm, F-Sa noon-2:30pm and 6:30-11:30pm, Su 6:30-11pm.*

LA BRACE
♦♈ PIZZERIA ❸

1 rue Franklin ☎02 736 57 73

You'd expect to find all types of cuisine in the EU quarter, but there's certainly a lot of Italian places. La Brace is renowned for its authentic Italian pizzas and pastas, and if you walk past the storefront you'll spot the chef through the window, poised over a traditional stone oven; he's there all day and night, so you know that your pizza will be cooked by an expert. The Italian waiters will take your

food · place schuman

order from either outside on the street or inside the restaurant, which is sometimes complete with guitar music and singing. If you want a real pizza surprise, try the Segreto Pizza—we can't tell you what's on it, because the ingredients are top secret!

[M]Schuman $ Pizzas €10-14. Pastas €12-14. Meats €18-24. Open M-Sa noon-3pm and 7-11:30pm.

RESTO SIMBA — AFRICAN ❷

13 Leuvensesteenweg ☎02 688 43 26 www.lsctraiteur.be

Situated inside Belgium's Musée Royal de l'Afrique Centrale, Resto Simba offers a few special menu offerings beyond the sandwiches and pastas you might find in the museum's cafeteria. Take a seat among the African art and statues and tuck into some African cuisine. Dishes include Madagascar chicken, *scampi nin* (a Kenyan curry), and *Croq'Simba* (chicken in palm nut sauce; something tells us that the dish isn't called the "Simba" back in its motherland). Other sandwiches and baguettes are also available.

Line 1 to [M]Montgomery. Or tram #44 to Tervuren. $ African food €7.80-16.20. Sandwiches €3. Toasted baguettes €5.50-7.50. Open Tu-Su 11:30am-3pm. Kitchen opens at noon.

THE SUSHI FACTORY — SUSHI ❶

44 Bvd. Charlemagne ☎02 230 74 32 www.sushifactory.be

If you fancy something a little **fishy,** or if you're just craving a Japanese salad, then this sushi shop in the Schuman area is just what the doctor ordered. There are two menus available. The small menu comes with a soup, Japanese salad, and four sushi choices *(€10)*. The big menu option offers soup, salad, and seven different types of sushi *(€12)*. The EU crowd can't get enough of this conveniently placed sushi restaurant, so you might have to order your meal to go if there isn't enough room inside.

[M]Schuman. $ Set menus €10-12. Open M-F noon-8:30pm. Takeout available until 9pm.

BALTHAZAR — KOSHER ❶

63 rue Archimède ☎02 742 06 00

This kosher dining restaurant offers takeout pitas ideal for a lunch on the run or a snack in the seating area upstairs. The dinner options are more expensive than grabbing a pita for the road. A nice change from the English-themed brasseries and Italian restaurants in the area.

[M]Schuman. $ Pitas €5-8. Entrees €12-22. Open M-F noon-2pm and 6:30-11pm, Sa 6:30-11pm, Su noon-2pm and 6:30-11pm.

EPONYME — CAFE, WINE, CHOCOLATIER ❷

6 rue de Trèves ☎02 513 02 10 info@eponyme.be

Is it a library? A chocolate shop? A cafe? Eponyme has managed to cram all of these things into one tiny room. Sit and enjoy a coffee and chocolate while reading one of the numerous cooking or travel books the shop specializes in. If you're really in the mood to splurge, ask to taste one of the expensive wines or champagnes on the list. Everything sold in the shop is high-quality, and the calm jazz music in the background makes Eponyme stand out.

[M]Maelbeek. Just off Place du Luxembourg. i Credit card min. €5. $ Coffees and teas €2-3. Wine €9-14 per glass. Champagne from €30 per glass. Open M-F 11am-7pm.

KARSMAKERS — BAGELS ❶

20 rue de Trèves ☎02 502 02 26 www.karsmakers.be

No one is in a hurry in Karsmakers, as the Eurocrats head for a light lunch and nibble at the bagel and salad offerings from the big blackboard at the front of the shop. The long-halled lounge area also has an outdoor terrace where suited and booted ladies and gentlemen chat in many different languages and discuss extremely important matters—red or white wine with that salmon bagel? Although the bagels aren't cheap, they come well stuffed and can be catered to your requests.

➡ Ⓜ*Maelbeek. Just off of Place du Luxembourg.* Ⓢ *Bagels €4-6.50.* ⏰ *Open M-F 7am-6pm, Su 10am-4pm.*

ARTHUR'S TEA HOUSE 🚬🍸 TEA HOUSE [1]

26 rue de Trèves ☎02 502 89 37

Just a few steps away from the very English-feeling Place du Luxembourg, this quaint little teahouse is cluttered with jewelry and artwork by local artists. Continue out to the back, where a large glass roof and indoor water feature makes for a comfortable place to enjoy a cuppa somethin'. Although Arthur's is a haunt of the ladies who lunch, if you want a high quality tea or coffee, leave the beers of the square behind and head here. Just know that you'll pay a price *(€3.50 for a pot of tea!).*

➡ Ⓜ*Maelbeek. Just off of Place du Luxembourg.* Ⓢ *Drinks €2.50-5.* ⏰ *Open M-Th 7am-7:30pm, F 7am-8pm.*

LA ROSTICCERIA FIORENTINA 🚬🍸 BRASSERIE [2]

43 rue Archimède ☎02 734 92 36

Established in 1962, the team at La Rosticceria Fiorentina knows what they are doing and will charge you for it. The small and intimate setting makes the restaurant an ideal place for a first date (better go ask out that sexy Eurocrat) away from the crowded squares a bit further on, so you can have the privacy you want. The staff is attentive, and if you sit outside you may be lucky enough to have your meal delivered to you via the front door of the connecting house.

➡ Ⓜ*Schuman.* Ⓢ *Pasta €8-15. Meat entrees €14.50-24.50.* ⏰ *Open M-F noon-2pm and 6:30-10pm, Su noon-2pm and 6:30-10pm.*

SNACK PITTA JOURDAN 🍴 KEBABS, PITA, FAST FOOD [1]

43-33 Place Jourdan ☎02 231 09 86 🖥www.pittajourdan.com

In a square with slightly expensive seafood and Italian restaurants, Snack Pitta Jourdan might be the best option for a quick budget dinner of greasy kebab. Don't expect haute cuisine or even plates, but you can expect something cheap *(most meals under €9)* and fast. Vegetarian options are available in addition to the Halal meat.

➡ Ⓜ*Schuman. Place Jourdan is just down rue Froissart.* Ⓢ *Sandwiches €6.80-7.50. Entrees €10-13.50.* ⏰ *Open M-Th 11am-3am, F-Sa 11am-4am, Su 11am-3am.*

nightlife

We encourage you to samples as many 🍺**good Belgian brews** as humanly possible, but remember: the Metro stops at midnight. Don't forget to plan around it, particularly if you're hoping to club your way through the Upper Town area. The cheapest and most popular bars are in Brussels's **Lower Town,** which features a decent mix of tourist traps and well-kept local secrets. **Upper Town** nightlife is less vibrant and more expensive. Bars and lounges for 30-somethings are in abundance, but there aren't that many hubs for students; even the students of Brussels University migrate en masse to the Lower Town for their nightly fix. For a more "European" experience, head to **Place Schuman** or **Place Luxembourg** (that's PLux to the Eurocrats), where young men in suits will undoubtedly ask you what you do and how much you make. Don't be put off by this attitude; they are a friendly bunch in the EU.

LOWER TOWN

GOUPIL LE FOL
♥ ♈ CABARET

22 rue de la Violette
☎02 511 13 96

This eclectic *estaminet* (a cafe where the owner is continually present) is the most fantastic, and best hidden, bar you will step into during your time in the Lower Town. From the outside, this pub-like building looks a bit odd, with a few eccentric items in the window—including a stuffed fox—and a sign explaining that the bar will not serve Coca-Cola to its patrons (without alcohol, that is). Step inside and you are thrown into a world of revolution, literature, and art where pictures of the Belgian Royal Family hang from the walls, a library of philosophical thought crowds shelves, and rooms full of artwork are at your disposal. The brilliant owner, Abel, sees his bar as one where people can come in groups or alone to reflect on life, admire the art, and have a slow and quiet drink, while the best of French and Belgian music plays in the background. Goupil le Fol is packed with an intellectual crowd of alternative students and older art lovers, and Abel counts the Prince of Spain and the Prince of Belgium as people who have walked through his doors.

❧ ⓂBourse. From the Grand Place, head down rue des Chapliers and take a left onto rue de la Violette. ⓘ Reservations may be required for the weekend. ⓢ Beer €3-6. ☒ Open daily 6pm-6am.

BONNEFOOI
♥ ♈ BAR

8 rue des Pieriès
☎048 762 22 31 ◻www.bonnefooi.be

Bonnefooi is one of the most pleasant finds in Brussels, and thanks to its location in an unobtrusive side street off the center, it lacks the tourists who frequent other bars in the area. Even more impressively, the bar is open every night until 8am; the punters at Bonnefooi really know the meaning of an all-night party. Despite the crazy kick-out time, the bar fosters a relaxed atmosphere. The gallery balcony is great for people-watching as locals order from a long list of beers (the Rochefort 8 is a popular and smooth beer). There is a different event going on here every night, from an acoustic session to a DJ-ed dance mix to a jazz performance. Check the board inside the bar for details.

❧ ⓂBourse. Just off of bd. Anspach. ⓢ Beer €2-4. Cocktails €7. ☒ Open daily 6pm-8am.

MUSIC LOUNGE
♥ ♈ JAZZ BAR

50 rue des Pierres
☎02 513 13 45 ◻themusicvillage@skynet.be

One of Brussels's very hip jazz bars, the Music Lounge is popular with all ages and hosts a wide range of jazz throughout the week. The youth jazz section tries to stick to traditional jazz rather than fusion or modern interpretations, so the Music Lounge will suit most jazz purists. The relaxed atmosphere and artsy clientele provide a chill setting to begin a night or end it in style. Check the website or a leaflet for concert details.

❧ ⓂBourse. Just off Grand Place. ⓘ Cover charge depends on the concert; student discounts available. ⓢ Drinks €2-7. ☒ Doors open at 7pm. Concerts start M-Th 8:30pm, F-Sa 9pm, Su 8:30pm.

DELIRIUM
♥ ♈ BAR

4A Impasse de la Fidélité
☎02 514 44 34 ◻www.deliriumcafe.be

Situated just opposite the female Manneken Pis, Delirium is the number one stop for anyone visiting Brussels; expect to be drinking among fellow tourists, but no matter—this is the bar that anyone, local or visitor, will recommend. The bar has over 2000 beers on tap, and you can ask your knowledgeable server to bring you their favorite for a real taste of Belgium (though be warned, you may end up with a very strong 10% beer!). The bar is packed nightly with students, so you'll need to shout to be heard and use hand gestures to order. Don't worry about your rudimentary French or Flemish, as you will most likely be surrounded by English speakers anyway. The interior makes you feel a little like you're inside a brewery, and the giant wooden barrels make for a quirky change from the traditional tables in other bars.

✚ ⓂBourse. Just off rue des Bouchers. Ⓢ Beer €2-6. Ⓩ Open M-Sa 10pm-4am, Su 10pm-2am.

ZEBRA
📍 ⛾ BAR

35 Place St. Géry ☎02 513 51 16

One of St. Géry's most popular hangouts due to its lively atmosphere and top-notch mojitos (€7), Zebra is a guaranteed fun night out in the busy square. The bar itself is small, but the terrace outside means a lot of people can get served at Zebra. In fact, Zebra is one of the few bars that stays busy year round, thanks to the outside heaters, so even in the middle of January you'll find people outside sipping their drinks and chilling to jazz. On the weekends, Zebra plays host to jazz performances and other free concerts, which are a good way to start the night or just hang for the evening. The decor can get pretty funky; check out the lollipops in Perspex cases around the windows, and the gumball machine stuck on top of a rather eclectic pile of old books.

✚ ⓂBourse. Just off rue Orts. Ⓢ Beer €2-4. Cocktails €7. Ⓩ Open daily 11am-3am.

CAFÉ DES HALLES
📍 ⛾ BAR

Place St. Géry

Set up in what used to be a shopping precinct, Des Halles is now a quirky and lively bar which showcases local pieces of artwork and hosts numerous events, including screenings of films and sporting events projected onto a large screen. Cozy up on one of the many leather sofas inside or, during the summer, head to the terrace to lounge in one of the deck chairs by the faux-beach. Since Des Halles isn't really a typical bar, many families come here, and little kids are a common sight—though they don't really seem to get in the way. For big sporting events, arrive early to get a good spot, otherwise you'll be seated on the other side of the screen watching a reversed image, which is never too fun.

✚ ⓂBourse. Head down rue Praet to reach the square. Des Halles is in the center. Ⓢ €3-8. Ⓩ Open daily 10am-1am.

L'ARCHIDUC
📍 ⛾ JAZZ BAR

6 rue A. Dansaert ☎02 512 06 52 ▣www.archiduc.net

Dating back to before WWI, L'Archiduc is renowned for its jazz concerts and Art Deco interior. Though the prices are a little higher than other bars in the areas (€4-12), the intricate and historic decor make those few extra euros worth it. Grab a spot in the gallery style balcony area for a good spot of people watching; L'Archiduc draws a good mix of locals and jazz loving tourists. On weekends the bar doesn't really pick up until 11pm, so we recommend paying Archiduc a visit near the end of your night for a classy drink or three.

✚ ⓂBourse. Head down rue Orts, which leads to rue A. Dansaert. 𝒊 Free concerts May-Aug M 11pm. Ⓢ Drinks €3-12. Ⓩ Open daily 4pm-5am.

LE BELGICA
📍 ⛾ BAR

32 rue du Marché au Charbon ▣www.lebelgica.be

Although Le Belgica does not fly the rainbow flag officially, the bar is situated in Brussels's main gay district, and the small bar flows out onto the street on the weekends with a mainly male clientele. The friendly owner sees Le Belgica as open to everyone, but women may feel somewhat out of place in this male-dominated bar scene. Cheap beer is readily available, as are cocktails; the bar prides itself on its special lemon shooter Genera, which will chill the back of your throat and refresh your tired body. The busy atmosphere means out-of-towners should feel welcome. The friendly local clientele will be more than willing to engage you in a conversation, just don't expect to find a seat inside after 11pm on the weekend.

✚ ⓂBourse. Ⓢ Beer €2. Cocktails €6.50. Ⓩ Open Th-Sa 10pm-3am, Su 8pm-3am.

EL METTEKO 🍸 BAR

88 Bld. Anspach ☎02 512 46 48 💻www.metteko.com

Surprisingly, El Metteko rocks out harder than the music bar next door—you never quite know what sounds you'll hear coming from this diverse and lively bar. The neighborhood institution is popular with locals because of its cheap dishes and is a bit of a tourist hotspot because of the cheap alcohol and central location. Luckily the tourists don't seem to dominate the scene, and you'll find yourself among friendly company at the cramped long tables. The stained-glass window above the bar is a nice effect, but it does feel somewhat out of place in this otherwise modern interior. Make sure you adhere to the advice in the menu—gentlemen must always be polite to the ladies and, very importantly, watch out for pickpockets in this area.

➔ ⓂBourse. Just past the Bourse on the left. ℹ Happy hour cocktails €4. $ Beer €3-5. Cocktails €5-6. ⏰ Open daily 11am-midnight. Happy hour 4-6pm.

LE ROI DES BELGES 🍸 CAFE, BAR

35 rue Praet ☎02 513 51 16

Although Le Roi des Belges is open all day every day for snacks and a coffee, the place really livens up at night, when an artistic crowd gathers inside to discuss philosophy, art, and life. When all the other bars around are showing big sporting events on TV you can be sure that the folks at Le Roi des Belges will be discussing Kierkegaard. Upstairs you can grab a window seat and watch the bustle of Place St. Géry unfold in front of you, as people come and go to the various bars surrounding the square. Take care on the spiral staircase leading to the second floor—those coming down might have to make room for people coming up.

➔ ⓂBourse. ℹ DJs Th-Sa. $ Drinks €3-7. ⏰ Open daily 9pm-1am.

MEZZO 🍸 BAR

Place St. Géry ☎02 511 33 25 💻www.mezzo.be

With a slightly more relaxed crowd (including some children), this bar is a chill venue for some quiet beers with a group of friends. A gigantic mirror at the far end of the bar makes the space feel big and open despite its limited size. You may feel the need to rearrange some of the tables, though, as they aren't really well suited for big groups. The fruity beers and the English speaking staff will help get your night started off well.

➔ ⓂBourse. Just off of rue Orts. $ Beers €3-4. Cocktails €7. ⏰ Open M-Th 4pm-2am, F-Sa 4pm-6am, Su 4pm-2am.

MAPPA MUNDO 🍸 PUB

2-6 rue du Point de la Carpe ☎02 513 51 16

From outside, Mappa Mundo looks like a disappointing pub-style bar filled with English tourists looking to recreate their local watering hole back home. But escape the tourists in the front rooms and head out back to the little wooden caverns, or even upstairs, and you'll find an oriental-style setting with low hanging lamps and private seating booths. Enjoy your drink while catching up with news from around Europe from the stash of newspapers from other countries.

➔ ⓂBourse. Just off of rue Orts. $ Drinks €2-7. Cocktails €7-10. ⏰ Open M-Th 11am-2am, F-Sa 11am-3am, Su 11am-2am.

ROYAL THÉÂTRE TOONE 🍸 PUB

66 rue du Marché aux Herbes ☎02 511 71 37 💻www.toone.be

One of Brussels's hidden gems, the Toone is a marionette-themed pub hidden down a covered walkway in a very old building. The puppets dangle over head as you sip your beer or munch on the chips and cheese served at the bar. A great quirky place to have a friendly beer and conversation. Performances still take place next door.

♯ Ⓜ️*Bourse.* Ⓢ *Beers €3-6. Food €4-6.* 🕐 *Open Tu-Su noon-midnight.*

ENFACE
♥ ✸ Ψ BAR

1-3 rue St. Géry

In the busy St. Géry there are many bars to choose from, but this triangular-shaped watering hole sitting on the corner of the street is a somewhat hip hangout with low seats, hanging drapes, and large doors and windows that give a very open feeling to the place. Known as "Enface" because it directly faces a tapas bar (its reference point, apparently), the bar provides a quiet and calm atmosphere. The mixed crowd that comes here ranges from young locals to older people and, of course, some tourists.

♯ Ⓜ️*Bourse. On the corner of rue Borgval, opposite the tapas bar.* 𝑖 *Credit card min. €15.* Ⓢ *Beers €2.50-4.* 🕐 *Open M-Sa 3pm-2am.*

PURE BAR
♥ Ψ BAR

46 rue des Pierres ☎0473 48 55 47 ◼️www.pure-bar.be

For a very relaxed experience—maybe a little too relaxed, actually—head to the Pure Bar just off of the Grand Place. Here you can smoke a variety of hookah pipes *(Pure Sheesha €8; Superior €15),* or sip on some creatively named cocktails as you recline in the red pillows around the floor. The house music adds an interesting vibe to the restaurant, and the cheap shooters *(€2.50)* mean that a trip to Pure doesn't have to be relaxed at all. The hostess can also offer you ◼️**balloons** of helium for a very funny (and squeaky) 15 seconds of fun.

♯ Ⓜ️*Bourse. Just off Grand Place.* Ⓢ *Drinks €2.50-10. Sheesha €8-15.* 🕐 *Open daily 2pm-2am.*

A LA MORT SUBITE
♥ Ψ BAR

7 rue Montagne-aux-Herbes Potagères ☎02 513 13 18 ◼️www.alamortsubite.be

Don't be put off by the name—A La Mort Subite ("Sudden Death") will not actually leave you cold and clammy, unless you go way overboard with the extremely strong 10% beers. The turn-of-the-century decor hasn't changed much from when the bar, now populated by an older crowd, first opened in 1910. The variety of beers on tap will keep you happy, but the crowd may not be ideally suited for all students; be prepared to engage in conversations with some older locals and even expats. But the setting and the true *zinneke* atmosphere (a *zinneke* is a typical person from Brussels) means that the time you spend in the A La Mort Subite won't be so painful after all.

♯ Ⓜ️*Bourse. From the Grand Place, head up to the Galleries St. Hubert. A la Mort Subite is through the galleries on the corner.* Ⓢ *Drinks €3-8.* 🕐 *Open M-Sa 11am-midnight, Su noon-midnight.*

CELTICA
♥ Ψ SPORTS BAR

55 rue du Marché aux Poulets ☎02 514 22 69 ◼️www.celticpubs.com

Sports bars are not uncommon in Brussels, but bars like Celtica are hard to come by. Locals know that Celtica offers the cheapest beer and the most generous happy hour in all of Brussels *(€1 before midnight, €2 after midnight, for any beer!),* and the bar draws a healthy mix of hip, young Belgian teenagers and an older student crowd. Celtica is also a sure fire place to find a party every day of the week, with DJs, live acoustic music, and bands gracing one of the two floors Monday through Sunday. For the real party goers, head upstairs to the dance floor, where the cheap beer will mean you can excuse your poor dance moves the next morning.

♯ Ⓜ️*Bourse. Just off of Bvd. Anspach.* Ⓢ *Beer €2-5.* 🕐 *Open daily 1pm-very late.*

CLASSIC ROCK BAR
♥ Ψ BAR

55 rue Marché au Charbon ☎02 512 15 47 ◼️www.rockclassic.be

This is quite simply a bar with a specific niche, and you'll feel very out of place unless your music of choice is, obviously, rock. Heavy metal also makes the playlist, and the dress code seems to be mainly black T-shirts and long ponytails (for the guys). The tunnel leading into the bar gives it a dark atmosphere and the various caverns underground will ensure that any wannabe Rock God will find a home in this Classic Rock Bar.

☼ ⓂBourse. Just off of rue du Midi. ⓈDrinks €3-8. ⌚ Open daily 8pm-6am.

CAFÉ WALVIS
●ϒ BAR

209 rue Dansaert ▦www.cafewalvis.be

Located in the far end of the Lower Town near the canal in the east of Brussels, Café Walvis is popular with a mid-20s crowd that comes here for the free concerts and expansive terrace. The recent transformation of the area into a hub of immigrants from other areas in the EU means you'll be drinking with a mix of nationalities; expect a good political debate on top of your beer and jazz. Situated a short walk from the HI Youth Hostel, this is great for those travelers who don't fancy the 20min. trek into the center.

☼ ⓂComte de Flandre. On the other side of the canal, just off of Bld. Barthélémy. ⓈBeer €2-5. Other drinks €2-8. ⌚ Open M-Sa 9am-3am, Su noon-1am.

UPPER TOWN

▨ FUSE
●ϒ▼ CLUB

208 rue Blaes ☎02 511 97 89 ▦www.fuse.be

Fuse is one of Brussels's biggest and liveliest clubs, so if you want to escape the calm and casual bar scene in the Lower Town for pounding music and drinks that will make your dancing excusable, this is the place to go. The large dance floor in the main room is a great place to lose your dignity; just make sure that's the only thing you end up losing there. Every month one of the biggest gay events in Europe, La Demance, takes place at Fuse. With male strippers, drag queens, and a lot of semi-naked clubbers, La Demance is infamous in Belgium, and guys travel from just about everywhere to party it up into the early hours.

☼ ⓂPort de Hal. ⓈCover Sa before midnight €5, after midnight €10. Drinks €4-10. ⌚ Hours vary, generally open Th-Sa 11pm-late. Check the website for schedule.

▨ LA FLEUR EN PAPIER DORÉ
●ϒ PUB

55 rue des Alexiens ☎02 511 16 59 ▦www.lafleurenpapierdore.be

This pub just off of the Sablon area counts the artist Magritte and the Tintin cartoonist Hergé among its former clientele. Nowadays, the pub fills it small nooks with locals and artsy types looking for inspiration from the smoke-stained walls (although smoking is now banned inside) and the temporary art exhibits. You can really feel the history in this kooky little pub; La Fleur hosted Magritte's first exhibition after the war, and the pub is now protected by the Belgian government, presumably for the artsy neurotics of the future.

☼ ⓂGare du Midi. ⓈBeer €2-7. ⌚ Open Tu-Sa 11am-midnight, Su 11am-7pm.

THE FLAT
●ϒ LOUNGE, BAR

12 rue de la Reinette ☎02 502 74 34 ▦www.theflat.be

A popular hangout for locals just getting off work and a good place to start your night, The Flat is exactly what it sounds like it is. The layout upstairs resembles an upscale flat that you might find in London or NYC: a spacious living room, a dining area, a grand bathroom, and even a bedroom. Enjoy your mojito from inside the bath, or sip your wine laid out on the bed. Downstairs, a DJ mixes music Thursday through Saturday, and each night three cocktails are selected to have their price fluctuate—as the prices drop dramatically or suddenly shoot up, you'll be reminded of the career on Wall Street that you're never going to have anymore.

☼ ⓂLouise. ⓈDrinks €3-10. ⌚ Open W-Sa 6pm-2am.

KARAOKE SABLON 🍸 KARAOKE BAR

34 rue St. Anne ☎02 512 40 94 💻www.karaokesablon.be

Off a side alley from the Sablon area, this smoky karaoke bar is full of locals until the wee hours of the morn who really feel that they could impress Simon Cowell and company with their talents. Karaoke Sablon specializes in French music, so expect to hear tone-deaf renditions of Edith Piaf as often as you hear The Beatles. Do not despair—just about any song you can think of is in their encyclopedic playlist, and something you can rock out to is bound to come up. A mixed crowd ranging from children to grandmothers hit the tiny stage, which comes complete with a stool for the slow ballads. This quirky bar will put a smile on your face, even if you just sit and watch the regulars belt it out.

🧭 Ⓜ Louise. $ Drinks €3-6. ⏰ Open Tu-Sa 9pm-4am.

LA SAMARITAINE 🍸 CABARET, BAR

16 rue de la Samaritaine ☎02 511 33 95 💻www.lasamaritaine.be

As you descend the steep steps down an alley off of Sablon Square, you'll know you aren't heading to any ordinary cabaret; La Samaritaine looks a bit like a converted wine cellar, and you can hear the music down the street. The underground bar is a fantastic local favorite frequented by the young, the old, and the artsy, who cheer on songs, dance numbers, and theater in cavernous rooms. You can catch a cappella concerts and other live performances here while enjoying some remarkably cheap drinks *(cocktails €6)*. Some tickets sell out quickly, so check online and ring up in advance to reserve your spot in Brussels's most interesting cabaret.

🧭 Ⓜ Central Station. $ Tickets €12, students €8. Drinks €2-7. ⏰ Bar opens on performance nights at 7:30pm. Check program for detailed hours.

BAR DU MARCHÉ 📶 🍸 BAR, CAFE

12 rue A. Dewitte ☎02 644 04 00 💻www.bardumarche.be

This smoky bar caters to the type of cool crowd that won't be seen without a cigarette in hand and the latest fashion in their wardrobe. Arts and philosophy are more likely to be the topic of conversation here than sports or politics, and the 20-somethings seem to all be regulars with their set groups, which might be difficult for a lone traveler to penetrate. But the bar has a very artsy vibe to it and is a great place to hang out with a group of friends, or just grab a mid-afternoon coffee and access the free Wi-Fi (the password is champagne; this says it all really). The bar hosts free jazz concerts on Sunday evenings.

🧭 Ⓜ Port de Namur. Just off of Place Flagey, via Chausée d'Ixelles. $ Beer €2-4. Cocktails €7. ⏰ Open daily 10am-3am.

CAFÉ BELGA 🍸 BAR

18 Place Flagey ☎02 460 35 08

Café Belga's sprawling terrace stretches across the far corner of Place Flagey, a lively square with fountains in the middle, and attracts a diverse crowd looking for a quiet beer or meeting up with friends. The chic crowd of Av. Louise makes their way down here, as do the Eurocrats from the EU area, but the bar also packs full of students and a generally younger crowd. Many expats working in Brussels find a comfortable home here, so if you're tired of speaking French or Flemish and just need a chat in English, this place will probably sort you right out. A younger crowd prefers to drink from cans they bought at the local *tabac*, and sit by the nearby canal, but it's warmer and more comfortable by the heated terrace, and worth the few extra euro.

🧭 Ⓜ Port de Namur. Place Flagey is off of Chausée d'Ixelles. $ Beer €2-5. ⏰ Open daily 8am-3am. Terrace open M-W 8am-midnight, Th-Sa 8am-1am.

L'ULTIME ATOME

BAR, BRASSERIE

14 rue St. Boniface ☎02 511 13 67

This brasserie serves food late into the night, but is full of drinkers after 9pm, especially among the English-speaking expats who flock here by the dozens. The bar has a terrace with a view of the St. Boniface church, which provides an ideal setting to make some Eurocratic friends or get into a conversation with some fellow Americans. We recommend you give your Flemish a try or brush up on your French with the locals who come here to sample the beers on tap. Luckily the bar is far enough out of the center that you'll avoid all the tourists, who tend to drink as much as they can in as short a time possible.

[M]Port de Namur. Just off Chausée d'Ixelles. $ Beer €2-5. Cocktails €7. Open M-Th 11am-12:30am, F-Sa 11am-1am, Su 11am-12:30am.

PEOPLE

BAR

11 Ave. Toison D'Or ☎02 511 64 05 www.peoplebar.be

People is certainly a bar for the people; this place really takes all kinds, from the young students who pack inside on the very popular student nights, to the older crowd that enjoys a quiet drink on the expansive outside terrace. The modern interior's green and pink flowered wallpaper makes for a soothing place to drink when the weather outside isn't ideal for drinking al fresco; the bar has a great selection of beers and drinks both on tap and in bottles. Thursday through Saturday, a DJ keeps the night going with pop and recent hits, and the relaxed vibe continues onto the dance floor. Wednesday night is specifically for students.

[M]Louise. $ Beer €2.50-5. Cocktails €7.50-9. Open daily noon-1am.

SAZZ'N'JAZZ MUSIC ROOM

JAZZ BAR

241 rue Royale ☎0475 78 23 78 www.sazznjazz.be

This jazz bar has something going on almost every night of the week, be it talks by visiting filmmakers, documentary screenings, or, of course, jazz concerts. Sazz'n'Jazz is not your traditional Jazz lounge, but you will surely be able to find something on their schedule which will keep you entertained. The bar wants to be a home for new and rising artists from all backgrounds, and you can expect to have a night of good entertainment and music no matter who's playing.

[M]Botanique. $ Prices depend on show. Check website for show times.

RECYCLART

BAR, UNDERGROUND

25 rue des Ursulines ☎02 289 00 59 www.recyclart.be

The youth of Brussels got a massive skate park built on top of the train station in this area, and the downstairs station area has been taken over by Recyclart, which holds club nights, concerts, and DJ nights. There are no set open hours or event times, so you have to check the venue or the website beforehand to see what's going on. The venue is definitely innovative and different from some of the bars you will find in the Grand Place.

[M]Gare Centrale. $ Cover is either free or €5; check which events have cover on the website. Hours depend on events. Cafe open Tu-F 11am-5pm.

DRAFT BAR

BAR

231 Av. de le Couronne

If, for whatever reason, you find yourself so south of the center you start to wonder if you're ever going to find a bar again, the Draft Bar might be your saving grace. In an area of Ixelles where nightlife is extremely lacking, this cozy pub and its foosball table serves up cheap drinks and small food plates which will keep you watered while you work out how to get back to civilization.

$ Beer €2-5. Food €4-8. Open M-W 10am-midnight, Th-Sa 10am-3am.

LA PORTE NOIRE

◆✝ BAR

67 rue des Alexiens

☎02 511 78 37 ▣www.laportenoire.be

If you like to feel like you might suffocate, then La Porte Noire is definitely a good stop to make on the far side of the Upper Town. Bang in the middle between the two main areas of Brussels, this dark bar has a unique character and caters to all ages, but the lack of windows may make you want to run back up the steep staircase very quickly, even before your drink has arrived.

✦ ⓂGare Centrale. ⓈBeer €2-5. ☒Open M-Sa 5pm-3am.

PLACE SCHUMAN

Place Schuman isn't the most lively of places for the student traveler, but it does have a happening club (Soho) and is *the* place to network and exchange business cards. Expect expats, suits, and EU workers, as well as an awful lot of English speakers.

▦ OLD OAK IRISH PUB

◆✝ IRISH PUB

26 rue Franklin

☎02 735 75 44

In an area full of English-speaking expats and corporate Eurocrats, this jolly Irish pub caters less to men in suits with BlackBerries and more to a young European crowd. The candlelight and low-timbered roof will make you feel like you left Brussels far behind and ended up in Ireland itself. The staff will immediately talk to you in English; if you're really in need of it, why not get a team together for the Pub Quiz on Monday nights.

✦ ⓂSchuman. ⓈDrinks €2-5. ☒Open daily noon-1am.

▦ THE WILD GEESE

◆✝ PUB

2-4 Av. Livingstone

☎02 230 20 07

In an area full of Irish pubs and bars packed with English speakers, The Wild Geese adds a little variety to the European center's night scene. The bar is large and open with round wooden tables and benches tucked in corners. Enjoy a beer outside on the expansive terrace, or head upstairs for a more reclusive spot. A DJ works the floor Thursday through Saturday nights, and the bar's middle-aged patrons are replaced by a swarm of young technocrats, who party until the early hours of the morning before deciding to stumble back to their luxury hotels. We're not bitter.

✦ ⓂMaelbeek. ⓈBeer €2.50-4. ☒Open M-W noon-1am, Th-Sa noon-3am, Su noon-1am.

FAT BOY'S SPORTS BAR

◆✝ SPORTS BAR

5 Place du Luxembourg

☎02 511 32 66 ▣www.fatboys-be.com

Fat boys don't frequent the TV screens of this bar—unless, perhaps, they're showing a sumo wrestling championship, which is completely possible. The owner boasts over 7000 sports channels, 11 inside screens, and two outdoor screens, and as a result is able to show five live games simultaneously. Every major sporting event is shown here, be it soccer, American football, baseball, or cricket; if there's a game on that you want to catch, chances are that Fat Boy's will be showing it. When people aren't shouting at the screen for a goal or a touchdown, the bar also hosts live music to keep the punters happy.

✦ ⓂMaelbeek. *i* Credit card min. €15. ⓈBeer €2-5. ☒Open daily 11am-late.

THE HAIRY CANARY

◆✝ ENGLISH PUB

12 rue Archimède

☎02 230 13 36

If you get bored of Belgium beer and want to visit England without paying the Eurostar fare, then this is perhaps the pub to head to. With Cadbury's posters on the wall, the BBC playing on the TV, and numerous signs in English, The Hairy Canary feels as if it was picked up out of England and dropped in the Schuman area. The friendly barman won't offer you a menu but will talk you through the different options, including the liquor lining the shelves and the beers on tap. If you hear any language other than English spoken here, you might not be in the right place.

 # [M]Schuman [$] Beer €2.50-5. Cocktails €7-9. ⏰ Open daily noon-late.

SOHO 🎟🍸 CLUB

47 Bvd. du Triomphe ☎02 649 35 00 💻www.soho-club.be

Soho is one of Brussels's liveliest clubs, situated just out of the center and near the EU district. If you're bored with the city's laid-back bars and fancy a real dance with some loud music, you'd better get yourself here. The 20-something crowd is a perfect match for the student traveler and a welcome break from the older geopoliticos found in the area. Expect a wide variety of music and theme nights and a dance floor that is big enough to get lost in—hopefully people won't be able to notice your not-so-cool dance moves. Taking a taxi home after you leave is advisable, as the distance back to the center is a bit of a walk, and the Metro stops a little after midnight.

 # [M]Hankar. Take Line 5 toward Hermann-Debroux. [$] Cover €10. Drinks €5-10. ⏰ Open Th-Sa 11pm-late.

THE MEETING POINT 🎟🍸 PUB

49 rue du Taciturne ☎02 230 28 02

Compared to the crowded and somewhat intense settings of the other bars in the area, The Meeting Point really is the ideal place to grab a drink and have a quiet rendezvous with a friend. The small corner terrace is a good spot for a beer at night, and the nooks inside the bright and cheery pub also are a great way to have a good catch up with someone. Don't expect to be surrounded by English and American speakers here; French and Flemish speakers are just as common as the Anglophones, so practice your language skills and leave the English for one of the EU's Irish pubs near Schuman.

 # [M]Maelbeek. [$] Beer €1.75-3.50. ⏰ Open daily 10am-1am.

RALPH'S BAR 🎟🍸 BAR

13 place du Luxembourg ☎02 230 16 13 💻www.ralphsbar.be

The center of Place du Luxembourg can be overwhelming and confusing, as the swarms of suits invade the various bar terraces and the parties overflow into the streets of the square. Ralph's Bar has a little more class than some of the Irish pubs around the corner, but it still manages to keep a relaxed atmosphere inside. The modern furniture is a great place to lounge after a day exploring the parks of the European area. Mingle outside on the terrace with the Eurocrats who will undoubtedly be making a pit stop after working just across the road.

 # [M]Maelbeek. [$] Beers €2.50-5. ⏰ Open daily 10am-1am.

THE GRAPEVINE 🎟🍸 BAR

11 Place du Luxembourg ☎02 280 00 17

This place has certainly made its way through the grapevine—European workers mob the bar for a drink and a quick bite to eat after work. The Grapevine's outdoor seating overflows onto the property of the bar next door, which seems to attract fewer visitors—the locals clearly know something we don't. The interior resembles more of a French brasserie than a modern Belgian bar, so ditch the Belgian beer for wine and mingle. Make sure you're carrying some business cards, as the Grapevine is an ideal place to network.

 # [M]Maelbeek. [$] Beer €2.50-4. ⏰ Open daily 9am-midnight.

THE BEER FACTORY 🎟🍸 BAR

6 Place du Luxembourg ☎02 513 38 56 💻www.brasserie-beer-factory.be

One of the more relaxed bars in this bustling square, The Beer Factory can be summed up by the painted picture of a man grinning over a generous pint on the wall. Although it isn't a massive space and doesn't actually produce any beer of its own, the Beer Factory has a cool rounded bar topped with a metal pipe "hat" to make it look like a brewery.

⚡ Ⓜ*Maelbeek*. *i Credit card min. €10.* Ⓢ *Beer €2-5.* ⏰ *Open M-F 10am-11:30pm.*

JAMES JOYCE

⦿ ⚲ IRISH PUB

34 rue Archimède
☎0497 48 89 41

Named after the Irish poet and writer James Joyce, this pub was the first Irish pub to be opened in the Schuman area and was quickly followed by many more. But as they say, the original is always the best. This small pub extends out the back, and you can place yourself at one of the many booths to enjoy your cheap drinks in the company of a mixed crowd; all ages and all nationalities seems to frequent James Joyce, but you won't feel as Eurocratic as you would in a place like, say, The Grapevine. On the weekends the pub stays open until 7am.

⚡ Ⓜ*Schuman.* Ⓢ *Beer €1.80-3. Cocktails €7-9.* ⏰ *Open M-Th 2pm-2am, F-Sa 2pm-7am, Su 2pm-2am.*

JORDAN'S

⦿ ⚲ CLUB, LOUNGE

49-50 Place Jourdan
☎02 230 74 66 🖥www.jordans.be

Jordan's is an after-work club, although it doesn't seem to have the pomp associated with such an establishment. The chill atmosphere and chic furniture make it an ideal place to relax and forget about the day (even if you weren't at work). Try one of their special cocktails *(€8)*, including classics or Jordan's specials such as Kiss Kool and Birdie Nam Nam.

⚡ Ⓜ*Schuman. Place Jourdan is just down rue Froissart.* Ⓢ *Drinks €2-8.* ⏰ *Open M 11:30am-3pm, Tu-F 11:30am-3pm and 5pm-late, Sa 5pm-late.*

KITTY O'SHEA'S

⦿ ⚲ IRISH PUB

42 Charle Magne
☎02 280 27 33

A young and hip crowd seems to frequent Kitty's, so despite all the English speakers you may forget that you are drinking with international uppity-ups flying it high in Brussels. Although this Irish pub seems to lack a real sense of the Irish, its corner terrace offers a relaxed place away from the EU center to enjoy your pint in peace.

⚡ Ⓜ*Schuman.* Ⓢ *Beer €2-4.* ⏰ *Open daily noon-1am.*

O'FARRELLS

⬗ ⚲ IRISH PUB

7 Place du Luxembourg
☎02 230 1887

Yet another Irish themed pub to keep you entertained with its quirks and larks. O'Farrells is located on the bustling Place Lux, so you have a lot of choices, but this is the only official Irish pub in the square. The large outside terrace is popular in the summer, and the fact that the European Parliament is a stone's throw away means the local clientele are likely to speak as many languages as the pub serves beers.

⚡ Ⓜ*Maelbeek.* Ⓢ *Beer €2-5.* ⏰ *Open daily 10am-3am.*

arts and culture

Brussels is a hotbed of theater, popular music, and opera, and hosts numerous music and film festivals throughout the year. Make sure you pick up the free weekly culture publication **Agenda** from the Tourist Office, or the free magazine **BruXXL** (available in English), both of which print schedules of all the hot arts and culture events in the city.

OPERA

THEATRE ROYALE DE LA MONNAIE
Place de la Monnaie

🞄 LOWER TOWN
☎070 23 39 39 🖳www.lamonnaie.be

Brussels's Opera House performed numerous sold-out shows in 2010, including a wildly popular production of *Macbeth*. Performances range from classical opera to chamber music performances. Student rush tickets and discounts of up to 50% are available, but performances sell out quickly, especially in June.
➿ Ⓜ De Brouckère. *i* Box office at 23 rue Léopold. Ⓢ Tickets from €20. ⌚ Box office open Tu-Sa 11:30am-5:30pm.

THEATER

THEATRE NATIONAL
111-115 Bld. Emile Jacqmain

🞄 LOWER TOWN
☎02 203 53 03 🖳www.theatrenational.be

The Theatre National is the official home to a wide range of productions, including well known plays and experimental theater. The seats in this modern building on Bld. Jacqmain sell out quickly, and the theater recently announced that the 2011 season will include three original plays.
➿ ⓂRogier. Ⓢ Tickets €19, students and under 26 €9. ⌚ Box office open Tu-Sa 11am-6pm.

BEURSSCHOUWBURG
20-28 rue Ortz

🞄 LOWER TOWN
☎02 550 03 50 🖳www.beursschouwburg.be

The Beursschouwburg is a haven for up-and-coming artists and prides itself on supporting newcomers to film, theater, and dance. Contemporary theater is the name of the game here, but you can also catch films, documentaries, dance performances, and temporary exhibits.
➿ ⓂBourse. Ⓢ Tickets €12, students €10. ⌚ Box office open M-F 10am-6pm.

THEATRE ROYAL DU PARC
3 rue de la Loi

🞄 UPPER TOWN
☎02 503 30 30 🖳www.theatreduparc.be

If you're game for a laugh, then get yourself down to the Parc and pick up a ticket to see stand-up or scripted comedies. The early 2011 season includes *La Poupée Titanic*, a reenactment of the Titanic with puppets.
➿ ⓂParc. Ⓢ Tickets €5-150, student rush €9.50. ⌚ Box office open Sept-May daily 11am-6pm; June-Aug M-F 11am-6pm.

CIRQUE ROYAL
81 rue de l'Enseignment

🞄 UPPER TOWN
☎02 218 20 15 🖳www.cirque-royal.org

Cirque Royal isn't actually a circus, but given its wide range of shows, it's surprising that a circus doesn't make it onto the docket. Expect to see comedies, ballets, popular French and European singers, operas, and traditional theater gracing the stage. Prices and student discounts for individual shows depend on the visiting company.
➿ ⓂGare Centrale. Ⓢ Depends on show. ⌚ Box office open M-F 10am-6pm.

BOZAR
18 rue Ravenstein

🞄 UPPER TOWN
☎02 507 82 00 🖳www.bozar.be

Bozar isn't just a brilliant sight to visit during the day for its exhibits—it also hosts visiting artists and performances in dance, music, theater, and film throughout the year. Expect quality cultural events to match the stunning and political exhibits. For more information, make sure you grab a copy of the Bozar Magazine, which lists the venue's current offerings.
➿ ⓂParc. Ⓢ Depends on performance. Student discounts offered. ⌚ Box office open Sept-June M-Sa 11am-7pm; July-Aug M-F 11am-5pm.

TOONE
66 rue du Marché aux Herbes

🞄 LOWER TOWN
☎02 511 71 37 🖳www.toone.be

This old and traditional puppet theater uses marionettes to create funny and enjoyable performances for the young or young at heart. Shows range from Shakespearean productions to modern comedies. Shows start at 8:30pm and usually run Thursday to Saturday, with a Saturday matinee at 4pm.

✱ ⓂBourse. *i* Booking in advance by telephone or online is advised. Ⓢ Tickets €10, students €7. Student discount not available F-Sa evenings. ⏰ Telephone lines open noon-midnight. Shows last approx. 2hr.

CONCERT VENUES

LE BOTANIQUE
✱¥ UPPER TOWN

Bvd. du Jardin. 29-31 Botanique ☎02 218 37 32 ▣www.botanique.be

The Botanical Gardens make for a beautiful stroll during the day, but things get a little raunchier at night, when the grand building that towers above the gardens hosts some of the best concerts in the city. Three different stages provide an intimate performance space for artists from the UK, continental Europe, and, on occasion, the States; in 2010, heavyweight performers included Ellie Goulding, Marina and the Diamonds, and Kate Nash. Brussels's student crowd can't get enough of Le Botanique, and in recent years it's become the city's most popular venue for live music. Make sure you check out a concert there when you head to Brussels.

✱ ⓂBotanique. Ⓢ Prices vary by show. ⏰ Box office open daily 10am-6pm.

L'ANCIENNE BELGIQUE
✱¥ LOWER TOWN

110 Bvd. Anspach ☎02 548 24 24 ▣www.abconcerts.be

L'Ancienne Belgique is one of the coolest concert venues in Brussels and is regularly mobbed by local students. Performances range from alternative to rock to pop; in 2010, Goldfrapp, Bullet for my Valentine, Funeral for a Friend, and Plan B all graced the stage. Regular free concerts are another plus at this awesome venue.

✱ ⓂBourse. *i* Box office at 23 rue Streen. Ⓢ Generally free; some concerts around €10. ⏰ Box office open M-F 11am-6pm.

MERCEDES HOUSE
✱ UPPER TOWN

22-24 rue Bodenbroek ☎02 400 42 50 ▣www.mercedeshouse.be

You don't have to be in the market for a new whip to check out one of the Mercedes House's monthly concerts. Jazz and classical performers play evening recitals for the patrician crowd seated around the House's seriously swanky cars. Dress to impress. Combine the show with dinner at their ritzy brasserie (€70).

✱ ⓂGare Centrale. *i* Tickets should be purchased online or by phone. Ⓢ Tickets from €15.

CINEMAS

CINEMA ARENBERG
⊛ UPPER TOWN

26 Galerie de la Reine ☎02 512 80 63 ▣www.arenberg.be

Cinema Arenberg is an eclectic little venue that shows European and American films. Catch that movie you missed in the States, or be a little more cultured and head to a Spanish or French documentary. Full schedule and prices can be found online.

✱ ⓂGare Centrale. *i* Film schedule available online. Ⓢ Tickets €8, students €6.60.

FLAGEY
✱ HEYSEL

Place St. Croix ☎02 641 10 20 ▣www.flagey.be

Situated in the hip Place St. Croix and surrounded by bars and 20-somethings, Flagey plays it smart and caters directly to the young and alternative crowd. The theater is home to the Brussels Film Festival, but the venue also offers live music and debates for its mixed audience. Ticket prices vary depending on event, but discounts for under 26 are available.

✱ ⓂLouise or tram #81 to Flagey. Ⓢ Prices vary depending on performance or film. ⏰ Box office *open M 5-8pm, Tu-Sa 11am-10pm, Su 3-8pm.*

STYX

⊛ UPPER TOWN

72 rue de l'Arbre Bénit

☎02 512 21 02

Styx traditionally claims to be the smallest cinema in Europe, and although this may not be entirely true anymore, it is certainly the smallest in Brussels. The little independent cinema offers a good mix of foreign and French films, and you can also find some American award-winners here a year or so after their official releases.

⧣ Ⓜ*Louise.* Ⓢ *Tickets from €6.* 𝄞 *Depends on films.*

festivals

BRUSSELS FILM FESTIVAL

⊛ SUMMER

Place St.-Croix

☎02 641 10 20 ▣www.fffb.be

European filmmakers flock to the city in late June to screen some of the most promising up-and-coming independent movies of the year. The competition takes place at Flagey, the independent cinema just off of Flagey square, and tickets for the films are available individually, as well as for the final awards ceremony.

⧣ *Tram #81 to* Ⓜ*Louise.* Ⓢ *€7 per film, under 26 €5. 5-film screen pass €25.* 𝄞 *Box office open M 5-10pm, Tu-Sa 11am-10pm, Su 5-10pm.*

COULEUR CAFÉ

⬥ SUMMER

▣www.couleurcafe.be

Snoop Dogg headlined the Belgian music festival here in 2010, though the rest of the performances were dominated by French and Belgian artists. The music festival draws in young people from all over Europe; many of its performances focus on fusion music and Afro-Caribbean sounds. The Couleur Café celebrated its 20th festival in 2010 and is set to continue going strong in 2011.

Ⓢ *1-day ticket €34; 3-day €73, with camping €88.* 𝄞 *Last weekend in June.*

FÊTE DE LA MUSIQUE

SUMMER

▣www.conseildelamusique.be

Considered by some to be a national holiday (it's actually treated as such in France), the Fête de la Musique is an annual jackpot for music lovers that features a variety of musical styles and performers. Stages are set up by the Royal Palace throughout the city, and the musicians perform around the clock. For more information on the 2011 lineup check the website.

Ⓢ *Free.* 𝄞 *3rd weekend in June.*

BRUSSELS JAZZ MARATHON

SPRING

▣www.brusselsjazzmarathon.be

The Brussels Jazz Marathon sets up five outdoor stages in the Grand Place, Place Ste. Catherine, Sablon, Marché aux Poissons and Place Fernard Cock, and provides free jazz shows for all to enjoy. Expect fusion, modern, and traditional jazz from both venerated musicians and up-and-coming stars.

Ⓢ *Free.* 𝄞 *Late May.*

BRUSSELS SUMMER FESTIVAL

⬥ SUMMER

▣www.bsf.be

The 10-day Brussels Summer Festival regularly draws music fans from across Europe, and will be celebrating its 10th anniversary in August 2011. Big European names hit the stage and entertain the mainly student crowd on outdoor and indoor stages; your ticket gets you in to all the performances in the city center.

brussels

Tickets can be bought online, from FNAC stores (🖥*www.fnac.be*), or at 🖥www.ticketnet.be.

$ Presale €20, during festival €30. ⏰ 10 days in early Aug.

walking in a winter wonders-land

Whether you're Christian, Jewish, Muslim, or Jain, there are few who can resist the undeniable charm of the **Winter Wonders** festival that occurs every winter in Brussels. Lasting from the middle of December until early January, the Winter Wonders festival, also known as Plaisirs d'Hiver or Winterpret, is the perfect way to get in the holiday spirit. The first Winter Wonders festival was in 2004, but it is obvious that it is quickly becoming a fixture in the wide array of Brussels festivals. An ice skating rink, a giant Ferris wheel offering breathtaking views of the city, and a Christmas tree à la Rockefeller Center are only some of the things that a visitor can look forward to at this festival, where entrance is free of charge. There are also more than 200 stalls selling food and holiday tchotchkes; warm up with a delicious cup of mulled wine, squeeze in some last-minute holiday purchases, or find the energy for some ice-skating by chowing down on some hearty Belgian fare.

There's a reason why *A Christmas Carol* didn't take place in Brussels: between the mood music, the smiling faces, the surreal lighting, and the ideal location, even Scrooge would be won over by the almost tangible holiday spirit at the Winter Wonders festival.

BROSELLA SUMMER

🖥www.brosella.be

This classic folk festival takes place over a weekend in mid-July and is entirely free. The festival dates back to 1977, and has provided concerts, workshops and master classes ever since. Special events are available for kids. All concerts take place at the Groentheater, which is near the Ossegem Parc (near Atomium). Check the website for full agenda and listings.

🚇 [M]Heysel. $ Free. ⏰ Mid-July.

shopping

SHOPPING MALLS

CITY2 LOWER TOWN

123 rue Neuve ☎02 22 11 40 60 🖥www.city2.be

Situated just off of rue Neuve, Brussels's central shopping mall dedicates an entire floor to the department store Fnac, and hosts a variety of clothes, electronics, and jewelry shops. A food hall is also located on the first floor. The mall includes an H and M, Sports World, and GB supermarket for your daily needs.

🚇 [M]Rogier. ⏰ Open M-Th 10am-7pm, F 10am-7:30pm, Sa-Su 10am-7pm.

GALERIE PORTE LOUISE UPPER TOWN

235 Galerie de la Porte Louise ☎02 2 512 97 12 🖥www.galerieportelouise.com

Situated in a more expensive shopping area, this mall is the place to go for independent designers, expensive jewelry, and high-class fashion. Small boutiques line the walkway, including a pooch pampering shop where the posh bring their lap dogs to be spoiled rotten. If you're on a budget you'd better stick to window shopping. The mall can be accessed from the lucrative shopping street of Av. Louise or off the main road Av. de la Toison d'Or.

🕈 ⓂLouise. 🕐 Open M-Sa 6:30am-9pm (most shops open from 9am), Su 9am-9pm.

MARKETS

MAROLLES FLEA MARKET
⬤ MAROLLES

Place du Jeu de Balles

The biggest flea market in Brussels. Anything and everything is on sale here, from pocket watches to plastic pins, stuffed squirrels to ferret skins. The local vendors will happily bargain with you, but don't try to out-haggle them—they do this job seven days a week and know all the tricks. The best deals go down early on, so if you want a chance of finding treasure amid all that junk, get there shortly after the market opens.

🕈 ⓂGare du Midi. *i* Most vendors only accept cash. 🕐 Open daily 7am-3pm.

CHOCOLATE SHOPS

PLANÈTE CHOCOLATE
⬥ LOWER TOWN

24 rue du Lombard ☎02 511 07 55 🖳www.planetechocolat.be

One of the most renowned chocolate shops in Brussels (and that's really saying something), Planète Chocolate displays an infinite array of handmade chocolate creations, including detailed chocolate bouquets. For a small fee (€7), you can arrange a trip to their "chocolate salon" and watch the local Oompa-Loompas brew the house specialties, learn a little chocolate history, and then—wait for it—try some of their creations. Call in advance to arrange your visit.

🕈 ⓂBourse. Ⓢ €7 for chocolate salon. 🕐 Open M-Sa 10am-6:30pm, Su 11am-6:30pm.

LA MAISON DES MAITRES CHOCOLATIERS
⬥ LOWER TOWN

4 Grand Place ☎02 888 66 20 🖳www.mmcb.be

This isn't just any chocolate shop. The 10 chocolate craftsmen employed here work tirelessly to invent scrumptious new tastes and treats, then sculpt their creations into increasingly eccentric shapes—we particularly enjoyed the life-sized chocolate baby in the window. The most innovative chocolatier you'll ever see, with the prices to match—but it's worth checking out, if only to see the flowing waterfall of chocolate behind the front desk.

🕈 ⓂBourse. 🕐 Open daily 10am-10pm.

CLOTHING

RUE NEUVE
⬥ LOWER TOWN

rue Neuve

Rue Neuve is Brussels's main shopping district. Big brand names are tucked between the small cafes and mom-and-pop shops. including H and M, C and A, and Pimkie. On the weekends, the street is packed with students and local families looking for a bargain.

🕈 ⓂRogier or ⓂDe Brouckère. Rue Neuve is between the two. 🕐 Shops usually open M-Sa 10am-6pm. Some shops open Su.

BLENDER01
⬥ LOWER TOWN

18 rue des Chartreux ☎02 503 61 83 🖳www.facebook.com/Blender01

The guy who owns this shop, Alexis, personally selects designs and gadgets from retailers, and then sells them to the general public. The result is an exceptionally unique collection; currently Blender01 exclusively stocks several designers, including Grenoble native HixSept L'Oiseau Gris, who makes some rather stylish male clothing. Pieces include a hoodie with a Lego-man printed onto the hood, and a pair of wooden sunglasses (€130). Although some items, like the glasses, are expensive, other pieces are more affordable, particularly when it comes to the quirky wallets and bags.

✤ ⓂBourse. 🕙 Open Tu-Sa 11am-7pm, Su 2-6pm.

FOXHOLE
LOWER TOWN

4 rue des Riches Claires ☎477 20 53 36 ✉info@foxholeshop.com

FoxHole specializes in the 1970s and '80s vintage gear; this is the place to go if you're looking for a really garish plaid shirt or just something cool and retro. The prices are student friendly, and many of Brussels's hip arts students buy their clothes here. Expect everything from shoes to bags to shell suits, as well as some really cool hats.

✤ ⓂBourse. 🕙 Open Tu-Sa 12:30-6:30pm.

WHAT?
LOWER TOWN

74 rue du Marché au Charbon ☎02 513 83 00 ✉www.what-shop.com

Say whaaaat? You might actually find that phrase on a T-shirt here in this tiny but plentiful emporium of quirky T-shirt designs. Expect retro styles, movie references, and Hello Kitty patterns, in addition to the general "I ♥ Brussels" fare.

✤ ⓂBourse. 🕙 Open M-F noon-7pm, Sa 11am-7pm, Su 1-7pm.

EPISODE
LOWER TOWN

28 rue de la Violette ☎02 513 36 53 ✉www.episode.eu

For affordable vintage clothing, including '80s shell suits, a great range of hats, and stone-washed Levis, then head up to Episode, a chain with stories throughout Europe's major cities. Treat yourself to some plaid and a genuine gas mask. Prices are cheaper here than some vintage shops, and most items aren't too expensive.

✤ ⓂBourse. 🕙 Open M 2-7pm, Tu 1-7pm, W-Sa 11am-7pm.

SOHO
UPPER TOWN

6 Place Stephanie ☎02 503 14 69 ✉www.sohofashion.be

All the designs in this shop are imported directly from Italy. Incredibly, the selection isn't overpriced, and most of the items are within a student price range. The funky decor is a collision of old and new styles: the shelves are made out of co-opted computer chip boards, and the floors are a mosaic of traditional tiles.

✤ ⓂLouise. ⑤ €15-150. 🕙 Open daily 10am-7:30pm.

MONSET
UPPER TOWN

4 Galerie de la Reine ☎02 511 41 33

Brussels sure likes its hats, and numerous shops offering to fill its head-wear fixation dot the city center. This small independent store provides both the area's most affordable stylish hats, as well as some more expensive options—people in Brussels will sure shell it out for swank, apparently. The store also sells a fashionable range of umbrellas and canes.

✤ ⓂGare Centrale. ⑤ €40-400. 🕙 Open M-Sa 10am-6pm.

BOOKS

BOZAR BOOKSHOP
UPPER TOWN

15 rue Ravenstein ☎02 514 15 05 ✉www.bozarshop.com

After exploring the exhibits and performances of the Bozar Center, make sure you head to the bookstore out back. Thick stacks of books, postcards, and DVDs make this place a cave of wonders for art lovers and bookworms alike.

✤ ⓂParc. 🕙 Open daily 10am-10pm.

BRÜSEL
LOWER TOWN

122-124 Bvd. Anspach ☎02 513 72 35 ✉www.multibd.com

Comic books have a strong Belgian heritage, and Brüsel makes sure you don't forget it—the walls here are covered in cardboard cutouts and posters of French and Belgian comic superstars. Don't expect to find Superman or the X-Men here—this is the home of Tintin, Asterix, and Obelix.

🚏 [M]Bourse. ⏰ Open M-Sa 11am-7pm.

LIBRAIRIE VAN DER ELST 🎫 UPPER TOWN

55 rue de la Madeline ☎02 511 82 54 💻librairievanderelst@hotmail.com

With shelves full of first editions, dated magazines, French newspapers, and rare copies of old books, Van Der Elst retains the comfortingly musty feel of an old library in the age of the Kindle.

🚏 [M]Gare Centrale. ℹ Books also bought here. ⏰ Open Tu-Sa 10am-6:30pm.

PASSA PARTA 🎫 LOWER TOWN

46 rue Antoine Dansaert ☎02 502 94 60 💻www.passpartabookshop.be

Passa Parta has one of Brussels's biggest collections of multilingual books. The extensive children's section also provides a diverse reading experience, and the store often holds author events and guest speakers.

🚏 [M]Ste.-Catherine. ⏰ Open M-Sa 11am-7pm, Su noon-6pm.

MUSIC

DR. VINYL 🎫 LOWER TOWN

1 rue de la Grande Île ☎02 512 73 44

Dr. Vinyl will see you now in this small, hip record store. Though most stores in the area specialize in second-hand vinyls and older, retro music, Dr Vinyl prides himself on selling new and cutting-edge music on vinyl. DJs of tomorrow should come to the Doctor for a check-up and spin some of their own music on the decks that line the edge of the shop. If you're not sure how a record player works and just need some new iPod headphones, the Doctor will also happily point you in the direction of other music shops in the area.

🚏 [M]Bourse. ⏰ Open M-Sa noon-8pm.

JUKE BOX SHOP 🌟 LOWER TOWN

165 Bld. Anspach ☎02 511 67 51 💻info@jukebox.be

The (self-proclaimed) best shop in Brussels for vinyls, EPs, and LPs, the Juke Box Shop prides itself on its alternative collection. Every musical taste is catered to, but the Shop's collection specializes in psychedelic, soul, chansons, and new-wave, making this store a little different from the others in the area. They buy, sell, and trade records.

🚏 [M]Bourse. ⏰ Open M-Sa 11am-6pm.

VEALS AND GEEKS 🎫 LOWER TOWN

8 rue des Grand Carmes ☎02 511 40 14

Bring your old Dungeons and Dragons set; geeks rule here. Veals and Geeks stocks a well-chosen, if small, collection of records, ranging from the Beatles to Metallica, but is better known for its secondhand Game Boys, band T-shirts, and DVDs.

🚏 [M]Bourse. ⏰ Open daily 11am-8pm.

JEWELRY

BETTY DE STEFANO 🎫 UPPER TOWN

17 rue Lebeau ☎02 511 46 13 💻www.collectors-gallery.com

Betty de Stefano is located near the Beaux-Arts area of town, so expect some very *beaux* pieces of jewelry from the 20th century. The small shop also specializes in diamonds, and Betty herself will help advise you on the perfect piece to match your outfit.

🚏 [M]Gare Centrale. Just off of Place de la Justice $ Prices vary. ⏰ Open W-Sa 11am-6pm, Su 11am-3pm.

LUXIOL

LOWER TOWN

221 Chaussée d'Ixelles ☎02 648 77 14

Still going strong after 21 years, Luxiol is a small but bright shop with a diverse range of handmade jewelry. Luxiol also specializes in classic wooden toys and precious stones.

[M]Louise. $ Prices vary. ⏰ Open Tu-Sa 10:30am-6:30pm.

LA VIE EST BELLE

LOWER TOWN

4 rue Jules Bouillon ☎02 513 89 98

The earthy vibe that pervades this little shop is reflected in its jewelry collection, which is vaguely South Asian and very intricate; expect lots of greens, purples, and precious stones. Walk away with a small piece of Asia without actually leaving Brussels.

[M]Louise. ⏰ Open M 2-6:30pm, Tu-Sa 11am-6:30pm.

AFRICAN MUSEUM GIFT SHOP

PLACE SCHUMAN

13 Leuvensesteenweg ☎02 769 52 11 🖥www.africanmuseum.be

This neat little shop specializes in African goods, with a fair-trade collection of necklaces, bracelets, and rings that have been imported from countries across the African continent. The artisans' intricate carvings and detail work make the shop an ideal place to pick up a stunning and unique piece of jewelry. The shop also sells precious stones, soapstone figures, and wooden carvings.

In African Museum. Line 1 to [M]Montgomery or tram #44 to Tervuren. ⏰ Open Tu-F 10am-5pm, Sa-Su 10am-6pm.

essentials

PRACTICALITIES

- **TOURIST OFFICES: Central Office** sells the **Brussels Card,** which includes free public transport, a city map, and museum access for 24hr., 48hr., or 72hr. *(€24/€34/€40.)([M] Bourse, East corner of Grand Place ☎02 513 89 40 🖥www.brusselsinternational.be ⏰ Open daily in summer 9am-6pm, in winter 10am-2pm.)* There is also a second, less central office location. *(2-4 rue Royale ☎02 513 89 40 ⏰ Open daily 10am-6pm.)*
- **CURRENCY EXCHANGE: CBC Automatic Change.** *(7 Grand Place ☎02 547 12 11 ⏰ Open 24hr.)* **Moneytrans** also offers currency exchange *(6 rue Marché-aux-Herbes ☎02 227 18 20).*
- **LAUNDROMATS: Washing 65.** *(65 rue du Midi ⏰ Open daily 7am-9pm.)* **Wash Club.** *(68 rue du Marché au Charbon $ €4 per 8 kg. ⏰ Open daily 7am-10pm.)*
- **INTERNET:** Free Wi-Fi in **McDonald's** and **Quick** on rue de Neuve. **CyberCafés.** *(66 rue du Midi and 86 Bld. Emile Jacqmain $ €1.50 per 30min. ⏰ Open daily 9am-10pm.)*
- **POST OFFICE: Central Office** *(1 Bvd. Anspach ☎022 012345 ⏰ Open M-F 8:30am-6pm, Sa 10am-4pm.)*
- **POSTAL CODE:** 1000

EMERGENCY!

- **LATE-NIGHT PHARMACIES: Pharmacie Fripiers** is closest to the Grand Place. *(24b rue des Fripiers ☎02 218 04 91 ⏰ Open M-Sa 9am-7pm.)* **Stanby Pharmacies** can be reached at all hours by phone only. *(☎0800 20 600 ⏰ Open 24hr.)*

GETTING THERE

By Air

The **Brussels airport** *(☎090 07 00 00 💻www.brusselsairport.be)* is 14km from the city center. **Shuttles** run between the airport and **Midi Train Station.** *(💻www.voyages-lelan.be $ One-way €13, round-trip €22. ⏰ Every 30min. 4am-11:45pm.)*

By Train

Brussels has three main train stations: **Gare du Midi, Gare Centrale,** and **Gare du Nord** *(☎02 555 25 55; 💻www.scnb.be).* All international trains stop at Gare du Midi, and most stop at Gare Centrale and Gare du Nord as well. Gare Centrale is the stop which will bring you closest to the center and most accommodations. Brussels can be reached from **Antwerp** (*$ €6. ⏰ 45min.*); **Bruges** (*$ €12. ⏰ 45 min.*); **Liège** (*$ €19. ⏰ 1hr.*); **Amsterdam, the Netherlands** (*$ €43. ⏰ 3hr.*); **Paris, France** (*$ €55-86. ⏰ 1hr.*). **Eurostar** (*💻www.eurostar.com)* runs to **London, UK.** (*$ €60-240. ⏰ 2hr.*).

GETTING AROUND

By Foot

Getting around Brussels is **👍cheap and simple** because you can do (almost) the whole city by foot and won't need to step onto the Metro unless you head to the Atomium or further on the outskirts.

By Bike

Remember, cars rule the roads in Brussels and bikes are only advisable for the truly brave. If you want to bike around the city there are **villo** (bike rental) points situated at key locations in Brussels; the first half hour is free and then you pay incrementally for each half hour afterward *(💻www.villo.be).* **Signposts** are strategically placed in the center to direct you to sights, museums, and points of interest in Brussels.

By Metro

The Metro system rings the city, with a tram running vertically through the middle and two Metro lines running east to west. The bus system also connects the various quarters of the city such as Ixelles and the European Area. All public transport in Brussels is run by **STIB (Société des Transports Intercommunaux Bruxellois)** *(☎070 23 2000 💻www.stib.be $ €0.30 per min. ⏰ M-Th 5:30am-12:30am, F-Sa 5:30am-3am, Su 5:30am-12:30am).* Hence, all tickets are valid for the Metro, the tram, and the bus. A **Ten-Voyage ticket** *(€12.30)* is probably the best deal.

By Taxi

If you want to take a taxi after the Metro stops running, you can call **Taxi Bleus** *(☎02 268 00 00)* or **Taxis Orange** *(☎02 349 43 43.)* Taxi prices are calculated by a fixed price per kilometer *(€1.35-2.70)* and a fixed base charge *(€2.40-4.40).*

brussels 101

HISTORY

Marshes Meet the Middle Ages

All that Duke Charles of Lower Lotharingia wanted was a private island in the River Senne. Unfortunately, the peasant riff-raff followed.

It seems that the site the Duke chose for his pet project Bruocsella, "the village in the marshes," was a little too perfect. Located on a flourishing trade route between the manufacturing centers of Flanders and Cologne, Brussels promptly became a vibrant trading hub in its own right after its founding in 979. To protect their investments, the nobility and an increasingly influential merchant class constructed the first fortifications around the city in the 12th century. The wall was named **La Petite Ceinture,** "The Small Belt," making Brussels the first capital in history to exclude the plebian masses by surrounding itself with a "Beltway." Having acquired this most important medieval status symbol, Brussels was poised to be a successful European metropolis.

Capital Gains

But that didn't mean it was a stable metropolis. Over the next hundreds of years, control of Brussels pinballed from empire to empire, from one royal family to the next. From the Dukes of Burgundy to the Habsburgs, the region's rulers were veritable who's who of medieval Europe. Holy Roman Emperor Charles V made Brussels the capital of his empire, and transformed the city into a beacon of refinement and elegance. His bloodthirsty successor, **Phillip II,** ruled from Spain, and was considerably less tasteful. As Martin Luther's Protestant teachings spread throughout Europe, Philip's army entered Belgium in 1567 to enforce Catholic doctrine. His military compelled locals to return to the warm embrace of the Church through several thousand executions, which culminated in the beheading of two nobles in Brussels's central marketplace.

For the next several centuries, ruling powers used Brussels as a pawn in an elaborate geopolitical chess game; heads rolled, and kings and queens were knocked off with alarming frequency. Brussels was hit hardest in 1695, when the French military nearly leveled the entire city and destroyed most of its institutions. The city rebuilt and flourished under the Austrian rule that followed, and got their revenge on the French 120 years later. In 1815, enemy forces defeated Napoleon at ⚔Waterloo, which took place just a swift gallop by cavalry from the capital's walls.

Free at Last!

Or...maybe not. After Napoleon's defeat in 1815, Belgium was incorporated into the United Kingdom of the Netherlands and technically freed from foreign rule. Belgians remained a minor, culturally incompatible part of their fledgling independent nation, and the country did not last long. The politically conscious people of Brussels revolted and declared independence, and on July 21, 1831, the new king of Belgium, **King Léopold I,** marched triumphantly into the city, ushering in a period of great wealth and success.

A More Perfect Union

After a rather sleepy century, the next big event to affect Brussels was WWII. Though Belgium was conquered by Germany in an embarrassing 18 days in 1940, Brussels was left largely unscathed by the war in comparison to the rest of Europe. In 1949, a new kid came to town: the North Atlantic Treaty Organization or **NATO,** a military alliance of countries against the Soviet Union. Finally, the little city that could had some serious international clout. More influence came in the 1960s, when Brussels became the capital and political center of the

12TH CENTURY
City builds its first wall.

1357-1379
A new and improved wall is built. Now they're going places.

1229
Law and order comes to Brussels when Henri I publishes the Brussels charter.

1695
French forces destroy the city.

1760
Roller skates are born when one Belgian replaces ice skate blades with wheels.

1847
Europe's oldest shopping center opens in Brussels.

1910
Brussels World
Exhibition.

European Economic Community, now the ◨**European Union**—though the buzz-kill that is Strasbourg, France, claims the capital title as well. The organization's arrival catalyzed a construction spree of unimaginative buildings, and the influx of bureaucrats gave Brussels a household necessity that remains in vogue today: red tape.

CUSTOMS AND ETIQUETTE

Two Nations, Indivisible...

1940
Nazis invade Belgium.

The Kingdom of Belgium is made up of two fiercely independent regions: French-speaking **Wallonia** (Wallonie, *en français*) to the south, and **Flanders** (Vlaanderen) to the north, which speaks Flemish, a form of Dutch. Brussels is located in the heart of Flanders, but is part of the "French Community"—one of the three official institutions that govern cultural affairs for the speakers of the country's languages. This capital city snub has caused Flemish blood to boil more than a few times. As recently as 2006, television stations were filled with images of Flemish revolution—albeit a fake revolt designed to spur discussion of the language issue. Independence parties routinely receive voter support. Belgians sometimes joke—none too jokingly—that their country is really two nations united under one king. Even in a city that has long been accustomed to politicians and hot-button issues, this is one issue tourists would be wise not to bring up in conversation, regardless of their native tongue.

1949
NATO is formed,
bringing diplomats by
the planeload.

1960S
Brussels becomes
political center of the
EU. More diplomats.

Lost in Translation

Apologies to the Flemish: French is the language of the day here. While there are two official languages, about 90% of people speak French. When giving or receiving directions, it helps to be picky about which language to use. On signs, all streets are listed as one long name made up of two languages, beginning with French and words such as "rue," and ending with the Dutch "straat." When looking for a street, Brussels residents will use only their preferred tongue. Of course, since Brussels is an international city filled with diplomats from across Europe, many people speak English as well.

1971
A Brussels court
sentences wannabe
lord Alexis Brimeyer
to jail for falsely
claiming nobility.

Slow Food Nation

Dining in Europe is not exactly a race against the clock. Meals are a social occasion; sandwich joints that (to an American eye) appear to be ideal stops for a lunch on the go provide seating, and patrons are expected to use it. Munching and multitasking is frowned upon, too. There's no better way to raise the ire of a Belgian shopkeeper than to chomp potato chips while strolling through his store, leaving lingering crumbs and some bad breath behind.

1987
Feminist groups erect
a peeing female
statue, Jeanneke
Pis...in an alley.

Merci for Smoking

No, really—thanks! As in much of continental Europe, smoking is not banned in Brussels establishments. And people do smoke. Most restaurateurs and barkeepers aren't about to keep customers away, so non-smoking sections can be hard to find, and ventilation in centuries-old stone buildings is often

brussels

sub-par to say the least. In public spaces including railway stations, public transportation, and—in case Someone above is watching—churches, smoking is barred.

FOOD AND DRINK

Street Cart/Calorie Chart?

What would the American diner be like without the influence of Belgium? A visit to Brussels reveals that Americana may not be so, well, American after all. Throughout Belgium, vendors with small carts sell **frites**—despite their American name, the Belgians invented the French fry first. Unlike the hometown drive-thru, these fries are always crispy and piping hot, because Belgians cook them twice, including right before they are served. Joining their fried friends on the streets of Brussels are the famous **Belgian waffles,** but hold the maple syrup—these babies are glazed with sugar or topped with ice cream and fruit. Have the Belgians declared war on unclogged arteries? If so, they're winning; these treats prove impossible to resist.

Chocolat, Chocolat, Chocolat

There are no Oompa-Loompas, but Brussels is likely home to more than a few slightly mad chocolatiers. It certainly has a number of chocolate factories and quaint sweet shops. In his Brussels kitchen in 1912, Jean Neuhaus invented the **praline,** the quintessential Belgian chocolate, when he filled chocolate shells with cream and nut pastes. Today, though still made largely in independent boutiques, chocolate accounts for hundreds of millions of dollars of Belgium's exports. If you're expecting any love back home, be sure to bring a box or ten home for that special someone.

A Healthy(er) Option...

With all its calorie-filled snacks, your inner entrepreneur might think that fat camp and vitamin shakes could find a niche here. But somehow the citizens manage to remain remarkably fit; now figure out how to export that success to the States, and you're golden. Even Brussels has some healthy options. After all, Brussels lent its name to a well-known vegetable, the **Brussels sprout,** reviled by children the world over. In Brussels they know how to cook them right, the way Mom just never could. Still craving that side of fries? **Moules frites,** mussels in wine sauce with fries, is a popular dish served at many Brussels brasseries and cafes.

Beer!

Need we say more? It's the de facto national drink of Belgium—8700 different varieties are produced in the country. Nowhere will you find more brews than in the bars and cafes of the cosmopolitan Belgian capital. Ordering wine at a Brussels brasserie is basically like ordering beer in Napa Valley. Brussels bars serve beer in all colors (a Flemish red, anyone?) and flavors (do raspberry and peach beer sound appealing?). Brussels even has beer museums, like the Brussels Gueuze Museum, that double as operating breweries and feature remnants of beer making from the middle ages.

FESTIVALS AND FOLKLORE

Is there anyone who doesn't love a good parade? The people of Brussels have certainly loved them for quite a while—since 1549, at least. That's the year when Emperor Charles V and his entourage entered the city in a spectacle not matched since—even though the citizens try every year, in a festival known as Ommegang.

Back to the...Past

Don't even try to count the number of rose petals and floats in the parade at **Ommegang.** Hours of preparation go into recreating period costumes and setting the scene as the vast square that is Brussels's Grand Place becomes the town square of 500 years ago. Giant catapults a'firing and armored knights a'fighting keep the kids entertained in the medieval village brought to life by 1400 performers. In Brussels in July, this village is the site to see—and it's free!

mey bloom-boom pow

Just because it's called a May pole doesn't mean that a May pole festival needs to happen in May. For proof of this fact, make sure not to miss the ◼Meyboom festival in Brussels, an annual tradition that takes place in early August.

Like many other historical explanations for Belgian traditions, the story of the Meyboom festival is often disputed. Some will tell you that in 1213 the people of Brussels were in the midst of celebrating a wedding when they came under attack from the army of neighboring Ghent. Despite being caught off guard, Brussels managed to win the battle, and the Meyboom celebration commemorates this victory. There are also those who will insist that the same wedding ceremony was ambushed by a group of rowdy youths from Leuven; fortunately, these wedding crashers were swiftly dealt with. A town decree entitled the newlywed couple to plant a tree on the saint's day of their savior, St. Laurence, each year. A large tree, carried by the "buumdroegers" participating in the festivities, departs from the Place du Grand Sablon at approximately 2pm, accompanied by costumed giants carried by the "poepedroegers."

But beware! The Meyboom tree must not, by any means, arrive at its final resting place in the Grand Place later than 5pm. In 1939, the people of Brussels received an unwelcome scare, as natives of Leuven stole the Meyboom tree in the midst of the festivities. Fortunately, the fast-acting Brussels quickly chopped down a replacement tree and planted it before the historical 5pm deadline. This annual tradition is a UNESCO-recognized folklore event, and in 2008 Brussels celebrated the 800th planting of the Meyboom tree.

Belgians Go Marching In

Since they have stayed home on Mayday in May for hundreds of years, in 2000 Brussels scheduled another spring parade, **Zinneke**, that fills the void. Zinneke features citizens who work for months in workshops, or Zinnodes, to prepare the parade. No judges are needed to see how spectacular it is. Zinneke is a full-blown, contemporary street opera with over 4000 performers, and more vibrant colors than a 64-box of crayons. But check your calendar—to trick tourists, this celebration only takes place every even-numbered year.

brussels

EXCURSIONS

This may be a book about Brussels and Amsterdam, but we'd be remiss in our duty if we didn't showcase some of the other noteworthy cities just a short train ride away. If you're looking for some history and medieval beauty, head to Bruges, Maastricht, or Utrecht. Bruges is probably the most picturesque, Maastricht has the advantage of the only hilly land in the Netherlands (as much as all that flatness makes biking a cinch, it can get a bit boring), and Utrecht is home to an exciting and student-friendly nightlife scene. The Hague may be more staid, but as the most important city in the world for international law and home to the Dutch government (and royal family), it's an international political and diplomatic heavyweight to rival Brussels. Finally, Rotterdam adds a jolt of modernity and multiculturalism to the mix, with avant-garde art and cheap food nestled in the shadows of the city's crazy post-WWII architecture.

None of these destinations are by any means tourist-free, but their sights are a bit quirkier, their locals a bit easier to find, and their beer a bit cheaper. While any of the towns could easily be done as a daytrip from one of the larger cities (except, perhaps, Maastricht, which requires a longer train ride), they could also each fill a few days with enjoyable exploration. Along the way, enjoy the rolling Belgian and Dutch countryside dotted with cows and windmills. As much awesomeness as there is in the largest cities of the Low Countries, these other destinations offer a more complete picture of the Netherlands's and Belgium's diversity and charm—meaning all the more potential enjoyment for the traveler willing to hit the road and explore new surroundings.

greatest hits

- **DAM GOOD ARCHITECTURE.** Rotterdam's filled with rocking modernist buildings to replace those razed in WWII. Try the Cube Houses on for size—you might just want to move in (p. 211).

- **WHERE DREAMS COME TRUE.** It's not Orlando, but Bruges (p. 176) certainly does feel like Disney World. Tourists, castles, more tourists...we can't promise you'll see Mickey, though.

- **RULE THE WORLD.** Wannabe world leaders, watch your step: you don't want to end up in the dock at The Hague's International Court of Justice (p. 189).

If you've bought this book and are looking for student life, you're probably planning to go to Amsterdam. But don't limit your perspective! Belgium and the Netherlands offer a multitude of great opportunities for young people outside of the city on the Amstel. Start in **Rotterdam.** This town parties hard each night, the bars along Witte de Withstraat being one of the best examples. During the day, you can appreciate the kind of modern architecture that makes your parents frown and wish for the days when Corinthian order was as risqué as buildings got. Speaking of parents, if they decide to tag along with you during your trip, maybe take them to the quieter stops of **Bruges** or **The Hague.** Maybe they'll become so engrossed with the former's pretty canals and the latter's international importance that you can leave them there and head off to find a few more people your own age. You could do far worse than going to **Utrecht.** Try to be there on a Thursday, when many clubs offer free entry with a student ID. With 60,000 students around, though, any night is a great time to be in town. Or try **Maastricht** for another town with plenty of students, if fewer lively bars and clubs. What's clear though is that, wherever you head in the Low Countries, you're in one of the world's most student-friendly regions.

bruges ☎050

Bruges is often called the "Venice of the North" thanks to its beautiful canals, but we prefer to think of it as the Disney World of Belgium. The buildings here are so well-preserved that they feel as if they were built just a few years ago, despite being hundreds of years old; the sidewalks are so clean that you'll wonder if anyone actually lives here. The cobbled streets are also clogged with tourists wearing fanny packs and toting Nikon cameras, but don't let them put you off. There's a reason this city is such a hotspot. Bruges can lay claim to being the best-preserved medieval city in Europe, with entire blocks dating back to the 12th and 13th centuries. There is a small but plentiful selection of museums, ranging from the history of the *frite* to collections of art by famous Flemish painters.

It's easy to get caught in the tourist trap when visiting Bruges. If you step a bit farther out of the center of town and head down some of the beautiful side streets, however, you'll find restaurants serving cheap and tasty Flemish cuisine, shops selling beer glasses and proper Belgian lace, and bars and pubs that the average tourist would never stumble across. Bruges can be visited in the American tourist way, or the *Let's Go* local way—and we suggest you try the latter.

ORIENTATION

Bruges is very easy to navigate, thanks to two centrally located squares and a pair of large landmarks. The city is also surrounded by a canal which cuts through the center of the city, so you can always follow the water if you get lost. **The Markt** is the center of town, and is recognizable by the large **Belfry tower,** which can be seen from almost any part of town. Four of Bruges's main roads emanate from the Markt: St. **Jakobstraat** to the northwest, **Vlamingstraat** to the northeast, **Wollestraat** to the southeast, and **Steenstraat** to the southwest. East of the Markt along **Breidelstraat** is **the Burg,** the second main square in Bruges, which sports the **Town Hall** and **Holy Blood Chapel.**

excursions

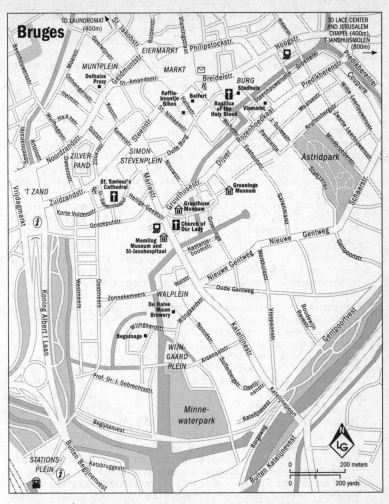

Bruges

TO LAUNDROMAT (400m)

TO LACE CENTER AND JERUSALEM CHAPEL (400m), T'JANSHUISMOLEN (800m)

EIERMARKT

MUNTPLEIN

Delhaize Proxy

MARKT

Breidelstr.

BURG

Stadhuis

Koffieboontje Bikes

Belfort

Basilica of the Holy Blood

Vismarkt

SIMON-STEVENPLEIN

'T ZAND

ZILVER-PAND

St. Saviour's Cathedral

Astridpark

Groeninge Museum

Gruuthuse Museum

Church of Our Lady

Memling Museum and St-Janshospitaal

Nieuwe Gentweg

Gentweg

WALPLEIN

De Halve Maan Brewery

Nieuwe Gentweg

Oude Gentweg

Beguinage

WIJN-GAARD PLEIN

Prof. Dr. J. Sebrechtsstr.

Minne-waterpark

Koning Albert I Laan

STATIONS-PLEIN

Beginnenvest

0   200 meters
0   200 yards

bruges · accommodations

Hoostrat runs from the Burg to the east, and **Biezelstraat** runs from the Burg to the south. When listing directions, we will use these two squares as starting points for finding other locations. All sights, restaurants and bars can be reached by a short walk from these squares.

ACCOMMODATIONS

Thanks to Bruges being a hotspot for young travelers, there is an abundance of youth hostels in the city center and just outside the city walls. The following are the best value hostels, but there are a few other hostels you can find a room in. You won't need to worry about shelling out for three- and four-star hotels in Bruges.

CHARLIE ROCKETS

HOSTEL ❶

19 Hoogstraat

☎050 33 06 60 ▪www.charlierockets.com

It's all American at Charlie Rockets, so you'll feel right at home in this hostel off

Bruges's main square. The large dorm rooms are spacious and the bathrooms are clean and modern, but Charlie really outshines the competition with its rocking bar, which is actually one of the highlights of a night out in Bruges. Save yourself the trouble and literally live at the bar.

➡ Hoogstraat runs southeast from the Burg. i Breakfast and sheets included. Free Wi-Fi. $ 6- to 8-bed dorms €17-20. ⏰ Reception 6am-4am.

BAUHAUS — HOSTEL [1]

133-145 Langestraat — ☎050 34 10 93

This hostel, budget hotel, and bar complex spans 12 houses on one of Bruges's historic streets, and as the owner explains it, "it's never easy to turn old 16th-century houses into youth hostel accommodations." The house front outside may be medieval, but rooms inside are definitely modern, with all the comfort and privacy a 21st-century backpacker could want. The lively bar is a great place to begin your night; just try not to get lost in the labyrinth of corridors leading back to your room.

➡ From the Burg, head east along Hoogstraat, which leads into Langestraat i Breakfast and sheets included. Towels available to rent. Free Wi-Fi. $ 4- to 8-bed dorms €15-22; singles €30-34; doubles €19-25; triples €18-24. ⏰ Reception 9am-11pm.

SNUFFEL — HOSTEL [1]

47-49 Ezelstraat — ☎050 33 31 33 💻www.snuffel.be

With a name like **Snuffel,** you know you aren't checking into your standard hostel. The dorms' doors are festively painted with bright colors and zany cartoon characters, and the murals continue into the rooms; you might discover some fantastic artwork hovering above your bed, or even better some photography taken by locals of the sights of Bruges. In keeping with the slightly "out there" feel, the showers are down an old winding staircase and operated by pulling a chain. They may not be modern, but they're definitely a novelty. The bar on the bottom floor boasts several chess and checker sets.

➡ From Markt, head up St. Jacobstraat which leads into Ezelstraat i Breakfast and sheets included. Free Wi-Fi. $ 4- to 12-bed dorms €15-22. ⏰ Reception 7:30am-midnight. No lockout.

EUROPA — HOSTEL [1]

143 Baron Ruzzettelaan — ☎050 35 26 79 💻www.vjh.be

The Europa hostel is bright and cheerful with extremely spacious dorms, despite the fact that the corridors feel a little bit like the set on *ER*. Although Dr. Green isn't going to burst through the main entrance any time soon, the hostel has other perks. It feels quite modern, and the lounge and bar area serve a good breakfast compared to most hostels. The main center of Bruges is a good 20min. walk away, which means you see a lot of the city, but the walk can get a bit annoying after a while.

➡ From the train station, take bus #2 to Wantestraat (just by the Texaco Garage). i Breakfast and sheets included. No towels. Wi-Fi or internet access €5 per 30min., IYHF card holders €3 per 30min. $ 4-bed dorm €17.80; 6-bed €15.70. Singles €31; doubles €22. ⏰ Reception 7:30-10am and 1:30-11pm.

CAMPING MEMLING — CAMPGROUND [2]

109 Veltennwey — ☎050 35 58 45 💻www.campingmemling.be

This very leafy campground is situated in an area that's nearly as pretty as Bruges itself. They can accommodate cars, caravans, tents, and mobile homes. Chalets are also available for rent in the summer. The center of Bruges is a short bike ride away or a 25min. walk. Showers and electricity are included in the price (an extra €2 for tent pitches).

➡ From the train station, take bus #58 or 62 to Vossensteert. Get off at Vossensteert and head down Veltennwey for about 300m. i Wi-Fi €1 per hr. $ €5 per car. €14 per tent. 4-person chalet July-Aug €63. Electricity €2 per tent. ⏰ Reception 8am-11pm.

SIGHTS

There are 16 prominent museums in Bruges, all of which are run by the local **Musea Brugge** organization. You can buy a three-day combo ticket which will get you into all of them *(€15, under 26 €5)*, but some of the museums are small and anticlimactic, and some of the city's best museums are not included in the combo pack. We've narrowed it down to a few must-sees for you:

BELFORT

TOWER

7 Markt ☎050 44 87 78 www.museabrugge.be

It is imperative that you climb the Belfort on your visit to Bruges—if you feel you have the athletic stamina, that is. This 83m high structure isn't so easy to climb if you aren't in tip top shape (we joke, but it's still quite a challenge). Fortunately there are rooms on your way up where you can learn about the tower and catch your breath. The **treasury room** showcases the fascinating history of the structure, and the exhibit in the **clock room** examines the mechanics of the giant clock outside. At the final stop in the **carillon,** you can catch a glimpse of the tower's 47 bells, which chime every hour on the hour. The panoramic view of Bruges and beyond from the top of the tower is more than worth the hike. Neatly labeled arrows are pasted to ledges of the stone windows and point you in the direction of the great cities of Europe and Belgium; they say on a clear day you can see the North Sea, but we aren't so convinced.

Grand Markt. ℹ Not part of the combo-ticket. $ €8, under 26 €4, seniors €6. ⏰ Open daily 9:30am-5pm. Last entry 30min. before close.

HOLY BLOOD CHAPEL

CHURCH

10 Burg ☎050 33 67 92

This small and simple church has one main draw which brings religious visitors and tourists by the thousands every year: a vial containing what the church claims to be the blood of Christ. The prized possession is displayed every day from 2-4pm; head up the flight of stairs and pay your respects (or even kiss!) the glass container containing one of Christianity's most prized possessions. In mid-May, the city of Bruges holds the annual Holy Blood Procession, a tradition dating back to the 14th century. The Bruges faithful reenact the passion and resurrection of Christ as the blood is paraded round the city center. Tickets for the event must be purchased in advance; more information can be found at www.ticketsbrugge.be.

In the southwest corner of the Burg. $ Free. ⏰ Open daily Apr-Sept 10am-noon and 2-6pm; Oct-Mar 10am-noon and 2-4pm.

FRIET MUSEUM

MUSEUM

33 Vlamingstraat ☎050 34 01 50 www.frietmuseum.be

It makes sense for Belgium to have a *frites* museum (*friet* in Flemish)—you're in the french fry's hometown, after all. The Friet Museum examines the history of the potato which is not as silly as it sounds; you'll discover a lot about the politics of sustainability and fair trade as well and pick up some other quirky facts. Did you know that ketchup originally came from China, for instance? Belgians will forever remind you that it's only called a *French* fry because Americans don't get out much; apparently, some Americans were offered the greasy snack by a few French-speaking Belgians during WWII, and got a little confused. "Walloon fry" doesn't have the same ring to it anyway. Make sure you grab some traditional fries in the cafe in the museum's basement on the way out.

Vlamingstraat is north off of the Markt. ℹ Not part of the Museum Pass. $ €6, students €5, ages 6-12 €4, ages 3-6 €1. ⏰ Open daily 10am-5pm.

GROENINGE MUSEUM

ART GALLERY

12 Dijver ☎050 44 87 43 www.museabrugge.be

The Groeninge Museum houses Bruges's best collection of Flemish and Belgian artists from the 15th-20th centuries. As you move through the rooms, you'll begin to appreciate the talent that went into some of these obscure religious paintings, particularly Provost's various intriguing depictions of the life of Saint Nicolas. We particularly enjoyed the Flemish Primitives (that's a painting style, not a racial slur, though we enjoyed the Flemish too). Be sure to stop and admire Vernet's "Shipwreck," which is particularly stunning. The museum also houses a Magritte for those who take their art like they take their men: surreal and begging for psychoanalysis. The ticket also gets you access to the temporary exhibition in the Arentshuis as well as The Forum, which is Bruges center for contemporary art.

*From the Markt, head south along Wollestraat and cross the bridge. Take a right onto Dijver and through the archway on your left. **i** Closed for renovation until Apr 2011. $ €8, seniors €6, ages 6-25 €1. Open Tu-Su 9:30am-5pm.*

CHURCH OF OUR LADY

CHURCH, MUSEUM

Mariastraat ☎050 44 87 78 www.museabrugge.be

The Church of our Lady houses some of Bruges's most glorious treasures including one of the very few Michelangelo statues outside of Italy. The intricate and beautiful **Madonna and Child** can be found on the baroque altar to the south of the church, with a replica of **The Last Supper** hanging above it. Many visitors pray at the feet of this masterpiece, and many others just whip out their camera instead—we'll leave it up to you to decide what to do. After exploring the church's grand interior, you can visit the museum *(€2, students €1)* to see more religious artwork from the 16th century, as well as decorative tombs for Mary of Burgundy and Charles the Bold. Although the church has no number on the street, it is pretty easy to find its steeple, which is 122m high and dominates the Bruges skyline; when in doubt, just look up and you'll find the right building.

From the Markt, head west along Seenstraat to Simon Stevenplein. From this square, head south down Mariastraat. The church is just before the bridge. $ Church free. Museum €2, students €1. Open M-F 9:30am-4:50pm, Sat 9:30am-4:40pm, Su 1:30-4:50pm.

FOOD

Bruges is brimming with restaurants, but most are overpriced with small portions thanks to the touristy nature of the town. Large groups of brasseries cluster around the **Markt,** offering cheap daily menus to the foreigners who flock in from across the globe. Don't fall for these traps—head a little further out from the Markt and try the local specialties, which will be kinder on your wallet and your stomach.

PAS PARTOUT

TRADITIONAL [1]

1 Jeruzalemstraat ☎050 33 51 16 srpaspartout@busmail.net

This restaurant used to be a three-star Michelin restaurant where it cost a fortune just to look at the menu, but a few years ago it was taken over and turned into a social service project, in an attempt to serve high-quality food to those who wouldn't normally be able to afford it. Now the older locals of Bruges come to Pas Partout to have cheap meals *(under €10)* of the highest quality in the area. Although the setting is plain and the atmosphere is pretty nondescript, you will not regret taking your lunch at this hidden treasure.

From the Burg, head along Hoogstraat to the east, cross the bridge and continue onto Molenmeers. Turn left onto Jeruzalemstraat just past the laundrette and continue right to the end of the road. $ Meals €3-10. Open M-Sa 11:45am-2:15pm.

MÉDRAD

TRADITIONAL, BELGIAN [1]

18 Sint Ammandstraat ☎050 34 86 84

Médrad has a history which goes back all the way to the 1930s, when the current owner's grandparents first opened their first little restaurant in Bruges. Food has been in the family for generations, and in 2003 the current owner moved back into what was once her parents' house to reopen the doors of Médrad. Locals started flocking back almost immediately, and after a look at the menu we can see why. The specialty spaghetti (€3) comes with cheese, vegetables, and plenty of ground beef—and this is just one of the small dishes. If you're really hungry try the large dishes, if you dare. The true definition of a neighborhood favorite, this isn't a well kept secret, so you may want to book a table the day before to guarantee one of the cheapest lunches in Bruges.

✴ *Just off of the Markt.* ⓘ *Reservations recommended.* Ⓢ *Spaghetti €3-5.50. Meals €2-10. Sandwiches €2.50-4.* ⏱ *Open Tu-Sa 11am-8:30pm, Su 12:30-8:30pm.*

DE HOBIT

✴✦ TRADITIONAL ❷

8 Kemelstraat

☎050 33 55 20

One restaurant to rule them all; that is, if you love meat. De Hobit is decorated in Lord of the Ring posters, and the recently closed Tolkein pub across the road does makes this feel like Middle Earth in the center of Bruges. De Hobit prides itself (as explained humorously in their menu) on the fact that people put on a lot of weight and get addicted to the plentiful meat dishes they serve up. One of the best dishes is the spare ribs, which are "all you can eat" (€18); after each rack is devoured the waitress will bring you another half rack until you request it to stop. Vegetarian options are few and far between but available.

✴ *From the Markt, head west along Steenstraat and take a right onto Kemelstraat.* ⓘ *Credit card min. €30. Call 2 days before your birthday for a free cake.* Ⓢ *Meals from €15-21.* ⏱ *Open daily 6-11pm.*

GRAND KAFFEE DE PASSAGE

✴✦ BELGIAN ❷

26-28 Dweerstraat

☎050 34 01 40 ▣www.passagebruges.com

The Grand Kaffee is deeply traditional, and proud of it. Portraits of family members spanning the generations hang on the walls, and the large interior feels much more like a homey living room than restaurant. Make sure you try one of their various stews, such as the beef stew with beer sauce (€14) or the "Waterzooi," an all-in-one stew with chicken, leeks, carrots, celery, onions and potatoes (€13). The menu even looks like a storybook, and the intricate writing is translated into English to make choosing even easier.

✴ *From the Markt, head down Steenstraat which leads into Zuidzandstraat. Dweerstraat is on your right.* Ⓢ *Meals €10-20.* ⏱ *Open daily 5-11pm.*

'T GANZESPEL

◍✦ TRADITIONAL, BELGIAN ❶

37 Ganzenstraat

☎050 33 12 33

Prepare to be welcomed into 't Ganzespel like family. Pull up a chair in what feels like an old living room and wait for the soup to be dished into your bowl out of a large pot, just like they used to do it back in the day. Once you've devoured your delicious soup (which is free with all main meals) you can choose from a selection of pastas, steaks, and traditional daily specials, including chicken and beef stews. The carved geese that line the walls lend a little quirkiness to this hidden Bruges classic.

✴ *From the Burg, head along Hoogstraat and into Langestraat. Ganzenstraat is 1st on your right after the bridge.* Ⓢ *Daily special €9.35. Meals €9-16.* ⏱ *Open F-Su 6:30-10pm.*

EL CHURRASCO

✴✦ STEAKHOUSE ❷

76 Vlamingstraat

☎050 34 68 28

If you're bored with Flemish food, head to El Churrasco to sample some proper South American food "grilled the Argentinian way." Most of the meat in El Churrasco is imported from Argentina, and the lamb is shipped in straight from New Zealand; that sizzling mixed grill (€20.50) won't be any ordinary feast. Although this is a more expensive night out, the high quality makes the extra few euro well worth your while.

✴ *From the Markt, head north on Vlamingstraat, El Churrasco is on the corner at the intersection* with Academiestraat. $ Beef entrees €16-26, chicken €15-16, fish €17-23. ⏰ Open M noon-3pm and 6pm-midnight, W-Su noon-3pm and 6pm-midnight.

CAFÉ VLISSINGHE 🍴🍸 CAFE, BAR ❷

2 Blakesstraat ☎050 34 37 37 🖳www.cafevlissinghe.be

This cafe isn't any old Flemish eatery—it's the oldest Flemish cafe in Bruges, and only the locals really know about it. The rustic kitchen and meticulously preserved 16th-century decor (!) makes this place a real time warp. Rest up on a sofa or large armchair by the fire or, on a sunny day, head to the garden and drink a cool beer from the large selection. The menu will keep you satisfied with basic sandwiches, panini and cheeses.

✈ From the Burg, head along Hoogstraat to the east, cross the bridge, and continue onto Molenmeers. Turn left onto Jeruzalemstraat just past the laundrette; the 4th road on the left is Blakesstraat. $ Food €3.50-8. Drinks €2-7. ⏰ Open W-Sa 11am-late.

MARKT FRITES 🍴 FRITES ❶

Markt, by the Belfry

Although these two rival *frite* sheds look like they are one and the same, there is actually a war of the *frites* being waged here as the two stands vie for customers. Both places charge identical prices for their hot potatoes, but we reckon that the one on the left, Sharsa, has the slightly tastier fries. But if the line is too long, the offerings at Mi-resto (the right hand side) aren't too bad.

✈ South corner of the Markt. $ Frites €2.25-2.75. Sauce €0.60. ⏰ Mi-resto open M-Th 9am-3am, F-Sa 9am-7am, Su 9am-3am. Sharsa open July-Aug M-Th 10am-5am, F-Sa 9am-7am, Su 10am-5am; Sept-June M-Th 10am-3am, F-Sa 9am-7am, Su 10am-3am.

DA VINCI 🍴 ICE CREAM ❶

34 Geldmunstraat

Locals rave about the ice cream here, and during the summer you'll have to fight to get to the counter to put in your order. Da Vinci serves all the usual suspects, but you can also sample some more adventurous flavors like melon and banana or something truly extravagant like tiramisu and Ferrero Rocher.

✈ Just off of the Markt. $ 1 scoop €1.20, 2 scoops €2.40, 3 scoops €3. ⏰ Open daily 11am-11pm.

NIGHTLIFE

Nightlife in Bruges is pretty easy-going, so don't expect thumping clubs and 6am kick-outs all across the city. Locals enjoy a quiet drink in some very well hidden spots, while the tourists congregate near the **Markt** to down cheap pints and trashy drinks. For a real Belgian experience, head to some of the more local spots we've listed, but you're not in Kansas anymore (by which we mean a college frat house): drink slowly, calmly, and show respect to the owner.

👍 **LUCIFERNUM** 🍴🍸 RUM BAR, ABSINTHE BAR

8 Twijnstraat

If you walk past Lucifernum during the day, you might idly wonder why someone would ring such a stately old house with barbed wire and scaffolding (the building used to be the mayor's residence and was briefly owned by the Free Masons). But ring the bell here on a Saturday night, and the doors of Lucifernum swing open, unleashing a series of the weird and wonderful. Willy Restin, the owner of the bar and a local Mephistopheles (in a good way), wanders round in a tux with a drink in hand as he ushers his guests into the parlor. The Cuban-style rum bar serves very strong but tasty mojitos, which you can enjoy in a very red bar area that's heavily decorated with trinkets Willy picked up over the years. During the summer months, the crowds head outside to lounge in Willy's garden, which feels more like the backyard of someone's house. Try get here on the first Saturday of the month, when local expert Maria opens up an 👍**Absinthe Bar** in a room just off of one of the corridors. Locals consider this to be one of the hidden gems of Bruges, so don't turn up expecting to down shots and stumble out wasted. Pay Willy and his friends some respect and treat this treasure for what it is: an absolutely fantastic venue for you to channel your inner Oscar Wilde. Keep in mind that Willy doesn't let his place fill up passed capacity, so don't arrive too late if you want to get in.

⌗ *From The Burg, head along Hoogstraat. Take a left up Kelkstraat and turn right onto Twijnstraat. Ring the doorbell (indicated with a sign).* *i* *Entry to either bar includes a free drink. No official dress code, but leave your sneakers at the hostel.* Ⓢ *Rum Bar cover €5; includes 1 free drink. Absinthe Bar cover €6; includes 1 drink. Drinks €5-6.* Ⓣ *Open Sa 9pm-late.*

'T POATERSGAT
⊛(ᵖ)⅃ BAR

82 Vlamingstraat
✉info@poetersgat.be

Three years ago, the owner of this bar bought the underground passage which connects the church above with the outside world. The owner claims that the monks that used to live in the church used the passage to sneak out, change into civilian clothes, and head down to the brothel at the end of the road. Nowadays the brothel no longer exists, but the underground passage is home to 't Poatersgat and still keeps the locals of Bruges pretty happy. Those who aren't in the know often miss the rabbit hole of an entrance; the door is embedded in the wall of the church, very low down, and many say the only way to find it is to "stumble down the steps by chance." (Be careful not to hit your head if you've had a few drinks already.) Definitely one of the most interesting places to grab a drink during your stay in Bruges.

⌗ *Vlamingstraat is just off the Markt.* *i* *Free Wi-Fi.* Ⓢ *Beer €2-5.* Ⓣ *Open daily 5pm-late.*

DE GARRE
⊛⅃ PUB

1 De Garre
☎050 34 10 29

They say no one just stumbles across De Garre—if you manage to find it, you were destined to visit. That's because De Garre is one of Bruges's best hidden pubs. Located down a small alleyway between the Markt and the Burg, De Garre is the only place to sample the smooth and tasty De Garre beer *(€3)*. This 12% beer is a strong brew, so strong that the pub only allows you to have three in one sitting; of course, if you're not having some sort of medical problem after three of these it'll be an achievement. Inside, the two-story house-like seating area is very typical of Belgian watering holes, and the cheese which comes with every beer helps the drinks along nicely. Make sure you head here for a pint of something special and a local setting.

⌗ *De Garre is just off of Breydelstraat, in between the Markt and the Burg.* Ⓢ *Beer €2-3.50.* Ⓣ *Open daily noon-midnight.*

CHARLIE ROCKETS
⊛⅃ HOSTEL, BAR

19 Hoogstraat
☎050 33 06 60 ▣www.charlierockets.com

We've never seen this anywhere else: in Bruges, the bars in some of the local hostels become hotspots in and of themselves come nightfall. Charlie Rockets is the busiest of the hostel bars in the city center. Covered in license plates and with an American motorcycle hanging from the ceiling, Charlie is unabashedly American, and the '60s music that blasts out over the jukebox gives the bar a quirky retro vibe. It's a great place to meet fellow travelers if your hostel isn't the home of the party.

⌗ *From the Burg, head along the southeast road, which is Hoogstraat.* Ⓢ *Drinks €2-6.* Ⓣ *Bar open 8am-4am.*

THE VINTAGE
⊛⅃ BAR

13 Westmeers
☎050 34 30 63 ▣www.thevintage.be

With its '70s wallpaper and a moped hanging from the ceiling, this fantastic little bar is a place to go if you want some serious "Booze and Music" (their words, not ours—though we wish they were). Classics from the '60s, '70s, and '80s play over the sound system, while the wireless radio and old-school television set make you question whether you're still in the 21st century. Grab a comfy chair in the small living room area. Just don't put your feet up on the table—it may feel like your house, but it isn't!

➡ Just opposite the Tourist Office. $ Beer €2-6. ⏰ Open daily 11am-2am.

THE CLASH

🍸 ROCK BAR

78 Langestraat — 💻www.thecrash.be

Although The Clash is a classic rock bar by design, the music won't blow your ears off and the clientele won't be banging their heads violently in your direction; in fact, you might catch some mellow Coldplay or Oasis interspersed with the heavy metal. If you're in for a good night you can pick up a meter of beer *(€19)*, which consists of 13 glasses of Jupiter placed in a 1m beer glass—just make sure you balance it properly. The small bar area is funky and welcoming, with a flickering chandelier, an overflowing trophy shelf, and a series of old records stuck above the bar. Even more impressive is the ceiling covered in empty Jupiter cans—beer mats are scrawled with messages to the owner and then stuck in between them. If you're drinking a Jupiter, you should also make sure to add to the collection of bottle stickers on the wall by the door.

➡ From the Burg, head along Hoogstraat, which runs into Langestraat. ⏰ Open M-Th 9pm-late, F 4pm-late, Sa-Su 9pm-late.

DE REPUBLIEK

🍸 BAR

36 St. Jakobsstraat — ☎050 34 02 29

De Republiek hosts a mixed crowd. The indoor seating area is populated by Bruges's teenagers, who grab drinks here before heading out back to the cinema next door. The expansive terrace is home to a more mature crowd, but finding a seat here in the summer can be difficult. The chill atmosphere and the whimsical cocktails mean De Republiek is more local and less touristy than some of the bars closer to the Markt. Get in touch with your inner Lady GaGa and order a *Poker Face* (tequila-based cocktail), or go with a battle of the sexes and get the ladies a *Wonder Bra* (gin, Cointreau, and pineapple) while the lads drink *Smooth Patrick* (vodka, rum, Midori, passion fruit, orange, and lime).

➡ St. Jakobsstraat is just off the northeast corner of the Markt. $ Beer €2.40-6. Cocktails €7.50. ⏰ Open daily 10:30am-3am.

SHOPPING

SWEET SHOP

CANDY, CHOCOLATE

48 Peperstraat

We wouldn't pick out a sweet shop if it wasn't a proper Belgian institution, and the woman who owns this shop really is just that. Angelea Puype is a 92-year-old local who has been serving sweets here since the 1950s, and the locals have a friendly name for her—*Omaatje*—which literally means "little granny." This tiny sweet shop is off the beaten track and sells all your classics, as well as more modern candies and chocolates to keep your sweet tooth happy. And just because Omaatje is old doesn't mean she is slow. She's sharp as a sour strawberry lace.

➡ From the Burg, head along Hoogstraat to the east, cross the bridge and continue onto Molenmeers. Continue right onto Peperstraat and the shop is halfway down the road. $ Sweets from a few pennies up to €2 or €3. ⏰ Open daily 10am-6pm.

THE CHOCOLATE LINE

CHOCOLATIER

19 Stevinplein — ☎050 34 10 90 💻www.thechocolateline.be

Among all the chocolate shops in Belgium, this one has some of the best items to take home beyond the luxury chocolates and sweets. For an interesting night with your significant other, why not pick up some chocolate body paint (with a free brush) or some chocolate lipstick? The window displays change with new chocolate creations and statues, so pop in and see what these guys have created this time.

Stevinplein is just off of Stevinstraat, south west of the Markt. i Credit card min. €10. $ Chocolate €4-50. ⏰ Open M 10:30am-6pm, Tu-Sa 9:30am-6pm, Su 10:30am-6pm.

ESSENTIALS

Practicalities

- **TOURIST OFFICES: In and Uit Brugge**. *(Concertgebouw 34 't Zand ☎050 44 46 46 💻www.bruges.be/tourism ⏰ Open daily 10am-6pm.)* A smaller location can be found in the train station, **Stationsplein.** *(⏰ Open M-F 10am-5pm, Sa-Su 10am-2pm.)*
- **ATMS:** There are 24hr. ATMs in **The Markt,** on **Vlamingstraat,** and in **Simostevi-plein.**
- **INTERNET:** There is free **Wi-Fi** at the train station.
- **LAUNDROMATS: Wash Casino,** 151 Langestraat. *(⏰ Open daily 6am-10pm. $ €4 for 8kg; €0.50 per 20min. drying.)* **Wassaloon Happyram,** 10 Ezelstraat. *(⏰ Open daily 6am-10pm. $ €4 for 7.5kg, €8 for 15kg; €1 per 15min. drying.)*
- **POST OFFICE:** 5 Markt. *(☎022 012345 💻www.depost.be ⏰ Open M-F 9am-6pm.)*
- **POSTAL CODE:** 8000

Emergency!

- **LATE-NIGHT PHARMACIES: 24hr. pharmacy hotline** *(☎0900 10 500).*
- **HOSPITALS/MEDICAL SERVICES: Hospital A.Z St.-Jan** *(☎050 45 21 11).*

Getting There

Bruges is really only reachable by train, but its **train station** has services that run to several Belgian and international cities and the three stations in **Brussels.** *($ €13. ⏰ 50min.)* To reach Bruges from other major European cities, you will have to change at Brussels Midi/Zuid or Brussels Nord. *(Ticket office open June-Aug M-Sa 10am-7pm, Su 10am-7pm; Sept-May M-Sa 10am-6pm, Su 10am-7pm.)*

Getting Around

Bruges is a rather simple city for tourists to navigate, thanks to the abundance of pedestrian walkways and bike lanes; in fact, you'll find more bikes on the road than you will cars, especially in the center. Most visitors tackle the city by foot, heading from the station into the center and exploring the cobbled streets and densely clustered sights. If you're hoping to explore further afield, or if you have more time to spend in Bruges, then renting a bike may be a good idea. Try **Ropellier Bikes** at 26 Mariastraat. *(☎050 34 32 62 $ €4 per hr., €8 per 4hr., €12 per day. ⏰ Open daily 9am-7pm.)* **Bruges Bike Rental** offers a student discount on single-day rentals. *(17 Desparsstraat ☎050 61 61 08 $ €4 per hr.; €6 per 2hr.; €8 per 4hr.; €12 per day, students €8. ⏰ Open daily 10am-10pm.)*

The **bus** system in Bruges is run by **De Lijn,** whose office is at the train station *(Stationsplein. ☎070 220 200; €0.30 per min. 💻www.delijn.be).* Buses #1, 6, and 11 go from the station into the town center. Buses #58 and 62 stop at Memling Campsite. Bus #2 stops at Europa HI Youth Hostel. Tickets are valid for 1hr. *(€1.20 if bought at the station booth, €2 if bought on board.)*

the hague *den haag* ☎070

The official name of The Hague is *'s Gravenhage*, translating to "The Count's Domain." That's a pretty awesome name for a city, so we're going to be using it for the rest of this introduction. The Count's Domain was birthed when **Floris IV**, Count of Holland, decided around 1230 that the land surrounding the pond that is now the Hofijver would be a good place to go hunting. Later Counts agreed that this was a nice tract of land, so they built more palaces here. Over time, this became an important administrative center for the Counts of Holland. After a bit of messy political history, The Count's Domain officially became the home of the government of the Dutch Republic and the residence of the House of Orange in the 16th century. In order for the national government to control the area, The Count's Domain didn't officially become a city until the Napoleonic period.

Today, while Amsterdam is the capital of the Netherlands, The Count's Domain is the seat of government. The two chambers of Parliament meet in the **Binnenhof,** where Floris started the whole thing by building his hunting lodge. Queen Beatrix lives in the palace on Noordeinde and opens Parliament every third Tuesday in September from the **Ridderzaal** (Hall of Knights). Besides being an epicenter of national politics, The Count's Domain is extremely important for international matters, serving as the home of all embassies to the Netherlands, the judicial body of the UN, the UN's tribunal on the former Yugoslavia, the International Criminal Court, and EU organizations like EUROPOL.

If all this makes The Count's Domain sound important (as though you weren't tipped off by the regal name), that's because it is. This is a city full of politicians, diplomats, and businesspeople. Unsurprisingly, it feels a bit more sedate than the other large Dutch cities. However, its international character makes it a pleasure for travelers, as you're pretty much guaranteed to find someone from your own country mixed in with all the locals. It's also got top-notch museums, loads of parks, a few lively night spots, and a great beach resort just 15min. away.

ORIENTATION

Coming into The Hague, you'll probably be arriving at **Den Haag Centraal** or, if you're sleeping at the Stayokay, **Holland Spoor.** The former station marks the eastern border of the city center, while the latter marks the southern. The Hague's real heart is the area around the palatial **Binnenhof,** the Dutch Parliament (the surrounding area is called **Buitenhof**). This is the main area for sights, museums, and some good but slightly pricey restaurants. North of here, the city gets increasingly more residential, although it's in this part of town that you'll find the **Vredespaleis** and the **Gemeentemuseum/GEM/Fotomuseum** complex. South and west of Buitenhof are the more commercial areas with the best shops, food, and nightlife. Running south from Buitenhof is **Spui,** which heads toward the **Stayokay,** lined first with theaters, then with some cheap takeout restaurants. West of Buitenhof is the busy shopping area on **Grotemarktstraat** and the surrounding streets. This region gives way to the popular nightlife area around **Grote Markt.** Northwest of Buitenhof a tangle of small streets like **Molenstraat** and **Papestraat** contains more relaxed bars and good restaurants. Fifteen minutes north of the city by tram, you'll find the beach town of **Scheveningen.**

ACCOMMODATIONS

With so many people rolling into The Hague on business, there are few rooms for those seeking a cheap roof over their heads. Budget hotels tend to be either quite plain or located outside the city center. The Stayokay, the one hostel in town, is a good option. If you're looking for a little liveliness, there's always the Jorplace beach hostel in nearby **Scheveningen.** (But if you're really looking for liveliness, you may want to think twice about visiting The Hague...)

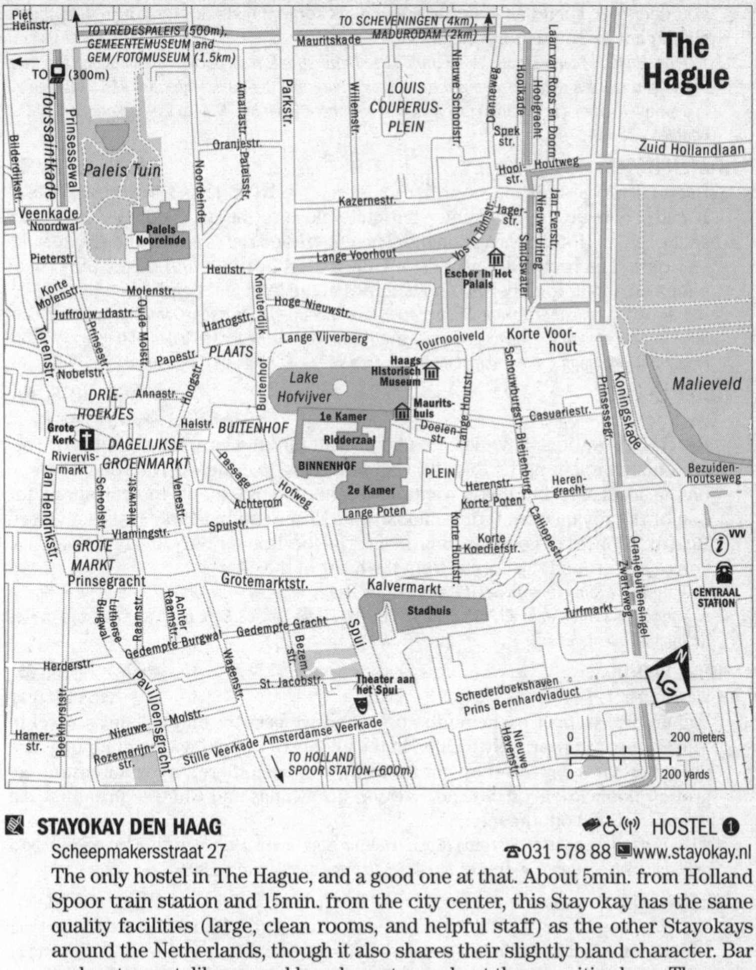

STAYOKAY DEN HAAG

💳♿📶 HOSTEL [1]

Scheepmakersstraat 27 ☎031 578 88 🖥www.stayokay.nl

The only hostel in The Hague, and a good one at that. About 5min. from Holland Spoor train station and 15min. from the city center, this Stayokay has the same quality facilities (large, clean rooms, and helpful staff) as the other Stayokays around the Netherlands, though it also shares their slightly bland character. Bar and restaurant, library, and laundromat round out the amenities here. There are no lockers in the rooms, but you can rent one in the lobby.

*# From Holland Spoor station, make a right when exiting. Follow the tram tracks straight to Rijswijkseplein, then make a right after crossing the canal. Or, from Den Haag Centraal, take tram #17 to Rijswijkseplein. **i** Breakfast included. Private rooms also available. Wi-Fi €3 per hr. $ 4- to 8-bed dorms from €20. ⏰ If you plan to stay out past 1am, make sure to get a special night key from reception (deposit of €50, passport, or credit card required).*

JORPLACE BEACH HOSTEL

💳🚭📶 HOSTEL [1]

Keizerstraat 296 ☎033 832 70 🖥www.jorplace.nl

Located in Scheveningen, the beach town 15min. away from The Hague, this is a great option if you want a bit more bustle and fun than the Stayokay. And if you want to go to the beach, of course. The rooms are quite plain, but the water is 5min. away. Plus, the lively hostel bar is a great hangout spot. With public transportation, you can easily explore the sights of The Hague from here. If you decide to spend all summer surfing, as some guests do, look into Jorplace's significant discounts for long stays.

✈ *From Holland Spoor station, take tram #1 to Keizerstraat. Walk back in the direction the tram came, and make a right onto Keizerstraat. From Den Haag Centraal, take tram #16 to Buitenhof and switch to tram #1.* *i* *Breakfast included. Internet €2 per hr.* Ⓢ *4- to 20-bed dorms €19-30; doubles €35-60.*

STATEN HOTEL
➡Ⓧ⟨⟨ʸ⟩⟩ HOTEL ❷

Frederik Hendriklaan 299 ☎035 439 43 ▣www.statenhotel.nl

Located outside the city center but quite close to the excellent Gemeentemu-seum, Staten Hotel calls a residential neighborhood full of shops and restaurants its home. The rooms are attractively decorated in white and dusky pink, with plants all about. Family-run, and it shows in the kind and helpful service.

✈ *Tram #17 (from either Holland Spoor or Den Haag Centraal) to Museon/Gemeentemuseum. Continue walking toward the museums, make a left onto Frederik Hendriksplein, and then a right onto Frederik Hendriklaan.* *i* *Breakfast included. Free Wi-Fi.* Ⓢ *Singles €45-70; doubles €77-83.*

HOTEL LA VILLE
➡Ⓧ⟨⟨ʸ⟩⟩ HOTEL ❷

Veenkade 5 ☎034 636 57 ▣www.hotellaville.nl

Recent renovations have left this hotel with ultramodern, all-white decor (oc-casionally broken up by the odd wall print here and there). The rooms can be on the small side, but if you want more space to stretch out, you can spring for one of the royal suites (with minibar *and* Nespresso machine, just like Queen Beatrix's house) or go for an apartment. The location is pretty ideal for the price: you're just around the corner from the heart of the city.

✈ *Tram #17 (from either Holland Spoor or Den Haag Centraal) to Noordwal. The hotel is ahead on your left.* *i* *Breakfast €12.50 per day. Free Wi-Fi.* Ⓢ *Singles €45; doubles €80; royal suites €125. Apartments €115.*

HOTEL WAHDO
➡Ⓧ⟨⟨ʸ⟩⟩ HOTEL ❹

Wagenstraat 127-129 ☎036 260 11

Wahdo prides itself on being the first (and we suspect only) Chinese hotel in The Hague. Appropriately located in the middle of Chinatown, so dumplings are never too far away—and by not far away, we mean there's a restaurant on the ground floor. Rooms have cherry-wood furnishings and Chinese prints on the linens to round out the look.

✈ *Tram #1, 8, 9, or 10 to Bierkade (Oost). Walk up Spui, make a left onto Stille Veerkade, then a right onto Wagenstraat.* *i* *Free Wi-Fi.* Ⓢ *Singles and doubles from €80.*

DELTA HOTEL
➡Ⓧ⟨⟨ʸ⟩⟩ HOTEL ❸

Anna Paulownastraat 8 ☎036 249 99 ▣www.deltahotel.info

Delta Hotel is conveniently located between the Vredespaleis and the more central sights to the south. Rooms have a minimalist, modern design and fur-nishings. A leafy little "zen patio" that has a few umbrella-adorned tables sits adjacent to the breakfast rooms.

✈ *Tram #17 to Elandstraat (Oost). Make a right onto Elandstraat, walk until the canal, and make a left onto Anna Paulownastraat.* *i* *Free Wi-Fi.* Ⓢ *Doubles €80-85.*

SIGHTS
👁

As the political center of the Netherlands and one of the most important diplomatic cities in the world, The Hague is full of political and historic heavyweights. How-ever, there's more to learn about here than wars, peace treaties, and Parliamentary disputes. A few excellent art museums dot the city, and if all the political power is making you feel a little bit inadequate, compensate by feeling (at least physically) superior to the miniature sights of Madurodam.

👍 VREDESPALEIS (PEACE PALACE) — GOVERNMENT

Carnegieplein 2 ☎030 242 42 🖥www.vredespaleis.nl

It might be difficult to think of **Tsar Nicholas II** as a big supporter of international peace and demilitarization. But he and 👍**Andrew Carnegie** were the two big players behind the construction of this formidable building dedicated to the promotion of cooperation between nation states. The Peace Palace is home to both the **International Court of Justice (ICJ)** (the judicial organ of the United Nations) and the lesser-known **Permanent Court of Arbitration (PCA)** (an older court for settling interstate disputes). At the time of construction, the opulence of the palace was meant to represent the power of the idea of international peace. Unfortunately, that goal is still pretty much just an ideal, but a great deal of interesting and important work is still done within the building's walls. There are two ways to get yourself inside: attend a session of the ICJ (the PCA hearings are usually closed to the public) or take a tour around the building. (There is a third way to get inside: being on trial there. But note that *Let's Go really* does not approve of crimes against international justice.) The hearings can certainly be a bit dry for those with no interest or experience in legal matters but give a better idea of the functioning of the court than the tours, which focus more on the history, architecture, and art of the building.

*➜ Tram #1 or 10 to Vredespaleis. You can't miss the place. **i** To attend a session of the ICJ, check the website's calendar (🖥www.icj-cij.org) or call ☎030 223 23. Unless it's a very high-profile case, you do not need to make reservations to attend. Bring a passport or driver's license for entry. Reservations must be made for the tours, recommended at least a week in advance. $ Tour €5, under 13 €3. 🕐 Tours May 1-Sept 30 M-F at 10, 11am, 2, 3, 4pm.*

👍 MAURITSHUIS — MUSEUM

Korte Vijverberg 8 ☎030 234 56 🖥www.mauritshuis.nl

The outside of this museum, an elegant 17th-century building next to the Binnenhof and the water of the Hofijver, is so pretty that you may not want to actually go inside. But that would be foolish, as this is one of the best collections of Dutch Golden Age art in the country (and the world). Concentrated in just two floors, you've got works by **Rubens, Van Ruisdael, Holbein, Hals,** and **Steen.** The most famous pieces in the collection are Rembrandt's *The Anatomy Lesson of Dr. Tulp*, and Vermeer's luminescent 👍**Girl with a Pearl Earring** and *View of Delft*. Given that only 36 works by Vermeer exist, this is a pretty good showing. The museum often organizes temporary exhibitions that bring more of his paintings (or other artists from the same period) within its walls.

➜ Tram #10 or 17 to Buitenhof. Walk along the water and make a right at the end; the museum is straight ahead of you. $ €12, under 18 free, with Museumjaarkaart €1.50. 🕐 Open Apr-Aug M-Sa 10am-5pm, Su 11am-5pm; Sept-Mar Tu-Sa 10am-5pm, Su 11am-5pm.

👍 GEMEENTEMUSEUM — MUSEUM

Stadhouderslaan 41 ☎033 811 11 🖥www.gemeentemuseum.nl

A perfect counterpoint to the Mauritshuis, this museum is the home of a wide collection of 19th- and 20th-century art, with a special focus on Dutch and other Northern European artists. A great selection of German Expressionist works gives way to a large body of paintings by **Piet Mondrian,** including his last work, *Victory Boogie Woogie*. Other De Stijl artists, members of the Hague School, and some contemporary painters like Francis Bacon make appearances here, and rotating exhibitions of recent pieces provide even more diversity to the collection. Besides painting and sculpture, there are some well-designed historic rooms intended to display the applied arts in the contexts for which they were intended. You'll also find significant fashion and music collections. Downstairs are the **Wonderkamers** (literally "wonder-rooms"), which sound a bit gimmicky but are really quite fun. Each main room contains a jumble of pieces from the museum's collection, organized by theme and color rather than time period (so you can find an evening gown next to a piece of modern art next to an ancient instrument). Other areas of the floor contain interactive exhibits, like a number of rooms with various kinds of DJ equipment where you can manipulate computer samples or play music on a touch-sensitive giant metal ball. The instructions are all in Dutch, but that makes experimenting and poking around all the more fun. Plus, surprisingly few people visit the museum, so you can make as much noise as you want.

🚋 *Tram #17 to Gemeentemuseum/Museon. The museum is just across the street.* $ *€10, under 18 or with Museumjaarkaart free.* ⏰ *Open Tu-Su 10am-5pm.*

BINNENHOF AND RIDDERZAAL ♿ GOVERNMENT

Binnenhof 8a ☎036 461 44 💻www.binnenhofbezoek.nl

This complex of palace-like buildings next to the waters of the Hofijver is one of the most central and photogenic sights in The Hague. And it's important, too! This is the home of Dutch democracy, where the upper and lower chambers (the *eerste kamer* and *tweede kamer*) of Parliament live. The earliest building was originally built in the 13th century as a hunting lodge (there's a joke about the bloodthirsty nature of politics in there somewhere), but the Dutch parliament has been meeting here in some form or another since the 15th century. Also in the complex is the **Ridderzaal,** or Hall of Knights, where Queen Beatrix officially opens Parliament each year on the third Tuesday in September (after traveling to the hall in a gilded carriage). Guided tours, which begin with a video on the history of the Binnenhof, can take you through the Ridderzaal and the **First or Second Chambers of Parliament** (except when they are in session). The tours are pretty lengthy and will tell you all you'd ever want to know about the workings of the Dutch political system. If you don't fancy a lecture, you can still wander through the courtyard of the Binnenhof and peek into the windows of the Ridderzaal. On the other hand, if you *really* want to get a feel for Dutch politics, you can attend meetings of the **Tweede Kamer,** the "lower" but more important house of Parliament. Plenary sessions are held Tuesday through Thursday *(enter at Lange Poten 4)* and committee meetings Monday through Thursday *(enter at Plein 2).* Keep in mind that Parliament is in recess during the summer. You do not need to make a reservation to attend but bring a passport or driver's license.

🚋 *Tram #1 to Centrum, or #10 or 17 to Buitenhof. It's the giant castle-like building by the water.* ℹ *Reservations recommended for the guided tours.* $ *Tour of Ridderzaal €4, Ridderzaal and a chamber of Parliament €6.* ⏰ *Tours M-Sa 10am-4pm.*

GEM/FOTOMUSEUM ♿ MUSEUM

Stadhouderslaan 43 ☎033 811 33, 033 811 44 💻www.gem-online.nl, www.fotomuseumdenhaag.nl

You'll find the distinct operations of GEM and the Fotomuseum housed in the same building, which is part of the Gemeentemuseum complex designed by Berlage. GEM is a place for contemporary art, exhibiting works by modern international artists in painting, video, performance art, and other forms of mixed media. The Fotomuseum is perhaps more accessible to the casual visitor, with photos from the early part of the 20th century to the present and a special emphasis on works involving the human figure.

🚋 *Tram #17 to Gemeentemuseum/Museon. The museum is across the street, to the left if you're facing the Gemeentemuseum.* $ *Entrance to both €6, students €4, under 18 or with Museumjaarkaart free.* ⏰ *Open Tu-Su 10am-6pm.*

ESCHER IN HET PALEIS MUSEUM

Lange Voorhout 74 ☎042 777 30 💻www.escherinhetpaleis.nl

Most people are familiar with at least a few of M. C. Escher's works (trust us, you are—they're the ones where you're always going up stairs), but it's incredibly illuminating to see an extensive selection of his prints and drawings and trace his progression as an artist at this informative museum. His earlier pieces are beautiful black-and-white engravings, many of them landscapes or architectural scenes, with increasingly exaggerated perspective. As you continue on through the museum, his fascination with infinity and eternity develops and you see more of the tessellations (collections of planes arranged without gaps between them, officially called "isohedral tiling"—try whipping that one out at your next cocktail party) and optical illusions for which he became famous. And there's more to see here than what's hanging on the walls: the museum (whose name means "Escher in the Palace") sits in a palace that was built for Queen Beatrix's great-grandmother. Most of it maintains its original luxurious style, and plaques on the walls discuss its architecture and decoration. We suspect that some things, like the giant crystal chandelier in the shape of a skull and crossbones, have been added more recently.

 # Tram #10 or 17 to Koorte Voorhout. Walk toward the Hofijver and make a right onto Lange Voorhout. $ €7.50, ages 7-15 €5, under 7 free. ⏰ Open Tu-Su 10am-5pm.

GROTE KERK ♿ CHURCH

Kerkplein ☎030 286 30 💻www.grotekerkdenhaag.nl

A stunning 15th-century church in the center of The Hague, Grote Kerk is all the more visually impressive when compared to its chain-store and large-bar surroundings. It doesn't have regular hours but is generally open in the afternoon for some part of the summer, and you can also gain entry by coming to one of the organ concerts and dance performances held here. Check the website for a list of upcoming events.

 # Tram #17 to Gravenstraat. Walk a few blocks down Riviervismarkt. $ Most events are free. ⏰ Varies by event.

HAAGS HISTORISCH MUSEUM ♿ MUSEUM

Korte Vijverberg 7 ☎036 469 40 💻www.haagshistorischmuseum.nl

Just across the street from the Mauritshuis, in a similarly lovely 17th-century building, is the historical museum of The Hague. Perhaps less impressive than its artsy neighbor, it still offers an interesting exposition of The Hague's (and for that matter, the Netherlands's) history, beginning with the 1560 rebellion against Spain. Besides the permanent collection of artifacts, paintings, and photographs, there are numerous rotating temporary exhibitions that explore other issues in the history or culture of The Hague. These can vary anywhere from series of 3D photos of the city to in-depth explorations of The Hague's political scene.

 # Tram #10 or 17 to Buitenhof. Walk down the length of the water; the museum is ahead on the corner with Korte Vijverberg. $ €5, under 18 or with Museumjaarkaart free. ⏰ Open Tu-F 10am-5pm, Sa-Su noon-5pm.

MADURODAM ♿ MINIATURE CITY

George Maduroplein 1 ☎041 624 00 💻www.madurodam.nl

How can the Netherlands be made even more picturesque? By shrinking it! This park contains models of virtually every famous Dutch sight and architectural stereotype—canals, windmills, gabled houses—at a 1:25 scale. Complete with tiny trees, moving trams, drawbridges, and even water skiers, this place isn't exactly highbrow culture, but it's remarkably intricate and offers the opportunity to get all Godzilla-like. This is all probably more fun if you've already been to a lot of the sights on display here, but then again, it can also save you from having to spend the train fare to visit the real-life versions.

 # Tram #8 or 9 to Madurodam. $ €14.50, over 65 €13.50, ages 3-11 €10.50, under 2 free. ⏰ Open daily May-Aug 9am-11pm; Sept-Apr 9am-6pm.

COFFEESHOPS AND SMARTSHOPS

The Hague doesn't have much of a coffeeshop scene—the few that are here aren't as bare bones as the ones in Rotterdam, but you won't find anything near the concentration or luxury of the Amsterdam shops.

EUPHORIA

🚫♿ SMARTSHOP

Schoolstraat 11

☎035 625 51 💻www.euphoria.nl

It's kind of surprising that a city with so few coffeeshops has such a good smartshop. Euphoria cuts the crap, stocking the same good selection of smoking gear (bongs, water pipes, etc.) as Amsterdam smartshops but eschewing the kitschy souvenirs those outposts hawk. Herbal enhancers like philosophers' stones, herbal XTC, and salvia are also available.

🪧 From the Grote Kerk, walk 1 block down Riviervismarkt toward Buitenhof and make a right onto Schoolstraat. Ⓢ Herbal XTC €8-14; philosophers' stones €17 per dose. ⏰ Open Tu-W noon-7pm, Th-Sa noon-9pm, Su noon-6pm.

THE GAME

🚫♿ COFFEESHOP

Nieuwstraat 4

☎034 505 74

As far as coffeeshops in The Hague go, this is one of the better ones. A spacious interior, a cool mural behind the bar, and sparkling lights complete the chilled-out look that is enjoyed by locals and tourists alike.

🪧 Walk down Buitenhof toward Riviervismarkt and make a left onto Nieuwstraat. Ⓢ Weed and hash €4-11 per g. ⏰ Open M-Th 11am-1am, F-Sa 11am-1:30am, Su 2pm-1am.

FOOD

The Hague does have some budget options, but they are largely the kind of places best for 3am pizza or post-clubbing shawarma. You can find them in the streets surrounding the **Grote Kerk** and along **Spui** (which is conveniently on your way home if you're stumbling back to the Stayokay). A higher quality but slightly more expensive meal can be enjoyed at one of the number of good restaurants around **Molenstraat.** Restaurants with terraces by the Binnenhof offer nice views, and **Chinatown,** the area surrounding Wagenstraat, is chock full of Asian restaurants.

👍 HNM CAFE

💳♿🍸⛅ CAFE, FUSION ❷

Molenstraat 21a

☎036 565 53

HNM is somewhat along the lines of a classic *bruin cafe*, but with brighter chairs, larger windows, and more international food. Try the Thai chicken soup or the pasta Bolognese and enjoy the decidedly eclectic mix of indie and electronic music playing overhead. The place is popular with locals from the surrounding offices and businesses.

🪧 From Binnenhof, walk through Plaats square, make a right onto Noordeinde, and a left onto Molenstraat. Ⓢ Sandwiches and appetizers €3-8. Entrees €11-14. ⏰ Open M-W noon-midnight, Th-Sa noon-1am, Su noon-6pm.

👍 VERY ITALIAN PIZZA

💳♿🍸⛅ ITALIAN ❷

Kettingstraat 13-15

☎036 545 41 💻www.veryitalianpizza.nl

Dozens of different oven-baked pizzas and pastas can satisfy just about any craving for a mixture of carbs, cheese, vegetables, and meat. Very Italian's pale wood interior and sidewalk patio are both quite large, yet both manage to fill up easily with groups of locals and tourists enjoying a bottle of wine and a *schaal* (a huge helping that serves four) of pasta.

🪧 Walk down to the end of Buitenhof, away from the water toward Riviervismarkt, and make a left onto Kettingstraat. Ⓢ Pizzas and pastas €5-10. Schaals €21-36. ⏰ Open daily 11am-1am.

BAKLUST

💳♿ VEGETARIAN ❶

Veenkade 19

☎075 322 74 💻www.baklust.nl

This cheery little cafe feels like a homey kitchen, with colorful decor, cool comic posters on the wall, and nice wooden tables. The food is all vegetarian, with many vegan options, but that doesn't mean your menu is limited. From a fake-meaty seitan sandwich to delicate quiches, everything is cooked to perfection. Their tarts and other bakery items are particularly mouth-watering.

➜ Tram #17 to Noordwal. The restaurant is at the beginning of the canal. $ Sandwiches €3.50-6. Entrees €4-10 🕑 Open Tu-Su 10am-6pm.

HARVEST 🚭♿🍸 CHINESE ❷

Sint Jacobstraat 1 ☎039 209 60

At the edge of Chinatown, this simple restaurant offers an excellent selection of dim sum. The pork buns are doughy, the dumplings steamy, and the rice flour rolls slippery. Harvest serves other noodle, rice, meat, and vegetable dishes as well, but who can resist the siren call of dim sum? Bring a large group so you can try a variety of dishes without killing your digestive system.

➜ Tram #2 or 6 to Spui. Walk south on Spui and make a right onto Sint Jacobstraat; Harvest is at the corner with Wagenstraat. $ Dim sum €2.50-4. Entrees €8-13. 🕑 Open daily noon-midnight.

LOS ARGENTINOS 💳♿🍸 ARGENTINIAN ❸

Kettingstraat 14 ☎034 685 23 💻www.los-argentinos.nl

This rough wood-paneled, bar-like spot boasts the best steaks in town—just ask the locals. If steak isn't your thing, entrees like grilled salmon should fit the bill, but don't come here expecting a good salad.

➜ Walk down to the end of Buitenhof, away from the water toward Riviervismarkt, and make a left onto Kettingstraat. $ Steaks €10-20. 🕑 Open daily 3pm-midnight.

DISHY ESPRESSO BAR 🚭♿ COFFEE, SANDWICHES ❶

Nordeinde 21 ☎039 226 92 💻www.dishy.nl

A sleek coffee bar that serves up excellent espresso and a small selection of good sandwiches, bagels, and pastries, Dishy Espresso Bar takes its coffee very seriously, using fancy machines and fancy beans, and the prices are incredibly reasonable given the quality.

➜ From Buitenhof, walk along the water away from the Binnenhof, make a left onto Hartogstraat and a right onto Noordeinde. $ Sandwiches €3-5. Coffee from €1.80. 🕑 Open M 8am-5pm, Tu-F 7am-5pm, Sa 8am-5pm, Su 10am-5pm.

NIGHTLIFE

Given the city's reputation as a center for business and politics, nightlife in The Hague is perhaps livelier than one would expect. You'll only find a handful of clubs, but some of the larger bars turn into dance spots late on weekend nights. The best places to go for boisterous crowds are the bars around **Grote Markt,** which have large terraces from which people spill out into the square. Near **Oude Molstraat,** a number of excellent bars and *bruin cafes* offer the working men and women of The Hague a place at which to drown their geopolitical sorrows.

👍 **BOTERWAAG** 💳♿🍸☀ BAR

Grote Markt 28 ☎036 238 62 💻www.boterwaag.nl

The vaulted ceilings in this large bar make it feel like you're drinking in a cathedral, which seems appropriate given that so many of the excellent Belgian beers they serve were brewed by monks. Not as rowdy as many of the places along Grote Markt, Boterwaag is the place to come for a drink and an excellent soundtrack of indie and post-punk music. During the day, try their nice selection of sandwiches at lunch and vaguely Mediterranean-Asian fusion dishes at dinner.

➜ Tram #2 or 6 to Grote Markt. Or from Buitenhof, walk straight down the square with your back to the Hofijver, follow signs for Grote Kerk, and then make a left at the church. $ Beer from €2.20. 🕑 Open M-W 10am-1am, Th-Sa 10am-1:30am, Su 10am-1am.

DE PAAS

BAR

Dunne Bierkade 16a ☎036 000 19 www.depaas.nl

With 10 beers on tap and 160 in the bottle, plus a selection of 25 *jenevers*, this is a good place to get sozzled or just appreciate a well-made drink. It's cozy inside during the winter (you'll be mesmerized by the bottles lining the back of the bar), but in the warmer months, you can sit on a leafy platform floating in the canal. Young and old locals frequent the place, which is filled with fewer business types than bars closer to the city center.

Tram #1, 8, 9, or 10 to Bierkade (Oost). Walk 1 block south on Spui, then right onto Bierkade, which becomes Dunne Bierkade. $ Beer from €2.20. Open M-Th 3pm-1am, F-Sa 3pm-1:30am, Su 3pm-1am.

DE PAAP

BAR, CONCERT VENUE

Papestraat 32 ☎036 520 02 www.depaap.nl

De Paap is simply the best rock cafe in town, attracting a fairly diverse group of rock, punk, funk, and cover bands. Artsy young locals enjoy rocking out and dancing in the bar's tastefully dim and slightly grungy interior. After the live acts end, the music keeps going until late, either with a DJ or whatever the bartenders feel like playing.

Tram #17 to Gravenstraat. Walk up Hoogstraat and left on Papestraat. $ Beer from €2. Open Th 7pm-4am, F 5pm-5am, Sa 7pm-5am.

PAARD VAN TROJE (TROJAN HORSE)

CLUB, CONCERT VENUE

Prinsengracht 12 ☎036 018 38 www.paard.nl

Probably the largest and most diverse nightlife spot in the city, Paard van Troje hosts an assortment of bands and DJs. Things die down a bit in the summer, but at least that means there is usually no cover. Some nights are more concert-y, some more club-y—generally dancing will get going, like the siege of Troy under the cloak of darkness, after 1am. The building is pretty remarkable, with a multi-level interior designed by the famous Dutch architect **Rem Koolhaas.**

Tram #2 or 6 to Grote Markt. The club is just a block or so away; head left if you are facing the bars on the main square. $ If there is cover, usually €5-12; free entrance with student ID on Th. Most summer events free. Beer from €2.20. Hours depend on event; check website for details. Pretty reliably open Th-F 11pm-4am, Sa 11pm-5am.

LA GRENOUILLE

BAR, JAZZ CLUB

Molenstraat 13 ☎036 001 17

A small French-feeling bar tucked into one of the quaintest areas of The Hague, La Grenouille hosts live jazz some nights. Even when there's no band, a melodious selection of jazz classics plays over the stereo.

From Buitenhof, walk up Kneuterdijk away from Binnenhof; make a left onto Hartogstraat, a right onto Noordeinde, then a left onto Molenstraat. $ Beer from €2. Open M-Th 3pm-1am, F-Sa 3pm-2am, Su 3pm-1am.

SUPERMARKT

BAR, CLUB

Grote Markt 25 ☎034 569 99 www.grotemarktdenhaag.nl/supermarkt

This place calls itself a bar and "poppodium," which means that both live bands and DJs play pretty much every kind of popular music, from soul and Irish punk to deliciously cheesy '80s and '90s hits. Given how tightly packed the bars are on the square, there's a surprising amount of space at the back for dancing. Supermarkt isn't as clubby as Paard and has a more laid-back crowd.

Tram #2 or 6 to Grote Markt. Or from Buitenhof, walk straight down the square with your back to the Hofijver; follow signs for Grote Kerk and then make a left at the church. $ Beer from €2.30. Open W 9pm-1am, Th-Sa 9pm-3am.

ARTS AND CULTURE

The Hague is a city for serious things like politics and diplomacy, but even suits need to have fun sometimes. As a result, the city offers a few good venues for highbrow events like opera and dance performances. The Count's Domain is also surprisingly big on pop music, evidenced by the often cheesy soundtrack of its clubs and its hosting of the largest free pop festival in Europe.

PARKPOP — FESTIVAL

Zuiderpark ☎052 390 64 www.parkpop.nl

One of Europe's largest free festivals, Parkpop draws huge crowds and very good rock, pop, and hip-hop acts. Past performers have included Juliette Lewis, Orishas, The Bangles, and Nena. Held in late June every year.

Tram #8 or 9 to Zuiderpark. The festival also runs special buses and trams from both Centraal Station and Holland Spoor. $ Free. ⏰ Late June. Festival events run from 1-9:30pm.

THEATER AAN HET SPUI — MUSIC, THEATER, DANCE

Spui 187 ☎034 652 72 www.theateraanhetspui.nl

A large performance complex that hosts all kinds of experimental theater, modern dance, music (classical, jazz, and pop), and opera. Some theater performances are in Dutch, but there are plenty in English as well.

Tram #1, 8, 9, or 10 to Spui. $ Tickets usually €10-20; often student discounts of €4-5. ⏰ Box office open Tu-F noon-5pm. Theater open Sept-June.

FILMHUIS DEN HAAG — FILM

Spui 191 ☎036 560 30 www.filmhuidenhaag.nl

This large movie theater in the center of town runs a remarkable program of international art house and independent movies, aiming to screen films that wouldn't be played in ordinary theaters. Some nights there are premiers; at other times they screen classics, and sometimes the theater also organizes retrospectives. Unfortunately, most of the films are foreign and only have subtitles in Dutch; however, all films originally in English are shown un-dubbed.

Tram #1, 8, 9, or 10 to Spui. $ Tickets €7.50-9; €1.50 student discount Tu-Su. Filmhuis ticket entitles you to free public transport 2hr. before the show up through the last transport on the day of your ticket. ⏰ Box office open M-F 1-10pm, Sa-Su 4-10pm.

ESSENTIALS

Practicalities

- **TOURIST OFFICES: VVV** provides hotel reservations for a small fee, maps, tickets to museums and attractions, and information on discount passes. The **Haags Uitburo,** in the same office, keeps information about cultural events and performances in the city. *(Hofweg 1 ☎036 188 60 www.denhaag.nl Across from the Binnenhof, just south of Buitenhof. Look for the signposts. ⏰ Open M-F 9:30am-6pm, Sa 9:30am-5pm, Su 11am-6pm.)*
- **INTERNET: Bibliotheek Den Haag.** *(Spui 68 ☎035 344 55 www.bibliotheekdenhaag.nl Tram #2 or 6 to Spui. It's next to the large dance theater, across from the church. $ Free Wi-Fi. Internet €2.80 per hr. ⏰ Open June-Aug M noon-8pm, Tu-F 10am-8pm, Sa 10am-5pm; Sept-May M noon-8pm, Tu-F 10am-8pm, Sa 10am-5pm, Su noon-5pm.)*

Emergency!

- **POLICE: Politie Haaglanden** is the regional police department for The Hague. *(Jan Hendrikstraat 85. ☎0900 88 44 www.politie.nl/haaglanden Tram #2 or 6 to Grote Markt. It's on the 1st street to the left if you're facing the square. ⏰ Open 24hr.)*

- **LATE-NIGHT PHARMACIES: Dienstapotheeks** are the 24hr. pharmacies. They rotate depending on the day. To find the nearest one in your neighborhood, check at your closest pharmacy or call ☎034 510 00. Alternatively, head to the **Apotheek Leyenburg.** *(Leyweg 295 ☎035 985 06 🚏 Tram #6 or bus #21, 23, 26, 27, 31, 34, 35, 36, 37, or 86 to Leyenburg. The pharmacy is 2 blocks down Leyweg. ⏰ Open M-F 5:30pm-midnight, Sa-Su 9am-midnight.)*
- **HOSPITALS/MEDICAL SERVICES: Bronovo Hospital** is the general hospital for residents and visitors to The Hague. *(Bronovolaan 5 ☎031 241 41, expat phone line ☎031 240 16 💻www.bronovo.nl 🚏 Tram #22, 23, or 28 to Bronovo Ziekenhuis. ⏰ Open 24hr. Expat line operates M-F 8am-4:30pm.)*

Getting There

Trains are by far the best option for getting to The Hague from within the Netherlands and Belgium. The two useful stations in The Hague are **Den Haag Centraal** and **Holland Spoor** (usually listed as Den Haag HS). Holland Spoor is most helpful if you are staying at the Stayokay hostel. Trains from **Amsterdam Centraal** *($ €10.10. ⏰ 1hr., 1-6 per hr.)* and **Rotterdam Centraal** *($ €4.30. ⏰ 30-45min., 1-6 per hr.)* stop at both stations. Trains from **Utrecht** *($ €9.70. ⏰ 35-40min., 1-6 per hr.)* stop at Den Haag Centraal, where you can hop on a train to Holland Spoor—easier and cheaper than taking a tram between the stations.

Getting Around

HTM *(💻www.htm.net)* is the public transport network for The Hague, Scheveningen, and Delft. You can find information about tickets, maps, and timetables on their website, along with a journey planner. Most points of interest in The Hague lie within an easily walked area, but if you are staying in a hotel outside the center, want to visit one of the more distant museums, or intend to check out the beach at Scheveningen, the tram network is your best bet. HTM still uses the **strippenkaart** system that has gone out of style in Amsterdam; you can purchase the tickets *(€7.60 for 15 strips)* at the train station and then present the tickets to be stamped by the driver or stamp them yourself on the tram. Most rides within The Hague will cost two to three strips. However, the easiest way to pay for transport is the **OV-chipkaart,** which is becoming increasingly universal in the Netherlands. As in Amsterdam, make sure to tap in and tap out of all transport vehicles you board. Rides will cost you €0.78 plus €0.15 per km. Tram #17 is a helpful line that hits Holland Spoor (passing right by the Stayokay), Den Haag Centraal, the city center, and the Gemeentemuseum. The limited **night bus network** only has a few stops within the city center, so you should probably give up hope and either walk or take a cab. Or, take a **bike,** which you can rent from the following companies.

RIJWIELSHOP DEN HAAG

Koningin Julianaplein 10 ☎038 532 35 💻www.rijwielshopdenhaag.nl

This bike rental company offers the best prices in town and the most extensive opening hours of any shop we've seen, so you can get your wheels no matter what time you need them.

🚏 Located by Den Haag Centraal. Go to the station hall and down the staircase by the flower store; the bike shop is on your right. i €50 deposit required. $ €6.50 per day, including insurance; €32.50 per week. ⏰ Open M-Sa 4:40am-2am, Su 6:10am-2am.

RENT A BIKE THE HAGUE

Noordeinde 59 ☎032 657 90 💻www.rentabikethehague.nl

This company rents good quality bikes and also sells new and used models. Will also provide biking route maps and picnic baskets.

🚏 Tram #1 or 10 to Kneuterdijk. Make a left onto Heulstraat and then a right onto Noordeinde. i €50 deposit required, plus ID. $ €10 per day. 10% discount for a week, 40% reduction for a month. ⏰ Open M-F 9am-6pm, Sa 9am-7:30pm, Su 9am-6pm.

utrecht ☎030

First settled under the Romans around the turn of the millennium, Utrecht was, for a long time, the Netherlands's cultural and religious capital. Given its ideal placement in the center of the country, the city is a good staging ground for all kinds of festivals and events and remains at the heart of Dutch life even though it is no longer the country's capital. Remnants of the city's religious past live on in the beautiful medieval churches and the stunning Domkerk. Not being the modern-day capital, however, means that Utrecht is small, easily accessible, and pedestrian friendly. Its rows of old-fashioned houses, church spires, and long walkways lining canals set below street level make it quite the *belle ville.* But we wouldn't have you thinking it's all sweetness and quiet here: with one of the Netherlands's largest universities and a student population pushing 60,000, Utrecht's got great nightlife and a buzzing, youthful feel. This makes it the ideal stop for those who want to experience the Netherlands at its most picturesque without totally leaving the urban jungle behind.

ORIENTATION

Arriving at Utrecht Centraal, you'll enter the city through the gargantuan Hoog Catharijne shopping center. Unless you're tempted to do some shopping, follow the signs toward **Vredenburg** and eventually emerge at a square about a 5min. walk from the city center, or **Museumkwartier.** This part of town, a long strip bordered on the west by **Oudegracht** and on the east by **Nieuwegracht canal,** contains the most points of interest in the city. **Domtoren,** Utrecht's most easily recognizable landmark, is located smack-dab in the middle of the two canals (well, in the middle of where Nieuwegracht would be if extended just a little bit farther). The primary east-west street is the many-named **Vredenburg/Lange Viestraat/Potterstraat,** which then becomes **Nobelstraat** after Janskerkhof. While Utrecht is an affluent and peaceful city, the area around Utrecht Centraal is best avoided at night.

ACCOMMODATIONS

Utrecht is a pretty swanky town, and this is immediately apparent when you're trying to find a hotel in the center that's under €200 a night. Fortunately, **Strowis** has great dorms and private rooms, and there are a few really excellent hotels on the city's outskirts. Still, inexpensive deals are few and far between, so reserving ahead is strongly recommended. If you don't mind staying a bit far from town, try the **Stayokay Bunnik,** a complex of 19th-century villas in a forest area 5km from Utrecht. *(Rhijnauwenselaan 14b ☎065 612 77 ▦www.stayokay.com ⌂ Dorms from €20.)*

▨ STROWIS   ♦⊗(ᵗᵖ) HOSTEL ❶
Boothstraat 8   ☎023 802 80 ▦www.strowis.nl

Run by the same former squatters' organization as the ACU, Strowis is a beautiful hostel located right in the city center. It's got high ceilings, brightly-painted walls, and spotless dorms and bathrooms. The bar and common area on the ground floor are better fitted for a hotel, as are the French doors opening onto the lovely garden. Unlike a hotel, however, Strowis provides a kitchen for use noon-9:30pm. If you want to experience Utrecht's lively nightlife, though, keep in mind that the hostel has a curfew, so you'll have to be back by 2am (3am on weekends) or stay out until 7am when it reopens for the day.

⌗ *From the train station, pass through the Hoog Catharijne shopping center and follow signs for the Vredenburg exit. Make a left through the square and turn right onto Lange Viestraat. This will become Potterstraat and then Lange Jansstraat, which will bring you to the Janskerk square. Make a left onto Boothstraat.* ℹ *Breakfast €7. Free lockers available in the basement. Free Wi-Fi and computer.* ⑤ *4- to 14-bed dorms €15.50-18.50; singles and doubles €60.* ⌂ *Curfew M-Th 2am, F-Sa 3am.*

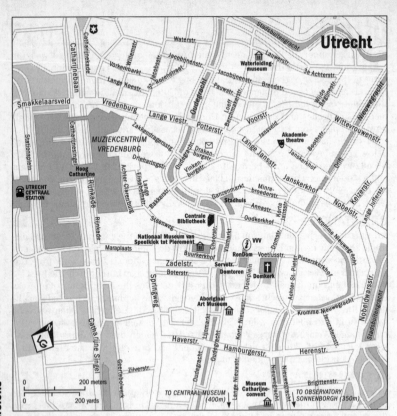

Utrecht

▧ DE ADMIRAAL

⬅⊗⊗((ŋ)) HOTEL ❸

Admiraal van Gentstraat 11   ☎027 585 00 🖳www.hoteldeadmiraal.nl

This hotel is about a 20min. walk from the city center, but don't let the distance put you off. For one thing, it's located in a very pleasant residential area near a leafy canal, and for another, it's an incredibly beautiful and well-designed place. The rooms are filled with art far more interesting than your average hotel wall hangings, the furniture is modern and comfortable, all linens and towels are ecologically friendly and specially made for the hotel, and a huge garden with quirky statues and verdant hedges sits to the back of the building. Ask for a room with a garden-view terrace. The warmth and hospitality of the owners, who invite guests to enjoy a free drink with them each day at 6pm, further enhance the surroundings.

✤ Bus #8 from Busstation Stadsvervoer at Centraal Station to Jan van Galenstraat. The stop is at the corner of Admiraal van Gentstraat; the hotel is a few blocks down the street. *i* Breakfast €10. All rooms with coffeemaker and fridge ensuite. Free Wi-Fi. Ⓢ Singles €70, with bath €90; doubles €110.

▧ HELLO B AND B

⬅⊗⊗((ŋ)) HOTEL ❷

Herenweg 32   ☎022 692 124

It's hard to tell that there is a hotel in the middle of the long line of houses here, and this non-commercial feeling continues inside, where you'll feel like a guest in a welcoming home. The rooms are incredibly cozy, with hearty wood furniture and floral patterns on walls and bedspreads. Moreover, the staff is laid-back and very accommodating to guests who roll in and out. Close to Utrecht Centraal, about a 15min. walk to the city center (a nice stroll along the Oudegracht).

From Centraal Station, walk through the Hoog Catharijne shopping center to Vredenburg. Make a left as soon as you get out, and walk along Catharijnebaan. Just after the roundabout when the street becomes Amsterdamsestraatweg, make a right onto Herenweg. ***i*** *Breakfast included. Kitchen available for use. All rooms with shared bath. Free Wi-Fi.* Ⓢ *Singles €45; doubles €65.*

VAN DIJK APARTMENTS APARTMENTS [3]

Pelikaanstraat 19 ☎062 458 3715 www.vandijkapartments.nl

Two apartments that each sleep up to three people, both with a large, newly renovated space and elegant modern furnishings. Kitchens are especially well equipped, while the ground-floor apartment also has a small garden available for use. Both are located just a few blocks away from the mouth of the Oudegracht and the beginning of the city center.

Tram #6, 8, 24, or 29 to Vondellaan. Walk down Vondellaan, cross the canal, make a left onto Albatrosstraat, and then a right onto Pelikaanstraat. ***i*** *Towels and linens €12.50 plus €30 cleaning fee. Free Wi-Fi.* Ⓢ *Apartments €75-80.*

B AND B UTRECHT CITY CENTER HOSTEL [1]

Lucas Bolwerk 4 ☎065 043 4884 www.hostelutrecht.nl

This hostel comes with about everything you'd expect from a hostel, both the good and the bad. With the price of a bed, you also gain access to a kitchen continuously stocked with basic food, a common area with TV and movies, and a music corner with loads of instruments. Nevertheless, the dorms are extremely basic, and some travelers report that they can get very stuffy in the summer months, even in the mild climate of the Netherlands. Keep in mind that there are also no lockers available for use.

From the station, pass through the Hoog Catharijne shopping center to Vredenburg. Keep going down the street as it changes names; after passing the Janskerk, make a left onto Lucas Bolwerk. ***i*** *Breakfast included. Linens €2.50, towels €1. Free Wi-Fi and computers.* Ⓢ *Dorms €20.50-21.50; singles €60; doubles €70.*

HOTEL OORSPRONGPARK HOTEL [4]

F. C. Donderstraat 12 ☎027 163 03 www.oorsprongpark.nl

Few hotels have exteriors as charming as this place's gleaming white, green-trimmed facade. The rooms aren't terrifically exciting, but the spots of bright pink in the curtains and blankets liven things up a bit. Views of the nearby canal and park through large windows are especially lovely. It's about a 15min. walk from the city center.

Bus #4 or 11 from station Stadsvervoer or bus #50, 52, or 74 from station Spreek at Utrecht Centraal to Oorsprongpark. The hotel is just to the left on F. C. Donderstraat. ***i*** *Breakfast included. Free Wi-Fi.* Ⓢ *Singles €95; doubles €115.*

SIGHTS

Utrecht's medieval history and importance for Dutch Christianity have left it with a whole lot of churches, and you could spend an extremely pleasant day wandering from one to another. Though their interiors have a certain austere similarity, their exteriors are generally quite striking. Helpfully, a few of the city's museums delve into the history behind the city's religious legacy. Others contain somewhat incongruous museums with exhibits on Aboriginal art, waterworks, and street organs.

DOMKERK AND DOMTOREN CHURCH

Domplein ☎023 600 10 (tour reservations) www.domkerk.nl, www.domtoren.nl

At 369 ft., this intricate Gothic spire belonging to Utrecht's cathedral is the tallest church tower in all of the Netherlands. Churches have stood on this spot, dedicated to St. Martin, since the seventh century. The current incarnation took quite a while to build (1254-1520), but the results were definitely worth it. Besides its unique height, it is distinguished by being the only Dutch church built in the Northern French Gothic style, which can be seen in its characteristic pointed arches and large windows. Unfortunately, Utrecht didn't have much time to enjoy the completed church: a massive tornado blew through Domkerk in 1674, taking the nave with it. The tower and church have remained separated ever since, though the original nave plan is marked into the ground of Dom Square. The church is open to visitors, so you can enter to observe its altarpieces bearing the marks of the 16th century's iconoclastic violence, its huge 19th-century organ, and the tomb of sea hero **Admiral van Gendt.** Make sure to stop by the peaceful cloister next door. If you want to go inside the tower, the only way to do so is as part of an hour-long guided tour. It begins at the VVV office on the square, where you can purchase tickets. Reservations are recommended, especially during the busy summer months. The tour, recounting history and anecdotes along the way, will take you to the top of the tower, from which you can see all the way to Amsterdam (and even Rotterdam) on a clear day.

⇟ Coming from Utrecht Centraal, walk down Vredenburg, cross the Oudegracht, and continue to Janskerkhof, where you make a right onto Korte Jansstraat. Seriously, though, it's the tallest thing around—you'll be able to find it. $ Church free. Tour €8, students and seniors €6.50, under 13 €4.50. ⏰ Church open May-Sept M-F 10am-5pm, Sa 10am-3:30pm, Su 2-4pm; Oct-Apr M-F 11am-4pm, Sa 11am-3:30pm, Su 2-4pm. Tower tours Apr-Sept every hr. M noon-4pm, Tu-Sa 11am-4pm, Su noon-4pm; Oct-Mar every other hr. M noon-4pm, Tu-Sa 11am-4pm, Su noon-4pm.

CENTRAAL MUSEUM

👍♿ MUSEUM

Nicolaaskerkhof ☎023 623 62 💻www.centraalmuseum.nl

This is the Netherlands's oldest municipal museum (dating from 1838), housed in a complex of pavilions constructed in a medieval cloister. The collection's eclectic mix tells the story of Utrecht's artistic and cultural development. Particularly notable is the selection of 17th-century Caravaggist painters, like **Hendrik ter Brugghen** and **Gerrit van Honthorst.** A modern art wing with works by Surrealist artists and Magic Realists such as **Pyke Koch** also merits mention. Contemporary pieces by Dutch artists are shown in temporary exhibitions as well, though watch out—some Dutch contemporary artists like to paint *really* creepy pictures of distorted faces. On the top floor, you'll find a group of archaeological pieces from Utrecht's Roman and medieval past. The museum oversees a large holding of pieces by the *De Stijl* designer Gerrit Rietveld, which are located at the UNESCO World Heritage Site **Rietveld Schroderhuis,** to the east of the city. You can make reservations for tours of that house through the museum. Across the street from the main museum complex, the **dick bruna huis** contains an exhibit about Dick Bruna, a cartoonist and artist most famous for his iconic rabbit character, Miffy. A ticket to the Centraal Museum includes admission to the dick bruna huis.

⇟ From Domkerk, head south on Korte Nieuwstraat, which becomes Lange Nieuwstraat. Turn right onto Agnietenstraat; it becomes Nicolaaskerkhof. $ €9, students and ages 13-17 €4, seniors €7.50, under 12 and with Museumjaarkaart free. ⏰ Open Tu-Su 11am-5pm.

CATHARIJNECONVENT

👍♿ MUSEUM

Lange Nieuwstraat 38 ☎023 138 35 💻www.catharijneconvent.nl

In honor of Utrecht's history as the Christian center of the Netherlands, this convent has been converted into a museum dedicated to the treasures of Dutch Christianity. Here you'll find beautiful religious paintings by artists like Rembrandt and **Frans Hals,** while in the treasury, ornate chalices and illuminated manuscripts explain the development of Christianity in the Netherlands and Utrecht in particular. The information throughout the exhibits is presented in

excursions

Dutch, but a detailed English program will help guide you through. Impressive temporary exhibits bring out items from the museum's collection and put them in context with more modern works and loosely related themes. The recent exhibit entitled "Gold" explored the religious and secular history of the precious metal.

🚶 From Domkerk, walk down Korte Nieuwstraat, which then becomes Lange Nieuwstraat. $ €11.50, under 18 €7.25, with Museumjaarkaart €2.50. ⏰ Open Tu-F 10am-5pm, Sa-Su 11am-5pm.

JANSKERK ♿ CHURCH

Janskerkhof ☎023 216 16 💻www.janskerkutrecht.nl

Somewhat more austere than the neighboring Domkerk, Janskerk (the church of St. John) is a lovely medieval house of worship worth a visit just to see its vaulted ceiling. This is one of two churches remaining from a cross-shaped set that Bishop Bernold built around Domkerk. Construction on Janskerk's nave and transepts began in the 11th century, while the choir dates back to the mid-16th century.

🚶 From Domkerk, walk down Korte Jansstraat to Janskerkhof. $ Free. ⏰ Open Tu-F noon-5pm, Sa noon-4:30pm.

MUSEUM FOR CONTEMPORARY ABORIGINAL ART 🎟♿ MUSEUM

Oudegracht 176 ☎023 801 00 💻www.aamu.nl

This is the only museum in Europe dedicated to Australian Aboriginal art. Works on display date from 1970 to the present and are made in diverse styles and materials ranging from tree bark and linen to multimedia video presentations. Two to three exhibits are held each year, many in conjunction with contemporary art museums like CoBrA.

🚶 From Domkerk, walk down to Oudegracht and make a left; it's about a block down, on the near bank of the canal. $ €8, under 12 and seniors €5, with Museumjaarkaart free. ⏰ Open Tu-F 10am-5pm, Sa-Su 11am-5pm.

NATIONAAL MUSEUM VAN SPEELKLOK TOT PIEREMENT 🎟♿ MUSEUM

Steenweg 6 ☎023 127 89 💻www.museumspeelklok.nl

The Museum of Musical Clocks and Street Organs is every bit as quirky as it sounds. While you can wander among the instruments on your own, make sure to arrive in time for one of the tours (available in English) led by energetic guides who will tell histories and anecdotes about the instruments and get many of them playing as well. Props to the staff for their chirpiness—if we worked here, we think we'd go insane from all the loud sounds leaping about this noisy place. You can see (and hear) an intricate clock with a tree full of twittering birds, a tremendous-sounding and gaudy player organ from a fairground, a pianola whose mechanism also plays three violins (you can observe the interior working away as it plays—quite the impressive sight), and a large dancehall organ that serenades the group with a sultry samba. The fact that most of them can only play a few songs over and over again really makes one appreciate the invention of the jukebox and record player, though modern contraptions don't have quite the same eye-popping proportions and color schemes as these guys.

🚶 From Domkerk, walk to Oudegracht, cross, and make a right. About a block down, make a left onto Steenweg. $ €9, seniors €8, under 12 €5, with Museumjaarkaart free. ⏰ Open Tu-Su 10am-5pm. 1 45min. tour per hr., on the hour.

COFFEESHOPS AND SMARTSHOPS

Utrecht is home to a few coffeeshops, though not as many as one might expect in a place this packed with students.

👍 **COFFEESHOP ANDERSON** COFFEESHOP

Vismarkt 23 ☎023 286 65

Coffeeshop Anderson is more touristy than many Utrecht shops, but that's just because of its prime location and its two large and well-decorated smoking rooms, one of which has a window overlooking the canal. Many patrons linger over juice and joints for hours while playing games of backgammon or chess. Four types each of weed and hash.

✳ *From Domkerk, walk to Oudegracht and make a right; it's just on the corner.* Ⓢ *€10 gets you 1-1.6g weed or hash; joints €3.50-5.* Ⓞ *Open M-W 10am-11pm, Th-Sa 10am-midnight, Su noon-11pm.*

BORDEAUX ROOD
Voorstraat 81

◉⅋ COFFEESHOP
☎023 696 86

The name makes Bordeaux Rood sound like an establishment in Amsterdam's Red Light District, but other than some red velvet curtains, there's little resemblance to a bordello here. Small but quality selection of weed with many popular strains.

✳ *From Domkerk, walk behind the church to get to Oudekerkhof and continue onto Drift; make a left onto Voorstraat; the shop is 1 block down, just before Boothstraat.* Ⓢ *Weed and hash €4-12 per g.* Ⓞ *Open M-W 10am-10pm, Th-Sa 10am-11pm, Su noon-10pm.*

FOOD

Eating in Utrecht is a delight for the stomach but certainly not for the bank account. **Museumkwartier** tempts with one elegant bistro after another. None are exorbitantly expensive (€25-30 for a meal, perhaps), but they're not exactly budget-traveler friendly. On Voorstraat and Nobelstraat, you can find some less expensive shawarma and pizza spots. The proliferation of sandwich cafes provides good lunch options, but if you really want to have a tasty dinner on the cheap, you're best off staying in a hostel with a kitchen and making it yourself.

BIGOLI
Schoutenstraat 7-12

◉⅋♈ ITALIAN, DELI ❶
☎023 688 48 ▣www.bigoli.nl

This Italian deli and sandwich shop sets out a mouthwatering display case full of meats, cheeses, and spreads. You can pick up a sandwich to go (we're fans of the one with bresaola, Parmigiano, and pine nuts drenched in olive oil) or stock up on deli items, pastas, oils, and wine.

✳ *Just off Neude square, in the direction of Domkerk.* Ⓢ *Sandwiches €3-4. Most deli ingredients €1-3 per 100g.* Ⓞ *Open M 11am-6pm, Tu-W 10am-6pm, Th 10am-9pm, F 10am-6pm, Sa 10am-5pm.*

STAMPOT TO GO
Nobelstraat 143

◉⅋ DUTCH ❶
☎022 323 62 ▣www.stampottogo.nl

Disappointed by the dearth of fulfilling Dutch comfort food in a sea of shawarma and pizza joints, the owner of this sleek green and white shop took matters into her own hands and opened a place where you can get classic Dutch food to go. **Stampot,** the main star, is a Dutch dish made with mashed potatoes and vegetables (broccoli, asparagus, and cabbage) and often served with meatballs or sausage. For a cheap and filling meal, it's one of your best options in Utrecht.

✳ *From Domkerk, walk down Korte Jansstraat to the Janskerk and make a right onto Nobelstraat.* Ⓢ *Stampot €5-6.* Ⓞ *Open M-W 4-8:30pm, Th 4-9pm, F 4-8:30pm. Closed most of July.*

RESTAURANT SWEETIE
Predikherenstraat 21

◉⅋♈ CHINESE, SURINAMESE ❷
☎023 227 24 ▣www.restaurant-sweetie.nl

One of the most popular ethnic restaurants in the city, Restaurant Sweetie has an impressive menu of dishes that are a mix of Chinese and Surinamese cuisine (leaning more toward the latter)—think lots of rice and noodles, satays, and rotis. They also offer a three-course menu that's a full €5 less than most of the other ones you'll see advertised around town.

✳ *From Domkerk, walk down Schoutenstraat toward Neude, cross the square, and head down Predikherenstraat, which splits to the left off of Voorstraat.* Ⓢ *Entrees €9-17. 3-course menu €17.50.* Ⓞ *Open Tu-Su 4-10pm.*

excursions

HET NACHTRESTAURANT

SPANISH ❷

Oudegracht 158 ☎023 030 36 💻www.dewinkelvansinkel.nl/nachtrestaurant

Run by the swanky and mellifluously-named Winkel van Sinkel *grandcafe,* this restaurant by the Oudegracht boasts a particularly striking setting in an arched cellar below street level. If you're walking by the canal at night, you can't miss the soft neon glow or the stylish patrons nibbling tapas on "the lounge-y pillows. Standard meat, fish, and vegetable tapas options available.

From Domkerk, go to Oudegracht and make a right. It's just below the Winkel van Sinkel cafe, at water level. $ Tapas €2.75-6. ⏰ Open M-F 6pm-"late," Sa-Su 5pm-"late."

ZIZO

CAFE, SANDWICHES ❶

Oudegracht 281-283 ☎023 004 63 💻www.zizo-online.net

This lunch cafe is part of a complex staffed almost entirely by men and women with cognitive disabilities and that includes a colorful gift store and a copy service. The menu consists of large sandwiches made fresh to order, salads, soups, and tarts. Also has a selection of homemade desserts that are extremely popular with the families that fill the cheery room.

On Oudegracht, near the Catharijneconvent. $ Sandwiches, soups, and tarts €2.75-4.75. Salads €9.90. ⏰ Open Tu-F 10am-5pm, Sa 10am-4:30pm.

NIGHTLIFE

For a picturesque medieval town, Utrecht sure does have some bumping nightlife, thanks in large part to the thousands of students that call it home. Thursday is a big night for clubbing, as many establishments grant free entrance with a student ID. Things are a bit bigger and more glam on Friday and Saturday evenings. In the summer, many places reduce their number of events, but most stay open to serve the needs of summer-school students. If you don't feel like dancing, the bar scene is still a whole lot of fun. Check out the streets of the **Museumkwartier** for bar-cafes and the **Oudegracht** for beautiful terraces along the canal. **Janskerkhof** has something of a monopoly on student bars, with a number of them clustered in a corner just down the road from the student club, **Woolloo Moolo** *(Janskerkhof 14),* that's run by a local fraternity.

TIVOLI

CLUB, CONCERT VENUE

Oudegracht 245 ☎0900 235 84 86 💻www.tivoli.nl

Utrecht's premier spot for good music and a good night, Tivoli hosts all kinds of bands, mainly indie rock and some blues, reggae, and hip-hop acts. Three nights a week, local and international DJs spin house, electro, hip hop, and pop to keep the crowd moving. With a capacity of 1000, it can get quite crowded—it's mainly packed with students, especially on Thursdays, when they get in free. There's a second, smaller location farther south of the city called Tivoli De Helling.

From Domkerk, walk down to Oudegracht and make a left. It's 2 blocks after Haverstraat. i 18+. $ Cover €4-10; students free Th with student ID. Beer from €2.30. ⏰ Open Th-Sa 11pm-5am; other times depend on concerts.

ACU

BAR, CLUB, CONCERT VENUE

Voorstraat 71 ☎023 145 90 💻www.acu.nl

A political and cultural center born out of a squatters' organization a few decades ago, ACU runs Hostel Strowis, a vegan cafe a squatters' information meeting *(W 8-9pm),* and also this bar, club, and concert space. Concerts of mainly punk, metal, and hardcore music are held here Fridays and some Saturdays; the "alternative discotheque" happens Fridays, Saturdays, and occasional Thursdays with an eclectic sound that ranges from New Wave to thrash to reggae. Whatever the music, you can be assured of cheap beer and an interesting dreadlocked and tattooed crowd. It certainly makes a nice break from the glitzier lounges and frattier bars of the Utrecht post-dinner scene.

➔ *From Domkerk, walk down Korte Jansstraat, cross the square, head down Boothstraat, and make a left onto Voorstraat.* $ *Cover free-€5. Beer from €1.40.* ⏰ *Open Tu-W 6-10pm, Th 6pm-3am, F 9pm-4am, Sa 11pm-4am, Su 6-11pm. Vegan cafe open Tu-Th 6-9pm, Su 6-9pm.*

KAFE BELGIË — BAR

Oudegracht 196 ☎023 126 66

It's a safe bet that any bar referencing Belgium in its name will have a good beer selection. True to form, this bar delivers—within its simple stucco interior you'll find 20 beers on tap and over 200 bottled varieties. Seriously, the menu is a thing of beauty; it has been known to cause men and women to weep tears of **beery joy.** Many of the brews are Belgian, some are Dutch, a few are German, and even a couple of stragglers from the US and the UK make their way onto the list. Enjoy your pint amid a faithful crowd of locals young and old.

➔ *From Domkerk, walk down to Oudegracht and make a left. It's on the near bank of the canal, just past the Aboriginal Art Museum.* $ *Beer from €2.* ⏰ *Open daily noon-1am.*

'T OUDE POTHUYS — BAR, JAZZ CLUB

Oudegracht 279 ☎023 189 70 💻www.pothuys.nl

A sunken, candlelit bar with live jazz, blues, or funk every night, 't Oude Pothuys is somewhat labyrinthine. It's got a stage-filled bar area, a restaurant, and a canalside terrace from which people have been known to take a drunken dive after a long night of carousing.

➔ *From Domkerk, walk down to Oudegracht and make a left. The bar is the one on the far side of the canal, at the corner with Korte Smeestraat.* $ *Beer from €2.10.* ⏰ *Open M-W 3pm-2am, Th-Sa 3pm-3am, Su 3pm-2am. Live music nightly 11pm.*

STUDENTCAFE'T PAKHUIS — BAR

Janskerkhof 21 ☎023 049 43 💻www.hetpakhuis.nl

Run by students, enjoyed by students. Early in the evening, the outdoor terrace is packed with people enjoying a meal. As the night progresses, the crowd moves into the bar and onto the small dance floor in the back. Music is a cheesy and fun sampling of pop, rock, and hip hop from the past few decades. Basically, if the bartenders and their friends feel like listening to it, they'll put it on.

➔ *From Domkerk, walk down Korte Jansstraat to Janskerkhof. The bar is on the far, left side.* $ *Beer from €2.20.* ⏰ *Open W 6pm-1am, Th-Sa 6pm-4am.*

MONZA — CLUB

Potterstraat 16-20 ☎065 53 93 814 💻www.clubmonza.nl

Though the crowd and music here change heavily from night to night, Monza is slightly trendier and maintains a more mainstream sound than nearby Tivoli. Some nights it's house, others electro, '80s and '90s hits, or R and B. Every event is quite the production, with massive video displays projecting great visuals behind the DJs. To get to the smoking room, you have to climb a luxurious double staircase of red velvet, which is worth it no matter how much you love or hate cigarettes.

➔ *From Domkerk, walk down Korte Jansstraat to Janskerk, make a left, and continue down the street just past Neude square.* $ *Cover F-Sa €10-15. Beer from €2.50.* ⏰ *Open Th-Sa 11pm-5am.*

HOFMAN — BAR

Janskerkhof 17a ☎023 024 70 💻www.hofman-cafe.nl

One of the ring of student-friendly bars around Janskerkhof (how so much revelry ended up next to a church, we have no idea), during the day, Hofman functions as a restaurant and cafe, and at night, it serves as the setting for all kinds of festivities—debates, improv theater, live bands, and DJ dance parties. They advertise as having a different musical style each night, but you can expect a similar mix of funky disco, '80s and '90s hits, some Latin music, and contemporary songs. Basically, it's what we like to think of as comfort dance music. The 20-somethings who pack in to drink and dance certainly seem to enjoy it.

⇆ From Domkerk, walk down Korte Jansstraat to Janskerkhof. The bar is on the far side of the square. ℹ Live bands on M. DJ dance parties on Sa-Su. Ⓢ Beer from €2.20. Th beer from €1.50. ⏰ Open M-W 11am-1am, Th 11am-3am, F-Sa 11am-4:30am, Su 11am-1am.

DE WINKEL VAN SINKEL
💳🚫🍸⛅ BAR, CLUB

Oudegracht 158 ☎023 030 30 🖥www.dewinkelvansinkel.nl

It's hard to miss the enormous, pillared facade of this *grandcafe*. By day, the tables on the sidewalk patio serve as prime people-watching territory. By night, the tables are equally nice, but a few Saturday nights a month the place turns into the Nachtwinkel club, generally playing oldies mixed in with a bit of dance-y house here and there.

⇆ From Domkerk, head to Oudegracht and make a right. Ⓢ Club cover €10-12.50. Beer from €2.30. ⏰ Bar open M-W 11am-midnight, Th-F 11am-1am, Sa 11am-10:30pm, Su noon-midnight. Club open Sa 11pm-5am.

FESTIVALS 🎆

Thanks to its central location, Utrecht is a popular site for festivals celebrating everything from children's theater to electronic music. Besides the more established fairs that fllow, new ones are always popping up around the city. Keep an eye out for posters around town, ask at the VVV, or grab a copy of *NL30*, which is free at most stores.

TWEETAKT
💳♿ SPRING

☎079 900 80 🖥www.tweetakt.net

The Netherlands's national youth theater festival, Tweetakt features performers from international locations like Belgium, Spain, and the United States. Some shows are intended for audiences as young as four, with some performers not much older.

⏰ Held yearly in Mar.

FESTIVAL A/D WERF
💳♿ SPRING

☎023 158 44 🖥www.festivalaandewerf.nl

This contemporary theater festival is held at a dozen venues around the city in the last week of May. Comes with visual art exhibits, debates, and free musical events in Neude square.

⏰ Last week of May.

NIGHT FEVER
💳🚫 SUMMER

🖥www.night-fever-utrecht.nl

Friday and Saturday of the second weekend in June, put on your best disco gear and head out for this celebration of dance classics. Live performances are held outdoors in Ledig Erf and near the Stadhuis, with many clubs also participating in the event.

Ⓢ Some events free; some clubs charge cover. ⏰ 2nd weekend in June.

MIDZOMERGRACHT
💳🚫▼ SUMMER

☎06 22 92 86 90 🖥www.midzomergracht.nl

Festival in the middle of June that aims to promote GLBT diversity and awareness with movies, theater, debates, concerts, and more.

⏰ About a week in the middle of June.

LIEF FESTIVAL
💳♿ FALL

Locatie Recreatiegebied Strijkviertel 🖥www.lieffestival.nl

Early in September, this one-day festival springs up in a multistage park outside of Utrecht. It draws a number of electronic DJs, some big names (Sander Kleinenberg, John Dahlback), and other up-and-comers.

↔ *Special buses travel to the festival site from Utrecht Centraal.* $ *Tickets €25-40.* ⏰ *1st weekend in Sept.*

NEDERLANDS FILM FESTIVAL ♿ FALL

☎023 038 00 💻www.filmfestival.nl

At the end of September, Utrecht fills with the attendees of this large festival dedicated to Dutch film. Over 400 movies are shown, with the highest honor of the **"Golden Calf"** given out in various cinematic categories. Golden Globe just really doesn't compare as a name for an award, does it?

↔ *Around town; many showings held in the Beatrix Theater at Jaarbeursplein 6a.* ⏰ *End of Sept.*

SMARTLAPPEN FALL

💻www.smartlappenfestival.nl

Utrecht already has a pretty lively nightlife scene, but come the end of November, things really get rowdy. Thanks to the Smartlappen festival, 🎵**folk-singing** and stein-drinking take over literally dozens of bars around the city.

$ *Free.* ⏰ *Last weekend in Nov.*

ESSENTIALS

Practicalities

- **TOURIST OFFICES: VVV** provides free city maps as well as information about cultural events, museums, and sights and can recommend or make hotel reservations. This is also the starting point for the Domtoren tours. *(Domplein 9 ☎0900 128 87 32 💻www.utrechtyourway.nl ↔ Across from Domkerk. ⏰ Open M noon-6pm, Tu-W 10am-6pm, Th 10am-8pm, F 10am-6pm, Sa 9:30am-5pm, Su noon-5pm.)*

- **INTERNET: Openbare Bibliotheek Utrecht.** *(Oudegracht 167 ☎028 618 00 💻www.bibliotheek-utrecht.nl ↔ From Domkerk, walk to Oudegracht, cross the canal, and make a right. $ Free Wi-Fi. Internet €3 per hr. ⏰ Open M 1-9pm, Tu-W 11am-6pm, Th 11am-9pm, F 11am-6pm, Sa 10am-5pm.)*

Emergency!

- **POLICE: Politie Utrecht** is the local police bureau. *(Kroonstraat 25 ☎0900 8844 💻www.politie.nl/utrecht ↔ From Vredenburg, walk down Willemstraat to the end of the street and turn left, then follow Kroonstraat as it curves to the right. ⏰ Open 24hr.)*

- **LATE-NIGHT PHARMACIES:** As with other cities in the Netherlands, Utrecht has no officially designated late-night pharmacy. Stores share the responsibility on a rotating basis; head to the nearest one, and if it's not open, there will be a sign on the door directing you to the closest open pharmacy. A centrally-located option is **De Liefde's Centraal Apotheek.** *(Voorstraat 6 ☎023 101 13 ↔ At the beginning of Voorstraat, across from Neude square.)*

- **HOSPITALS/MEDICAL SERVICES: Universitair Medisch Centrum Utrecht** is the medical center of the University of Utrecht and has a number of hospitals located near the university campus to the east of the city center. *(Heidelberglaan 100 ☎088 75 555 55 💻www.umcutrecht.nl ↔ Buses #10, 11, 12, 30, 31, 32, 71, and many more to Academisch Ziekenhuis. The stop is right at the hospital. ⏰ Open 24hr.)*

Getting There

Trains are the best option for getting to Utrecht. Passenger-carrying locomotives roll into **Utrecht Centraal,** an easy walk from the city center, from **Amsterdam** *($ €6.70. ⏰ 30min., 1-4 per hr.),* **Rotterdam** *($ €9.10. ⏰ 40min., 1-4 per hr.),* and **The Hague.** *($ €9.70. ⏰ 35-40min., 1-6 per hr.)* There are no direct trains from Brussels, so change in Rotterdam. To get here from **Maastricht,** you have to switch trains at Hertogenbosch, and it'll cost you more for the privilege. *($ €22.20. ⏰ 2½hr., 2 per hr.)*

Getting Around

Virtually every point of interest in Utrecht is within walking distance of Domkerk, the focal point of the city center. If you do choose to take public transportation (useful if you're staying in a hotel a bit farther away), you'll want to make use of Utrecht's **bus** system, run by **GVU.** (Find maps and timetables at www.gvu.nl.) There are two bus stations underneath Utrecht Centraal train station, **Busstation Stadsvervoer** and **Busstation Streek.** Pretty much every bus in the city stops at one of these two stations; check the maps in the station to figure out which one you need. The **OV-chipkaart** that works in Amsterdam is also the easiest method of payment on Utrecht transport. You'll use it to check-in and check-out of buses *(trips €0.78 to start and then €0.15 per km. 1- to 3-day ticket €6-12. Single-use tickets, valid for 1hr., €2.50-3.50).* Most public transportation runs from 6am-midnight. For **bike rental,** try **Laag Catharijne,** which rents bikes, sells new and secondhand bikes, and also provides bike storage. *(Catharijnesingel 34 ☎023 167 80 www.laagcatharijne.nl Located in front of the Hoog Catharijne shopping center. $ Bike rental €7 per day. Open M-F 7am-9:30pm, Sa 8am-6:15pm.)*

rotterdam ☎010

If you've spent a lot of time in other parts of the Netherlands, you may have forgotten what a skyscraper looks like. **Rotterdam** is here to remind you. It's strategic importance as a port city drew Nazi attention during WWII, and in May 1940, a massive bombing campaign razed virtually the entire city center. The reconstruction effort that followed in the postwar period focused on building a modern, revitalized city, and those efforts have left an indelible mark, creating a legacy of fascinating architecture and cutting-edge art that continues to this day. Rebuilding also imbued Rotterdammers with a fierce sense of city pride, most evident when you hear them talk about Amsterdam, their bitter rival in soccer and just about everything else. There's certainly a lot for the port city's residents to be proud of: Rotterdam, in addition to being a center for architecture and culture, boasts terrific festivals, live music, and some of the hippest nightlife you can imagine—all with an extremely laid-back attitude. The city is also home to both the largest port in Europe and the largest immigrant population in the Netherlands—and a host of delicious ethnic eateries. While other Dutch cities may have a certain fairy tale quality that comes from their quaint houses and leafy canals, Rotterdam feels more real. Maybe this helps explain why most people who live here, whether homegrown locals or expats, can't imagine living anywhere else.

ORIENTATION

Rotterdam is the second-largest city in the Netherlands, but pretty much all points of interest lie within a fairly small perimeter. The two main arteries are **Coolsingel/Schiedamsedijk,** which passes the main historical museums as it runs south from **Stadhuis** to the **Erasmus Bridge,** and **Westblaak/Blaak,** which stretches from the Erasmus Medical Center west toward the Cube Houses, passing Museumpark and the principal art museums along the way. These two roads intersect at **Beurs,** a huge commercial center filled with lots of shopping and fast food. Just west of Beurs, Witte de Withstraat and Oude Binnenweg provide nice streets to wander, and the streets north of the Cube Houses around the Laurenskerk also present nice sidewalks upon which to stroll. They're full of good restaurants, stores, and bars. The area west of **'s-Gravendijkwal** is best avoided at night.

Rotterdam

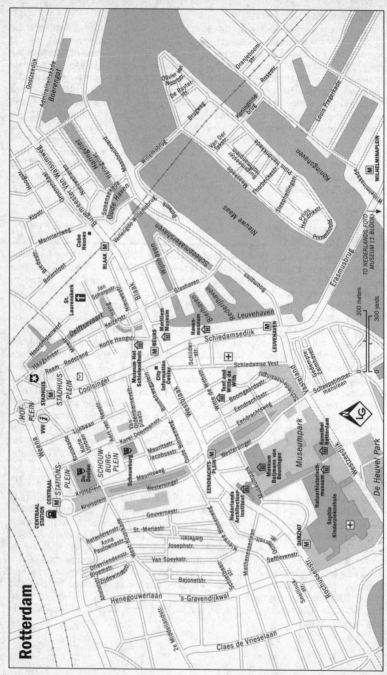

ACCOMMODATIONS 🏠

The accommodations in Rotterdam pretty accurately reflect its split between business-focused industrial city and youthful cultural hotspot. Some really excellent hostels can be found here in addition to a few reasonably priced hotels. The vast majority of the latter, however, are rather impersonal and expensive hotel complexes full of business travelers.

👍 ROOM HOSTEL
💳🚭📶 HOSTEL [1]

Van Vollenhovenstraat 62 ☎028 272 77 💻www.roomrotterdam.nl

Ask anyone who has stayed here about the hostel, and the first thing they'll mention is the fun-loving and extremely kind international staff. Everyone who works here loves the hostel and loves Rotterdam—and they'll help you to do the same as you chat over a beer in the popular hostel bar. The rooms aren't half bad, either. Each room—the Port Room, the Club Room (complete with disco dancer mural), and the Dutch Delight Room—is decorated with a different theme. The bathrooms are some of the cleanest we've ever seen in a hostel. Events are organized throughout the week, like movie nights, tours of the city, and Dutch snack tastings.

➔ Tram #4 or 7 to Westplein. Walk back the way the tram came and then 1 block up Van Vollenhovenstraat. ℹ Breakfast included. Well-equipped kitchen available for use. Free lockers. Free Wi-Fi. [$] 4- to 10-bed dorms €18.50-25.50; doubles €50-55. ⏰ Reception 24hr.

👍 STAYOKAY ROTTERDAM (HI)
💳♿📶 HOSTEL [1]

Overblaak 85-87 ☎043 657 63 💻www.stayokay.com

Stayokay Rotterdam is covered in one of the most architecturally unique roofs you'll ever have over your head—the hostel is located in some of Rotterdam's Cube Houses. The whole hostel embraces this ultramodern aesthetic: the lobby and bar are glossy and bright orange, and the rooms are done up in space-age white and gray. Walls and windows slant at crazy angles, thanks to the shape of the houses. True to the standard of Stayokays everywhere, the rooms are impeccably clean. However, note that there are no lockers in the dorms themselves, though they are by each room entrance. All chambers, be they dorms or private, have their own shower and toilet.

➔ Ⓜ Blaak. Exit the station and look up; you'll see the houses. It's easiest to find the hostel if you go under the houses toward the water and follow the signs up the ramp. ℹ Breakfast included. Private rooms available. All-female dorms available. Free Wi-Fi. [$] Beds €20.50-31. HI discount €2.50 per night.

HOTEL BAZAR
💳🚭📶 HOTEL [3]

Witte de Withstraat 16 ☎020 651 51 💻www.bazarrotterdam.nl

Enjoy exquisitely decorated rooms based on the Middle East, Africa, and South America. It's not gimmicky in the least: the colors of each theme are vibrant and the furnishings lovely. Plus, you're right in the heart of the nighttime action on Witte de Withstraat.

➔ Tram #7 or 20 to Museumpark. Walk away from the water down Witte de Withstraat. ℹ Breakfast included. Free Wi-Fi. [$] Singles €70; doubles €80-130.

SKYLINE HOTEL
💳🚭📶 HOTEL [2]

's-Gravendijkwal 70-72 ☎043 640 40

Skyline is surprisingly nice for the price, with a location that's conveniently near both Centraal Station and the bustling area by Witte de Withstraat and the Binnenwegs. Wood floors, modern furniture, and tastefully coordinated wallpaper and linens make the rooms feel very classy. A brightly tiled bar is downstairs.

➔ Tram #4 to 's-Gravendijkwal. Walk a few blocks north. ℹ Breakfast €7 per day. All rooms with ensuite bathroom. Free Wi-Fi. [$] Singles €49; doubles €75; triples €95.

HOME HOTEL

ჯ☒⒨ HOTEL ❸

Witte de Withstraat 38   ☎041 121 21 ▪www.homehotel.nl

The design here might not be unique, but the rooms are distinguished by that rarest of commodities: a kitchenette. (A Spar supermarket is conveniently nearby.) The rooms are extremely large, with multiple couches and more of a studio apartment feel.

✦ *Tram #7 or 20 to Museumpark. Walk away from the water down Witte de Withstraat.* *i* *All rooms with ensuite bath. Free Wi-Fi.* ⑤ *Singles €70; doubles €100. Discounts for longer stays.*

SLEEP-IN MAKFEES

☺☒⒨ HOSTEL ❶

Schaatsbaan 41-45   ☎024 091 58 ▪www.sleep-in.nl

If you want the most minimal and phenomenally cheap accommodations possible, head to this hostel run by the Use-It people. They have two dorms: a 24-bed female dorm and a 120-bed mixed dorm. Yeah, 120 people, sleeping in rows and rows of plain bunk beds in a cavernous room. To be fair, it only fills up during popular event weekends like the North Sea Jazz Festival. A relaxed common space and bar has comfy couches and a pool table.

✦ *From Rotterdam Centraal, walk west on Weena and make a right onto Schaatsbaan; it's at the very end of the street.* *i* *Breakfast included. Limited bed linens available for rent; staff recommends you bring your own sleeping bag. Free Wi-Fi.* ⑤ *Dorms €10.* ☼ *Open July-Aug and for the International Film Festival in Jan. Lockout 11:30am-5pm.*

SIGHTS

👁

Rotterdam's architecture is one of its most famous attractions, and the postwar explosion of modernity has given the city not just an impressive skyline but also a vibrant contemporary art scene. More historical art awaits at ▧**Museum Boijmans van Beuningen,** one of the best museums in the Netherlands, and the city's fascinating and complex history as an important port town and then as a war victim is explained in great detail at the various historical museums located near Beurs.

▧ MUSEUM BOIJMANS VAN BEUNINGEN

ჯ♿ MUSEUM

Museumpark 18-20   ☎044 194 00 ▪www.boijmans.nl

Absolutely one of the foremost art museums in the Netherlands, Boijmans van Beuningen boasts a collection that spans hundreds of works and multiple centuries but nothing in the exhibits feels superfluous. The museum is split into two sections: the permanent collection and the contemporary exhibition halls. Consider visiting them on separate days so that you don't suffer from an art overload. If you don't have the luxury of giving the museum two days, focus on the permanent collection, as there's much more modern art to be found elsewhere in the city. The permanent collection begins with medieval art from Italy and Northern Europe, then has a few rooms with works by Dutch masters like Bruegel, **Bosch,** and Rembrandt. Further along, there are rooms of Impressionism, a terrific group of Surrealist works (Dalì and Magritte in particular, thanks to a previous museum director who snapped up a bunch of Surrealist paintings and sculptures early on), and a remarkable set of Expressionist pieces, notably those by **Kandinsky.** The lower floor is dedicated to applied arts and design, with all kinds of furniture, glassware, and other functional objects on display that span roughly the same period as the paintings and sculptures above. In May 2010, the museum opened a new exhibition space for contemporary art in a former submarine wharf in the harbor. See ▧www.submarinewharf.com for more details.

✦ ⓂEendrachtsplein. *Walk south on Westersingel and make the first right; you'll see the flags of the museum.* ⑤ *€10, students €5, under 18 or with Museumjaarkaart free. Free entrance on W.* ☼ *Open Tu-Su 11am-5pm.*

NETHERLANDS ARCHITECTURE INSTITUTE (NAI)

MUSEUM

Museumpark 25 ☎044 013 58 en.nai.nl

It's appropriate that a city with architecture as interesting as Rotterdam's would be home to one of the best institutes for architecture in the world. The glass and steel building, designed by **Jo Coenen,** contains an exhibition space, library, and a huge architecture archive. The museum is scheduled to re-open from construction in January 2011. When it does, it will feature a segment dedicated to the Institute's conception of "architecture as consequence"—the idea that architecture can be promoted as a solution to many of the world's social and environmental problems. On the upper level, a permanent section called "the birth of the city" will take visitors through the progression from an initial swamp to the appearance of buildings to the development of the diverse elements that comprise the urban and suburban environment. The library is open to the public and holds an intense collection of architecture books in a variety of languages. The archive is not casually accessible, but if you want to see something from their holdings of architectural models, paintings, drawings, and architects' correspondence, inquire at the library desk. A ticket to the NAI includes entrance to **Sonneveld House** *(free while the museum is under construction),* a prime example of Dutch Functionalism built in 1933. With a special emphasis on space, light, and color—plus the most cutting-edge technology of its day—the house is a visual wonder, and the excellent audio tour will talk you through its importance to architectural history.

[M]Eendrachtsplein. Walk south on Westersingel and make the 1st right; it's just past the Boijmans Museum. $ €8, students and seniors €5, under 18 or with Museumjaarkaart free. Museum and Sonneveld House open Tu-Sa 10am-5pm, Su 11am-5pm. Library open July-Aug M-F 10am-5pm; Sept-June M-Sa 10am-5pm.

KUBUSWONIG (CUBE HOUSES)

ARCHITECTURE

Overblaak 70 ☎041 422 85 www.kubuswonig.nl

These exceptionally weird additions to Rotterdam's architecture were designed by **Piet Blom** in 1982 as a new sort of housing complex. Bright yellow cubes, rotated and set atop concrete columns, form a "forest," with commercial establishments on the lower promenade and residences inside the cube. If you're staying at the Rotterdam Stayokay, you'll already be familiar with the interior of the buildings, but if you want to get an idea of what an actual house would be like inside, then head to the **Show Cube (Kijk-Kubus).** Here, you can see how its three slightly claustrophobic floors make an interesting use of space and angles.

[M]Blaak or tram #21 to Station Blaak. Trust us, you'll know the houses when you see them. i While there are ramps up to the level of the houses, the Show Cube is not wheelchair-accessible. $ €2.50, over 65 €2, under 12 €1.50. Show Cube open daily 11am-5pm.

KUNSTHAL

MUSEUM

Westzeedijk 341 ☎044 003 01 www.kunsthal.nl

Rem Koolhaas, a super famous Dutch architect and contender to design the NAI, was the brain behind this striking building that houses an excellent contemporary art museum. Exhibits on photography, painting, sculpture, media, and any combination of the four pass through the three floors here. The museum is somewhat more accessible than the über avant-garde Tent and Witte de With galleries. Unfortunately, virtually all of its information is in Dutch, but you can read a little bit about the exhibits before or after you see them on the English version of the website.

Tram #8 to Kievitslaan. The museum is about a block in the opposite direction of the park. $ €10, students €5.50, ages 6-18 €2, under 6 free. Open Tu-Sa 10am-5pm, Su 11am-5pm.

ST. LAURENSKERK
♿ CHURCH

Grote Kerkplein 15   ☎041 314 94. ◼www.laurenskerkrotterdam.nl

This magnificent 17th-century building seems out of place in modern Rotterdam. It was virtually destroyed in the 1940 bombing, but its remains became a symbol of the wartime city. Since those tragic years, the building has been restored to its original design, a huge, vaulted neo-Gothic structure with amazing space and light. Don't miss the vibrantly painted red and gold organ over the back of the church—concerts are held here a few times a month. At one end of the church, there's a small cafe, which strikes us as a European take on those giant American megachurches that have Starbucks at the edge of the aisles.

✝ Ⓜ Blaak or tram #21 to Station Blaak. Facing the Cube Houses, walk to your left; you'll see the church tower a few blocks up ahead. ◫ Open Tu-Sa 10am-4pm.

MUSEUM HET SCHIELANDSHUIS (HISTORICAL MUSEUM)
✈♿ MUSEUM

Korte Hoogstraat 31   ☎021 767 67 ◼www.hmr.rotterdam.nl

This excellent museum on the history of Rotterdam lies in one of the few buildings of the city center that survived the bombing. The permanent collection on the first floor consists of a well-designed exhibit that takes you on a tour of the growth, destruction, and rebuilding of the city. Artifacts, photos, and videos are arranged around the path that's studded by little numbered stations. Point your audio tour handset at one of the stations to learn about a particular moment in time or historical subject. (This system is pretty baller. Isn't technology fun?) The other floors contain rotating art or media exhibits about the city such as collections of paintings and photographs depicting the damage of the 1940 bombing or models showing what the city might have looked like if different plans had been followed during the rebuilding effort.

✝ Ⓜ Beurs or tram #8, 23, or 25 to Churchillplein. Walk down Blaak and make a left onto Korte Hoogstraat. Ⓢ €5, under 17 or with Museumjaarkaart free. ◫ Open Tu-Su 11am-5pm.

HET PARK
♿ PARK

Het Park

Yes, Rotterdam is famous for its hyper-urban glass and steel architecture, but this 19th-century park (simply called "The Park") in the southwest corner of the city center is a nice place to see real trees, as opposed to the yellow cube "forest" that is the **Kubuswonig**. A rectangle with a 1.8km perimeter, it's full of grassy meadows, meandering paths, bubbling brooks, and some lovely shrubberies. On a sunny day, basking Rotterdammers add to the fauna.

✝ Tram #8 to Kievitslaan. ◫ Open 24hr.

COFFEESHOPS AND SMARTSHOPS

Of the few coffeeshops in Rotterdam, virtually all are merely takeout spots—none of the comfy, pillow-strewn interiors familiar to smokers in Amsterdam here. On the plus side, the weed and hash do tend to be slightly cheaper. Head to **Nieuwe Binnenweg** to find numerous shops.

REEFER
Ⓢ♿◕ COFFEESHOP

Oppert 1   ☎041 226 13

This is one of the only coffeeshops in Rotterdam where people—virtually all locals—actually stick around after buying their weed. The large smoking room (tobacco allowed) has couches, pool, foosball, and free computers. An eclectic music selection ranges from trancey house to R and B to cheesy '90s girl ballads.

✝ Tram #7 or 8 to Meent. Walk down Meent and make a right onto Oppert. 𝒊 Extremely strict about ID, make sure to have it with you. Ⓢ Weed and hash €4-12 per g; joints €2.50-3.50. ◫ Open daily 10am-midnight.

excursions

PLUTO

COFFEESHOP

Nieuwe Binnenweg 181 ☎043 667 68

The large window display of hookahs and bongs makes this place seem a lot larger than it really is. In fact, it's pretty much just a takeaway spot. However, Pluto stocks a more extensive selection of wares than most Rotterdam shops and also sells Philosopher's Stones (psychedelic truffles).

Tram #4 to 's-Gravendijkwal. Walk about a block east on Nieuwe Binnenweg. $ Weed and hash €4-14 per g; Philosopher's Stones €10-13 per dose. ⏰ Open M-Th 9am-midnight, F-Sa 9am-1am, Su 11am-10pm.

FOOD

Eating is a pleasure in Rotterdam, whose international character brings in a plethora of affordable ethnic options. For cheap Chinese and shawarma, check out **Witte de Withstraat,** where the stores are conveniently open as late as most of the bars. Slightly nicer sit-down ethnic places are to the north on **Nieuwe Binnenweg.** The area north of the Cube Houses, behind the Laurenskerk, is full of interesting cafes.

BAGEL BAKERY

BAGELS, MEDITERRANEAN [1]

Schilderstraat 57a ☎041 121 560

Both businesspeople and tourists pop into this fresh and airy restaurant with plenty of outdoor seating to enjoy bagels and a variety of toppings (all kinds of cream cheese, mozzarella and tomato, tuna with olive tapenade, etc.). If you're around for dinner, lots of delicious tapas and *mezze*, plus salads and other entrees are ready to please your palate.

[M]Beurs or tram #8, 23, or 25 to Churchillplein. Walk south on Schiedamsedijk and make a right onto Schilderstraat. $ Bagels €2-8. Entrees from €11. ⏰ Open Tu-W 9am-5:30pm, Th-F 9am-10 pm, Sa 10am-10pm, Su 10am-5:30pm.

FAFI

CHINESE, INDONESIAN [1]

Witte de Withstraat 93b ☎041 400 02

Just what every bar-filled street needs: a Chinese greasy spoon where you can satisfy your drunkies with some pork fried rice. This one ups the ante by adding even more kinds of noodles and curries to its extensive menu. Prices may be slightly higher than one would expect, but the portions are gigantic and the food is freshly made. You can eat at the plastic tables in the store or take your food to go.

Tram #7 or 20 to Museumpark. It's right on the corner with Eendrachtsweg. $ Sandwiches €2-3. Entrees €7-12. ⏰ Open M-Th 11:30am-2am, F-Sa 11:30am-4am, Su 2pm-2am.

BAZAR

MIDDLE EASTERN [2]

Witte de Withstraat 16 ☎020 651 51 www.bazarrotterdam.com

Sibling restaurant to the one in Amsterdam's De Pijp neighborhood and connected to the hotel next door. Festive Arabian fairytale decor (including some very cool glass and beaded lanterns) makes Bazar's dining room feel quite magical, while the tables running the long length of the outside are a prime place from which to watch the action on Witte de Withstraat. The food is a mix of Middle Eastern and Mediterranean fare, with an assortment of dishes that includes falafel salads, Turkish pizzas, fancy kebabs, and baked vegetarian plates with eggplant and tofu all adding up to a true "bazar" of dining opportunities.

Tram #7 or 20 to Museumpark. Walk away from the water down Witte de Withstraat. $ Sandwiches and lunch entrees €4-10. Dinner entrees €12-16. ⏰ Open M-Th 8am-1am, F 8am-2am, Sa 9am-2am, Su 9am-midnight.

LEBKOV AND SONS

CAFE, SANDWICHES [1]

Stationsplein 50 ☎024 006 17 www.lebkov.com

You can find this purveyor of top-notch sandwiches in a random corner next to the train station. The light and spacious interior is a tempting place to take a break from the neighborhood action, and the benches outside are ideal for catching some sun. When it comes to the food, the selection of sandwiches on wonderfully plump bread is mouth-watering (especially the decadent sandwich of the week), though the store also does soups, salads, and desserts.

➜ *Facing Rotterdam Centraal, it's on the left of the main square.* $ *Sandwiches €2.25-3.50.* ⏰ *Open M-F 6am-7pm, Sa 9am-5pm.*

DE SMAAK VAN AFRIKA

🚭♿🍸⛅ AFRICAN ❷

Goudsesingel 342a ☎021 355 66 🖥www.desmaakvanafrika.nl

In an area full of ethnic restaurants, De Smaak van Afrika may be the most fun. Brightly colored patterns intermix with cozy wood in the lively interior, an ideal setting for trying dishes from both the eastern and western sides of the continent. The eastern dishes include various kinds of stews and vegetables served with *injera* (flat bread), the western ones include things like spicy *piri piri* shrimp. Don't miss out on the imported, fair-trade African fruit beer in flavors like banana and coconut. At lunch, a smaller menu of sandwiches and *injera* rolls is available.

➜ *Tram #7 or 8 to Meent. The restaurant is just east of the intersection.* $ *Sandwiches €4-5. Dinner entrees €10-13.* ⏰ *Open daily noon-midnight. Kitchen closes at 11pm.*

LOOK

💳♿🍸 MEDITERRANEAN ❹

's-Gravendijkwal 140b ☎043 670 00 🖥www.restaurantlook.nl

This restaurant's name is the Dutch word for "garlic," but Look isn't just trying to be cute: the name really does describe the restaurant's ethos. All dishes, taking Italian, French, and Spanish influences, are built around the use of this pungent plant. The flavor complements rather than overwhelms dishes like prawns, steak, or pasta. There's even garlic ice cream, served with chocolate cake. The decor is, appropriately, mostly an elegant white.

➜ *Tram #4 to 's-Gravendijkwal. The restaurant is 1 block south.* $ *Appetizers €5.50-11.50; entrees €12.50-19.50. 3-course meal €24.50-26.* ⏰ *Open W-Su 5:30-11pm.*

NIGHTLIFE 🎭

Nightlife in Rotterdam is painted as the only Dutch scene to rival Amsterdam's. Its main difference (and drawback) is that nightspots tend to be clustered in neighborhoods separated from each other by a lot of dead space, so most Rotterdammers head to one area and stay there for the night. It's by no means impossible to walk between them, but some travelers may find it a bit dodgy, especially as the night progresses. The **Witte de Withstraat** and **Oude Binnenweg** area offers a fantastic bar scene, with live music or sweet stuff on the stereo at practically any watering hole you hit up. Establishments here are stylish but laid-back, with the same mod-urban feel that permeates the city. Student nightlife is centered on **Oudehaven,** in the west of the city. As a result, it can be a bit dead here during the summer and early in the week. (Apparently Rotterdam students actually do work during the week—who knew?) For clubs, head to the area near **Kruiskade and Stadhuis** just south of the station. Some might find the dance music a bit disappointing, but on a weekend night, this is the place to be seen. In front of Stadhuis, check out the complex of massive bars whose loud techno and cheesy pop bleed into each other. Rotterdam's GLBT nightlife isn't as extensive as Amsterdam's, but there are a few good bars and clubs surrounding **Van Oldenbarneveltstraat.**

👍 DE WITTE AAP

🚭♿🍸⛅ BAR

Witte de Withstraat 78 ☎041 495 65 🖥www.dewitteaap.nl

As cute and cool as its headphones-wearing monkey logo (the name means "The White Ape"), De Witte Aap is filled with a sizeable crowd of urban-artsy locals lingering on the street patio or along the curvaceous bar pretty much every night of the week. Besides the friendly bartenders and the overall air of hip-dom, the main attraction here is the well-chosen soundtrack of mashed-up hip hop.

Tram #7 or 20 to Museumpark. Walk straight down Witte de Withstraat. $ Beer from €2. ⏰ Open M-Th 4pm-4am, F-Sa 4pm-5am, Su 4pm-4am.

DIZZY — BAR, JAZZ CLUB

's-Gravendijkwal 127 ☎047 730 14 www.dizzy.nl

An established institution in a city renowned for the largest jazz festival in Europe, Dizzy has quite the reputation. With jam sessions on Monday, live jazz Tuesday and Thursday, funk DJs on Friday, and Brazilian jazz on Saturday, there's no shortage of things to hear. Even on the nights without live performances, the large bar and restaurant invites hepcats to hang out under the portraits of all kinds of jazz greats or on the backyard garden patio.

Tram #4 to 's-Gravendijkwal. $ Beer from €2.20. ⏰ Open M-F noon-2am, Sa 4pm-2am, Su 4-11pm. Music usually starts at 10pm.

DE SCHOUW — BAR

Witte de Withstraat 80 ☎041 242 53

A stubbornly simple and local bar plastered with old concert posters and photographs, De Schouw is full of regulars enjoying a drink and possibly a game of chess. Attached to the exterior is **de Aanschouw Rotterdam,** quite possibly the smallest gallery in the world—it's just a glass box with a single piece of art inside. Every Friday, the art changes in an official ceremony at 8:30pm with the artist present. It must be a very proud moment in his or her life. Today De Schouw, tomorrow the Louvre!

Tram #7 or 20 to Museumpark. Walk away from the water down Witte de Withstraat. $ Beer from €2. ⏰ Open M-Th 11am-1am, F-Sa 11am-3am, Su 11am-1am.

CATWALK — CLUB

Weena Zuid 33 www.catwalkclub.eu

This intimate, welcoming club (wait that sounds really sexual in a way we don't intend) sits in a former pedestrian tunnel near Rotterdam Centraal and is cheaper and less about being seen than some of the area's other clubs. The narrow space is filled with soft red lighting, some loungey-chairs, and truly excellent trance and house. The DJ is the focal point of the room, and that reflects how seriously they take the music. Dancing alongside you, you'll find a stylishly laid-back group of diverse students and locals.

Tram #4, 7, 8, 21, 23, or 25 to Weena. Walk away from the roundabout, left onto Lijnbaan, and right onto Weena Zuid. $ Cover €5. Beer from €2.20. ⏰ Usually open Th-Sa 11pm-whenever the people go home (they have a 24hr. license). Check website for specific events.

ROTOWN — BAR, CONCERT VENUE

Nieuwe Binnenweg 19b ☎043 626 69 www.rotown.nl

On nights without live music, the vast interior can feel a bit empty, but when a band or a DJ takes the stage, you'll be surrounded by a very cool, young crowd. The music is pretty diverse and leans toward indie, electro rock, dub soul funk, or whatever new genres the crazy kids are listening to these days.

[M]Eendrachtsplein. Walk to the northern end of the square and make a left onto Nieuwe Binnenweg. $ Cover for concerts €5-15. Beer from €2. ⏰ Open M-Th 11am-1am, F-Sa 11am-3am, Su 11am-1am. Concerts usually start around 9pm, DJ sets around 11pm.

GAY PALACE — CLUB

Schiedamsingel 139 ☎041 414 86 www.gay-palace.nl

No false advertising here—this is, in fact, a palace fit for a queen. The largest gay club in Rotterdam attracts a pretty mixed crowd of partygoers with one thing in common: their fondness for the dance floor. You'll find mostly men but quite a few women as well, all shaking it under the big paper lanterns and neon lights.

Tram #7 or 20 to Museumpark. Walk down Witte de Withstraat, make a right when you get to

Bazar, and keep right on that street as it loops around Ⓢ *F cover varies by event; Sa cover €5 before midnight, €10 after.* ☒ *Open some F; check website or flyers. Otherwise open Sa 11pm-5am.*

OFF_CORSO
●●⊗♈ CLUB

Kruiskade 22 ☎028 073 59 ▣www.offcorso.nl

A well known and popular fixture of the Rotterdam night scene, this place can be hit-or-miss depending on your taste in music. Some nights are techno, some are hip hop/R and B, and their most popular parties play '80s and '90s music. Check the website or at least ask at the door before heading in. You don't want to find that you're headed to the hip-hop party when you're decked out in your best candy raver gear. It's housed in an old movie theater that retains significant vestiges of its former purpose, so at least you can enjoy the space, if not the dancing.

⚡ *Metro or tram #21 or 23 to* Ⓜ*Stadhuis. Kruiskade runs diagonally off the western side of Coolsingel.* Ⓢ *Cover €10-15. Beer from €2.20.* ☒ *Usually open F-Sa 11pm-5am; check website or flyers to be sure.*

STRANO
➹⊗♈▼ BAR, CLUB

Van Oldebarneveltstraat 154 ☎041 258 11 ▣www.cafestrano.nl

Trendier than most bars (gay and straight) in Rotterdam, this is a good place to see and be seen by other male partiers while you sip excellent cocktails. When the night and the Top 40 and dance music gets going, the crowd moves right off the red leather couches and starts shifting to the beats.

⚡ Ⓜ*Eendrachtsplein. Walk to the top of the square on the right and continue on Mauritsweg, then make a right onto the impossible-to-pronounce street.* Ⓢ *Cocktails €7.* ☒ *Open M-W 4pm-2am, Th 4pm-3am, F-Sa 4pm-6am, Su 4pm-4am.*

ARTS AND CULTURE
♫

Rotterdam is full of exciting cultural events, especially when its various festivals erupt. To find out what's on, look for posters around the city or ask at the **VVV**, which publishes *R'Uit*, a guidebook with listings of performances.

◪ NORTH SEA JAZZ FESTIVAL
➹♿♈ FESTIVAL, JAZZ

Ahoy Complex, Zuiderpark ☎0900 1010 2020 (€0.45 per min.) ▣www.northseajazz.com

One of the largest jazz festivals in the world, North Sea draws over 70,000 people to three days of top-notch music. Past performers have included Stevie Wonder, Norah Jones, B. B. King, Questlove, Joss Stone, ◪**Herbie Hancock,** and many more. Besides numerous types of jazz, hip hop, soul, blues, funk, and other genres are featured. Alongside the official concerts at Ahoy, the days surrounding the festival are full of performances at smaller venues across Rotterdam.

⚡ Ⓜ*Zuidplein. Walk down Metroplein to Zuiderpark.* Ⓢ *Day tickets €88; 3-day pass €204. Some concerts require an extra €15 ticket.* ☒ *Usually held the 2nd weekend of July.*

INTERNATIONAL FILM FESTIVAL ROTTERDAM
➹♿ FESTIVAL, FILM

Karel Doormanstraat 278b ☎089 090 90 ▣www.filmfestivalrotterdam.nl

Holland's largest film festival, with two weeks in late January to early February of independent, international film. Everything from avant-garde performance art to documentaries to slightly more mainstream fare is screened here at 24 venues across the city. All films are shown in their original languages, most with English subtitles.

⚡ *To get to the festival's main office, take tram #4, 7, 8, 20, 21, 23, or 25 to Kruisplein. Walk to the far side of the square and make a right onto Karel Doormanstraat. Directions to the actual screenings vary by venue; the website has a good map.* 𝒊 *Central box office during the festival is in De Doelen.* ☒ *Festival runs late Jan-early Feb.*

ROTTERDAMSE SCHOUWBURG THEATER, OPERA, DANCE

Schouwburgplein 25 ☎041 181 10 🖥www.rotterdamseschouwburg.nl

The city's premier performing arts venue, Rotterdamse Schouwburg is the stage for all kinds of opera, dance, and theater performances. Most drama is performed in Dutch, but an international theater festival runs here every October. This cube-like white building facing a massive square is worth a visit for the architecture, even if you don't attend a performance.

Tram #4, 7, 8, 20, 21, 23, or 25 to Kruisplein. Walk across the square to the theater. $ Tickets €6-40. ⏰ Box office open daily noon-7pm.

DE DOELEN LIVE MUSIC

Schouwburgplein 50 ☎021 717 17 🖥www.dedoelen.nl

The Netherlands's largest concert venue, rebuilt in its modern incarnation after the original was destroyed in the 1940 bombing, De Doelen is the official home of the Rotterdam Philharmonic Orchestra. The musical fun doesn't stop there: it also serves as a performance space for hip hop festivals, pop performances, jazz and world music, and more.

Tram #4, 7, 8, 20, 21, 23, or 25 to Kruisplein. Walk across the square to the theater. $ Tickets free-over €50. ⏰ Box office open M-Th 10am-6pm, F 10am-7pm, Sa-Su 10am-6pm. Venue open 2nd week of Aug-3rd week of July.

ESSENTIALS

Practicalities

- **TOURIST OFFICES: Use-It** is a great one-stop shop for everything you could need in Rotterdam. It publishes *Simply the Best,* a free pamphlet to the city that includes information on everything from practical concerns to museums to nightclubs. The store also offers bike rentals, internet usage, and Wi-Fi. It can make last-minute hotel bookings for the same day for up to 65% discounts and has its own hostel in the summer. Moreover, it stocks maps, party flyers, and small necessities like rain ponchos and earplugs. Impressed yet? *(Schaatsbaan 41-45 ☎024 092 58 🖥www.use-it.nl Leaving Rotterdam Centraal, walk toward the tram stops. Make a right onto Weena, keep going for a few blocks, then make a right onto Schaatsbaan. Use-It is at the very end of the street, on the left. $ Bikes €6 per day. Wi-Fi free. Internet €0.80 per 15min. ⏰ Open May 15-June Tu-Su 9am-6pm; July-Aug M noon-5pm, Tu-Su 9am-6pm; Sept 1-Sept 15 Tu-Su 9am-6pm; Sept 16-May 14 Tu-Sa 9am-5pm.)* **VVV** provides accommodations bookings for a small fee, transport and city maps, and information about all kinds of events around the city. It also offers internet for a fee. *(Stationsplein 45 ☎0900 403 4065 🖥www.vvvrotterdam.nl Leaving the train station, head toward the tram stop and make a right onto Weena; and the office is on your right. $ Internet €4 per hr. ⏰ Open M-Sa 9am-5:30pm, Su 10am-5pm.)*
- **INTERNET:** Both **tourist offices** above provide internet, including **free Wi-Fi** at **Use-It. Bibliotheek Rotterdam** has free internet on the sixth floor. Bring your ID to open a user account and you'll get 30min. of internet use. (If the interwebz aren't busy, you can ask to extend your time.) *(Hoogstraat 110 ☎028 161 14 🖥www.bibliotheek.rotterdam.nl Metro or tram #21 to Ⓜ Blaak. Walk behind the station with the Cube Houses on your right; the library is on the large square next to the Laurenskerk. ⏰ Open July-Aug M 1-8pm, Tu-F 10am-8pm, Sa 10am-5pm; Sept-June M 1-8pm, Tu-F 10am-8pm, Sa 10am-5pm, Su 1-5pm.)* Internet is also available at the **VVV** and **Use-It.**

Emergency!

- **POLICE: Politie Rotterdam-Rijnmond** is the local police department. *(Doelwater 5 ☎0900 88 44 🖥www.politie-rotterdam-rijnmond.nl Metro or tram #21 or 23 to Ⓜ Stadhuis. It's 1 block south of Hofplein, on the right. ⏰ Open 24hr.)*

- **LATE-NIGHT PHARMACIES: Night Pharmacy** is open late and on weekends. *(Schiedamsedijk 80 ☎043 399 66 🚊 [M] or tram #8, 23, or 25 to Leuvehaven. Walk up Schiedamsedijk toward the Maritime Museum; the pharmacy is on the left. 🕐 Open daily 5:30pm-8am.)*
- **HOSPITALS/MEDICAL SERVICES: Erasmus MC** is the large hospital complex quite close to the city center. *('s-Gravendijkwal 320 ☎070 401 45 💻www.erasmusmc.nl 🚊 Tram #8 to Erasmus MC. 🕐 Open 24hr.)*

Getting There

Both national and international **trains** roll into **Rotterdam Centraal.** You can check timetables at all stations or at 💻www.ns.nl. From **Amsterdam Centraal** *($ €13.30. 🕐 1hr.-1hr. 15min., 1-7 per hr.),* **Brussels** *($ €25.50. 🕐 1hr. 10min., 1 per hr., 8am-9pm.),* **The Hague** *($ €4.30. 🕐 30 min., 1-5 per hr.),* and **Utrecht** *($ €9.10. 🕐 40 min., 1-4 per hr.).* You can also theoretically fly into the small Rotterdam international **airport,** serviced by **budget airlines** like Transavia and City Jet, but it's easy to get there from Amsterdam's Schiphol Airport *($ €10.70. 🕐 45 min., 1-5 per hr.),* where you'll have many more flight options.

Getting Around

RET is the transport network for Rotterdam. Their website *(💻www.ret.nl)* includes good maps, timetables, and a journey planner. There are numerous **Metro** lines in the city; the D line runs north-south, with Rotterdam Centraal as its northern terminus, and the A, B, and C lines run east-west, intersecting D at Beurs. However, since there are only a few Metro stops within the city center, it is much more convenient for tourists to use the **tram** network. The **OV-chipkaart** that works in Amsterdam is also the easiest method of payment on Rotterdam transport. Use it to check-in and check-out of buses, trams, and the Metro *(trips €0.78 to start and then €0.15 per additional km. 1- to 3-day ticket €6-12. Single-use tickets, valid for 1hr. on tram and bus or 2hr. on tram, bus, and Metro €2.50-3.50).* Most public transportation runs from 6am-midnight. There is a **night bus** network, **BOB** *(tickets €4.50).* The somewhat confusing tangle of buses intersect at Rotterdam Centraal. See maps at tram and bus stops or 💻www.bob-bus.nl. However, given the price of tickets, you're probably better off just dragging someone from your hostel out with you and sharing a cab home at the end of the night. As with most Dutch cities, **biking** is the most popular and convenient method of transportation. You can rent bikes at most hostels and hotels or at **Use-It** (see **Practicalities**) for €6 per day *(€50 deposit required).*

maastricht ☎043

The capital city of the southern province of Limburg, Maastricht is not like the rest of the Netherlands. The flatlands recede into rolling green hills, and then into mountains and networks of caves; soft-core drug use is decidedly less in your face, and the local cuisine has a definite Belgian and German feel to it. In fact, Limburg shares more borders with more European countries than it does with other provinces of the Netherlands, and it's little wonder that the city was once so well fortified. Though cut in two by the river Maas, Maastricht was once encompassed by some formidable city walls. Today, the city still features well-preserved fortifications which date back to the 13th century.

Despite its differences from other cities in the Netherlands, Maastricht still retains the beauty that is associated with the country. Towering buildings and cobbled streets run throughout the city, and the center of town and its three main squares overflow with history. The laid back locals seem to not notice the tourists who flock to Maastricht on the weekends, and that's because a lot of them are Dutch

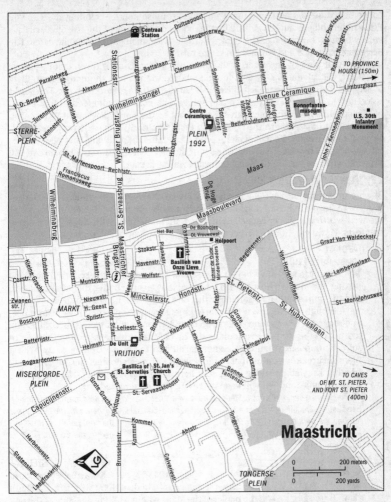

themselves and blend into the Limburg crowd. The city is less crowded during the week, but during summer weekends Maastricht becomes a hub of activity, as bars and restaurants pour into outdoor seating areas and onto the promenade by the river. Expect a chill bar scene and small traditional *kaffees* dominating the scene, rather than thumping dance clubs. If you're looking to have a relaxing few days away from the rest of the Netherlands or even Belgium, then Maastricht is the ideal place.

ORIENTATION

Maastricht is divided into two sections by the river **Maas,** which flows directly through the center of the city. The main pedestrian bridge is St. **Servaasbrug,** which connects the **train station** with the old center; from the train station, **Stationstraat** runs westward into **Wycker Burgstraat** and across the bridge to the promenade. This bridge leads to both **Maasboulevard,** which runs to the south of the city, and the **Promenade,** which runs to the north. The east side of the river by the station hosts some good bars, convenient hotels, and some more upscale establishments, including the Crowne Plaza hotel and restaurant. A little further south on this side of the river is **Céramique** area, which is comprised of the Centre Céramique, a small park, and some cafes. The **Bonnedantenmuseum** and **Province House** are further south.

The west side of the river is the location of Maastricht's three main squares: the **Markt, Vrijthof,** and **O.L. Vrouwe.** It is also home to the main shopping street, **Grote Straat,** and the **Tourist Information Office** (VVV) at the bottom of Grote Straat. The Markt is located in the north of the city, and serves as a point of intersection for several of Maastricht's main thoroughfares: **Boschstraat** to the north, **Hoenstraat** to the east, **Neuwstraat** and **Spilstraat** to the south, and **Grote Gracht** to the west. From the Markt, Grote Gracht runs to **Vrijthof,** which is full of restaurants and bars, and also houses the **Basilica St. Servatius.** To the south east of the city center is the small square of O.L Vrouwe, which is just off of Maasboulevard via **Plankstraat.**

ACCOMMODATIONS

Staying in Maastricht isn't cheap; the city doesn't have enough student and budget tourists to keep the hostel market strong. But there are a few cheaper options that are well worth the price, especially if you want something with a few more home comforts. If you can book a bed in the **Stayokay,** do it—you won't regret it.

STAYOKAY — HOSTEL [1]

Maasboulevard 101 — ☎043 750 17 90 💻www.stayokay.com/maastricht

If you want to stay anywhere in Maastricht, it's Stayokay; the beautiful riverside setting, the modern dormitories with spacious ensuite baths, the great facilities, and the unbeatable location make this one of the best hostels you will ever stay in. Although rooms are a tad more expensive than in other European cities, you're paying a very good price in comparison to the other games in town. Enjoy a drink on the terrace overlooking the River Maas or read a book in the beautiful park opposite, then take a short stroll into the center 10min. away. With a plentiful breakfast buffet that outdoes most European hostels, and an extremely friendly English speaking staff, stay here if you possibly can. The pool table, foosball table, and Wii will keep you more than entertained.

From the station, head down Stationsstraat, which becomes Wycker Burgstraat. Cross the St. Servaasbrug and take a left just after the S3evice shop. Continue along here with the river to your left and the park on your right. The hostel is on your left just after the boat hotel. [i] Breakfast and sheets included. Bring your own towel. Wi-Fi €2 per hr. $ 6-bed dorms from €27-34. Reception 24hr.

BOTEL — BOAT HOSTEL [1]

Maasboulevard 95 — ☎043 321 90 23 💻www.botelmaastricht.nl

I'M ON A BOAT! What do you get if you cross a budget hotel with a boat? That's right: Botel. Docked on the banks of the Maas within walking distance of the city center, this big blue boat is a great budget option, especially if the Stayokay is booked. Although the cabin rooms are not the biggest sleeping rooms you'll find in Maastricht, it's not often you can say you've stayed on a boat.

From the station, head down Stationsstraat which becomes Wycker Burgstraat. Cross the St. Servaasbrug and take a left just after the S3evice shop. Continue along here with the river to your left and the park on your right. The botel is on your left. [i] Breakfast €6; compulsory on weekends. Sheets and towels included. Free Wi-Fi. $ Singles €29-33; doubles €44-48. 3-person cabins €72; 4-person €96; 5-person €120; 6-person €144. Reception 10am-10pm.

HOSTEL OH LA LA — HOSTEL [2]

Van Hasseltkade 23 — ☎043 327 07 74 💻www.ohlalamosae.com

Oh La La indeed—who knows what room you'll get when you check in to the hostel on the banks of the Maas. Each room is decorated with its own character and is rather impressive—they even come complete with a kettle, toiletries and towels for you to enjoy. Channel your inner Emma Watson in the Burberry room, which comes with Burberry sheets, curtains and decoration. The golden room is fit for a king, and the very summery flower room will put you in the right mood to explore Maastricht in July and August.

✴ *Take a right at the foot of St. Servaasbrug and continue along the promenade, keeping to the left hand side. Climb a set of stairs by a statue of a globe and the hostel is at the bottom of another set of stairs.* *i* *Breakfast €8. Sheets and towels included. Free Wi-Fi.* Ⓢ *3- to 4-bed dorms €39-50.* Ⓩ *Reception 10am-1:30am. 24hr access.*

LE GUIDE
Stationsstraat 17A   🛩HOTEL ❷
☎043 32 61 76 📧www.leguide.nl

Situated close to the train station, Le Guide doesn't suffer from being cheap and dingy like most of the hostels by transportation hubs that we've reviewed. The rooms are bright and cheerful, and the walls are covered with renditions of Da Vinci's *Vetruvian Man*—clearly the owner is an art lover, or just a Dan Brown fan. Although some rooms don't have bathroom facilities ensuite, communal bathrooms are still private and just outside the door. The hotel places you about a 10min. walk from the center of town, along the lovely river promenade.

✴ *Head out of the train station's main entrance and walk straight down Stationsstraat.* Ⓢ *Singles €45-50; doubles €60-65.* Ⓩ *Reception 8:30am-7pm.*

HOTEL DE POSHOORN
Stationstraat 47   🛩(ᵗᵖ) HOTEL ❸
☎043 321 73 34 📧www.poshoorn.nl

This hotel is also situated near the train station but is slightly less appealing than Le Guide and a little more pricey. The large rooms and modern bathroom facilities might explain the price. The rooms vary widely in size but stay the same price, so you may be disappointed with your room's size or shocked at the amount of space you have in your bathroom. The brasserie downstairs is very traditional and a good place to start your day with a quiet beer.

✴ *Head out of the train station and walk straight down Stationsstraat.* *i* *Breakfast €6.75. Free Wi-Fi.* Ⓢ *Singles €57.50; doubles €70.* Ⓩ *Reception 10am-midnight.*

HOTEL HOLLA
Boschstraat 104-106   🛩(ᵗᵖ) HOTEL ❸
☎043 321 35 23 📧www.hotelholla.nl

Holla out loud and they might just hear you in the Markt, the center of Maastricht; you're that close to the historical center of the city. Unfortunately, the modern and swanky brasserie downstairs doesn't seem to be reflected in the tired rooms, which feel a bit stale and in need of a touch up of paint. They still feel clean and tidy, and the bathrooms are very modern. Given the ideal location, you should be able to live with the scratches in the paint.

✴ *Just north of the Markt.* *i* *Breakfast €9.50. Free Wi-Fi.* Ⓢ *Singles €62; doubles €76.* Ⓩ *Reception 8am-11pm.*

HOTEL DE LA BOURSE
Markt 37   🛩(ᵗᵖ) HOTEL ❸
☎043 321 81 12 📧www.hoteldelabourse.nl

Hotel de la Bourse's ideal location in the corner of the Markt puts the main sights of Maastricht at your doorstep. This is, of course, reflected in the hotel's price, and you may be wondering what you've paid for when you discover a small bathroom hidden behind what feels like a closet door in a modest sized room. Although nothing too special, this place might be worth the extra cash if you aren't up for walking out of the center. If you aren't bone idle, however, it may be better to choose a cheaper and less centralized option.

✴ *In the northeast corner of the Markt.* *i* *Breakfast included. Wi-Fi available.* Ⓢ *Singles €65; doubles €65; triples €132.* Ⓩ *Reception 8am-2am.*

maastricht . accommodations

SIGHTS 👁

Most of Maastricht's sights are churches and other religious buildings, but there a few good examples of modern architecture (such as the Province House) which are worth checking out. Make sure you take the trip south of the city to visit the **Caves** and surrounding area of **Mount St. Pieter.**

BASILICA OF ST. SERVATIUS — BASILICA

Keizer Karelplein

Compared to the other Basilica in Maastricht, St. Servatius is bright and grand (instead of dark and creepy like Van Onze Lieve Vrouwe) with a fascinating history stretching back to the death of St. Servatius in the 6th century. The plain tomb of the local saint can be seen in the crypt of the cathedral, and features one Europe's oldest alters. The attached museum and treasure room contain a series of religious relics that are decidedly more quirky than the stuff you'll find in other religious establishments. Look for the collection of foghorns that resemble animals (think of the Looney Tunes character Foghorn Leghorn—come to think of it, maybe this is where the inspiration come from), the busts of Servatius and other important Dutch figures, and the lavish treasure boxes.

➡ Entrance just behind the Vrijthof Square, along Keizer Karelplein. $ Entrance for Basilica, Museum and crypt €3.80, students €2.30, under 18 free. 🕐 Open daily 10am-5pm.

ZONNENBERG CAVE OF MT. ST. PIETER — 👍 CAVES

Slavante 1 ☎043 325 21 21 🖥www.vvvmaastricht.nl

Mount Saint Pieter is a great trip to do on a sunny day, especially since the cool manmade caves will give you an hour's break from the boiling Dutch sun. Take a boat trip from the center of Maastricht, then disembark and climb a grassy hill to reach a great restaurant, a brilliant view, and **The Zonnenberg Caves,** which date back to 1700. Although the caves won't be for everyone, the English tour is quite interesting, and the history of the limestone walls, carvings, and drawings make for a good afternoon trip away from the center. If you just want to go on a boat trip and feel the need to skip the caves, check out the sightseeing boat trip tours below.

➡ The ticket office for the boat is located along the promenade, to the right of St. Servaasbrug. You can walk to the caves, heading straight down Maasboulevard and following the river. Tickets for just the caves can be bought at the VVV office. $ Combination tickets of boat trip and entrance into the Zonnenberg caves; €12.15, under 12 €8.25. 🕐 Ticket office open daily 9am-5pm. The boat leaves dock 2 per hr. 10am-5pm. Tours are every hr. from noon at the caves. Tours in English are conducted every Sa at 2pm, during July and Aug only.

TOWN HALL — GOVERNMENT BUILDING

Markt

That big building you see in the center of the Markt is worth checking out, even if you can only look around the main lobby. Climb the steps through the grand gates and enter through a very large set of doors. The beautiful domed ceiling boasts a series of idealistic 17th-century murals, which portray the expulsion of human vice from heaven, and moral virtues receiving praise from God. We wonder what the mural would have looked like if the artist had painted a portrait of government in practice instead. Use the computer in the corner of the room for a virtual tour of the exterior and interior (in English).

➡ Center of Markt. [i] Contact the VVV tourist office to arrange a tour of the parlor rooms. $ Free. 🕐 Open M-F 8am-5pm. Tours arranged through tourist office.

BONNEFANTENMUSEUM — 👍 MUSEUM

Av. Céramique 250 ☎043 329 01 90 🖥www.bonnefantenmuseum.nl

Maastricht's biggest art museum juxtaposes a collection of wonderful classical pieces with the work of local and international modern artists. Look out for sculptures representing all types of emotions, collages of disembodied hands, and a plain white canvas that we found conceptually snarky. For those who prefer more classical artwork, the exhibit also houses classical artwork from the 16th-20th centuries which might be more to your taste. The current exhibits will remain on display until the end of 2011.

 # The gherkin-shaped building, a short walk from the Centre Céramique. i See website for up-to-date information about exhibits. $ €8, students €6, under 18 €2. ⏰ Open T-Su 11am-5pm.

ST JAN'S CHURCH CHURCH

Vrijthof 24

That red tower you can see from around the city is the main tower of St. Jan's Church, an annex to the Basilica built in the 17th century as a Protestant chapel. Nowadays, the church houses the most tombstones in Maastricht, so you're literally in the dead center of town *(groan)*. The 115 tombstones are dated but not named; most the deceased that are housed here died between 1378 and 1771. If you head down to the altar and look backwards you can see the grand organ, which was built in 1780 and was recently restored in the late 20th century. Make sure you climb the 43m.-high tower for a brilliant view of the sprawling city and river below.

 # Just behind the Vrijthof square. $ Free. Tower €1.50, under 12 €0.50. ⏰ Open daily 11am-4pm.

STADSPARK PARK

Stadspark, Maasboulevard

Maastricht's biggest park is home to some real beauties (both the people who frequent it and the natural sights). Centering on a big lake with a fountain in the middle, the city's old fortifications run through the park and continue along to the West, which you can climb and follow. The park itself has hills, bridges, and large green areas where you can spend a lazy afternoon. If you head further south following the former fortifications, you'll reach a deer park complete with a rangale of deer, some goats who share the compound with them, a couple of peacocks, and even a small aviary with a few doves and other birds. An ideal place for a nice romantic walk along the river bank—just watch out for the hissing geese, who don't like having their territory invaded.

 # Off of Maasboulevard, south of the St. Servaasbrug. $ Free.

COFFEESHOPS AND SMARTSHOPS

Remember: Maastricht isn't Amsterdam. Belgium has had a strong influence on the drug culture in Maastricht, and a few years ago the Mayor even tried to move the coffeeshops out of the town center (with little success). Maastricht has a few small shops in the center where you can have a coffee alongside hash, but these places are very strict on other drug uses and are strict on age as well (18+ only).

HEAVEN 69 ☕ COFFEESHOP

Brusselstraat 146

Blessed with the most suggestive name in Maastricht, Heaven 69 is a more modern and welcoming coffeeshop than some of Maastricht's other pot shops, and boasts a very smoke-free bar area. You have to descend into a small and cavernous bar to buy the other stuff; the younger local crowd smoking up down there is very friendly.

 # Brusselstraat runs off of the Vrijthof. $ Weed from €15. ⏰ Open daily 9am-midnight.

COOL RUNNING ☕ COFFEESHOP

Brusselstraat 35

With a Red Indian statue guarding the door, this narrow coffeeshop has a more traditional feel to it despite its cool and hip younger crowd. Grab a coffee at the bar and install yourself in one of the booths, or head through the sliding doors to the more specialized area where you can pick up the necessaries for a good night out.

➔ Brusselstraat runs off of the Vrijthof. $ Weed from €15. 🕐 Open M-Th 11am-11pm, F-Sa 11am-1am, Su noon-10pm.

FOOD

Eating in Maastricht is a mixed bag; restaurants are remarkably diverse, and range widely in quality. Expect to find standard French and Belgian fare with a touch of German influence now and again, in addition to the typical Dutch *Eetcafés*, which serve up good grub in a pub-like setting. Try and avoid the cheaper eats of the Markt and head a bit further out of the center for a real taste of the Netherlands and Western Europe.

L'HERMITAGE

🍴🍸 TEX MEX [3]

St Bernardusstraat 20 ☎043 325 17 77

With the postcards depicting Picasso's artwork and the various pieces of art scattered around the room, this intimate Tex-Mex restaurant offers a high class version of the greasy taquerias back in the States. It's hardly authentic, but it definitely tastes good. Choose from salads, meat dishes, tapas and even a few vegetarian meals. If you're after something really tasty, order the rack of ribs in BBQ sauce; you won't regret it.

➔ From the foot of St. Servaasbrug head left along Maasboulevard. Take a right onto Graanmarkt and then left onto Sint Bernardusstraat. $ Salads €9.50-11.50, Tex-Mex €11.50-16.20, meat dishes €14.50-21.50. 🕐 Open Tu-Su 5pm-late.

DE DIKKE DRAGONDER

🍴🍸 DUTCH, BELGIAN [3]

Platidstraat 21 ☎043 321 41 87 🖥www.dikkedragonder.nl

This rustic little restaurant is illuminated by low hanging lamps and flickering candlelight. Choose from a selection of sandwiches *(served until 6pm, €3-7)* or, for something more filling, try traditional Dutch dishes like the lambstrips *(€16.50)* or the in-house specialty rabbit cooked "the Maastricht way" *(€13.50);* the restaurant claims to have a secret recipe with special ingredients, and they're keeping it close to their chests.

➔ From Vrijthof, the street us in the south east corner. $ Light meals €3-11. Entrees €12.50-17. 🕐 Open M-Th 10am-2am, F-Sa 10am-3am. Kitchen closes at 9:30pm.

AMADEUS

🍴🍸 BRASSERIE [3]

Dominikanerkerkstraat 1a ☎043 356 05 92 🖥www.brasserieamadeus.nl

Situated in front of a large and retired cathedral (now a bookshop), Amadeus is a great spot for lunch or dinner, particularly if you sit outside. Although it is unknown whether Mozart actually ate here (the brasserie looks old, but not that old), it is worth popping in if you fancy a sandwich or a something more substantial. Amadeus has a range of "special sandwiches" that include roast beef, salmon, or vegetarian options *(€7-12),* but we recommend the large bowls of soup *(€4-6).*

➔ Just off of Vrijthof. $ Entrees €12-16. Smaller plates €4-12. 🕐 Open M 10am-late, Tu-Sa 9:30am-late, Su 11am-late.

LUNA RUSSA

🍦 ICE CREAM [1]

Hoogbrugstraat 45 ☎043 311 25 05

Forget the vanilla or chocolate options offered at other ice cream stores in the center; come over the bridge to Luna Russa, where you can sample eccentric flavors like cheese cake, brownie, and the bright blue "puflo-blue." For aspiring sophisticates, we recommend the mojito (flavor, that is).

➔ Just over the river Maas from the center, near Centre Céramique. $ 1 scoop €1.50, 2 €3, 3 €4.25. 🕐 Open daily 10am-11pm.

BRASSERIE BONHOMME

●🞄🍷🞄 BRASSERIE ❷

Maaspromenade 78 ☎043 325 89 25 ■www.bonhomme.be

This very swanky little brasserie is just the trick for a sunny afternoon by the Maas. Despite the upscale décor, great food, and a top notch presentation, the price tag here is extremely reasonable, with lunch meals under €8 for sandwiches and soups, and generous steaks or pork escalopes for under €17. The Brasserie's terrace is also an ideal spot to grab a drink or beer and watch the boats flow past on the river.

🍴 *Just to the right of St. Servaasbrug.* Ⓢ *Breakfast €9.50-12.50. Sandwiches €4.50-7.50. Entrees €4.50-17.* Ⓩ *Open Daily. Breakfast served 10am-noon. Full menu served noon-8pm.*

DE LANTERN EETCAFÉ

●🍷 CAFE ❸

O.L Vrouwplein 26 ☎043 321 43 26 ■www.lanteern.nl

Grab a table on the terrace in between the other restaurants in this area, where locals come for a night out with a few quiet beers and some top quality nosh for a great price. The waiters and waitresses here run in between the tables delivering steaming and meaty dishes such as sauerkraut, pork ribs with a delicious whiskey sauce, and other vaguely Germanic classic. Vegetarian dishes and English translation menu available. Also open for lighter bites and sandwiches at lunch.

🍴 *O.L Vrouwplein is off of Graanmarkt.* Ⓢ *Lunch €5-13. Entrees €10.50-16.50.* Ⓩ *Open daily 10am-2am.*

SLAVANTE

●🍷 BRASSERIE ❷

Slavante 1 ☎043 321 00 15 ■www.slavante.nl

Situated at the top of Mt. St. Pieter, this beautiful log cabin style restaurant is an ideal pit-stop for hungry cave explorers. Eating here is a great way to extend your day at the caves, and you could sit here all afternoon and watch the river and streets below. The beautiful views of the city alone make the restaurant worth the trip.

🍴 *Either take the boat run by Rederij Stiphout (see sights), or walking the restaurant is about 4km south of the city. Follow Maasboulevard by the river until you reach the mountain path for the Zonnenberg caves and follow the signs for the casino.* Ⓢ *Sandwiches €4-6. Entrees €8-15.* Ⓩ *Open in summer daily 10am-9pm; in winter M-Sa 10am-6pm, Su 10am-8pm.*

NIGHTLIFE

Maastricht is full of relaxed *kaffees* (pub-like interiors with an extensive beer list) and bars, where locals and tourists lounge on terraces and nurse a pint or three beneath the fading sun. There are some dance type clubs here, but don't expect the thumping "discotheques" of other cities—it's not like this is Amsterdam. The three main squares of Maastricht, the **Markt, Vrojthof,** and **O.L. Vrouwe,** each offer a different type of nightlife experience. Off of these squares are smaller and more quirky bars, and some of Maastricht's best bars can be found over the river around the streets off of **Stationsstraat** and **Wycker Burgstraat.** For a busy street near the center, head down to **Platidstraat** for a mix of bars, cafes and a club.

TAKE ONE

●🍷 BAR

Rechstraat 28 ☎043 321 64 23 ■www.takeonebiercafe.nl

We recommend that you bond with Peet's "victims"—that's how this bar's extremely eccentric owner refers to his willing customers. From the outside, this bar looks pretty innocuous, but once you see the international array of beer mats pasted on the walls, you'll know you've stumbled on a treasure. An ever changing beer list lines the wall behind the bar, and you can expect to find beers that other bars in Maastricht will never have the opportunity to stock, including multiple brews from Belgium. On weekends, the beer get flowing and the nuts on the tables end up all over the floor, but the bar's quirky enough to get away with it.

🍴 *From the train station head down Stationstraat. Rechstraat is on your right just before the bridge.* $ *Most beer €2-6.* ⏰ *Open M 4pm-2am, Th-Su 4pm-2am.*

IN DE KARKOL 🍴🍸 BEER GARDEN, KAFFEE

Stockstraat 5 ☎043 321 70 33

Like most of Maastricht's best places to grab a beer, In de Karkol looks extremely unassuming from the outside. A small snail sits in the window (the Karkol), and the door can be easily missed if you aren't looking for it. Like most hidden treasures, though, this bar is worth searching for; In de Karkol's been voted into the Top 10 best Kaffees in the Netherlands for so many years in a row, they've finally lost count. Locals line the bar and sit under framed photos that span generations, while the little beer garden outside is decorated with angels, presumably to keep local punters protected from heart and liver failure as they smoke their cigars and sup their drink.

✣ *Stockstraat is off of O.L. Vrouweplein.* $ *Beer €2-6.* ⏰ *Open M-Tu noon-midnight, Th-Sa noon-2am, Su noon-midnight.*

ZONDAG 🍴🍸 KAFFEE

Wyckerbrugstraat 42 ☎043 321 93 00 🖥www.cafezondag.nl

In Dutch, Zondag is Sunday, that laid back day of the week where you feel you can just kick back, relax and not worry about anything else. This slacker vibe radiates from Zondag, and fortunately the bar's open seven days a week rather than just on *zondag*. Modern art is displayed inside, rotating between local artists who want to show of their talents. Colorful chairs and tables line the streets outside, and on a weekend you will have to fight through crowds (or climb through a window) to reach the bar. Kick back with a drink, or even a snack served until 8pm, and imagine it was a lazy Sunday afternoon.

✣ *Straight down from the train station, on the corner on the right before the bridge.* $ *Drinks €2-6.* ⏰ *Open daily 10am-2am.*

KAFFEE DE KRINSPIEP 🍴🍸 KAFFEE

Muntstraat 45 ☎043 321 40 65

The jolly owner of this local watering hole looks a bit like a ruddy-cheeked Disney character; in our book that's a good thing. Grab a stool at the bar and work on your Dutch with the locals, or pull up a chair at one of the tables under the mix of musical instruments that hang from the ceiling.

✣ *Muntstraat is just to the right of the VVV.* $ *Beer €2.50-5.* ⏰ *Open M noon-7pm, T-Th 10am-11pm, F-Sa 10am-2am, Su 5-11pm.*

KAFFEE 'T PERREPLUKE 🍴🍸☁ KAFFEE

Kesselkade 47 ☎043 321 45 62

Sitting near the river Maas is a fine way to spend an evening, and this local Kaffee has a small outside seating which enables you to do just that. With a pleasant beer menu, and an even more pleasant staff, this local hangout attracts a younger crowd in the week who enjoy its vibrant interior and exterior.

✣ *Along the promenade, right of the St. Servaasbrug.* $ *Drinks €2.50-5.* ⏰ *Open W-Sa noon-late, Su 2pm-late.*

DEKADANS 🍴🍸☁ BAR

Kesselskade 62 ☎043 326 17 00 🖥www.dekadans.nl

The waterfront of the Maas is normally calm and quiet, but once the food stops being served and the music starts playing there's nothing calm about Dekadans. Most patrons head outside to the waterfront terrace on a summer's evening.

✣ *Near the foot of St. Servaasbrug.* $ *Drinks €2-6.* ⏰ *Open daily noon-late. Kitchen closes at 10pm.*

FESTIVALS

Maastricht is a hub of culture, and is a great resting point between some of Europe's biggest summer festivals thanks to its location near the Belgian-German border. For a rundown of what's happening, make sure you grab **Week in, Week Uit;** although it's in Dutch, you can pick out the titles and dates pretty easily, or ask a friendly local to translate for you. Some of the bigger festivals take place just over the border in Belgium, but getting there from Maastricht is pretty easy to do.

ROCK WERCHTER ● SUMMER

Haachtsesteenweg ☎+32 34 00 00 34 ▣www.rockwerchter.be

One of Europe's biggest and best festivals, Rock Werchter takes place every July just outside of Leuven, Belgium, but can be easily reached from Maastricht. 2010 headliners included Muse, La Roux, Green Day, and Arcade Fire, to name a few. *⌗ From Maastricht take the train to Leuven. Shuttle services will run from the station to the site. ⓘ Tickets for go on sale Dec-Jan. ⓢ Day pass €78; 4-day pass €180. Campsite tickets €18 per person.*

FESTIVAL ZOMERAVONDON SUMMER

▣www.ainsi.nl

This Maastricht summer favorite transforms the streets with live theater, dance, and music. In addition to the countless performances, the festival offers workshops for all age groups in the performing arts. Check online in the summer for details on how to get involved. *ⓢ Some events are free; others you have to pay for. ⓤ Mid-Aug.*

JAZZ MAASTRICHT PROMENADE ● FALL

▣www.jazzmaastricht.be

Maastricht is home to one of the largest jazz and cultural events in the whole of Europe. The center of the city is turned into a hub of jazz music, with live concerts being performed in various locations. Tickets for the events go on sale online at the website and you can find more specific information under their agenda. *ⓢ Prices vary by event. ⓤ Oct.*

ESSENTIALS 🔁

Practicalities

- **TOURIST OFFICE: VVV,** Kleine Staat 1, sells city maps *(€1.50)* with details of all the historical sights and tourist locations and a city guide *(€5)* with listings and extra information. (Although the Stayokay hostel gives this out for free). They also book tours of the caves, city walks, and tours of the local breweries. *(☎043 325 21 21 ▣www.vvvmaastricht.be ⓤ Open in summer M-Sa 9am-6pm, Su 11am-3pm; in winter M-Sa 9am-5pm.)*

- **INTERNET: The Centre Céramique.** *(Av. Céramique 50 ☎043 350 56 00 ⓤ Open Tu 10:30am-7pm, W 10:30am-5pm, Th 10:30am-7pm, F 10:30am-5pm, Sa 10am-3pm, Su 1-5pm.)* This is an exhibition center with a library on the bottom floor. It's free to entry the library, just grab a ticket from the machine and input the code to get access to one of the computer terminals. **Free Wi-Fi** is also available.

- **ATMS:** There's a 24hr. **ING Bank** ATM at Vrijthof 45. ATMs can also be found on the Markt.

- **LAUNDROMATS: Wasserij Huysman,** Boschstraat 82.

- **POST OFFICE:** There is a smaller **post office** at Stationstraat 60, near the train station. *(ⓤ Open M noon-5:30pm, Tu-F 9:30am-5:30pm, Sa 9:30am-1:30pm.)*

Emergency!

- **POLICE:** Sint Hubertuslaan 40.
- **HOSPITAL/MEDICAL SERVICES:** University Hospital Maastricht, P. Debyelaan 25. *(☎043 387 65 43)*

Getting There

Thanks to its close proximity to both Germany and Belgium, Maastricht is easily accessible by train from across Europe. If you need to catch a flight across the Pond, trains run direct to both Brussels or Dusseldorf North airports, which are bigger and offer more international destinations.

By Plane

The airport at Maastricht, **Maastricht Aachen,** offers commercial passenger flights to a collection of smaller European destinations, including **Malaga, Alicante, Faro, Pisa, Trapani,** and **Ankara.** To reach the airport from the center, take **bus #59** from the train station. *(⏰ 30min., every 30min. daily 5:40am-11:47pm.)*

By Train

Trains go to **Amsterdam Centraal NTH** *($€24.60 ⏰ 2hr.)* and **Brussels Midi BEL** *($ €23, under 25 €15. ⏰ 1hr. 15min.)* as well as other European cities. The station and ticket office are located at Stationsplein 27. *(☎0900 92 92 ⏰ Open M-Sa 7am-8pm, Su 7:15am-8pm.)*

Getting Around

The simplest way to get around the city center is by foot; large pedestrian areas, a riverside promenade and grassy parks all make Maastricht very easy to explore. With the **train station** a short walk from the historical center and roads connecting all the main squares of the city, you won't need to worry about buses or taxis unless you are making longer journeys.

By Bike

As in most of the Netherlands, a bicycle is the best way to travel if you want to blend in. Bike lanes line the streets and roads, and most pedestrian areas are accessible by bike as well. The best place to rent one is at the **train station shop.** *(Stainsplein 26 ☎043 321 11 00 $ €7.50-17.50 per day. ⏰ Open M-F 5:15am-1:15am, Sa 6am-1:15am, Su 7:15am-1:15am.)* Bikes can also be rented from **OrangeBike**, Sint Jacobstraat 4b. *(☎043 311 36 13 💻www.orangebike.nl $ €6 per 3hr., 10am-6pm costs €8.50 per 8hr., €9.50 per 24hr. ⏰ Open M 10am-6pm, Th-Su 10am-6pm.)*

By Bus

Ideal for a quick trip into the city's outer areas, Maastricht's buses all stop by **Veoila** in the city center. *(Parallelweg 59 ☎0900 331 05 50 $ €0.70 per min. ⏰ Open M-F 8am-6pm, Sa 9am-5pm.)* Maastricht is split into "zones," and each journey by bus costs one "strippen" for each zone that you pass through. A "strippen" doesn't convert into a set number of euros, so it's hard to know exactly how much your ride's going to cost. We can't really think of a more confusing system, actually. Tickets are bought on board and divided into strippen automatically; two strippen equal a round-trip ticket between two "zones" *(€1.60).*

By Taxi

They're not really necessary in Maastricht, unless you're making a journey to the airport or feel the need to be lazy. Taxis can be hailed on the street, and particularly cluster by the station.

ESSENTIALS

You don't have to be a rocket scientist to plan a good trip. (It might help, but it's not required.) You do, however, need to be well prepared, and that's what we can do for you. Essentials is the chapter that gives you all the nitty-gritty you need to know for your trip: the hard information gleaned from 50 years of collective wisdom (and that phone call to Utrecht the other day that put us on hold for an hour). Planning your trip? Check. Staying safe and healthy? Check. The dirt on transportation? Check. We've also thrown in communications info, meteorological charts, and a 🔖**phrasebook,** just for good measure. Plus, for overall trip-planning advice from what to pack (money and as little underwear as possible) to how to take a good passport photo (it's physically impossible; consider airbrushing), you can also check out the Essentials section of 🖥**www.letsgo.com.**

We're not going to lie—this chapter is tough for us to write, and you might not find it as fun of a read as 101 or Discover. But please, for the love of all that is good, read it! It's super helpful, and, most importantly, it means we didn't compile all this technical info and put it in one place for you (yes YOU) for nothing.

greatest hits

- **GET A VISA.** Or not, if your stay is less than 90 days. Europe's rules are quite complicated, so read inside (p. 230) for more details.

- **DON'T SMUGGLE IN ANY DRUGS.** Um, duh. Besides, the Netherlands's decriminalization policy means you can buy pot there (p. 234).

- **EURAIL BENELUX PASS.** Fix yourself up with unlimited rides on trains in Belgium, the Netherlands, and Luxembourg for five days (p. 239).

- **THE PROSTITUTION INFORMATION CENTRE.** Head to this helpful office in Amsterdam's Red Light District to find out all you need to know (and are afraid to ask) about "the world's oldest profession" (p. 237).

- **BRUSH UP ON YOUR LANGUAGE.** Learn the secrets of what Flemish actually is, how French got to the Low Countries, and pronunciation of Dutch consonants (p. 242).

planning your trip

- **PASSPORT:** Required of any citizens, of anywhere.
- **VISA:** Required of non-EU citizens staying longer than 90 days.
- **WORK PERMIT:** Required of all non-EU citizens planning to work in the Netherlands or Belgium.

DOCUMENTS AND FORMALITIES

You've got your visa and your work permit, just like Let's Go told you to, and then you realize you've forgotten the most important thing: your passport. Well, we're not going to let that happen. **Don't forget your passport!**

Visas

Those lucky enough to be citizens of the European Union do not need a visa in the Netherlands or Belgium. Citizens of all non-EU countries do not need a visa for short trips, but if your trip lasts more than 90 days, you will need one. Take note that this 90 day period begins when you enter the EU's **freedom of movement** zone (for more info, see **One Europe** below), so ask yourself if you really want to spend 89 days in Estonia, and apportion your time wisely. If you really can't pull yourself away from the wonders of Tallinn, contact your nearest Dutch or Belgian consulate or embassy (listed below for your convenience) for info on how to obtain a visa for an elongated stay.

It's a good idea to double-check entrance requirements at the nearest embassy or consulate of the Netherlands or Belgium for up-to-date information before departure. US citizens can also consult ▣travel.state.gov.

Entering the Netherlands or Belgium to study will generally require a special visa. For more information, see the **Beyond Tourism** chapter.

one europe

The EU's policy of freedom of movement means that most border controls have been abolished and visa policies harmonized. Under this treaty, formally known as the Schengen Agreement, you're still required to carry a passport (or government-issued ID card for EU citizens) when crossing an internal border, but, once you've been admitted into one country, you're free to travel to other participating states. Most EU states are already members of Schengen (excluding Cyprus), as are Iceland and Norway. For more consequences of the EU for travelers, see **The Euro** feature later in this chapter.

Work Permits

Admittance to the Netherlands or Belgium as a non-EU traveler does not include the right to work, which is authorized only by a work permit. For more information, see the **Beyond Tourism** chapter.

essentials

dutch consular services

- **IN AUSTRALIA: Consulate General.** *(Level 23, Westfield Tower 2, 101 Grafton St., Bondi Junction NSW 2022 ☎02 9387 6644 🖳www.netherlands.org.au ⌚ Open M-F 10am-noon.)*

- **IN CANADA: Consulate General.** *(1 Dundas St. W, Ste. 2106, Toronto, ON M5G 1Z3 ☎877-DUTCHHELP 🖳www.netherlandsembassy.ca ⌚ Open M-F 9am-noon.)*

- **IN IRELAND: Embassy.** *(160 Merrion Rd., Dublin 4 ☎01 269 3444 🖳www.netherlandsembassy.ie ⌚ Open M-F 8:30am-4:15pm.)*

- **IN NEW ZEALAND: Embassy.** *(Investment House, 10th fl., Wellington ☎04 471 6390 🖳www.netherlandsembassy.co.nz ⌚ Open M-Th 10am-12:30pm.)*

- **IN THE UK: Embassy.** *(38 Hyde Park Gate, London, SW7 5DP ☎020 7590 3200 🖳www.netherlands-embassy.org.uk ⌚ Open M-F 8:30am-noon, closed 1st and 3rd W each month. Appointments required, schedule one online.)*

- **IN THE USA: Embassy.** *(4200 Linnean Ave. NW, Washington, DC, 20008 ☎877-DUTCHHELP 🖳www.netherlands-embassy.org ⌚ Open M-F 9:30am-12:30pm. Appointments required, schedule one online.)*

Embassies in the Netherlands are situated in The Hague. The UK and the US have Consulate Generals in Amsterdam; their embassies do not offer consular services.

- **AUSTRALIAN CONSULAR SERVICES: Embassy.** *(Carnegielaan 4, 2517 KH The Hague ☎070 310 8200 🖳www.netherlands.embassy.gov.au ⌚ Open M-F 8:30am-5pm.)*

- **CANADIAN CONSULAR SERVICES: Embassy.** *(Sophialaan 7, 2514 JP The Hague ☎070 311 1600 🖳www.canada.nl ⌚ Consular section open Jan-May 16 M-F 10am-1pm and 2-4:30pm; May 17-Aug 27 M-Th 10am-12:30pm and 1:30-4:30pm, F 10am-1pm; Aug 28-Dec 31 M-F 10am-1pm and 2-4:30pm.)*

- **IRISH CONSULAR SERVICES: Embassy.** *(Scheveningseweg 112, 2584 AE The Hague ☎070 363 0993 🖳www.irishembassy.nl ⌚ Open M-F 10am-12:30pm and 2:30-5pm.)*

- **NEW ZEALAND CONSULAR SERVICES: Embassy.** *(Eisenhowerlaan 77N, 2517 KK The Hague ☎070 346 9324 🖳www.nzembassy.com/netherlands ⌚ Open M-F 9am-12:30pm and 1:30-5pm.)*

- **BRITISH CONSULAR SERVICES: Consulate General.** *(Koningslaan 44, Amsterdam ☎020 676 4343 🖳www.britain.nl 𝒊 Visa services by online appointment only. ⌚ Open M-F 9am-12:30pm and 2-3:30pm.)*

- **AMERICAN CONSULAR SERVICES: Consulate General.** *(Museumplein 19, 1071 DJ Amsterdam ☎020 575 5309 🖳amsterdam.usconsulate.gov 𝒊 All non-emergency visits require online appointment. ⌚ Open M-F 8:30-11:30am. Immigrant visa services available M-Tu 1:30-3pm, Th 1:30-3pm.)*

- **IN AUSTRALIA: Embassy.** *(19 Arkana St., Yarralumla, Canberra ACT 2600 ☎(0)2 6273 2501 ▣www.diplomatie.be/canberra ⌚ Open M-Th 9am-12:30pm and 1-4pm, F 9am-12:30pm and 1-3pm. Visa services available M-F 9am-noon.)*

- **IN CANADA: Embassy.** *(360 Albert St. Ste. 820, Ottawa Ontario K1R 7X7 ☎613-236-7267 ▣www.diplomatie.be/ottawa ⌚ Open M-Th 9am-1pm and 2-3pm, F 9am-2pm.)*

- **IN IRELAND: Embassy.** *(2 Shrewsbury Rd., Ballsbridge, Dublin 4 ☎01 205 7100 ▣www.diplomatie.be/dublin ⌚ Open M-F 9am-1pm and 2-3pm. Visa services available 9am-12:30pm.)*

- **IN NEW ZEALAND: Consulate.** *(Level 6 Leaders Building, 15 Brandon St., 6011 Wellington ☎04 974 9080 ⌚ Open T 2-4pm, Th 2-4pm and by appointment.)*

- **IN THE UK: Embassy.** *(17 Grosvenor Crescent, London SW1X 7EE ☎020 7470 3700 ▣www.diplomatie.be/london ⌚ Open M-F 9am-5pm. Passport services open M-F 9am-1pm.)*

- **IN THE USA: Embassy.** *(3330 Garfield St. NW, 20008 Washington, DC ☎202-333-6900 ▣www.diplobel.us ⌚ Open M-F 9:30am-noon.)*

- **AUSTRALIAN CONSULAR SERVICES: Embassy.** *(6/8 rue Guimard, 1040 Brussels }02 286 0500 ▣www.belgium.embassy.gov.au ⌚ Open M-F 8:30am-5pm. No visa section: visa services are handled by the Australian Embassy in Paris ☎01 40 59 33 00 ▣www.france.embassy.gov.au.)*

- **CANADIAN CONSULAR SERVICES: Embassy.** *(2 Av. de Tervueren, 1040 Brussels ☎02 741 0611 ▣www.ambassade-canada.be ⌚ Open M-F 9am-12:30pm and 1:30-5pm. Consular services open M-F 9am-noon. Afternoon hours for emergencies only.)*

- **IRISH CONSULAR SERVICES: Embassy.** *(180 chaussée d'Etterbeek, 1040 Brussels ☎02 282 3400 ▣www.embassyofireland.be ⌚ Open M-F 10am-1pm.)*

- **NEW ZEALAND CONSULAR SERVICES: Embassy.** *(Level 7, 9-31 Av. des Nerviens, Nervierslaan, 1040 Brussels ☎02 512 1040 ▣www.nzembassy.com/belgium ⌚ Open M-F 9am-1pm and 2-5:30pm.)*

- **BRITISH CONSULAR SERVICES: Consulate General.** *(9-31 Av. des Nerviens, Nervierslaan, 1040 Brussels ☎02 287 6248 ▣ukinbelgium.fco.gov.uk ⌚ Open M-F 9am-12:30pm and 2:15-4pm. Visa services open 9-11:30am.)*

- **AMERICAN CONSULAR SERVICES: Embassy.** *(27 bd. du Regent, 1000 Brussels ☎02 508 2111 ▣belgium.usembassy.gov ⌚ Open M-Th 1:30-3:30pm, F 9-11am.)*

essentials

TIME DIFFERENCES

Both the Netherlands and Belgium are 1hr. ahead of Greenwich Mean Time (GMT) and both observe Daylight Saving Time. This means that they are 6hr. ahead of New

York City, 9hr. ahead of Los Angeles, and 1hr. ahead of the British Isles. In Northern Hemisphere summer they are 8hr. behind Sydney and 10hr. behind New Zealand, while in Northern Hemisphere winter they are 10hr. behind Sydney and 12hr. behind New Zealand. Don't get confused and call your parents when it's actually 4am their time! Note that both countries change to Daylight Savings Time on different dates from some other countries, so sometimes the difference will be one hour different from what is stated here.

money

GETTING MONEY FROM HOME

Stuff happens. When stuff happens, you might need some money. When you need some money, the easiest and cheapest solution is to have someone back home make a deposit to your bank account. Otherwise, consider one of the following options.

Wiring Money

Arranging a **bank money transfer** means asking a bank back home to wire money to a bank in the Netherlands or Belgium. This is the cheapest way to transfer cash, but it's also the slowest and most agonizing, usually taking several days or more. Note that some banks may only release your funds in local currency, potentially sticking you with a poor exchange rate; inquire about this in advance. Both the Netherlands and Belgium are pretty well-organized countries, so transfers should go quite smoothly; you can thank your lucky stars you aren't in Italy. In addition to bank transfers, money transfer services like **Western Union** offer a faster and more convenient service than bank transfers—but are also much pricier. Western Union has many locations worldwide. To find one, visit ▣www.westernunion.com or call the appropriate number: in Belgium ☎0800 99 709, in the Netherlands 0800 023 5172, in Australia 1800 173 833, in Canada 800-235-0000, in the US 800-325-6000, and in the UK 0800 731 1815. Money transfer services are also available to **American Express** cardholders and at selected **Thomas Cook** offices.

the euro

Despite what many dollar-possessing Americans might want to hear, the official currency of 16 members of the European Union—Austria, Belgium, Cyprus, Finland, France, Germany, Greece, Ireland, Italy, Luxembourg, Malta, the Netherlands, Portugal, Slovakia, Slovenia, and Spain—is the euro.

Still, the currency has some important—and positive—consequences for travelers hitting more than one eurozone country. For one thing, money-changers across the eurozone are obliged to exchange money at the official, fixed rate and at no commission (though they may still charge a small service fee). Second, euro-denominated traveler's checks allow you to pay for goods and services across the eurozone, again at the official rate and commission-free. For more info, check a currency converter (such as ▣www.xe.com or www.europa.eu.int).

US State Department (US Citizens Only)

In serious emergencies only, the US State Department will forward money within hours to the nearest consular office, which will then disburse it according to instructions for a US$30 fee. If you wish to use this service, you must contact the Overseas

Citizens Services division of the US State Department. *(☎+1-202-501-4444, from US 888-407-4747)*

pins and atms

To use a debit or credit card to withdraw money from a cash machine (ATM) in Europe, you must have a four-digit Personal Identification Number (PIN). If your PIN is longer than four digits, ask your bank whether you can just use the first four or whether you'll need a new one. Credit cards don't usually come with PINs, so if you intend to hit up ATMs in Europe with a credit card to get cash advances, call your credit card company before leaving to request one.

Travelers with alphabetic rather than numeric PINs may also be thrown off by the absence of letters on European cash machines. Here are the corresponding numbers to use: 1 = QZ; 2 = ABC; 3 = DEF; 4 = GHI; 5 = JKL; 6 = MNO; 7 = PRS; 8 = TUV; 9 = WXY. Note that if you mistakenly punch the wrong code into the machine multiple (often three) times, it can swallow (gulp!) your card for good.

TIPPING

In both the Netherlands and Belgium, service charges are included in the bill at restaurants. Waiters do not depend on tips for their livelihood, so there is no need to feel guilty about not leaving a tip. Still, leaving 5-10% extra will certainly be appreciated. Higher than that is just showing off. Tips in bars are very unusual. Cab drivers are normally tipped about 10%.

TAXES

The quoted price of goods in both the Netherlands and Belgium includes **value added tax** (**BTW** in the Netherlands and **BTW** or **TVA** in Belgium). This tax on goods is generally levied at 19% in the Netherlands and 21% in Belgium, although some goods are subject to lower rates.

safety and health

GENERAL ADVICE

In any type of crisis, the most important thing to do is **stay calm.** Your country's embassy abroad is usually your best resource in an emergency; registering with that embassy upon arrival in the country is a good idea. The government offices listed in the **Travel Advisories** feature at the end of this section can provide information on the services they offer their citizens in case of emergencies abroad.

Drugs and Alcohol

It hardly needs to be stated that attitudes towards conscience-altering substances are quite different between Amsterdam and Brussels. Both have fairly liberal attitudes regarding alcohol, with legal drinking ages of 16 and booze widely available. Public drunkenness, however, is frowned upon and is a sure way to mark yourself as a tourist.

When it comes to drugs other than alcohol, as is so often the case, things get a little more interesting. Hard drugs are completely illegal in both countries, and possession or consumption of substances like heroin and cocaine will be harshly punished if caught. In the Netherlands, soft drugs like marijuana and mushrooms are

tolerated, and you are very unlikely to face prosecution for using them. Consumption is confined to certain legalized zones, namely coffeeshops (for marijuana) and smartshops (for herbal drugs). Both are heavily regulated but very popular: the number of smartshops in particular has exploded in recent years. When visiting a coffeeshop or smartshop for the first time, it may be a good idea to take a sober friend with you. Even experienced drug users may be surprised at the hotbox effect created in shops where the fumes of several pot-smokers accumulate. Having a friend to guide you home could turn out to be helpful if not absolutely essential.

Belgium's attitude toward even soft drugs is much more traditional and conservative. Marijuana is both illegal and not tolerated. Coffeeshops in Belgium are just that; the strongest substance you'll be able to buy is a simple *café noir*.

Prostitution

Just as with drugs, Belgium and the Netherlands have exceptionally different policies regarding prostitution. The sex industry is illegal in Belgium and probably always will be (Catholic morals live on). The "world's oldest profession" has, however, flourished in the Netherlands, particularly in the liberal capital of the world, Amsterdam. Prostitution in Amsterdam has always centered on what is today called the Red Light District, though it is practiced elsewhere in the city as well.

Legal prostitution in Amsterdam comes in two main forms. Window prostitution, which involves scantily clad women tempting passersby from small chambers fronted by a plate-glass window, is by far the most visible. Sex workers of this kind are self-employed and rent the windows themselves. Accordingly, each sets her own price. This form of commercial sex gave the Red Light District its name, as lamps both outside and inside the windows emit a red glow that, at night, bathes the whole area. Whether shopping or "just looking," be sure to show the women basic respect. Looking is fine and even expected, but leering and catcalling are absolutely uncalled for. Keep in mind that prostitution is an entirely legal enterprise, and windows are places of business. Most of the prostitutes whom you see belong to a union called "The Red Thread" and are tested for HIV and STIs, although testing is on a voluntary basis. Do not take photos unless you want to explain yourself to the angriest—and largest—man you'll ever see.

If you're interested in having sex with a window prostitute, go up to the door and wait for someone inside to let you in. Show up clean and sober; prostitutes always reserve the right to refuse their services. Anything goes as long as you clearly and straightforwardly agree to it beforehand. Specifically state what you want to get for the money you're paying—that means which sex acts, in what positions, and, especially, how much time you have in which to do it. Window prostitutes can set their standards; by no means are they required to do anything you want without consenting to it in advance. Negotiation occurs and money changes hands before any sexual acts take place. Always practice safe sex; a prostitute should not and will not touch a penis that is not covered by a condom. Don't ask for a refund if you are left unsatisfied: all sales are final. There is no excuse for making trouble; if anyone becomes violent or threatening with a window prostitute, she has access to an emergency button that sets off a loud alarm. Not only does it make an ear-splitting noise but it also summons the police, who invariably side with prostitutes in disputes. If you feel you have a legitimate complaint or have any questions about commercial sex, head to the extremely helpful Prostitution Information Centre and talk it through.

Another option is the recently legalized brothels. The term usually refers to an establishment centered on a bar. There, women—or men—who are available for hour-long sessions will make your acquaintance. These brothels, also called sex clubs, can be pricey. They are also controversial, and in the last few years the authorities have sought to close brothels associated with trafficking and criminal gangs.

essentials

The best place to go for information about prostitution in Amsterdam is the **Prostitution Information Centre.** (*Enge Kerksteeg 3, in the Red Light District behind the Oude Kerk,* ☎*020 420 7328 ▣www.pic-amsterdam.com ◷ Open Sa 4-7pm. Available at other times for group bookings, call ahead.)* Founded in 1994 by Mariska Majoor (once a prostitute herself), the center fills a niche, connecting the Red Light District with its eager frequenters. The center's staff can answer any question you might have, no matter how blushworthy the query.

---

travel advisories

The following government offices provide travel information and advisories by telephone, by fax, or via the web:

- **AUSTRALIA: Department of Foreign Affairs and Trade.** (}+61 2 6261 1111 ▣*www.dfat.gov.au)*

- **CANADA: Department of Foreign Affairs and International Trade (DFAIT).** Call or visit the website for the free booklet *Bon Voyage...But.* (}+1-800-267-8376 ▣*www.dfait-maeci.gc.ca)*

- **NEW ZEALAND: Ministry of Foreign Affairs.** (}+64 4 439 8000 ▣*www.mfat.govt.nz)*

- **UK: Foreign and Commonwealth Office.** (}+44 20 7008 1500 ▣*www.fco.gov.uk)*

- **US: Department of State.** (}888-407-4747 from the US, +1-202-501-4444 elsewhere ▣*travel.state.gov)*

PRE-DEPARTURE HEALTH

Matching a prescription to a foreign equivalent is not always easy, safe, or possible, so if you take **prescription drugs,** carry up-to-date prescriptions or a statement from your doctor stating the medications' trade names, manufacturers, chemical names, and dosages. Be sure to keep all medication with you in your carry-on luggage.

Immunizations And Precautions

Travelers over two years old should make sure that the following vaccines are up to date: MMR (for measles, mumps, and rubella); DTaP or Td (for diphtheria, tetanus, and pertussis); IPV (for polio); Hib (for *Haemophilus influenzae* B); and HepB (for Hepatitis B). For recommendations on immunizations and prophylaxis, check with a doctor and consult the **Centers for Disease Control and Prevention (CDC)** in the US or the equivalent in your home country. (☎*+1-800-CDC-INFO/232-4636 ▣www.cdc.gov/travel)*

getting around

For information on how to get to the Netherlands and Belgium and save a bundle while doing so, check out the Essentials section of ▣**www.letsgo.com.** (In case you can't tell, we think our website's the bomb.) For information specific to a certain city, see the **Getting There** and **Getting Around** sections for that city.

BY PLANE

For small-scale travel on the continent, *Let's Go* suggests ⬛budget airlines for budget travelers, but more traditional carriers have made efforts to keep up with the revolution. The **Star Alliance Europe Airpass** offers low economy-class fares for travel within Europe to 220 destinations in 45 countries. The pass is available to non-European passengers on Star Alliance carriers, including Brussels Airlines. (⬛*www.staralliance.com*) **EuropebyAir's** snazzy FlightPass also allows you to hop between hundreds of cities in Europe and North Africa. (☎*+1-888-321-4737* ⬛*www.europebyair.com* Ⓢ *Most flights US$99.*)

In addition, a number of European airlines offer discount coupon packets. Most are only available as tack-ons for transatlantic passengers, but some are standalone offers. Most must be purchased before departure, so research in advance. For example, **oneworld**, a coalition of 10 major international airlines, offers deals and cheap connections all over the world, including within Europe. (⬛*www.oneworld.com*)

budget airlines

The recent emergence of no-frills airlines has made hopscotching around Europe by air increasingly affordable. Though these flights often feature inconvenient hours or serve less popular regional airports, with ticket prices often dipping into single digits, it's never been faster or easier to jet across the continent. The following resources will be useful both for getting to Amsterdam and Brussels and for those ever-popular weekend trips to nearby international destinations. Be warned—these airlines try to squeeze their profit margins any way they can, and calling some of the phone numbers listed here will cost as much as a euro per minute, so it may be best to use their websites.

- **BMIBABY:** Flies from Birmingham and East Midlands in the UK to Amsterdam. (☎*0871 224 0224 for the UK, +44 870 126 6726 elsewhere* ⬛*www.bmibaby.com*)

- **EASYJET:** Flies from across Europe to Amsterdam, and from many destinations (but not from Britain) to Brussels. (☎*+44 871 244 2366* ⬛*www.easyjet.com.* Ⓢ *UK£50-150.*)

- **RYANAIR:** From multiple European locations to Brussels. (☎*0818 30 30 30 for Ireland, 0871 246 0000 for the UK* ⬛*www.ryanair.com*)

- **TRANSAVIA:** From all around the Mediterranean (and, bizarrely, Berlin and Innsbruck) to Amsterdam. (☎*020 7365 4997 for the UK* ⬛*www.transavia.com.* Ⓢ *From €49 one-way.*)

- **WIZZ AIR:** From across Eastern Europe to Brussels. (☎*0904 475 9500 for the UK* ⬛*www.wizzair.com*)

BY TRAIN

Trains in the Netherlands and Belgium are generally comfortable, convenient, and reasonably swift. Make sure you are on the correct car, as trains sometimes split at crossroads. Towns listed in parentheses on European train schedules require a train switch at the town listed immediately before the parentheses.

You can either buy a **railpass,** which allows you unlimited travel within a particular region for a given period of time, or rely on buying individual **point-to-point** tickets as you go. Almost all countries give students or youths (under 26, usually) direct discounts on regular domestic rail tickets, and many also sell a student or youth card that provides 20-50% off all fares for up to a year.

Eurail offers the Eurail Benelux pass *(🖳www.raileurope.com/rail-tickets-passes/eurail-benelux-pass/index.html)*, a railcard offering five days in one month of unlimited use of rail networks in Belgium, the Netherlands, and Luxembourg for $151 to those under 26. For more information on rail passes check out the **Rail Resources** feature.

rail resources

- **WWW.RAILEUROPE.COM:** Info on rail travel and railpasses.
- **POINT-TO-POINT FARES AND SCHEDULES:** 🖳www.raileurope.com/us/rail/fares_schedules/index.htm allows you to calculate whether buying a railpass would save you money.
- **WWW.RAILSAVER.COM:** Uses your itinerary to calculate the best railpass for your trip.
- **WWW.RAILFANEUROPE.NET:** Links to rail servers throughout Europe.
- **WWW.LETSGO.COM:** Check out the Essentials section for more details.

BY BUS

Though European trains and railpasses are extremely popular, in some cases buses prove a better option. Often cheaper than railpasses, **international bus passes** allow unlimited travel on a hop-on, hop-off basis between major European cities. **Busabout,** for instance, offers three interconnecting bus circuits covering 29 of Europe's best bus hubs. *(☎+44 8450 267 514 🖳www.busabout.com $ 1 circuit in high season starts at US$579, students US$549.)* **Eurolines,** meanwhile, is the largest operator of Europe-wide coach services. We get misty-eyed just thinking about their unlimited 15- and 30-day passes to 41 major European cities. *(☎020 560 8788 in the Netherlands, 02 274 1350 in Belgium 🖳www.eurolines.com $ High season 15-day pass €345, 30-day pass €455; under 26 €290/375. Mid-season €240/330; under 26 €205/270. Low season €205/310; under 26 €175/240.)*

BY BICYCLE

If you go to Amsterdam and never sit on a bike, you just haven't fully experienced the city. For information on renting a bike in Amsterdam, see **Amsterdam Getting Around.** Although bikes are less ubiquitous in Brussels, they are still widely used. See **Brussels Getting Around** for more information. You will need a sturdy **lock** (from US$30); bike theft is rampant in Amsterdam. If you're interested in a biking holiday and have too much money as well as too little ability to plan things yourself, **Austin-Lehman Adventures** *(PO Box 81025, Billings, MT 59108-1025 ☎1-800-575-1540 🖳www.austinlehman.com)* offers four cycling tours of the Netherlands and Belgium for US$2000-3000.

keeping in touch

BY EMAIL AND INTERNET

Hello and welcome to the 21st century, where you can check your email in most major European cities, though sometimes you'll have to pay a few bucks or buy a drink for internet access. **Internet cafes** and the occasional free internet terminal at a public library or university are listed in the **Practicalities** sections of cities that we cover. For lists of additional cybercafes in the Netherlands and Belgium, you can check out ■www.cybercaptive.com or ■www.netcafeguide.com. If you already have an internet connection, that is.

Wireless hot spots make internet access possible in public and remote places. Unfortunately, they also pose security risks. Hot spots are public, open networks that use unencrypted, unsecured connections. They are susceptible to hacks and "packet sniffing"—the theft of passwords and other private information. To prevent problems, disable "ad hoc" mode, turn off file sharing and network discovery, encrypt your email, turn on your firewall, beware of phony networks, and watch for over-the-shoulder creeps. Many (and the number increases almost daily) of hostels and hotels offer Wi-Fi either for free or a price, so you may even be able to check the internet from your bed.

BY TELEPHONE

Calling Home

Without a doubt, the cheapest, easiest, and downright coolest way to call home is ■Skype (■www.skype.com). You can even videochat if you have one of those new-fangled webcams. Calls to other Skype users are ■free; calls to landlines and mobiles worldwide start at US$0.021 per minute, depending on where you're calling. The only drawback of Skype is that it requires an active internet connection.

For those who can't find Wi-Fi or prefer to pretend that it's still the 20th century, **prepaid phone cards** are a common and relatively inexpensive means of calling abroad. Each one comes with a Personal Identification Number (PIN) and a toll-free access number. You call the access number and then follow the directions for dialing your PIN. To purchase prepaid phone cards, check online for the best rates; ■www.callingcards.com is a good place to start. Online providers generally send your access number and PIN via email, with no actual "card" involved. You can also call home with prepaid phone cards purchased in the Netherlands or Belgium.

Another option is a **calling card,** linked to a major national telecommunications service in your home country. Calls are billed collect or to your account. Cards generally come with instructions for dialing both domestically and internationally.

Placing a collect call through an international operator can be expensive but may be necessary in case of an emergency. You can frequently call collect without even possessing a company's calling card just by calling its access number and following the instructions.

international calls

To call to or from the Netherlands or Belgium, dial:

1. THE INTERNATIONAL DIALING PREFIX. To call from **the Netherlands, Belgium, Ireland, New Zealand,** or the **UK,** dial ☎00; from **Australia,** dial ☎0011; from **Canada** or the **US,** dial ☎011.

2. THE COUNTRY CODE OF THE COUNTRY YOU WANT TO CALL. To call **the Netherlands,** dial ☎31; **Belgium,** ☎32; **Australia,** ☎61; **Canada** or the **US,** ☎1; **Ireland,** ☎353; **New Zealand,** ☎64; the **UK,** ☎44.

3. THE CITY/AREA CODE. The city code for Amsterdam is }020, for Brussels it is ☎02. The codes for other cities are listed next to their headers in the Excursions chapter. If the first digit of the city code is a zero, omit the zero when calling from abroad (e.g., dial ☎20 from Canada to reach Amsterdam).

4. THE LOCAL NUMBER.

Cellular Phones

Sadly, the world refuses to be a simple place, and cell phones bought abroad, particularly in the US, are unlikely to work in the Low Countries. Fortunately, it is quite easy to purchase a reasonably priced phone. You won't necessarily have to deal with cell phone plans and bills; prepaid minutes are widely available, and phones can be purchased cheaply or even rented, avoiding the hassle of pay phones and phone cards.

The international standard for cell phones is **Global System for Mobile Communication (GSM).** To make and receive calls in the Netherlands or Belgium, you will need a GSM-compatible phone and a **SIM (Subscriber Identity Module) card,** a country-specific, thumbnail-size chip that gives you a local phone number and plugs you into the local network. Many SIM cards are prepaid, and incoming calls are frequently free. You can buy additional cards or vouchers (usually available at convenience stores) to "top up" your phone. For more information on GSM phones, check out ▪www. telestial.com. Companies like Cellular Abroad (▪www.cellularabroad.com) and OneSimCard (▪www.onesimcard.com) rent cell phones and SIM cards that work in a variety of destinations around the world.

BY SNAIL MAIL

Sending Mail Home

Airmail is the best way to send mail home from the Netherlands or Belgium. **Aerogrammes,** printed sheets that fold into envelopes and travel via airmail, are available at post offices. Write "airmail" or *"par avion"* on the front. Most post offices will charge exorbitant fees or simply refuse to send aerogrammes with enclosures. Surface mail is by far the cheapest and slowest way to send mail. It takes one to two months to cross the Atlantic and one to three to cross the Pacific—good for heavy items you won't need for a while, like souvenirs that you've acquired along the way or gifts you're obligated to send but don't care about people receiving promptly.

Sending Mail to the Netherlands or Belgium

Federal Express offers express mail services from most countries to the Netherlands and Belgium. (☎+1-800-463-3339 ▪www.fedex.com) Within the Netherlands and Belgium, postage is extremely reasonably-priced, and will generally cost less than a euro, unless you're sending a weighty package.

There are several ways to arrange pickup of letters sent to you while you are abroad, even if you don't have a fixed address. Mail can be sent via Poste Restante (General Delivery) to almost any city or town in the Netherlands or Belgium with a post office, and it is very reliable. Address Poste Restante letters like so:

Vincent VAN GOGH
Poste Restante
Amsterdam, the Netherlands

The mail will go to a special desk in the central post office, unless you specify a post office by street address or postal code. It's best to use the largest post office, since mail may be sent there regardless. It is usually safer and quicker, though more expensive, to send mail express or registered. Bring your passport (or other photo ID) for pickup; there may be a small fee. If the clerks insist that there is nothing for you, ask them to check under your first name as well. *Let's Go* lists post offices in the **Practicalities** section for each city.

climate

Amsterdam and Brussels have similar climates that are mild, temperate, and unpredictable. As in much of Northern Europe, the mostly snow free winters are chilly and wet, while the summers are warmish and wet. Basically, it's wet a lot. Hot summers are possible, but don't count on it. Rainfall is fairly consistent throughout the year, making a raincoat an essential thing to pack no matter what time of year you plan to visit. It's probably best not to complain about whatever the skies throw your way, since if you decided to travel to Amsterdam and Brussels, you clearly didn't come for the weather. Take another tour around the Rijksmuseum and forget the gray skies outside.

AVG. TEMP.(LOW/ HIGH), PRECIP.	JANUARY			APRIL			JULY			OCTOBER		
	°C	°F	mm	°C	°F	mm	°C	°F	mm	°C	°F	mm
Amsterdam	1/5	34/41	69	4/12	39/64	53	12/20	64/68	76	7/13	45/56	74
Brussels	-1/4	30/39	66	5/14	41/67	60	12/23	64/74	95	7/15	45/59	83

To convert from degrees Fahrenheit to degrees Celsius, subtract 32 and multiply by 5/9. To convert from Celsius to Fahrenheit, multiply by 9/5 and add 32. Or just use this chart. Yeah, we know you're just going to use the chart.

°CELSIUS	-5	0	5	10	15	20	25	30	35	40
°FAHRENHEIT	23	32	41	50	59	68	77	86	95	104

measurements

Like the rest of the rational world, the Netherlands and Belgium use the metric system. The basic unit of length is the meter (m), which is divided into 100 centimeters (cm) or 1000 millimeters (mm). One thousand meters make up one kilometer (km). Fluids are measured in liters (L), each divided into 1000 milliliters (mL). A liter of pure water weighs one kilogram (kg), the unit of mass that is divided into 1000 grams (g). One metric ton is 1000kg. It'll probably just be easiest if you check out this chart.

MEASUREMENT CONVERSIONS	
1 inch (in.) = 25.4mm	1 millimeter (mm) = 0.039 in.
1 foot (ft.) = 0.305m	1 meter (m) = 3.28 ft.
1 yard (yd.) = 0.914m	1 meter (m) = 1.094 yd.
1 mile (mi.) = 1.609km	1 kilometer (km) = 0.621 mi.
1 ounce (oz.) = 28.35g	1 gram (g) = 0.035 oz.
1 pound (lb.) = 0.454kg	1 kilogram (kg) = 2.205 lb.
1 fluid ounce (fl. oz.) = 29.57mL	1 milliliter (mL) = 0.034 fl. oz.
1 gallon (gal.) = 3.785L	1 liter (L) = 0.264 gal.

language

DUTCH

Dutch is the official language of the Netherlands, but in Amsterdam most natives speak English—and speak it well. Thanks to mandatory English education in schools and to English-language media exports, most locals have impeccable grammar, vast

essentials

vocabularies, and a soft continental accent that makes conversing relatively easy. Knowing a few key Dutch words and phrases can't hurt, particularly in smaller towns where English is not spoken as widely. Dutch spellings frequently resemble German, but pronunciation is very different. To initiate an English conversation, politely ask, "Spreekt u Engels?" (SPRAYKT oo ANG-les?). Even if your conversational counterpart speaks little English, he or she will usually try to communicate, an effort you can acknowledge with the appropriate words of thanks: "Dank u wel" (DAHNK oo vell).

Pronunciation

For those of you willing to take on the vagaries of the Dutch language, we salute you. Here are a few tips that will at least set you apart from most tourists, even if every Dutch person will still immediately realize that you have no idea what you're saying. Most Dutch consonants, with a few notable exceptions, have the same sounds as their English versions, sometimes rendering Dutch into a phonetic version of English colored by a foreign accent. Vowels are a different story. The combinations "e," "ee," "i," and "ij" are occasionally pronounced "er" as in "mother." Here are the other counterintuitive pronunciations:

PHONETIC UNIT	PRONUNCIATION	PHONETIC UNIT	PRONUNCIATION
au, ou, or ui	ow, as in "now"	g or ch	kh, as in "loch"
oo	oa, as in "boat"	ie	ee, as in "see"
v	between f and v	j	y, as in "yes"
w	between v and w	ee, ij or ei	ay, as in "layer"
aa	a longer a than in "cat"	oe	oo, as in "shoo"
eu	u, as in "hurt"	uu	a longer oo than in "too"

Phrasebook

ENGLISH	DUTCH	PRONUNCIATION
Hello!/Hi!	Dag!/Hallo!	Dakh!/Hallo!
Goodbye!	Tot ziens!	Tot zeens!
Yes	Ja	Yah
No	Nee	Nay
Sorry!	Sorry!	SOR-ee!
My name is...	Mijn naam is...	Mayn nahm iss...
Do you speak English?	Spreekt u Engels?	Spraykt oo ANG-les?
I don't speak Dutch	Ik spreek geen Nederlands	Ik sprayk khayn NAY-der-lans
I don't understand	Ik begrijp het niet	Ik ber-KHRAYP het neet
Good morning!	Goedemorgen!	KHOO-der-mor-khern!
Good evening!	Goedenavond!	KHOO-der-na-fondt!
Please/You're welcome	Alstublieft	Als-too-BLEEFT
Thank you	Dank u wel	Dahnk oo vell
EMERGENCY		
Go away!	Ga weg!	Kha vekh!
Help!	Help!	Help!
Stop!	Stop!	Stop!
Call the police!	Bel de politie!	Bel der poh-LEET-see!
Get a doctor!	Haal een dokter!	Haal ayn DOK-ter!
I'm sick	Ik ben ziek	Ik ben zeek
I'm lost	Ik ben verdwaald	Ik ben ferd-VAHLDT
QUESTIONS		
Who?	Wie?	Vee?
What?	Wat?	Vat?
When?	Wanneer?	Van-AYR?
Why?	Waarom?	VAR-ohm?

essentials

Where is...?	Waar is...?	Vahr iss...?
How do I get to...?	Hoe kom ik in...?	Hoo kom ik in...?
...the museum	...het museum	...het muh-say-um
...the church	...de kerk	...de kerk?
....the bank	...de bank	...de bahnk?
...the hotel	...het hotel	...het ho-TEL
...the shop	...de winkel	...de VIN-kerl
...the market	...de markt	...de markt
...the consulate	...het consulaat	het kon-sul-AAT...
...the train station	...het station	het staht-see-OHN
...the bus stop	...de bushalte	de BUS-hahlter
...the tourist office	...de VVV	de fay fay fay
...the toilet	...het toilet	het tva-LET
What time is it?	Hoe laat is het?	Hoo laht iss het?
Do you have...?	Heeft u...?	Hayft oo...?
How much does this cost?	Wat kost het?	Vat kost het?
ACCOMMODATIONS		
I have a reservation	Ik heb een reservering	Ik hep ayn res-er-VAY-ring
Single room	Eenpersoonskamer	AYN-per-sohn-kah-mer
Double room	Tweepersoonskamer	TVAY-per-sohn-kah-mer
How much per night?	Hoeveel kost per nacht?	Hoo-FAYL kost het per nakht?
FOOD		
We have a reservation	We hebben gereserveerd	Vay HEP-bern kher-ay-ser-VAYRT
Waiter/waitress	Meneer/mevrouw	Mer-NAYR/me-FROW
I'd like...	Ik wil graag...	Ik vil krakh...
May I have the check/bill please?	Mag ik de rekening	Makh ik der Ray-kern-inkh

BELGIAN

Psych! Belgian isn't actually a language. There are three official languages in Belgium: Dutch, French, and German. Hardly anyone speaks German, so you don't really have to worry about that one. Dutch is more commonly known in Belgium as Flemish (conjuring up nasty thoughts of throat mucus). While about 60% of the country speaks Flemish as its first language, French is more prevalent in Brussels. French-speaking has been increasing for centuries in the formerly Flemish-speaking city, and the relationship between the two languages is extremely controversial. It's probably best not to ask locals why, as chances are they are pretty opinionated about it. But if you want to start up a rigorous political discussion this might be the perfect place to start. Look out for lots of bilingual signs, although if you understand neither French nor Flemish you might not be able to tell the difference. Bear in mind that Belgian French and Flemish are not identical to the languages spoken in France and the Netherlands, and local vocabulary might be a little confusing to those who consider themselves competent in one or the other. Never fear however, for Brussels, like Amsterdam, is a cosmopolitan city where many people speak English, particularly in large hotels and restaurants.

Phrasebook

ENGLISH	FRENCH	ENGLISH	FRENCH
Hello!/Hi!	Bonjour!/Salut!	Do you speak English?	Parlez-vous anglais?
Goodbye!	Au revoir!	I don't speak French	Je ne parle pas français
Yes	Oui	I don't understand	Je ne comprends pas
No	Non	Good evening!	Bon soir!
Sorry!	Pardon!	Please	S'il vous plaît
My name is...	Je m'appelle...	Thank you	Merci

EMERGENCY			
Go away!	Allez-vous en!	I need a doctor	J'ai besoin d'un médecin
Help!	Au secours!	I'm sick	Je suis malade
Stop!	Arrêtez	I'm lost	Je suis perdu
Call the police!	Appelez la police!	Please release me from jail	Me libérer de prison, s'il vous plaît
QUESTIONS			
Who?	Qui?	...the shop	...le magasin
What?	Quoi?	...the market	...la marché
When?	Quand?	...the consulate	...le consulat
Why?	Pourquoi?	...the train station	...la gare
Where is...?	Où est...?	...the bus stop	...l'arrêt de bus
How do I get to...?	Comment puis-je arriver à...	...the tourist office	...l'office de tourisme
...the museum	...la musée	...the toilet	...les toilettes
...the church	...l'église	What time is it?	Quelle heure est-il?
...the bank	...la banque	Do you have...?	Avez-vous...?
...the hotel	...l'hôtel	How much does this cost?	Combien ça coûte?
ACCOMMODATIONS			
I have a reservation	J'ai une réservation	Double room	Une chambre double
Single room	Une chambre simple	How much per night?	Combien par nuit?
FOOD			
We have a reservation	Nous avons une réservation	I'd like...	Je voudrais...
Waiter/waitress	Serveur / serveuse	May I have the check/bill please?	L'addition, s'il vous plaît
L'AMOUR			
I love you	Je t'aime	You are an angel come to Earth	Vous êtes un ange descendu sur terre
You're so much more beautiful than my boyfriend/girlfriend	Tu es beaucoup plus beau/belle que mon copain/copine	Hello, I'm a thief, and I'm here to steal your heart.	Bonjour, je suis un voleur, et je suis ici pour voler votre coeur
The profound mystery of what you just said sets my soul on fire	Le mystère profond de ce que vous venez de dire s'enflamme mon coeur	Forgive me, Father, for I have sinned	Pardonnez-moi, mon Père, car j'ai péché

essentials

let's go online

Plan your next trip on our spiffy website, ◻www.letsgo.com. It features full book content, the latest travel info on your favorite destinations, and tons of interactive features: make your own itinerary, read blogs from our trusty Researcher-Writers, browse our photo library, watch exclusive videos, check out our newsletter, find travel deals, follow us on Facebook, and buy new guides. Plus, if this Essentials wasn't enough for you, we've got even more online. We're always updating and adding new features, so check back often!

BEYOND TOURISM

If you are reading this, then you are a member of an elite group—and we don't mean "the literate." You're a student preparing for a semester abroad. You're taking a gap year to save the trees, the whales, or the dates. You're an 80-year-old woman who has devoted her life to egg-laying platypuses and figuring out what the hell is up with that. In short, you're a traveler, not a tourist; like any good spy, you don't observe your surroundings—you become an active part of them.

Your mission, should you choose to accept it, is to study, volunteer, or work in the Netherlands or Belgium as laid out in the dossier—er, chapter—that follows. More general wisdom, including international organizations with a presence in many destinations and tips on how to pick the right program, is also accessible by logging onto the Beyond Tourism section of ◼www.letsgo.com. We leave the rest (when to go, whom to bring, and how many changes of underwear to pack) in your hands. This message will ▓**self-destruct** in five seconds. Good luck.

greatest hits

- **THE SAME THING WE DO EVERY NIGHT...** Try to take over the world. You can start in Brussels, which is home to both NATO and the EU (p. 251).

- **SPREEK NEDERLANDS:** Learn Dutch during the summer at an alma mater of past Nobel Prize winners (p. 250).

- **SELL YOURSELF:** No, we're not advocating prostitution. Market your mother tongue to pick up some moolah as a tutor of English (p. 254).

studying

There are two main ways to study abroad in the Low Countries: in small, private, language and culture programs that cater to international students studying abroad or at honest-to-goodness local universities that accept exchange students from foreign colleges. For the former, your best bet is to look into the programs offered by the international study-abroad organizations listed next. To study in a Dutch or Belgian university (these are generally divided into Dutch-speaking in the north and French-speaking in the south—though in academia you'll find many of the Dutch to be at least bilingual and the Belgians at least trilingual), you should first consult your own high school or college study-abroad office to see if they offer an exchange program with a Dutch or Belgian university. If not, get in touch with the universities directly to find out if you meet their academic and language requirements for exchange admission.

visa information

In order to apply for a student visa (US$216), you will need a passport (valid for 15 months), a criminal history record, a medical certificate, proof of sufficient funds to cover the cost of your stay, and an attestation from an academic institution acknowledging that you are accepted or registered as a student. For US citizens, visas generally take 1-2 weeks to process.

UNIVERSITIES

International Programs

AMERICAN FIELD SERVICE BELGIUM

71 W. 23rd St., 17th fl., New York, NY 10010 ☎+1-212-352-9810 🖳www.afs.org

AFS runs high school exchange programs that send students all over the world, including to both the northern Dutch-speaking and southern French-speaking regions of Belgium, to live with host families and attend local schools full-time. Also, on their website, they offer a vision for the year 2020, so you know they're in it for the long haul.

ℹ Programs to Belgium depart from New York. $ In 2010 the Flanders year-long program cost $10,500 and the French program cost $11,750, though prices vary by length and year. Check website for details. ⏰ "School Programs" lasts for a trimester, semester, or year. Intensive and summer programs last for 1-3 months.

COUNCIL ON INTERNATIONAL EDUCATIONAL EXCHANGE (CIEE) BELGIUM

300 Fore St., Portland, ME 04101 ☎+1-207-553-4000 🖳www.ciee.org

CIEE organizes study abroad programs for US high school and college students (as well as some programs for international HS students). Current programs in Belgium are based in Brussels, taught in English, French (at the Université Libre de Bruxelles), and Dutch (at the Vrije Universiteit Brussels), and cover topics ranging from the liberal arts (think cultural studies, film, philosophy) to business (language skills, management, economics, and that sort of thing).

ℹ Some programs have GPA or language requirements; check website for details. $ Costs for the Belgium programs range from $6200 for the summer to $14,750 for 1 semester to $28,400 for a year. ⏰ Summer programs run for 6 weeks from late May to mid-July; applications due Apr. 1. Longer programs range from 19-39 weeks, with applications due Apr 1 for fall semester and full-year programs and Oct 15 for spring semester programs.

GOABROAD.COM BELGIUM

324 E. Oak St., Fort Collins, CO 80524 ☎+1-720-570-1702 🖳www.volunteerabroad.com

The study-abroad section of the ubiquitous GoAbroad.com (see also **Working,** later in this chapter) offers easy-to-navigate listings of study-abroad opportunities in Belgium and elsewhere, including local university programs.

INTERNATIONAL STUDIES ABROAD
BELGIUM

1112 W. Ben White Bld., Austin, TX 78704 ☎+1-800-580-8826 ▨www.studiesabroad.com

ISA offers study-abroad programs at host universities across the globe, including at Vesalius College in Brussels. Classes at Vesalius are offered in both English and French.

i Current high school or college transcript required to apply. Minimum GPA of 2.50-3.00 applies for most programs. Ⓢ Summer tuition at Vesalius $4950, semester/trimester $14,500, academic year $26,000. ☒ Applications for fall and year-long programs due Apr 30, winter programs Oct 1.

YOUTH FOR UNDERSTANDING USA
BELGIUM

6400 Goldsboro Rd., Ste. 100, Bethesda, MD 20817 ☎+1-240-235-2100 ▨www.yfu-usa.org

YFU places American students in homestays abroad. Year- or semester-long Belgian programs in either Flanders (Dutch-speaking Belgium) or Wallonia (French-speaking Belgium) focus on art, fashion, sports, or tourism.

i Belgium programs have a language requirement. Ⓢ Tuition and fees vary by program; check website for up-to-date prices. ☒ Offers 3-8 week summer programs (leave in mid-June) as well as year-long and semester-long programs departing in either the summer or winter. Applications for summer departure programs due Apr 1, for winter departures Oct 1.

WEBSTER UNIVERSITY PROGRAM IN ENGLISH
NETHERLANDS

Boommarkt 1, 2311 EA Leiden ☎71 516 8000 ▨www.webster.nl

Netherlands campus of the international system of Webster schools. Provides business-oriented education for people interested in working in NGOs. Must score 550 on the TOEFL for applicants not from English-speaking countries. Graduate programs operate on Amsterdam campus.

Local Programs

UNIVERSITY OF AMSTERDAM (UNIVERSITY VAN AMSTERDAM)
NETHERLANDS

Binnengasthuisstraat 9, Amsterdam ☎20 525 8080 ▨www.studeren.uva.nl

Three-year bachelor's degree program in both sciences and humanities. Offers special degrees in finance and business-related fields. Tuition for Non-EU students approximately €9000 for two-term academic year.

LEIDEN UNIVERSITY (UNIVERSITEIT LEIDEN)
NETHERLANDS

Rapenburg 70, Leiden ☎71 527 2727 ▨www.leidenuniv.nl

Oldest university in the Netherlands, dating back to 1575, with a campus in Amsterdam. Includes an observatory, medical center, and academy of performing arts. Part-time programs available.

LANGUAGE SCHOOLS

The national languages of Belgium—French, Dutch, and German—are probably best studied from home, or if you're feeling particularly authentic, from France, the Netherlands, or Germany, but a few companies do offer language immersion classes in Belgium. Check out the following programs:

AAA EUROPA LANGUAGE SCHOOL ASBL
BELGIUM

717A Chaussée de Waterloo, B-1180 Brussels ☎02 347 44 11 ▨www.elsb.be

AAA Europa offers private, semi-private, group, and immersion courses in French, Dutch, and German.

Ⓢ Group courses in French start at €275, in Dutch €380; no group courses in German. Private courses, priced per hour, offered in French (€33), Dutch (€38), and German (€36). Hourly pricing varies by course length and time of day; check website for a detailed table.

EASY LANGUAGES
BELGIUM

28 rue de la Loi, 1040 Bruxelles, Belgium ☎02 230 01 90 ▥http://lvi.org

Easy Languages offers group, intensive, conversational, private, and culturally oriented courses in French (schools in Brussels and Bruges) and in Dutch (school in Antwerp). Classes are offered with or without student or "executive" accommodations.

Ⓢ *Dutch courses start at €250 for 1 week, €450 with homestay and meals. French conversational courses start at €95 for 1 week, intensive courses €295 for 1 week. Check website for detailed pricing tables.*

EUROLINGUA INSTITUTE
BELGIUM

Eurolingua Institute SA, Hong Kong Bank Building 6th fl., Samuel Lewis Ave., PO Box 0819-05911, Panama City, Panama ▥www.eurolingua.com

Eurolingua offers French and Dutch homestay programs in La Louvière in which students live with tutors and receive one-on-one language instruction.

Ⓢ *Homestays start at around US$1600.*

ITHA DUTCH LANGUAGE INSTITUTE
NETHERLANDS

Mathenesserlaan 253, Rotterdam ☎10 425 45 79 ▥www.itha.nl

Provides introduction in Dutch language and culture targeted at beginners including expatriates and international business students.

Ⓢ *Intensive 2-week individual courses €1250-1732.*

KATAKURA/WBLC
NETHERLANDS

Havikshorst 30, Amsterdam ☎20 612 2727 ▥www.katakura-wblc.nl

Small classes taught by native Dutch speakers. Two locations in Amsterdam and one in Düsseldorf. Also offers German, Italian, and Japanese classes. Private lessons and intensive courses available upon request.

SUMMER SCHOOL UTRECHT
NETHERLANDS

Kriekenpitplein 21-22, Utrecht ☎30 253 4400 ▥www.utrechtsummerschool.nl

Alma mater of past Nobel Prize winners, including **Gerard 't Hooft.** Summer school curriculum targeted at master's level students. Over 130 courses offered in various fields, such as culture, art and design, life sciences, and economics.

COOKING SCHOOLS

Not exactly known for its world-class gourmet fare, the Dutch claim fame to cheese, stews, and not much else. With cooking centered around seafood due to the prevalent farming industry around the coast, meat and vegetables on a Wednesday night is as exciting as it gets at the dinner table. Cooking schools in larger cities offer international styles for aspiring chefs—or at least, those who get sick of stew on bread after the fifth day in a row. With an established branch of Cordon Bleu in Amsterdam as well as other larger hotel and management schools offering crash courses in fine dining, the Dutch are trying to cultivate a bit more culinary flair.

HEAT AMSTERDAM
NETHERLANDS

Arnold Schönberglaan 9, Amsterdam ☎20 646 5158 ▥www.heatamsterdam.nl

Cooking studio gives courses for groups between 15 and 40 people. Classes include instruction in culinary styles such as Italian and Lebanese cuisine. Manage2Cook program offers management and communication skills, enhancement for local professionals seeking out-of-office training oriented around food and cooking.

Ⓢ *Tuition €62.50-72.50.*

HOTELSCHOOL THE HAGUE
NETHERLANDS

Prinses Irenestraat 59, Amsterdam ☎20 85 12 900 ▥www.hotelschool.nl

Internationally-oriented programs in hospitality, business, and management. Placements for graduates in the catering and consultancy industries. Restaurant

Le Début and Hotel Skotel in Amsterdam and The Hague both allow students to train on site while offering to the greater public.

LA CUISINE FRANCAISE NETHERLANDS

Herengracht 314, Amsterdam ☎20 627 87 25 💻www.lacuisinefrancaise.nl

Amsterdam campus of famous culinary and hospitality school Le Cordon Bleu Paris.

$ Basic 6-course wine program, taught in English, from €325.

volunteering

In the search for volunteer work, your best bet is to start on the internet. There are plenty of sites that host job and volunteer opportunities for a small fee to the poster, and they are generally free on your end. GoAbroad.com is an easy place to start.

POLITICS, PUBLIC SERVICE, AND GOVERNMENT

These two countries are ideal for volunteers looking to work in the public sector. With one of the highest-ranking civil liberties scores in the world, the Netherlands is a hotbed of human rights work. What Belgium lacks in size and organically farmable real estate it makes up for in political relevance. Brussels is home to both NATO (below) and the EU, and has active branches of many major international human rights organizations, including Amnesty International and Oxfam. If you're willing to put in work without that Friday paycheck—and without that work visa—consider some of the options below for volunteer work in the Low Countries.

AMNESTY INTERNATIONAL BELGIUM/NETHERLANDS

Kerkstraat 156, Antwerpen 2060 ☎03 271 16 16 💻www.amnesty.org, www.amnesty.be

Postbus 1968, 1000 BZ Amsterdam ☎20 626 44 36 💻www.amnesty.nl

One of the world's foremost human rights organizations. Contact the Brussels office for info about paid positions and volunteer work in Belgium. Volunteer positions in Amsterdam available in a Service Center that handles communication between Amnesty International and the general public. Send cover letter to personnel department at persona@amnesty.nl.

NORTH ATLANTIC TREATY ORGANIZATION (NATO) BELGIUM

Bld. Léopold III, 1110 Brussels 💻www.nato.int

Current students and recent graduates (within 1 year) who are nationals of a NATO member state and fluent in one official NATO language (English or French) with a working knowledge of the other can apply for internships at NATO headquarters in Brussels. Requirements and application details available at 💻www.nato.int/structur/interns/index.html. Paid positions are listed on the NATO website under "Jobs."

i Interns must be 21+ and have at least 2 years of university study or equivalent. $ Interns receive €800 per month. ⏰ Applications accepted Mar-June. Internships start in Sept or Mar and last for 6 months.

OXFAM INTERNATIONAL BELGIUM

R. des Quatre Vents 60, Brussels ☎02 501 67 00 💻www.oxfam.org

Oxfam is dedicated to reducing poverty and injustice around the world, focusing in particular on basic human rights, income inequality, and arms reduction. Contact the Brussels office for information about working and volunteering in Belgium.

MOVISIE INTERNATIONAL NETHERLANDS

Catharijnesingel 47, 3511 GC Utrecht ☎30 789 21 12 💻www.moivisie.nl

Nonprofit organization supported by the Dutch Ministry of Health, Welfare, and

Sport to promote citizenship participation through assistance to other volunteer and professional organizations. Works to eliminate domestic and sexual violence and promote social cohesion, and informal health care among families. Civic internships also available. Contact Sandra Kamerbeek at s.kamerbeek@movisie.nl for more information on opportunities.

UNICEF
BELGIUM

R. Montoyer 14 2nd fl., B-1000 Brussels   ☎02 513 22 51 ▣www.unicef.org

In addition to providing those little orange cardboard boxes to millions of trick-or-treaters each year, UNICEF works to further children's rights and health across the globe, focusing on survival and development (including immunizations and vaccinations), basic education, HIV/AIDS prevention, and policy advocacy. Get in touch with the Brussels office for information about volunteering or working in Belgium—unfortunately, as of September 2010, the English version of the Belgian branch's website (▣www.unicef.be) was under construction. The international (.org) website offers information on children's health by country.

WOMEN'S ISSUES

Thanks to legal prostitution, Amsterdam enjoys an income from international sex tourism that most first-world countries do not. While there are many rules and regulations intended to protect prostitutes and their customers, abuses still occur. International media outlets report that as many as 80% of prostitutes in the Netherlands are foreign, most without documentation, and research institutions estimate that human trafficking victims numbering in the thousands are smuggled into the Netherlands annually. Fortunately, the issue of women's rights is no longer a mere sidebar on business brochures. Organizations in Amsterdam and most other major cities have arisen in the last two decades to address these issues.

AIM FOR HUMAN RIGHTS
NETHERLANDS

Vinkenburgstraat 2A, 3512 AB Utrecht   ☎30 233 40 27 ▣www.aimforhumanrights.org

Targets measures against women's trafficking and domestic violence. Contacts Dutch politicians to advocate changes in public human rights policy. Volunteers must be fluent in both Dutch and English. Send letter of motivation and resume to hr@humanforhumanrights.nl; open applications saved for six months.

FEDERATIE ZAKENVRONWEN
NETHERLANDS

Bezeuidenhoutseweg 12, The Hague   ☎70 34 90 347 ▣www.federatiezakenvronwen.nl

This "Federation of Businesswomen" aims to increase women's entrepreneurial power in business industries through financial assistance and community support. Companies registered through the local chamber of commerce can join and pay ($45-250 per year) for various membership benefits including access to FZ networking events and political lobbying hearings.

IIAV
NETHERLANDS

Obiplein 4, Amsterdam   ☎20 665 13 18 ▣www.iiav.nl

The International Information Center and Archive for the Women's Movement. National library and documentation center preserving and archiving information on past women's movements to maintain cultural and historical legacy.

INTERNATIONAL TRAINING CENTER FOR WOMEN
NETHERLANDS

P.O. Box 3611, Amsterdam   ☎20 420 52 43 ▣www.euronet.nl/users/itw

NGO founded in 1990 to promote gender equality in the work force. Trains women in management and entrepreneurship skills. Also provides a youth summer school in creative empowerment and drama for both Dutch and non-Dutch citizens. Offers consultant services to both private and public businesses.

beyond tourism

WOMEN'S GLOBAL NETWORK FOR REPRODUCTIVE RIGHTS — NETHERLANDS

Marius van Bouwdijk Bastiaansestraat 56, Amsterdam ☎20 622 24 50 🖳www.wgnrr.org

International women's network emphasizing abortion rights and increased access to contraceptives for women globally. Comprised of local community organizations. Volunteering opportunities dependent on current projects and programs. Send resume and cover letter detailing office and program of interest to office@wgnrr.org.

ENVIRONMENTAL ISSUES

FRIENDS OF THE EARTH INTERNATIONAL — NETHERLANDS

P.O. Box 19199, 1000 GD Amsterdam ☎20 622 1369 🖳www.foei.org

World's largest grassroots environmental network, active in both environmental and social issues. Predominant campaigns include those for food sovereignty and biodiversity. Volunteers hired through need and availability of positions; email resume to web@foei.org.

GREENPEACE NETHERLANDS — NETHERLANDS

Jollemanhof 15-17, 1019 GW Amsterdam ☎800 422 3344 🖳www.greenpeace.nl

International organization aiming for environmental improvement. Employs about 500 volunteers in the Netherlands. Local volunteers, officers, and campaigners receive professional training before beginning. See website for more positions.

WORLD WIDE OPPORTUNITIES ON ORGANIC FARMS — BELGIUM

🖳www.wwoof.org

WWOOF works to put members in touch with host individuals or organizations engaged in organic farming, who offer room and board in exchange for a certain amount of work per week. Belgium does not currently have a national WWOOF organization, but it nonetheless hosts various WWOOF projects, which are listed at 🖳www.wwoof.org/newsite08.

ℹ Volunteers 18+. $ Membership fees vary by country; membership for WWOOF Independents (countries without national organizations) £15 per year, joint membership for 2 £25. ⏰ Duration and min. stay varies by project.

YOUTH AND COMMUNITY

WORLD VISION NETHERLANDS — NETHERLANDS

Zonnehof 38, 3811 ND Amsterdam t☎33 46 43 444 🖳www.worldvision.nl

Organization involved with underprivileged children's issues, including education, healthcare, and general standard of living. Supports AIDS education in Africa. Volunteer work includes administrative tasks at Amsterdam office or representation at concerts and other publicity events. Call for more information.

working

There's nothing particularly exotic about working in the Low Countries. If you're taking a gap year and need to fund your travels, consider teaching English; if you're a non-threatening (ideally female) 18- to 26-year-old, you might have great luck as an au pair—if you find a good family, you'll have a delightful time, ample pocket money, and as deep an immersion experience as you could ask for. Other work and volunteer opportunities in Belgium focus on international politics, especially in Brussels, which is home to both NATO and the EU. In general, when job hunting, start on the internet—because, really, where else are you going to look? C'mon. We've evolved.

more visa information

If you're an EU citizen—good news! You don't need a visa to work in Belgium or the Netherlands. If you are from outside the EU, however, and you intend to work as a salaried employee, you will need a work visa, which shares most of the requirements and fees of the student visa (see **Visa Information**), but which also requires a work permit from your employer. If you're traveling from the United States to au pair in Belgium and have a host family that is willing to sponsor you, special visa regulations might apply—consult ■www.diplobel.us and contact your local Belgian Embassy or Consulate General for more info. If you're traveling to the Netherlands, the Dutch Ministry of Justice's Immigration and Naturalization Service runs a helpful website at ■www.ind.nl, which is a good place to turn for advice.

For US citizens, visas generally take 1-2 weeks to process. Visit ■www.diplobel.us for application info and instructions on how to acquire all necessary forms.

LONG-TERM WORK

Teaching English

Although English remains compulsory in the national education system from elementary school onward, large Dutch cities still call on the services of expatriates lollygagging around waiting to make a euro or two. Most native Dutch request lessons from private companies to improve minute details, such as getting rid of the guttural accents and vestiges of Scandinavian pronunciation. Most English programs also target recent immigrants to the Netherlands.

There are plenty of opportunities to teach English in Belgium, but you won't be able to take advantage of them without a work visa—and to get that visa you'll need to find an employer willing to sponsor you (see **More Visa Information**). Also, bear in mind that Belgium has three national languages—so unless you speak French, Dutch, and German in addition to your impeccable English (you nerd), you'll want to localize your search. Here are a few good places to start looking.

GLOBAL ENGLISH

Senate Court, Southernhay Gardens, Exeter, UK ☎1392 411999 ■www.global-english.com

Teach general and business English to students. Global English follows English Level 2 TESOL curriculum. Hires freelance teachers and tutors. Pay rate ranging €18-25 per hour.

INTERNATIONAL SCHOOL OF BRUSSELS BELGIUM

Kattenberg-Botisfort 19, Brussels ☎02 661 42 11 ■www.isb.be

The ISB hires teachers for positions lasting longer than one full year. You'll need permission to work within Belgium—that is to say, a work visa and all the documentation that goes along with getting one.

OXFORD SEMINARS

244 5th Ave., Ste. J262, New York, NY 10001 ☎+1-800-779-1779 ■www.oxfordseminars.com

If you want to teach English abroad but don't know "their" from "there" from "they're," Oxford might be the place to start. (Or middle school—zing.) Oxford offers TESOL/TESL/TEFL certification courses in the US and Canada and then helps to place its graduates at ESL teaching jobs around the world, including in Belgium—as long as you've got a bachelor's degree to go along with your Oxford certification. The helpful website measures local cost of living by the price of a Big Mac.

$ TESOL/TESL/TEFL Teacher Training Certification Course $1095. ⏰ Courses generally take up 6 days over the course of 3 weeks. Check website for local course info.

TEACH ENGLISH ABROAD

240 Commercial St., Suite 4A, Boston, MA ☎1-800-352-1793 💻www.onlinetefl.com

Programs for academic purposes and business English. Salary ranges $20-35 per hour, depending on qualifications and experience. Requires TEFL and TESOL accreditation.

US DEPARTMENT OF STATE

2201 C Street NW, Washington, DC 20520 ☎+1-202-647-4000 💻www.state.gov/m/a/os

Leave it to Uncle Sam to monitor your every twitch and inhalation as you flirt naively with a freedom you'll never know. Er, that is, to link you to teaching opportunities in Belgium. The D of S maintains a directory of international schools abroad and offers helpful info on how to pursue teaching jobs. Just try to act normal when the suits come knocking.

Au Pair

Working as an au pair is a popular option for young women who want a professional and relatively stable job abroad as a modern nanny and maid. The job offers housing and a small stipend in exchange for the work. Au pairs in Belgium must be between 18 and 26 years old. If you're traveling from the United States to au pair in Belgium and you have a host family that is willing to sponsor you, special visa regulations might apply—see **More Visa Information.**

AU PAIR CONNECT

💻www.aupairconnect.com

More of the same: basic pairing service, and you'll have to pay to access contact info. Au pairs can search for families by nationality as well as by country, so if you want to au pair in Belgium but only get along with Luxembourgers, you're in luck.

$ Free to register and search, $45 for 3 months for access to contact info.

AU PAIR IN HOLLAND NETHERLANDS

Bilderdijkstraat 25L, Amsterdam ☎20 770 45 90 💻www.aupairinholland.nl

Seeks young adults ages 18-25 to assist with local families in childcare and other domestic duties. No smoking or alcohol usage. Email info@aupairinholland.nl.

AU PAIR SUPPORT BELGIUM VZW BELGIUM

Jan Mahieustraat 31, 8800 Roeselare, Belgium ☎32 51 22 32 02 💻www.aupairsupport.be

A non-profit Belgium-based au pair service. They will take care of work permit and visa paperwork for registered au pairs, and also offer to organize air travel.

GREAT AU PAIR

1329 Hwy. 395, Gardnerville, NV 89410 ☎+1-775-215-5770 💻www.greataupair.com

An easy-to-use, US-based organization that matches au pairs with families across the world. Make a profile and search for jobs. Also offers information on visas and immigration.

ℹ You can search for jobs without a membership, but must register to access contact info. $ Free registration offers functional access to site. For full access, 30-day membership $60, 90-day membership $120. Criminal background checks $45-75.

SUNNY AU PAIRS

☎+1-503-616-3026, +44 20 8144 1636 💻www.sunnyaupairs.com

Simple, convenient UK-based service that connects au pairs with families.

$ Free to register as an au pair; membership for host families starts at £70 for 6 months.

OTHER LONG-TERM AND SHORT-TERM WORK

GOABROAD.COM

324 E. Oak St., Fort Collins, CO 80524 ☎+1-720-570-1702 💻www.jobsabroad.com, www.internabroad.com

The jobs and intern sections of the ubiquitous GoAbroad.com (see also **Studying** and **Volunteering**) offers easy-to-navigate listings of private-sector short- and long-term jobs and internships.

INTERNATIONAL COOPERATIVE EDUCATION

15 Spiros Way, Menlo Park, CA 94025 ☎+1-650-323-4944 💻www.icemenlo.com

Provides full-time paid internships to US college students in a number of countries. Type-A workers rejoice: in addition to studying job-related vocabulary and current events, accepted students must write a five-page "paper of intent," a letter of introduction, a 10-page pre-departure paper, and a 15-page final report. So, uh, get to work.

[i] Applicants must be 18-30 years old. $ Application fee $250. Placement fee $900; includes some housing, work authorization, and visa application fees. Salaries $300-2300 per month. $100 extra for students with non-US passports or students outside the US at the time of application. See website for details. ⏰ Internships run 2-3 months in the summer or for 1-2 college semesters.

WORKAWAY

💻www.workaway.info

Workaway connects travelers with host families and organizations who offer room and board in exchange for a few hours of work per day *(generally 5hr. per day, 5 days per week)*. So it's kind of like a labor pimp with a heart of gold.

$ €18 for 2-year membership, €24 to sign up as a couple. ⏰ No min. stay.

SEASONAL JOBS 365

☎+1-202-657-6842, +44 20 8816 7936 💻www.seasonaljobs365.com

Seasonal Jobs 365 is a simple job hosting site that lists volunteer opportunities, seasonal and holiday work, and teaching jobs worldwide, including in Belgium.

$ Free to search; £25+ per month to post a job. ⏰ Short- and long-term opportunities available.

EXPAT EXCHANGE

P.O. Box 67, Bernardsville, NJ 07924 ☎+1-908-766-2733 💻www.expatexchange.com

Expat Exchange is more of a discussion board for expats across the globe than a job site, but it does have job listings.

tell the world

If your friends are tired of hearing about that time you saved a baby orangutan in Indonesia, there's clearly only one thing to do: get new friends. Find them at our website, 💻www.letsgo.com, where you can post your study-, volunteer-, or work-abroad stories for other, more appreciative community members to read. There's also a Beyond Tourism section that elaborates on non-destination-specific volunteering, studying, and working opportunities. If you liked this chapter, you'll love it; if you didn't like this chapter, maybe you'll find the website's more general Beyond Tourism tips more likeable, you non-likey person.

INDEX

index

index

index

V

W

Y

Z

index

MAP INDEX

MAP LEGEND

■ Sight/Service   ♜ Castle   ▢ Internet Cafe   ✪ Police

✈ Airport   ✝ Church   ▮ Library   ✉ Post Office

⌐ Arch/Gate   ⚑ Consulate/Embassy   Ⓜ Metro Station   ✡ Synagogue

§ Bank   ✝ Convent/Monastery   ⛰ Mountain   ☎ Telephone Office

⚓ Beach   ⚓ Ferry Landing   ☪ Mosque   ▲ Temple

🚌 Bus Station   (347) Highway Sign   🏛 Museum   ♆ Theater

✪ Capital City   ✚ Hospital   ℞ Pharmacy   ⓘ Tourist Office

                                                                            🚆 Train Station

The Let's Go compass
always points NORTH.   ⋯⋯⋯ Pedestrian Zone
                         ▨▨▨ Stairs   Park   Water   Beach

map index

LET'S GO!

THE STUDENT TRAVEL GUIDE

These Let's Go guidebooks are available at bookstores and through online retailers:

EUROPE

Let's Go Amsterdam & Brussels, 1st ed.
Let's Go Berlin, Prague & Budapest, 2nd ed.
Let's Go France, 32nd ed.
Let's Go Europe 2011, 51st ed.
Let's Go European Riviera, 1st ed.
Let's Go Germany, 16th ed.
Let's Go Great Britain with Belfast and Dublin, 33rd ed.
Let's Go Greece, 10th ed.
Let's Go Istanbul, Athens & the Greek Islands, 1st ed.
Let's Go Italy, 31st ed.
Let's Go London, Oxford, Cambridge & Edinburgh,
    2nd ed.
Let's Go Madrid & Barcelona, 1st ed.
Let's Go Paris, 17th ed.
Let's Go Rome, Venice & Florence, 1st ed.
Let's Go Spain, Portugal & Morocco, 26th ed.
Let's Go Western Europe, 10th ed.

UNITED STATES

Let's Go Boston, 6th ed.
Let's Go New York City, 19th ed.
Let's Go Roadtripping USA, 4th ed.

MEXICO, CENTRAL & SOUTH AMERICA

Let's Go Buenos Aires, 2nd ed.
Let's Go Central America, 10th ed.
Let's Go Costa Rica, 5th ed.
Let's Go Costa Rica, Nicaragua & Panama, 1st ed.
Let's Go Guatemala & Belize, 1st ed.
Let's Go Yucatán Peninsula, 1st ed.

ASIA & THE MIDDLE EAST

Let's Go Israel, 5th ed.
Let's Go Thailand, 5th ed.

Exam and desk copies are available for study-abroad programs and resource centers.
Let's Go guidebooks are distributed to bookstores in the U.S. through Publishers Group West and through Publishers Group Canada in Canada.
For more information, email letsgo.info@perseusbooks.com.

ACKNOWLEDGMENTS

TERESA THANKS: Veggie Planet pizzas and Petsi Pies coffee, Liza Flum's kitchen and bootleg TV and the rickety machines at the Central Square Y. I thank Joe Gaspard and my pod-mates for having my back, and my parents, bad music, and David Foster Wallace for getting me through. My uncle's '80s comic books and my grandpa's Chicago sundaes helped too.

BRONWEN THANKS: First off, let me bow down to the indefatigable 🔲**Beatrice.** You explored Amsterdam with the same open spirit that city is famous for—our readers are lucky to have you as their guide. My appreciation to Joe, Teresa, and super-ME Marykate, though if her name was Maryjane, this book would be even punnier. Finally, my biggest thanks must go to Chris and his ikonic brilliance.

JOE THANKS: The Let's Go office team and his RWs for their hard work. Special thanks go out to the Starbucks staff for keeping me well caffeinated, Bolt Bus for taking me back to Dix Hills, my brother and sisters for always being down to party, and to my mother for her continued support. The ladies of Harem Pod never failed to make me laugh, even when I was pulling my hair out. Lady Gaga should also be thanked for her part in keeping me happy; we could definitely have a bad romance.

CHRIS THANKS: 🔲**Bronwen,** for being the hardest-working person at LGHQ and an awesome person at the same time. Marykate, for remarkable patience in the face of an avalanche of questions. Beatrice, for a whole load of amity. Bourton-on-the-Water, for being the true "Venice of the North." Area 51, for three years of happiness. My family, for 22 years of the same. And PJ, for everything.

DIRECTOR OF PUBLISHING   Ashley R. Laporte
EXECUTIVE EDITOR   Nathaniel Rakich
PRODUCTION AND DESIGN DIRECTOR   Sara Plana
PUBLICITY AND MARKETING DIRECTOR   Joseph Molimock
MANAGING EDITORS   Charlotte Alter, Daniel C. Barbero, Marykate Jasper, Iya Megre
TECHNOLOGY PROJECT MANAGERS   Daniel J. Choi, C. Alexander Tremblay
PRODUCTION ASSOCIATES   Rebecca Cooper, Melissa Niu
FINANCIAL ASSOCIATE   Louis Caputo

DIRECTOR OF IT   Yasha Iravantchi
PRESIDENT   Meagan Hill
GENERAL MANAGER   Jim McKellar

LET'S GO
masthead

ABOUT LET'S GO

THE STUDENT TRAVEL GUIDE

Let's Go publishes the world's favorite student travel guides, written entirely by Harvard students. Armed with pens, notebooks, and a few changes of clothes stuffed into their backpacks, our student researchers go across continents, through time zones, and above expectations to seek out invaluable travel experiences for our readers. Because we are a completely student-run company, we have a unique perspective on how students travel, where they want to go, and what they're looking to do when they get there. If your dream is to grab a machete and forge through the jungles of Costa Rica, we can take you there. If you'd rather bask in the Riviera sun at a beachside cafe, we'll set you a table. In short, we write for readers who know that there's more to travel than tour buses. To keep up, visit our website, www.letsgo. com, where you can sign up to blog, post photos from your trips, and connect with the Let's Go community.

TRAVELING BEYOND TOURISM

We're on a mission to provide our readers with sharp, fresh coverage packed with socially responsible opportunities to go beyond tourism. Each guide's Beyond Tourism chapter shares ideas about responsible travel, study abroad, and how to give back to the places you visit while on the road. To help you gain a deeper connection with the places you travel, our fearless researchers scour the globe to give you the heads-up on both world-renowned and off-the-beaten-track opportunities. We've also opened our pages to respected writers and scholars to hear their takes on the countries and regions we cover, and asked travelers who have worked, studied, or volunteered abroad to contribute first-person accounts of their experiences.

FIFTY-ONE YEARS OF WISDOM

Let's Go has been on the road for 51 years and counting. We've grown a lot since publishing our first 20-page pamphlet to Europe in 1960, but five decades and 60 titles later, our witty, candid guides are still researched and written entirely by students on shoestring budgets who know that train strikes, stolen luggage, food poisoning, and marriage proposals are all part of a day's work. Meanwhile, we're still bringing readers fresh new features, such as a student-life section with advice on how and where to meet students from around the world; a revamped, user-friendly layout for our listings; and greater emphasis on the experiences that make travel abroad a rite of passage for readers of all ages. And, of course, this year's 16 titles—including five brand-new guides—are still brimming with editorial honesty, a commitment to students, and our irreverent style.

THE LET'S GO COMMUNITY

More than just a travel guide company, Let's Go is a community that reaches from our headquarters in Cambridge, MA, all across the globe. Our small staff of dedicated student editors, writers, and tech nerds comes together because of our shared passion for travel and our desire to help other travelers get the most out of their experience. We love it when our readers become part of the Let's Go community as well—when you travel, drop us a postcard (67 Mt. Auburn St., Cambridge, MA 02138, USA), send us an email (feedback@letsgo.com), or sign up on our website (www. letsgo.com) to tell us about your adventures and discoveries.

For more information, updated travel coverage, and news from our researcher team, visit us online at www.letsgo.com.

Distributed by Publishers Group West.
Printed in Canada by Friesens Corp.

Maps © Let's Go and Avalon Travel
Design Support by Jane Musser, Sarah Juckniess, Tim McGrath

ISBN-13: 978-1-59880-715-8
First edition
10 9 8 7 6 5 4 3 2 1

Let's Go Amsterdam & Brussels is written by Let's Go Publications, 67 Mt. Auburn St., Cambridge, MA 02138, USA.

Let's Go® and the LG logo are trademarks of Let's Go, Inc.

quick reference

YOUR GUIDE TO LET'S GO ICONS

☎	Phone numbers	⊗	Not wheelchair-accessible	❄	Has A/C
🖳	Websites	((ဂ))	Has internet access	⇅	Directions
💳	Takes credit cards	☁	Has outdoor seating	*i*	Other hard info
⊛	Cash only	▼	Is GLBT or GLBT-friendly	Ⓢ	Prices
♿	Wheelchair-accessible	⌙	Serves alcohol	⏰	Hours

PRICE RANGES

Let's Go includes price ranges, marked by icons ❶ through ❺, in accommodations and food listings. For an expanded explanation, see the chart in How To Use This Book.

NETHERLANDS	❶	❷	❸	❹	❺
ACCOMMODATIONS	under €36	€36-55	€56-77	€78-100	over €100
FOOD	under €8	€8-12	€13-17	€18-22	over €22

BELGIUM	❶	❷	❸	❹	❺
ACCOMMODATIONS	under €25	€25-40	€40-60	€60-80	over €80
FOOD	under €15	€15-25	€25-35	€35-45	over €45

IMPORTANT PHONE NUMBERS

NETHERLANDS: EMERGENCY ☎112			
Police (non-emergency)	☎0900 8844	Telephone Operator	☎0800 0410
ANWB	☎0800 0888	24hr. medical hotline	☎0900 503 2042

BELGIUM: POLICE ☎101, AMBULANCE AND FIRE ☎100			
Directory assistance	☎12 07	English-Language Crisis Line in Belgium	☎32 0264 84014

USEFUL PHRASES

ENGLISH	DUTCH	FRENCH
Hello/Hi!	Dag!/Hello!	Bonjour/Salut!
Do you speak English?	Spreekt u Engels?	Parlez-vous anglais?
I don't speak Dutch / French	Ik spreek geen Nederlands	Je ne parle pas français
How much does this cost?	Wat koost het?	Combien ça coûte?
Where is...?	Waar is...?	Où est...?
Get a doctor!	Haal een doktor?	Trouvez un médecin
Thank you	Dank u wel	Merci

TEMPERATURE CONVERSIONS

°CELSIUS	-5	0	5	10	15	20	25	30	35	40
°FAHRENHEIT	23	32	41	50	59	68	77	86	95	104

MEASUREMENT CONVERSIONS

1 inch (in.) = 25.4mm	1 millimeter (mm) = 0.039 in.
1 foot (ft.) = 0.305m	1 meter (m) = 3.28 ft.
1 mile (mi.) = 1.609km	1 kilometer (km) = 0.621 mi.
1 pound (lb.) = 0.454kg	1 kilogram (kg) = 2.205 lb.
1 gallon (gal.) = 3.785L	1 liter (L) = 0.264 gal.